George Francis Hill

A handbook of Greek and Roman coins

BAMBOO BOOKS

George Francis Hill

A handbook of Greek and Roman coins

Original published in 1899
Republished by Bamboo Books, 2020
Cover Design: Bamboo Books

ISBN: 978-5-519-68902-1

Dear Reader,

This is an exact replica of a book published in 1899. The book reprint was manually improved by a team of professionals, as opposed to automatic processed used by some companies. However, the book may still have imperfections such as missing pages, poor pictures, errant marks, etc. that were a part of the original text. We appreciate your understanding if the imperfection which can not be improved, and hope you will enjoy reading this book.

Our contacts:
request@bamboo-publishing.com
fb.com/bamboobooks

A HANDBOOK

OF

GREEK AND ROMAN COINS

G. F. HILL, M.A.

OF THE DEPARTMENT OF COINS AND MEDALS IN THE BRITISH MUSEUM

WITH FIFTEEN COLLOTYPE PLATES

London
MACMILLAN AND CO., Limited
NEW YORK: THE MACMILLAN COMPANY
1899

[*All rights reserved*]

Oxford
HORACE HART, PRINTER TO THE UNIVERSITY

PREFACE

THE attempt has often been made to condense into a small volume all that is necessary for a beginner in numismatics or a young collector of coins. But success has been less frequent, because the knowledge of coins is essentially a knowledge of details, and small treatises are apt to be unreadable when they contain too many references to particular coins, and unprofitably vague when such references are avoided. I cannot hope that I have passed safely between these two dangers; indeed, my desire has been to avoid the second at all risk of encountering the former. At the same time it may be said that this book is not meant for the collector who desires only to identify the coins which he happens to possess, while caring little for the wider problems of history, art, mythology, and religion, to which coins sometimes furnish the only key. It is meant chiefly as a guide to put students of antiquity in the way of bringing numismatics to bear on their difficulties. No attempt, therefore, has been made to avoid controversy where any profitable stimulus seems likely to be provided by the discussion of doubtful questions. The comparatively full references and the bibliography are also added with the aim of making the book an introduction to more advanced works, rather than a more or less self-contained statement of the elements.

PREFACE

Since the publication of François Lenormant's *La Monnaie dans l'Antiquité*—the last considerable work undertaking to cover the whole ground of ancient numismatics—the number of works of a general and special nature which cannot be neglected by the student has at least been doubled. Fresh catalogues of great collections, public and private, appear in rapid succession; a new quarterly, devoted entirely to Greek numismatic archaeology, has been established within the last year; and, above all, the Prussian Academy has begun to issue its Corpus of the coins of Northern Greece, which, it is to be hoped, will in time grow into a Corpus of Greek coins. Mommsen has said that he was driven to write his numismatic work because he felt that the help to history which he sought in coins 'was not to be found in a literature which, after Eckhel, has been left mostly to dilettanti and shopmen.' The publications of recent years show that his reproach is no longer so true as it was. It is now not too much to expect that all archaeologists should have at least some first-hand acquaintance with coins. If coins do not, like some other antiquities, throw much light on private life, their importance as public and official documents is inestimable. And it must not be forgotten that the number of coins of which the condition is practically perfect, and the authenticity beyond suspicion, is greater than we can find in any other series of antiquities:

> Le temps passe. Tout meurt. Le marbre même s'use.
> Agrigente n'est plus qu'une ombre, et Syracuse
> Dort sous le bleu linceul de son ciel indulgent;
> Et seul le dur métal que l'amour fit docile
> Garde encore en sa fleur, aux médailles d'argent,
> L'immortelle beauté des vierges de Sicile.

As regards the illustrations in the text, most of the blocks have been made from line-drawings by Mr. F. Anderson. This draughtsman, to whom students of classical antiquity owe so much, has made the drawings over enlarged photographs, adding nothing to what exists on the original. For

PREFACE vii

permission to use one of the drawings (Fig. 31), I have to thank the Council of the Society for the Promotion of Hellenic Studies. Except in a few cases, duly noted, the coins illustrated, both in text and plates, are all in the British Museum. The collotype plates have been executed by the Clarendon Press.

My indebtedness to the authorities, from whose works this volume is nothing more than a distillation, can be fairly well gauged by means of the footnotes, although it has been impossible to give chapter and verse for every statement not my own. These footnotes, as might be expected, show my deep obligations to the works of Head, Imhoof-Blumer, and Mommsen, as well as of the editor of this series of handbooks, Professor Percy Gardner. To the last indeed, both as writer and as teacher, I am under peculiar obligations, since to him I owe my introduction to the study of numismatics. Mr. Warwick Wroth has had the kindness to read the proof-sheets, and to make many valuable suggestions, and I have to thank Mr. H. A. Grueber also for similar assistance.

G. F. HILL.

BRITISH MUSEUM,
July, 1899.

CONTENTS

INTRODUCTION.

GENERAL SKETCH OF THE HISTORY OF COINAGE IN GREECE AND ROME.

	PAGE
§ 1. Early Stages of Exchange	1
2. Scope of Classical Numismatics	2
3. The Metallic Unit generally adopted	4
4. The Invention of Coinage	6
5. The Spread of Coinage to European Greece	8
6. The Extension of Coinage to Western Greece	8
7. Coinage adopted by the 'Barbarians'	9
8. The Regal Period	10
9. Revival of the Coinage of the Cities	11
10. Beginning of the Influence of Rome	11
11. Coinage under the Roman Empire	12

BOOK I.

CHAPTER I.

THE METALS.

§ 1. Quality of the Metals used for Coinage	13
2. Minor Metals and Alloys	16
3. The Sources of the Metals	18
4. The Testing of Metals in Antiquity	23
5. Oxide and Patina	25

CHAPTER II.

THE COIN AS A MEDIUM OF EXCHANGE. ORIGIN, DISTRIBUTION, AND RELATION OF COIN-STANDARDS.

	PAGE
§ 1. Theories of the Origin of Coin-Standards	26
2. Determination of Early Weight-Standards	28
3. Distribution of the Three Oriental Standards	33
4. The Aeginetic and Euboic-Attic Standards	34
5. Local Standards of Asia Minor	38
6. Local Standards of European Greece	40
7. The Western Mediterranean	41
8. Sicily	42
9. Roman Bronze	44
10. Roman Silver	53
11. Roman Gold	54
12. Etruria	55
13. Northern and Central Italy	59
14. Southern Italy	60
15. Coin-Denominations	64

CHAPTER III.

MONETARY THEORY AND PRACTICE.

§ 1. Aristotle's Conception of Money	67
2. The Quality of Ancient Money	68
3. Plated Coin	71
4. Precautions against Forgery	72
5. Protection by Tariff	73
6. Relative Values of the Metals	74

CHAPTER IV.

THE COINAGE AND THE STATE.

§ 1. Private Coinage	78
2. Nature of 'Temple Coinage'	80
3. Coinage of Monarchs	81
4. The Coinage and the Sovereign Power	82
5. Rome and her Subjects. Restriction of Gold	85
6. Restriction of Silver	87

		PAGE
§ 7. The Eastern Provinces under the Empire	. . . .	89
8. Roman Colonies		92
9. Delegated Coinage: the Satraps	. . . .	95
10. Military Coinage in the West	. . . .	97
11. Roman Military Coinage		98
12. Combined Coinages: Real and Complimentary Alliances	.	102
13. Commercial Unions		103
14. Political Unions		106
15. Other Alliances		114
16. Greek Colonies		116
17. Religious Combinations		117

CHAPTER V.

Monetary Officials.

A. Among the Greeks.

§ 1. Magistrates' Signatures and Symbols	119
2. The Athenian Monetary Officials	121
3. The Office of the Moneyer	124
4. Magistrates in Imperial Times	126
5. The Greek Mint	129

B. Among the Romans.

6. Roman Monetary Magistrates	131
7. Monetary Officials of Roman Colonies . . .	136
8. Roman Governors	138
9. The Roman Mint	139

BOOK II.

CHAPTER VI.

Fabric and Style.

§ 1. Struck Coins	143
2. Ancient Dies	149
3. The Development of Form of Struck Coins . .	151
4. Cast Coins	155
5. The Composition of the Type	158
6. Development of Style	160

CHAPTER VII.

The Meaning and Classification of Coin-Types.

	PAGE
§ 1. The Religious Theory and the Commercial Theory	166
2. Religious Types	169
3. Types representing the Issuing Authority	171
4. Types representing Local Features	173
5. Types representing Monuments	174
6. Historical Types	175
7. Canting Types	176
8. Ornamental Types	177
9. Imitative Types	177
10. Classification of Symbols	178

CHAPTER VIII.

Coin-Inscriptions.

§ 1. Inscriptions naming the Issuing Authority	180
2. Varieties of Titulature	181
3. Inscriptions naming the Type	185
4. Inscriptions giving the Reason of Issue	189
5. Mint-marks and Artists' Signatures	194
6. Names and Values of Coins	196
7. Dates	196
8. Graffiti	197
9. Abbreviations	197

CHAPTER IX.

The Dating of Coins.

§ 1. Dating by the Evidence of History	199
2. Coins bearing Dates	201
3. Dating by Style and Fabric	203
4. Weight and Quality	204
5. Types	205
6. Epigraphy	207
Greek	208
Roman	215
7. Finds	217

APPENDICES.

		PAGE
I.	Ancient Standards	222
II.	Equivalents in Troy Grains of Weights mentioned in the Text	226
III.	Roman Mint-marks	228
IV.	The Imperial Families	230
V.	Select Bibliography	242
	Key to the Plates	256
	Index of Subjects	273
	Index of Greek Words	289
	Index of Latin Words	293
	Plates I–XV	at end

LIST OF ILLUSTRATIONS IN THE TEXT

		PAGE
Fig. 1.	Bronze Coin (?) of Olbia (Sarmatia)	3
2.	,, ,, of the Colony of Nemausus	4
3.	Weighing Rings of Precious Metal (Egyptian Painting)	5
4.	Gaulish Imitation of Gold Stater of Philip II	10
5.	Iron Coin of Argos	17
6.	Babylonian Bronze Weight of 5 manahs	28
7.	Half-shekel of Jewish First Revolt	34
8.	Athenian *Chalcūs*	37
9.	*Aes rude* from Caere	44
10.	Reverse of Italian *aes signatum*	45
11.	Roman *as* of 10½ oz.	46
12.	*As* of 1⅓ oz.	48
13.	*As* of Augustus	50
14.	*Semis* of Lamia, Silius, and Annius	50
15.	*Follis* of Anastasius I	52
16.	Reverse of *Nummus* of Anastasius I	53
17.	*As* of Hatria	59
18.	Reverse of *as* of Commodus (Rome as a *Colony*)	94
19.	Reverse of 'Alliance-Coin' of Side and Delphi	102
20.	Semuncial bronze *semis*	133
21.	Gold Bar from Sirmio [Pesth Museum]	137
22.	Gold Bar from Sirmio [British Museum]	137
23.	Bronze of Antiochus IV of Syria	144
24.	Wall-painting in the House of the Vettii [Pompeii]	146, 147
25.	Bronze Coin of Paestum	148
26.	Die of Faustina II [Lyon Museum]	150
27.	Clay Moulds for casting Coins	157
28.	Coin of Apamea in Phrygia with Noah's Ark [Bibliothèque Nationale]	170
29.	Coin of Antiochia in Caria with Bridge	174
30.	Coin of Delphi with Agonistic Type	192
31.	Stater of Sicyon with Punctured Inscription	197
Plates I-XV		at end

NOTE ON ABBREVIATIONS

A REFERENCE to the Bibliography will make clear the abbreviated references to works by individual writers. The chief periodical and collective publications quoted in abbreviated form are as follows:—

Abhandl(ungen) der Kön(iglich) Sächs(ischen) Ges(ellschaft) d(er) Wiss(enschaften).
Amer(ican) Journ(al) of Arch(aeology).
Ann(ali) d(ell') Inst(ituto di Corrispondenza Archeologica).
Arch(äologische) Ep(igraphische) Mitth(eilungen) aus Oest(erreich-Ungarn).
Arch(äologische) Zeit(ung).
Athen(ische) Mitth(eilungen) = Mittheilungen des Kaiserlich Deutschen Archäologischen Instituts, Athenische Abtheilung.
Berl(iner) Akad(emische) Abh(andlungen) = Abhandlungen der Königlichen Akademie der Wissenschaften zu Berlin.
Berl(iner) Phil(ologische) Woch(enschrift).
B(ritish) M(useum) Cat(alogue of Greek Coins).
Bull(etin de) Corr(espondance) Hellén(ique).
C(orpus) I(nscriptionum) A(tticarum).
C(orpus) I(nscriptionum) G(raecarum) ed. Boeckh.
C(orpus) I(nscriptionum) L(atinarum).
'Εφ(ημερὶs) 'Αρχ(αιολογική).
J(ournal of) H(ellenic) S(tudies).
Journ(al) Internat(ional) d'Archéologie Numismatique).
Mém(oires) de l'Acad(émie) des Inscr(iptions).
Neue Jahrb(ücher) f(ür) Phil(ologie).
Num(ismatic) Chron(icle).
Num(ismatische) Z(eitschrift).
Rev(ue) des Ét(udes) Gr(ecques).
Rev(ue) Num(ismatique).
Rev(ue) Num(ismatique) Belge.
Rhein(isches) Mus(eum für Philologie).
Röm(ische) Mitth(eilungen) = Mittheilungen des Kaiserlich Deutschen Archäologischen Instituts, Römische Abtheilung.
Verhandl(ungen) der Berl(iner) Gesellsch(aft) für Anthrop(ologie, &c.).
Z(eitschrift) f(ür) N(umismatik).

INTRODUCTION

GENERAL SKETCH OF THE HISTORY OF COINAGE IN GREECE AND ROME

§ 1. *Early Stages of Exchange.*

TRADE in its development passes through three stages. Beginning as barter, or the direct exchange of commodity against commodity, it proceeds, as soon as it attains large proportions, to the stage of mediate exchange, conducted with the aid of a medium in which the value of exchangeable commodities can be expressed. In order to serve for the measuring of value, this medium should above all possess three qualities: intrinsic value, so that the possessor of it may feel secure of his power to exchange it for commodities when he wishes; high value, so that a small quantity of it may represent a large quantity of ordinary commodities; and divisibility, in order that accuracy of measurement may be obtained. A later development of this kind of exchange is seen when the medium of exchange is treated purely as such, and to save time and labour, the number of units of value contained in each piece of it is directly or indirectly[1] indicated. This obviates the necessity of repeatedly calculating the amount of the medium, and exchange is thus considerably facilitated. A still further development is that of the 'token,' a term which may

[1] Indirectly, by the genuineness of the piece being guaranteed by some mark of authority.

be taken, broadly, as meaning any medium of exchange which represents on its face a value which it does not intrinsically possess, but for which it is or should be redeemable. Thus under tokens would be included all token-coins, bank-notes, cheques, and the like. As these forms of money depend on credit—i. e. a fund assumed to be somewhere in reserve—this stage may be regarded as only a subsidiary development of the second stage. We may therefore tabulate as follows the stages in the development of trade:

I. Barter or Immediate Exchange.
II. Mediate Exchange.
   (i) By means of an uncoined medium.
   (ii) By means of a coined medium of full value.
   (iii) By means of tokens.

The study of numismatics in its accepted sense deals strictly with II, ii and iii (but with the latter only so far as the tokens assume the external form of coins proper). But its roots stretch down into the lower stages, and in dealing with monetary standards and types it is often necessary to go back to the days of early mediate exchange and even of barter.

§ 2. *Scope of Classical Numismatics.*

The table of contents will make it sufficiently clear under what main aspects the classical numismatist considers his subject. For the purpose of a working definition we may describe a coin[1] as follows. A coin is a piece of metal (or, exceptionally, some other convenient material) artificially rendered into a required shape, and marked with a sign as a guarantee that it is of the proper fineness and weight, and issued by some responsible authority; the prime object served by the piece being to facili-

---

[1] The Latin *cuneus*, from which, through the French, this word is derived, was used in the middle ages for the die for striking coins, and sometimes actually for the coin itself. The Greek word for coin, νόμισμα (meaning, like νόμος, in the first instance a regular custom or institution) has given, through the Latinized form *numisma*, the modern name of the science. The use of the word *medal* for an ancient coin is now old-fashioned in the English language, being properly restricted to commemorative or decorative pieces not meant to circulate as currency.

tate exchange, since it serves as an expression of the value of exchangeable commodities. By this definition those objects are excluded which serve other purposes than that of exchange, such, for instance, as drinking cups or ornamental rings of precious metals, which were made in days of barter, often according to a fixed weight[1]; or medals; or natural objects which have been used, and in some savage countries are still used, for the purposes of change, such as cowry-shells[2], 'cats' eyes,' and the like. But imitations in metal of such natural objects, as for instance the snail-shell money of the Burmese[3], or imitations of implements such as the knife-money and hoe-money of China[4], come strictly within the limits of the definition. Nevertheless, with this latter kind of coin the student of Greek and Roman coinage has practically nothing to do, the coins which concern him being almost entirely of a conventional shape.

FIG. 1.—Bronze Coin (?) of Olbia (Sarmatia); *Rev.* ⊙Y.

An exception may be found in the fish-shaped pieces from the north of the Euxine (Fig. 1). If these are coins, they differ from the ordinary Greek coin only in the fact that, instead of putting a fish-type on a flan of ordinary shape, the whole coin was made in the shape of a fish. Another explanation is suggested by the fact that a pig of metal was sometimes called δελφίς[5]. These fish-shaped pieces may be the degenerate representatives of similar-shaped pigs of bronze. The rings and ball-shaped pieces from Pannonia, and similar barbarous regions, hardly come within the province of Greek and Roman numismatics. The ham-shaped pieces of Nemausus (Fig. 2) were probably made for some religious purpose; the person who

---

[1] See for instance, Ridgeway, *Origin of Metallic Currency*, pp. 35 ff.; *Journ. Hellen. Stud.* xiii. p. 225 (a treasure from Mycenae), and Holm, *Griech. Gesch.* i. p. 257, Eng. trans. p. 214 (rings with the name of Eteandros of Cyprus).
[2] Ridgeway, p. 13. [3] Ib. p. 22. [4] Ib. p. 23.
[5] Ardaillon, *Les Mines du Laurion*, p. 111, who compares the French *saumon*.

would have liked to make an offering in kind, was able to give its equivalent in a coin the shape of which suggested the animal offered to his deity.

FIG. 2.—Bronze Coin of the Colony of Nemausus. *Obv.* Heads of Augustus and Agrippa. *Rev.* COL. NEM. Crocodile chained to palm-tree.

§ 3. *The Metallic unit generally adopted.*

It is unnecessary to dwell here upon the first stage of mediate exchange, through an uncoined medium. It is sufficient to recognize that it is in all cases presupposed by the next stage, with which commences our subject proper. It should, however, be borne in mind that the uncoined medium is not necessarily metal, but may be anything, from a stock-fish to an ox, which is capable of being regarded as a unit of calculation; which is, that is to say, of a generally recognized value [1].

It was, however, the *metallic* unit which developed into the coin, simply by having an official mark, a guarantee of genuineness and true weight, placed upon it. The stage in which the medium had to be weighed upon each occasion of exchange is illustrated by a few monuments and by a number of literary references. On more than one Egyptian wall-painting [2] a large

---

[1] For these primitive currencies see Ridgeway, *Origin of Currency*, ch. ii.
[2] Figured in *Zeitschr. für Ethnologie*, 1889, pp. 5 ff., in Ridgeway, *Origin of Currency*, p. 128, and in many other works. The illustration in the text is taken from Lepsius, *Denkmä'er*, iii. pl. 39 *d*.

pair of scales is represented, in which rings of metal are being weighed (Fig. 3). There is reason to suppose that in Greece in early times small bars of metal were in circulation, which

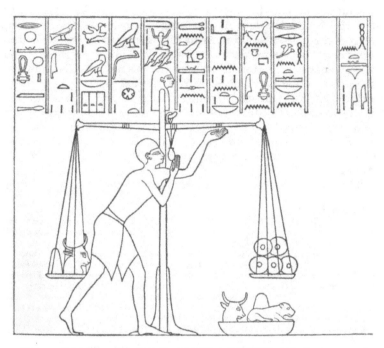

Fig. 3.—Weighing Rings of Precious Metal. (Fifteenth Century B.C.)

being of uniform size could be counted out instead of being always weighed[1]. But for aught we know these may have had some official mark, like the rings of Eteandros (above, p. 3, note 1), and have therefore been true coins.

[1] Plutarch, *Lysand*. c. 17 κινδυνεύει δὲ καὶ τὸ πάμπαν ἀρχαῖον οὕτως ἔχειν, ὀβελίσκοις χρωμένων νομίσμασι σιδηροῖς, ἐνίων δὲ χαλκοῖς· ἀφ' ὧν παραμένει πλῆθος ἔτι καὶ νῦν τῶν κερμάτων ὀβολοὺς καλεῖσθαι, δραχμὴν δὲ τοὺς ἓξ ὀβολούς, τοσούτων γὰρ ἡ χεὶρ περιεδράττετο. Cf. *Etym. Magn.* s.v. ὀβελίσκος. Pheidon of Argos is said to have hung up in the temple of Hera specimens of the ὀβελίσκοι which had served for money before his time. (But see below, p. 6, note 3.)

§ 4. *The Invention of Coinage.*

Of all those to whom the invention of coinage was, according to Julius Pollux [1], ascribed — the Athenians, the Naxians, Pheidon of Argos, Demodice, wife of Midas, the Lydians — only the third and the last have strong claims. As to Pheidon, Herodotus speaks of him as having given measures (i. e. presumably, a complete metrical system, including weights) to the Peloponnesians [2]. Herodotus himself does not mention coinage, the introduction of which is only attributed to Pheidon by later authorities, the earliest of whom is Ephorus [3]. The bulk of the evidence, both literary and numismatic, goes to show merely that the earliest silver coinage was the Aeginetic, but that the Aeginetic coinage was at the same time only an adaptation of something which already existed on the other side of the Aegean Sea.

The credit of inaugurating coinage in the Western world

---

[1] *Onom.* ix. 83.

[2] vi. 127 Φείδωνος δὲ τοῦ τὰ μέτρα ποιήσαντος Πελοποννησίοισι καὶ ὑβρίσαντος μέγιστα δὴ Ἑλλήνων ἁπάντων, ὃς ἐξαναστήσας τοὺς Ἠλείων ἀγωνοθέτας αὐτὸς τὸν ἐν Ὀλυμπίῃ ἀγῶνα ἔθηκε (cf. Pausanias, vi. 22. 2).

[3] Strabo (viii. p. 376) has: 'Ephorus says that silver was first coined in Aegina by Pheidon.' Elsewhere Ephorus (Strabo, p. 358) attributes to Pheidon 'struck coins not only of silver but of other metals.' This τό τε ἄλλο betrays Ephorus, unless we can suppose him to mean thereby the iron coinage which was afterwards used in some Dorian states, or the electrum Aeginetic coinage, of which a solitary specimen is extant. Neither alternative is likely, and the truth is that Ephorus combined the statement of the introduction of measures by Pheidon with the theory that the Aeginetic silver coinage is earlier than any other in the same metal. As to this theory, it is admitted by every numismatist. But as to the tradition that Pheidon was connected with the coinage, that can neither be proved nor disproved, with our present lights. No accumulation of quotations from later writers will strengthen the position of those who hold that Pheidon introduced coinage into Greece. [Of these late quotations, one from the *Etymologicum Magnum* is worth mentioning, s.v. Εὐβοικὸν νόμισμα: 'Pheidon, king of the Argives, was the first to strike gold money in Euboea, a place in Argos.' Yet even this has been taken seriously by some critics.] Pheidon's date is quite uncertain. It should be noted that by Herodotus Pheidon is mentioned in a context which makes the mention valueless as regards his date (the story of Agariste's suitors is only a Greek version of the Indian story of the shameless dancing peacock, and the personages are introduced regardless of chronology). For the other evidence see Busolt, *Griech. Gesch.* 2nd ed. I. p. 611 f.; Macan, note on Herod. l. c.; C. F. Lehmann, *Hermes*, 1892, p. 577 f.; Th. Reinach, *Rev. Num.* 1894, pp. 1-8 (where it is suggested that the ὀβελίσκοι dedicated by Pheidon were *standards*, and not obsolete coins)

almost certainly belongs to the Lydians[1]. There is direct literary tradition to this effect; and the provenance of the earliest and rudest coins, which clearly belong to Asia Minor, and being of electrum, may be supposed to come from the Tmolus district, bears out the tradition[2]. Again, the position of the Lydians as intermediaries between East and West, which enabled them to rise to a high state of civilization and luxury[3], makes it easy for us to accept the tradition. The earliest specimens seem, if we may judge by style, to go back well into the seventh century B.C., and there is nothing improbable in the suggestion[4] that we should 'ascribe to the seventh century B.C., and probably to the reign of Gyges, the founder of the dynasty of the Mermnadae and of the new Lydian empire, as distinguished from the Lydia of more remote antiquity, the first issues of the Lydian mint.' These issues are of electrum; but this fact can hardly be said to clash seriously with the words χρυσοῦ καὶ ἀργύρου in the account of Herodotus[5], of whom it is unfair to expect numismatic accuracy. The first Lydian coins of gold and silver are now usually attributed to the time of Croesus (the middle of the sixth century B.C., Pl. I. 8 and 9). The coinage of this famous ruler would naturally make an impression on the Greek mind which would cause it to forget the earlier electrum coinage.

What may be called the Ionian theory of the origin of Western coinage is not, however, out of accordance with the statement of Herodotus. This theory would attribute the early electrum coinage to the cities of the western coast of Asia Minor, leaving to the Lydians only the innovation of a coinage of pure gold and silver. There is, however, no tradition in favour of this view, and the Lydian tradition, confirmed

---

[1] Herodotus (i. 94) says of the Lydians: πρῶτοι δὲ ἀνθρώπων τῶν ἡμεῖς ἴδμεν νόμισμα χρυσοῦ καὶ ἀργύρου κοψάμενοι ἐχρήσαντο, πρῶτοι δὲ καὶ κάπηλοι ἐγένοντο. Julius Pollux (ix. 83) gives Xenophanes as the authority for the Lydian origin of coinage. This takes the tradition well back into the sixth century.

[2] On the evidence of the early Lydian coin-types see Curtius, *Ueber den relig. Charakter der gr. Münzen* (*Gesamm. Abhandl.* ii. pp. 455 f.) transl. by Head, *Num. Chron.* 1870, p. 91.

[3] Herodotus, l. c., Athen. xii. 515 d, xv. 690 b, c, &c.

[4] Head, *H. N.* p. 544.

[5] These words must mean 'of gold and of silver,' not 'of gold and silver mixed,' i. e. of electrum.

as it is by the circumstantial evidence already mentioned, must be allowed to hold the field.

§ 5. *The spread of Coinage to European Greece.*

If the Lydians invented coinage, the Greeks of the Ionian coast adopted it at an early period. For a very large series of coins, with types that are endless in variety, has to be distributed among the cities of the Asiatic Greeks. This coinage consists chiefly of electrum; but, as we have seen, gold and silver were introduced by Croesus, and gold was used even earlier by the great maritime city of Phocaea, in the period of its thalassocracy, B. C. 602-560 (Pl. I. 2). Farther east, at a slightly later date, Persia adopted gold and silver coinage from the Lydians. But as early as the seventh century the institution of coinage had made its way across the Aegean Sea. Its path is marked by a series of primitive issues which are grouped together as island-coins (Pl. II. 1 and 3). Of these the series which can be most satisfactorily attributed to a mint are the famous 'tortoises' of Aegina (Pl. II. 1). Somewhat different in general character, but hardly less early in date, are the primitive coins of Euboea (Pl. II. 4). Euboea is the starting-point of the coinage of two other great states: Corinth, which begins to coin towards the end of the seventh century, and Athens (Pl. II. 2), where the earliest coinage is probably to be associated with Solon. But besides passing westwards across the Aegean, the stream of coinage also in very early times went southwards across the Mediterranean to the rich Cyrenaica.

These are the lines along which Greek coinage first spread. In the islands and Greece proper, where little or no gold was found, the early coinage is of silver. In Cyrene, on the other hand, electrum is the material of the early issues.

§ 6. *The extension of Coinage to Western Greece.*

The middle of the sixth century saw a further extension of coinage. In the north it was introduced into Macedon and Thrace. Corinth had already extended her influence westwards, and the coinage of the important trading city of Corcyra

(Pl. II. 7) probably begins as early as B.C. 585, when it gained its independence. And the same influence passed across the Adriatic to Southern Italy. Meanwhile trade, extending westwards by another route round the Peloponnese, carried the invention to Sicily, whence it passed to Etruria. While coinage thus spread westward, it began to move eastward along the south coast of Asia Minor, where, in Lycia, Pamphylia, Cilicia, and the island of Cyprus, the beginnings of coinage date from the end of the sixth century. By the time of the Persian wars nearly all the important states of the Greek world were in possession of a coinage, with some few exceptions such as Lacedaemon and Byzantium[1]. The fifth century saw a still further extension of the limits, and an increase within the old limits of the number of cities possessing a coinage. In the latter half of this century begins the 'period of finest art.'

§ 7. *Coinage adopted by the 'Barbarians.'*

And at the same time the influence of Greece begins to be felt by the barbarians. The coinage of Carthage, struck largely for Sicily, begins about 410 B C. (Pl. XI. 5). To the same time, or perhaps to a somewhat earlier date, belong the first coinages of Tyre and Sidon. By the middle of the next century Rome has begun to coin, in bronze only, it is true. Bronze, indeed, came into use as a coined medium for the first time towards the end of the fifth or the beginning of the fourth century. Gold, which some few cities, such as Athens and Rhodes, had begun to coin either shortly before or shortly after 400 B.C., now becomes very important. The exploitation by Philip II of Macedon of the mines of Crenides gave him a gold coinage (Pl. VII. 2), the influence of which was of the most far-reaching kind. Not only did it pave the way for the still more abundant gold coinage of his son (Pl. VII. 5), but it was eagerly imitated by the barbarians who hovered above Greece. By the valley of the Danube and across central Europe Philip's gold and silver coins (Pl. VII. 1 and 2) were carried to the West, and from them were derived the most important classes of Gaulish coinage (Fig. 4). From Gaul the imitations passed to

---

[1] And these are perhaps not exceptions, for they may have had an iron coinage. See above, p. 5, note 1.

Britain, giving rise, after about two centuries of degradation, to the earliest British coinage. Curiously enough the gold of Alexander

FIG. 4.—Gaulish Imitation of gold stater of Philip II. (Weight: 7.9 grammes.)

appears to have almost escaped imitation by the barbarians, although they found his silver (Pl. VII. 4) much to their taste.

§ 8. *The Regal Period.*

From the time of Philip II it is the coinage of the kings both in the West and in the East that attracts most attention for a considerable period. Alexander's conquests carried the Greek civilization eastward, and soon after Alexander's death began the regal coinages of the Seleucidae in Syria (beginning with Seleucus I Nicator, B. C. 312–280, Pl. VII. 11) and of the Ptolemies in Egypt (Ptolemy I, Soter, took the title of king in 305 B. C., Pl. VII. 9); while somewhat later, about the middle of the third century, begin the independent coinages of Bactria (Diodotus, B. C. 250, Pl VIII. 1) and Parthia (Arsaces I, B. C. 249–247). In the west we have the important coinage of Agathocles of Syracuse (B. C. 317–289), who was followed, after a short interval of democracy, by Hicetas, Hiero II (Pl. XI. 6), and Hieronymus. In Greece there are the various successors of Alexander (such as Demetrius Poliorcetes, B. C. 306-283, Pl. VII. 7 and 10), and, especially important, Lysimachus, king of Thrace (Pl. VII. 6). Naturally enough, therefore, the chief feature of interest in this period is the portraiture of these rulers. Nevertheless, in spite of the dominance of the individual ruler, some cities, notably Rhodes (Pl. V. 5), retained their commercial and monetary importance; and it is noticeable that the chief currency of whole districts like Peloponnese consisted of federal coinages, of which the most famous instance is the coinage of the Achaean league (Pl. IX. 1). The coinage of Athens and Corinth either disappeared altogether or dwindled for a time.

§ 9. *Revival of the Coinage of the Cities.*

Towards the end of the third century began the new Athenian coinage (Pl. IX. 8) which surpassed the old in its extent. At this time the number of large silver coins in circulation must have been enormous; for besides the ordinary regal coinages, there were vast numbers of coins issued all over the East with the types of Alexander the Great, and, in Thrace, with those of Lysimachus. It is hard to disabuse oneself of the idea that these are regal coins ; we speak of them as 'Alexanders' and the like, and forget that they were issued by autonomous cities.

§ 10. *Beginning of the influence of Rome.*

A turning-point in the history of ancient coinage is the defeat of Antiochus the Great at Magnesia in 190 B.C. This is the date of the first decisive step taken by Rome to interfere in the affairs of the East. Already the Greek and Punic coinage of the West had lost all importance ; the Carthaginian coinage from the beginning of the Punic War to the destruction of the city is wretched in every way. There is no Sicilian coinage of any importance after the fall of Syracuse in B.C. 212 By the end of the third century the influence of Rome was making itself felt in the western part of northern Greece. So that, when Antiochus fell, the advance of Rome eastwards was imminent. The peculiarity of the coinage of the new period is the large size of the silver tetradrachms. This feature is commonest in Asia Minor (Pl. VIII. 10) and in Thrace (Pl. IX. 2), but it is also found, for instance, in the coinage of Athens (Pl. IX. 8) and the Macedonian district (Pl. X. 5). Coincident with the advent of the Roman domination is the gradual disappearance of gold from the Greek coinage. The last Ptolemy to strike gold was the fifth (Epiphanes), B.C. 204–181. Of the Seleucids, Demetrius I, Soter (B.C. 162–150), and Timarchus, the revolted satrap of Babylon (B C. 162), were the last to issue gold as a matter of course; but Alexander II, Zebina (B.C. 128–123), in an emergency, melted down the golden Victory that the Zeus of Antioch held in his hand, and made her into coins, of which one, and one only, is known to exist (Pl. VIII. 8)[1]. There are other instances of gold being issued at this period (see chapter iv. § 5), but the general rule is clear, that only Roman generals were allowed to strike gold coins. The gold coinage of Rome itself, as apart from the coins required by generals for the payment of troops, belongs to a later period. Rome could hardly be expected to allow the petty Greek state a privilege which she denied herself. The more direct interference of Rome with the ordinary Greek coinage is shown by the introduction of the coinage of the Macedonian Regions and the adoption of the Asiatic cistophori, which were made the standard according to which the other large coins of Asia Minor were tariffed.

§ 11. *Coinage under the Roman Empire.*

In the early days of the Empire, all autonomous coinage had died out in the West (all extra-Roman mints had been closed in Italy in B. C. 89); even in outlying parts such as Britain, the autonomous coinage entirely ceased before the end of the first century, A. D. In Greece proper, there is a bronze coinage of not very great dimensions, and of a somewhat inconsecutive character, down to the time of Gallienus. In the East, an important feature is the semi-Roman coinage of the three great mints, Caesarea in Cappadocia (Pl. XIV. 2), Antiochia in Syria (Pl. XIV. 7) and its assistant-mints, and Alexandria in Egypt (Pl. XIV. 5, 8). The latter remained open until the time of Domitius Domitianus (A. D. 296), longer than any other mint from which Greek coins were issued. The rest of the Greek imperial coinage consists of issues representing an enormous number of cities and colonies, especially in Asia Minor, down to the time of Gallienus (with a few instances of the time of Aurelian and Tacitus). The subsequent establishment of mints for striking purely Roman coins in all the provinces of the Empire marks the complete supremacy of the Roman coinage. The commencement of the Eastern Empire with Arcadius (A D. 395-408) did not affect this supremacy, which lasted until the barbarian invaders, not content with merely imitating Roman and Byzantine coins, began in the fifth century to make those changes out of which were to develop the coinages of mediaeval Europe.

[1] Wroth, *Num. Chron.* 1897, p. 23, Pl. V. 8.

BOOK I

CHAPTER I

THE METALS

§ 1. *Quality of the Metals used for Coinage.*

THE ancients were well acquainted with the art of refining and of alloying metals [1]. Of the three chief metals, gold (*A*) was used in a very pure state. The Persian darics were ·958 to ·970 fine; staters of Philip and Alexander ·997 fine. The gold of the Roman Republic was perfectly pure. The aurei of Augustus were ·998 fine, and the gold of the Roman Empire only began to lose its purity towards the time of Septimius Severus. The gold coinage of the Bosporus, under the Roman Empire, became rapidly debased, and after the time of Severus Alexander was practically mere copper with a tinge of gold.

Silver (*R*) was also used in a form much purer than that found in modern coins. The tetradrachms of Athens of the best period are from ·986 to ·983 fine; those of the succeeding age are somewhat less pure, but contain about ·002 of gold [2]. The staters of Aegina average ·960 fine; those of Corinth ·961 to ·936. The analysis of three drachms of Alexander yields:—

	Silver.	Gold.	Other Metals.
(1)	·991	·009	
(2)	·9885	·0005	·011
(3)	·9674	·0036	·029

[1] See especially Mongez, *Mém. de l'Acad. des Inscr.* tom. ix (1831), pp. 187 ff.; Lenormant, *La Monnaie dans l'Antiquité*, i. pp. 187 ff. (who gives other references). Ancient metallurgy, especially with regard to the mines of Laurion, is dealt with by Ardaillon, *Les Mines du Laurion*, pp. 59 ff.

[2] On the good character of the Athenian coinage see Hultsch, *Metrologie*, pp. 232 ff.; on the Macedonian, p. 248.

The silver of Magna Graecia of the early and best periods is of very good quality, though it not unfrequently falls below ·95 fine. Equally good results have been obtained for the East, although some of the smaller denominations, and the late coins of the Seleucidae, Lagidae, and Arsacidae are largely alloyed, the 'silver' coins of Ptolemy XIII, Auletes (B. C. 81-58 and 55-52), being made of copper slightly alloyed with silver. The silver of the Roman Republic was always of good quality except in the time of the civil war, when, for instance, the military issues of Marcus Antonius contained some twenty per cent. of copper. Under the Empire the history of the silver coinage is one of melancholy debasement [1]. Silver of a kind was issued by some provincial mints under the Empire, notably Alexandria in Egypt, Antiochia in Syria, and Caesarea in Cappadocia [2]. But the metal of these series rapidly degenerated into billon and bronze, therein resembling the coinage of Rome itself.

One of the most important metals used for coinage in antiquity was *electrum* (EL) or 'white gold' (ἤλεκτρος, ἤλεκτρον, λευκὸς χρυσός)[3], by which name the ancients designated any alloy (natural or artificial) of gold and silver, in which more than twenty per cent. consisted of the latter metal. The chief source of this mixed metal was Lydia, where it was yielded by the mountain-districts of Tmolus and Sipylus. It was regarded as a metal distinct from either gold or silver, for the purpose of coinage; but its actual composition seems to have varied within very wide limits[4]. It was used for coinage in the first place in Lydia, and very soon afterwards in several great cities of Asiatic Greece, in Cyrene, and perhaps in Aegina, Euboea, and even Athens. On the western side of the Aegean it was soon superseded by silver; but on the east its use was more enduring. It is found in Asia Minor in early times as far north as Cyzicus and Lampsacus, and as far south as Camirus in Rhodes. Two of the most important currencies of the fifth century were the electrum staters of Cyzicus (Pl. V. 8) and Lampsacus. The electrum of Mytilene

---

[1] See ch. iii. [2] See ch. iv.
[3] Blümner, *Technologie u. Terminologie d. Gewerbe u. Künste*, iv. p. 160.
[4] On the composition of electrum coins see Head, *Num. Chr.* 1875, p. 245 (*Metrological Notes on Ancient Electrum Coins*); 1887 p. 277 (*El. Coins and their Specific Gravity*); *Brit. Mus. Catal. Ionia*, pp. xxv ff.

(Pl. IV. 9) and Phocaea (Pl. IV. 8), in the form of sixths of the stater, exists in great quantities[1], and is somewhat later in date.

In the fourth century an electrum coinage is also found at Syracuse and at Carthage; at the latter place this metal was coined as late as the beginning of the second century. At the same time we find Capua coining electrum during her revolt from the Romans, who had themselves introduced the mixture some time before in their coins issued for Campania. These later issues of electrum seem to have partaken of a fraudulent character, and the metal was an artificial and not a natural product.

Copper was from the first days of its use in coinage almost always strongly alloyed with tin. The abbreviation Æ stands for copper and bronze indifferently. The smallest proportion of tin, so far as we can tell from the analyses hitherto made, is found in some coins of Massalia, although the copper in them can hardly, with Lenormant, be called 'absolument pur.' The analysis of these gives [2]—

            Copper 789
            Zinc 165
            Tin . . . . 28 } in 1000.
            Lead 12
            Silver 6

In other Greek bronze coins the proportion of tin is sometimes as large as sixteen per cent. Greek bronze coins contained a very slight amount of lead, not to speak of other metals in still more insignificant proportions[3]. The Roman bronze coins from the beginning contained lead in considerable quantity (twelve to twenty-nine per cent.). After Republican times the admixture of lead was discontinued until the time of M. Aurelius, when it was resumed. Under the Early Empire, however, it is necessary to distinguish between the metals used for the various denominations of coins. Thus the *sestertii* (Pl. XII. 11) and *dupondii* (Pl. XII. 9) were of brass (ὀρείχαλκος,

---

[1] But of the staters, only one (of Mytilene) is extant; the two known specimens of the Phocaean stater (Pl. I. 2) being of gold and belonging to an earlier period.
[2] Lenormant, i. p. 199; *Rev. Num Belge*, 1857, p. 319.
[3] Blümner, *Techn.* iv. p. 191.

orichalcum, aurichalcum, a mixture of copper and zinc); the *asses,* on the other hand, of pure copper[1].

§ 2. *Minor Metals and Alloys.*

Potin, as distinct from billon, which contains about one-fifth silver to four-fifths copper, is an alloy of copper, zinc, lead, and tin. It is not found as a monetary medium except in some late Gaulish coins, which are always cast, not struck, owing to the want of ductility characteristic of this composition[2].

A peculiar alloy of copper and nickel, in almost the same proportions as those employed in modern coinage, was used in the second century B.C. by some of the kings of Bactria, who thus anticipated the use of 'kupfernickel' by some 2,000 years[3].

A certain number of leaden coins have come down from antiquity, and the fact that they were used is attested by ancient writers[4]. The only known specimens earlier than the Christian era belong to the kings of Numidia. Besides these, leaden coins were issued, probably in the second or third century A.D., in Egypt, especially at Memphis, and in the first and second centuries A.D. in Roman Gaul. From actual leaden coins it is necessary to distinguish the leaden 'proof pieces,' struck with the dies afterwards used for the precious metals.

Tin coins are stated on good authority[5] to have been issued

---

[1] As Blümner, *Techn.* iv. p. 191, puts it: at the beginning of the Empire the proportion of tin falls, to rise again about 100 A.D. Zinc, which is wanting in Republican coins, is constantly found from shortly before the Christian era, in quantities of from ten to twenty per cent., and only begins to fail about the time of the thirty tyrants. Pliny (*N. H.* xxxiv. 4) is the authority for the distinction between the various denominations, and his statement, as Blümner (op. cit. p. 197) says, is partially confirmed by the analysis of the coins.

[2] Analysis: copper, sixty per cent.; zinc, ten per cent.; lead, twenty per cent.; tin, ten per cent.

[3] Flight, *Num. Chr.* 1868, p. 305. Nickel was known to the Chinese at an early period. Small traces of nickel have been found in modern times in association with copper at Kandahar, but not in sufficient quantity for coinage.

[4] Lenormant, i. p. 207. Polycrates of Samos is said to have deceived the Lacedaemonians with leaden coins plated with gold (Hdt. iii. 56, who, however, does not credit the story).

[5] Pseudo-Arist. *Oecon.* ii. 2. 20; Pollux, ix. 79. Polyaenus (iv. 10. 2) says that Perdiccas when fighting against the Chalcidians paid his troops by

by Dionysius of Syracuse. If the tradition is correct, all these pieces have disappeared[1]. False tin money is mentioned in the Digest[2]. A large hoard of tin denarii, of the time of Septimius Severus, was found at Lyons[3]; they were struck from dies otherwise used for silver, and were not plated. They appear in fact to have been meant by the government for circulation in Gaul.

Iron money is stated, also on good authority, to have been

FIG. 5.— Iron Coin of Argos. *Obv.* Forepart of Wolf. *Rev.* A. (From an electrotype in the British Museum.)

used at Byzantium[4] and at Sparta[5]. Lenormant holds that this was not money properly speaking, but bars or 'bricks' of iron circulating at their market price; in fact, the so-called iron money was a case of the survival of a premonetary medium of exchange. We know that the Spartan iron took the form of bars or spits (ὀβελοί, ὀβελίσκοι)[6]. Nevertheless there exist pieces of iron, purporting to be, and in every way resembling coins, with types which enable them to be attributed

striking χαλκόκρατον κασσίτερον, but this may mean copper plated with tin (*Zeit. f. Num.* 1898, p. 72).

[1] Probably by oxidation; Mongez, l. c. p. 200. J. P. Six has suggested that the so-called tin coins were composed of copper strongly alloyed with tin (*Num. Chron.* 1875, p. 28 ff.). A. J. Evans (*Num. Chron.* 1894, p. 219, Pl. VIII. Fig. 1) describes a coin of the same kind as the silver decadrachms of Euaenetus, but made of bronze, and showing traces of having been originally coated with a white metal, not silver, and probably tin. It is not a plated piece struck from one of the ordinary decadrachm dies; a special die must have been engraved for it. But Pollux speaks of a νομισμάτιον passing for four Attic drachms instead of one, whereas Mr. Evans' coin is a decadrachm; and the profit obtained by plating with tin instead of silver must have been so small as to make the fraud barely worth perpetration.

[2] x. 48. [3] Lenormant, i. p. 213.

[4] Pollux, vii. 105, ix. 78; Hesychius σιδόρεος. Aristoph. *Nub.* 249 et Schol.

[5] Plat. *Eryx.* 400; Plut. *Lycurg.* 9, *Lysandr.* 17 quoted above; Pollux, ix. 79.

[6] See above, p. 5, note 1. The Britons also used bars (or rods) of iron instead of money (Caes. *B. G.* v. 12).

to Tegea, Argos (Fig. 5), and perhaps Heraea[1]. They are of Aeginetic weight and their types are similar to those of the silver coins of these towns.

The glass pieces which are well known to students of Arabic numismatics have their analogy in certain pieces of this material dating from Roman Imperial and Byzantine times[2]. But there is no doubt that all these pieces alike are to be regarded not as coins but as coin-weights[3].

Wood, terra-cotta, and leather are mentioned by various writers as having occasionally been the material of money. There is no reason to doubt that a token coinage may have been issued in these materials. Terra-cotta casts of silver coins of various countries have been frequently found at Athens[4].

§ 3. *The Sources of the Metals.*

The sources of the metals which we have described are of some importance in the history of coinage since, in days of comparatively difficult communication, those metals as a rule which were most accessible in the neighbourhood would be made into coin. Thus the first coinage of Persia was largely a gold coinage, since the treasures of Central Asia were not far removed; the early coinage of Asia Minor was of the electrum from the Lydian mountains; that of Greece proper was of silver; that of Central Italy of bronze. Other facts less broad rest on similar bases; thus it is probably the nearness of the Crimea to the Asiatic gold mines that accounts for the high weight of the gold coins of Panticapaeum (Pl. V. 4), and the extraordinary continuance of a gold coinage (Pl. XIII. 3) in that part of the world even under the Roman Empire.

As to the distribution of the metals, we may take a brief survey, in geographical order, of the more important metalliferous districts in ancient times[5]. The metals we take in their natural order of precedence.

---

[1] Köhler in *Ath. Mitth.* 1882, pp. 2 and 377.
[2] Longpérier, *Rev. Num.* 1861, pp. 412, 413. The British Museum possesses a large number.
[3] See Lane-Poole, *Catal. of Arabic Glass Weights in the B. M.*, p. vii.
[4] See, on these materials, Lenormant, i. pp. 215, 220.
[5] In this we cannot do better than follow H. Blümner, *Techn. u. Termin. d. Gewerbe u. Künste,* iv (1887), where ample references to the authorities

In Africa there were two chief sources of gold; the mysterious interior, whence gold was brought by caravans to Egypt and Carthage; and the Abyssinian and Egyptian mountains. The island of Meroe was rich in gold and other metals; but most famous were the mountains between the Nile and the Red Sea, near Berenice Panchrysos, on the road from Assuan to Abu Hammed, near Olaki. The east coast of Africa, south of the Red Sea, was perhaps the land of Ophir.

In Asia, gold came from several places in Arabia; but far richer sources were the Altai Mountains and Siberia. The Indian supplies probably came from the region north of the Punjab. The fame of these districts came to the Greeks in the form of the well-known stories about the gold-digging ants, and the gold-guarding griffins. The gold mines of Armenia and Colchis were also important; the legend of the golden fleece not improbably originated in the practice of catching the gold dust by means of fleeces. In Asia Minor, there is record of a number of sources of gold, but their wealth was probably exaggerated. Gold was found in mines on Tmolus and Sipylus, and in the rivers Pactolus and Hermus which flowed from those mountains. These sources were already exhausted in Strabo's time. It is necessary also to mention the mines between Atarneus and Pergamum, near Abydus, Cremaste, Astyra, and Lampsacus; for these go a little way towards explaining the early gold and electrum currencies of the north-west corner of Asia Minor.

The tradition that the island of Siphnos possessed rich gold mines is supported by the fact that its inhabitants were unusually wealthy. The only other island to be mentioned here is Thasos, where, in the part lying opposite to Samothrace, the gold mines were early exploited by the Phoenicians. These mines belonged really to the same system as those of Thrace. In that country there were several important mines. Those at Skapte Hyle yielded as much as eighty talents a year in the beginning of the fifth century. We know that Athenian interests were strong in this district, and that the historian Thucydides owned mines there [1]. Daton was proverbially rich

will be found. For the distribution of gold in antiquity, see also W. Ridgeway, *Origin of Currency*, pp. 66 ff.

[1] The reference in Lucian (*De Sacrif.* 11) to statues made of Thracian gold hardly applies, as Blümner thinks, to Athens in particular.

in gold (Δάτον ἀγαθῶν). The mines called Asyla at Crenides (afterwards Philippi, Pl. VII. 3) became the chief source of the wealth of Philip II, yielding 1,000 talents a year. To these sources we may add Mount Pangaeus and the River Hebrus, and also the mines of Nisvoro in Chalcidice, which are still worked, though not for gold[1]. The other Thracian mines were worked as late as the fourth century A.D.

In Macedon it is necessary to mention the mines of Mount Bermion and of Pieria, as well as those near the Strymon, as far up as Paeonia. These were at first closed by the Romans, and afterwards (158 B.C.) reopened for the benefit of the Roman treasury.

The reports of gold in other parts of the Greek mainland are probably untrue. Even in Mycenaean times the gold which was buried in such quantities with the dead was probably imported from Asia Minor.

In Italy the most important gold mines were in Transpadane Gaul, especially near Aquileia, where the state took over the mines formerly belonging to the Taurisci.

Spain was a treasure-house of all the metals. The mines, which were first organized by the Phoenicians, and then passed to Carthage, and so to Rome, belonged in Imperial times mostly to the state. Gold was found in nearly all parts. In Gaul, too, all the metals were plentiful, gold especially being found in the mountain districts of the Northern Pyrenees, the Cevennes, and Switzerland. In Central Europe, the districts of Noricum, Dacia, Moesia (Hungary and Siebenbürgen) in the Danube district, as well as Dalmatia, where the gold mines were state-property, must be mentioned. The state also possessed gold mines in Britain (probably in South Wales).

Silver in ancient times was much less widely distributed than gold[2]. In Africa itself none was found, except in admixture with gold in the electrum mines of Aethiopia. In Asia we hear of it in Nabathaea, Northern India, Karmania, and Bactriana. The silver of Asia Minor was perhaps obtained by smelting the electrum. There were, however, silver mines

---

[1] W. C. F. Anderson, *A Journey from Mount Athos to the Hebrus*, p. 223 (in the Commemoration Volume of *University College, Sheffield*, 1897).

[2] It was, as Blümner (p. 29) notes, sometimes more costly than gold, as in Egypt (Lepsius, *die Metalle*—Berl. Akad. Abh. 1871—p. 51) and, as late as the days of Mungo Park, in Africa.

such as those at Balia in Mysia [1]; and a considerable amount of silver came from Colchis.

Of the Greek islands, Siphnos alone need be mentioned, and its store of silver was probably slight. On the mainland there were silver mines at Mount Pangaeus, and at Damastium in Epirus [2]. Elsewhere in Greece silver was scarce, except — important exception!—at Laurium [3] in Attica. It is probable that the great mines here were not properly worked until the time of Themistocles [4]. The mines belonged to the state, but were worked by contract. They were supposed to be quite exhausted by Strabo's time; nevertheless an attempt has been made in our own day to reopen them.

Italy possessed practically no silver. There were mines in Sardinia; but those between Populonia and Volaterrae were probably unknown to the ancients.

Spain was the great silver country of antiquity. Its silver mines [5] were worked by natives, Phoenicians, Carthaginians, and Romans; yet their output did not begin to fall off until Christian times. In Roman times the mines were at first in part the property of the Roman state; later a large number of them belonged to rich individuals, who paid a tax which yielded more profit to the state than the actual working of the mines by the government would have done. As silver was found in nearly all parts of the peninsula, it is unnecessary to specify the silver-bearing districts, except perhaps that of Osca, north of the Ebro, whence came the *argentum Oscense* often mentioned by Livy.

Of the remaining silver-bearing districts of Europe (Aquitania in Gaul, the district of the Mattiaci in Germany, Britain, Dalmatia, and Pannonia), only the last two are of any importance. The mines in these were the property of the state.

---

[1] W. C. F. Anderson, l. c.

[2] The miner's pick, hammer (τυπίς), and a block of metal with an attachment to enable it to be carried, are represented on the smaller coins. For specimens of the instruments, see Ardaillon, *Les Mines du Laurion*, pp. 21, 22.

[3] See the exhaustive work of E. Ardaillon, *Les Mines du Laurion dans l'Antiquité* (Bibl. des Écoles françaises), 1897.

[4] Silver was scarce at Athens in the time of Solon: Plut. *Solon*. 16.

[5] See the description of the mines in Diodorus Siculus, v. 36. One Euboic talent of silver could be won in three days; and in the time of Polybius no less than 40,000 men were at work in the mines of Carthagena.

The copper of antiquity came especially from two districts, Cyprus and Spain. But we have evidence of the finding of copper in Africa and Asia, as well as other parts of Europe. Thus, for Africa, although most of the copper used in Egypt came from the mines in the Sinaitic district, the metal was also found in the Thebaid and at Meroe [1]. The produce of such vaguely defined localities as 'the Numidian coast' and 'Libya' was probably unimportant. In Asia, Palestine, Edom, the Phoenician Lebanon, Chaldaea, and Karmania produced copper. In Asia Minor copper came from Cilicia, Cisthene in Mysia, the island of Chalcitis or Demonnesos, near Chalcedon, the district of the Mossynoeci on the south coast of the Euxine, and doubtless from several other places. The importance of Cyprus in respect of this metal is shown by the name borne by copper in a large number of languages. Whether copper gave its name to Cyprus or the island its name to the metal, matters little for our purpose; the latter alternative is, however, probably the true one. In the island, the most famous mines were at Tamassus (called Temesa in Homer), Amathus, Soli, Tyrrhias (?), and the promontory of Crommyon.

Legend fixed the discovery of copper at Chalcis in Euboea. We shall see that one explanation of the origin of the Euboic standard is based on the fact that copper was the staple product of the great Euboean cities. In Strabo's time the mine, which had possessed the peculiarity of producing iron and copper in conjunction, had given out. In the south of the island, on Mount Ocha, and perhaps in the north at Aedepsus, there are traces of copper mining. The sources of copper on the mainland of Greece were insignificant.

In Italy we must mention first the mines of Temesa in Bruttium. The similarity of name caused many critics in ancient times to suppose that Homer referred not to Temesa-Tamassus in Cyprus, but to the Bruttian city. Further north the mines of Elba (Aethalia) [2] and Volaterrae (the latter especially rich) produced the metal which was employed so largely in Italy, not only for bronze-work, as by the Etruscans, but also

---

[1] Copper was more important in the coinage of Egypt under the Ptolemies, than in that of any ancient state outside the Italian peninsula.

[2] The copper of Elba, however, gave out at a comparatively early date, and was succeeded by iron.

for the purposes of currency. The home produce was probably considerably supplemented by importation.

Spain, once more, takes an important position as a source of copper, which, next to silver, was probably her chief treasure. The region of the southern coast (Baetica) was especially rich, the most famous mines being at Cotinae in the Mons Marianus (Sierra Morena). The Rio Tinto mines which were also worked in antiquity were, however, probably not far behind in richness.

The amount of copper produced by Gaul and Germany was comparatively small. In Caesar's time, Britain used imported copper; but it appears that copper mines were anciently worked in Wales.

The chief source of tin in historical times lay in the Far West, in the 'Tin Islands.' These were probably the British Isles, or more accurately speaking South West Britain [1]. The metal came to the Mediterranean countries partly overland through Gaul to Narbo and Massalia, partly by sea to Spain, across the peninsula, and thence again by sea to its destination. In comparison with the British mines those of Spain and Gaul need hardly be mentioned.

Without going in detail into the source of the other metals, we may mention one fact which seems to bear on a numismatic question. The fact that the chief ancient source of iron, so far as the mainland of Greece is concerned, was in Peloponnesus, on the promontory of Taenarus, and in the range ending in Cape Malea, is not without significance in regard to the iron coinage of Peloponnesus.

§ 4. *The Testing of Metals in Antiquity.*

The description of the ancient methods of refining does not strictly come within the limits of our subject, and it is sufficient to refer to the treatment of these matters by Blümner [2].

It is probable that the ancients were much more skilful than ourselves at practically detecting the baseness of metal, apart

---

[1] That tin came thence as well as from the Spanish peninsula of course admits of no doubt. Where the ancients placed the 'Cassiterides' is another question.

[2] *Techn.* iv. p. 130 f. See also Gardner, *Types*, p. 17; Ridgeway, *Origin of Currency*, p. 81; and Mongez, op. cit. p. 188.

from a scientific assay. If the Chinese at the present day can test the purity of metals by sight, touch, sound, and smell, the Greeks were apparently as clever [1]. Copper, even when present in a small proportion only, betrays itself by its smell if the metal is warmed by friction. If the coin was plated, an obvious test was to stab the piece, and the marks of this test having been applied are to be seen on many ancient coins (Pl. II. 9). There is even authority for the use by the ancients of the touchstone to a degree which seems to us almost incredible [2]. Theophrastus [3] describes a stone, found especially in the river Tmolus, evidently the well-known 'Lydian stone' or βασανίτης λίθος, which could be applied as a test of not only refined metal, but also gold and silver when alloyed with copper (κατάχαλκος). By this means it was possible to tell what proportion was contained in the stater; the test revealed the presence of so small a proportion of alloy as a 'barley corn' (κριθή, i.e. $\tfrac{1}{72}$ obol?) in a stater. This test must surely have been carried out by the application of some reagent to the mark left on the touchstone, and not merely by noting its colour. But probably there is an element of fable in this account as in the account given in the treatise *De Fluviis* of the behaviour of the plant called *chrysopolis*, which grew near the Pactolus [4].

Silver was tested [5] by means of the touchstone, and also by the process of placing it on a red-hot iron shovel. Metal which under such conditions retained its clear white colour was pure; that which took a red hue was not so good; that which became black was worthless. There were, however, it would seem, methods of cheating this test. Another simpler test, when

---

[1] Epictetus, *Diss.* i. 20, 8 ὁρᾶτε καὶ ἐπὶ τοῦ νομίσματος ... ὅσοις ὁ ἀργυρογνώμων προσχρῆται κατὰ δοκιμασίαν τοῦ νομίσματος· τῇ ὄψει, τῇ ἁφῇ, τῇ ὀσφρασίᾳ, τὰ τελευταῖα τῇ ἀκοῇ· ῥάξας τὸ δηνάριον, τῷ ψόφῳ προσέχει κ.τ.λ.

[2] Ridgeway, in *Num. Chron.* 1895, pp. 104–109; Blümner, *Technol.* iv. p. 138.

[3] *De Lapid.* 46. Cf. Plin. *N. H.* xxxiii. 126 (the stone was called in Latin *coticula*, just as sometimes in Greek ἀκόνη). A piece of true metal, and the piece to be tested, were rubbed beside each other (παρατρίβειν) on the stone, and the colours of the streaks compared.

[4] Cap. vii. § 4. Πρὸς αὐτὴν γὰρ αἱ ἀστυγείτονες πόλεις τὸν ἀκέραιον χρυσὸν δοκιμάζουσιν. ἅμα γὰρ αὐτὸν χωνευθῆναι βάπτουσι τὴν βοτάνην· καὶ ἐὰν μὲν ἀνόθευτον τὸ χρυσίον ᾖ, τὰ φύλλα χρυσοῦται· ἐὰν δ' ἐφθαρμένον ὑπάρχῃ, τὴν ἠλλαγμένην ὑγρασίαν ἀποπτύει καὶ διατηρεῖ τῆς ὕλης τὴν οὐσίαν· καθὼς ἱστορεῖ Χρύσερμος ἐν γ´ περὶ Ποταμῶν. (Plutarch, *Moralia*, ed. Bernardakis, vol. vii. p. 295.)

[5] Blümner, *Techn.* iv. p. 153.

silver was polished, was to breathe upon it. Pure metal immediately threw off the moisture.

§ 5. *Oxide and Patina.*

On the nature of the metal, but still more on the character of the soil in which ancient coins have been buried, depends the quality of the surface which they now present. Gold suffers least of all the metals, but it is not uncommon to find gold coins, when freshly dug up, covered with a reddish deposit. This, however, is usually quite superficial. Silver of course becomes considerably oxidized under favourable circumstances. It is not uncommon for silver coins to be covered in addition with a greenish deposit from the surrounding earth, or possibly from bronze vessels in which they have been hoarded. But it is brass and bronze coins which are most affected by the circumstances of their burial. A very small percentage of the former retain their original bright yellow colour. In volcanic soils, such as those of South Italy, Sicily, and Thessaly, the effect of the sulphurous surroundings is happy, the rich green or blue porcelain-like patina which they impart being highly prized by collectors [1]. Other soils, again, such as that of many parts of Cyprus, are most destructive to metal.

[1] The dark bluish-green patina (such as that on a 'large brass' coin of Julia Domna in the British Museum, rev. type SPES) is rarer than the pale green.

CHAPTER II

THE COIN AS A MEDIUM OF EXCHANGE ORIGIN, DISTRIBUTION, AND RELATION OF COIN-STANDARDS

§ 1. *Theories of the Origin of Coin-Standards.*

THE least satisfactory department of ancient Numismatics is that which is occupied with questions of Metrology[1]. Rigid as may be the mathematical basis of this science, it is as yet impossible to erect on it a firm system into which the various measures adopted for coinage in ancient times can be safely fitted. Commercial interest and many other influences, at which we can only guess, combined to modify, often beyond recognition, the standards of weight which preceded the introduction of coinage.

Briefly regarded, the theories of the origin of coin-standards and weight-standards fall into two divisions. The one comprises theories according to which these standards are derived from a scientifically obtained unit or units; the other theory, for in this second division there is but one, regards man as making 'his earliest essays in weighing by means of the seeds of plants, which nature had placed ready to his hand as counters and weights[2].' The first object, it is supposed,

---

[1] F. Hultsch, *Griechische u. Römische Metrologie*, 2nd ed. 1882; J. Brandis, *Münz-, Mass- u. Gewichtswesen in Vorderasien*, 1866. Summary up to 1887 by Mr. B. V. Head in his *Historia Numorum*, pp. xxviii ff. For Roman coins especially, Mommsen-Blacas, *Histoire de la Monnaie Romaine*, and Samwer-Bahrfeldt, *Gesch. des ält. röm. Münzwesens*, 1883. See also Head's bibliography.

[2] W. Ridgeway, *Origin of Currency and Weight-Standards*, 1892, p. 387.

to which the art of weighing was applied, was gold, and the gold-unit all over the world was the amount equivalent in value to an ox. And this gold-unit was universally in the earliest times determined by weighing the metal against a certain number of grains of corn. That something like this was the origin of the weight-unit seems to be exceedingly probable, and the theory indeed so far meets with little opposition from the representatives of the 'scientific' school. Whether the weight was arrived at independently in various places by this method is another question. What concerns the metrologist, however, is the fact that at a very early period the Babylonians and the Egyptians had left this primitive system far behind. 'There is an interval of centuries between the two stages: (1) of the first introduction of the practice of measuring weight every time by a number of grains of corn, and (2) of the development or introduction of a scientific system with a fixed standard of weight—the origin and natural prototype of which were without influence on commerce and therefore a matter of no concern to it[1].' It was in Asia Minor, where Greece came into contact with the East, that coinage began, at a time when the scientific standards had long been in use for the weighing of metal. Whatever was the ultimate source of those standards, as applied to coins they can only be regarded as coming from the East. The unit of 8·42 grammes would not be employed by peoples in all parts of the world because that amount of gold was (if it was !) the equivalent of an ox, but because that unit was employed for the weighing of gold when the metal was first made into coin, and had continued to be employed as the use of coinage spread from East to West. It is sufficient for us to recognize that a fixed unit of weight had been already determined, whether by taking once for all the weight of a definite number of grains, or by some other process, as by weighing the amount of water contained in a certain cubic space.

[1] C. F. Lehmann, *Das altbabylonische Maass- u. Gewichts-system als Grundlage der antiken Gewichts-, Münz- u. Maass-systeme*, in the Transactions of the Eighth Oriental Congress at Stockholm, 1889. Other papers by this author which will be frequently referred to in the course of this chapter are *Altbabylonisches Maas u. Gewicht* in the *Verhandlungen der Berliner Gesellschaft für Anthropologie*, &c., 1889, pp. 245 ff., and *Zur Ἀθηναίων Πολιτεία* in *Hermes*, 1892, pp. 530 ff.

Admitting the existence of this developed system, we find that two countries, Babylonia and Egypt, dispute the claim of its origination. As, again, this question belongs to a stage prior to the history of our subject, it may be passed by. But, since coinage originated in Asia Minor and not in Egypt, it was the weight-system of Babylonia and its derivatives to which the early coin-weights belonged, and this system, therefore, so far as it concerns the coin-standards, must now be described [1].

§ 2. *Determination of Early Weight-Standards.*

The unit of weight was the *shekel* (σίγλος or σίκλος). This was $\frac{1}{60}$ of the *manah* or *mina* (μνᾶ), and this again $\frac{1}{60}$ of the

FIG. 6.—Babylonian Bronze Weight of 5 manahs.

highest weight of all, the talent (τάλαντον or load; the Semitic name was *kikkar*).

[1] I have already referred to the summary of the evidence as to the origin of the Greek coin-standards given by Mr. Head in his *Historia Numorum*. Since the publication of that work, the study has received a new development through the researches of Herr Lehmann (op. cit.). The latest contribution to the subject is by F. Hultsch, *Die Gewichte des Alterthums nach ihrem Zusammenhange dargestellt* (Abhandl. der Kön. Sächs. Ges. d. Wiss. xviii. no. ii. Leipzig, 1898).

THE COIN AS A MEDIUM OF EXCHANGE

To determine the amounts of these various denominations we are guided by various extant weights, mostly inscribed with their amounts.

BABYLONIAN WEIGHTS.

	Description of the weight.	Probable date.	Inscription (usually in cuneiform).	Weight in grammes.	Weight in grammes of resultant manah.
1	Bronze lion (Fig. 6)	?	'Five manahs of the king' in cuneiform, 'Five manahs weight of the country' in Aramaic.	5042	1008
2	,,	B.C. 850	'The Palace of Shalmaneser, king of the country, two manahs of the king' in cuneiform, and 'Two manahs weight of the country' in Aramaic.	1992	996
3	Stone duck	B.C. 1050	'The Palace of Irba-Merodach, king of Babylon, thirty manahs.'	15060·5	502
4	,,	?	'Thirty manahs of Nabusuma-libur, king of Assyria.'	14589 (broken)	About 500
5	,,	B.C. 2000	'Ten manahs'; and name of Dungi.	4986 (injured)	498·6
6	Stone cone		'One manah . . . imitation of the weight fixed by Nebuchadnezzar, king of Babylon' (B.C. 605-561), 'son of Nabopolassar after the pattern of the standard of Dungi' (B C. 2000).	978·309 (about 1·2 g. lost)	979·5
7	Oval stone		'Half manah,' &c.	244·8	489·6
8	,,		'Ur-nin-am.'	81·87	491·2
9	,,		'One-third manah in shekels. Palace of Nabu-sum-esir,' &c.	164·3	492·9

An examination of these weights reveals the following facts. In the first place, there are clearly two classes of manah, one the double of the other. Further, there is a distinction between the *royal* manah, represented by 1 and 2 (heavy), 3, 4, and 5 (light), and the *common* manah, represented by 6 (heavy), 7, 8, and 9 (light).

Of these, the common manah is probably the older, and the royal is derived from it. The raising of the norm was probably dictated by a principle of taxation, in accordance with which a certain percentage was added to all the common weights whenever payments were made to the royal treasury. In accordance with the Babylonian sexagesimal system, the addition was in the first instance $\frac{1}{24}$. This gives a heavy manah of 1022·9 g. to 1027 g. But in later times an addition of $\frac{1}{20}$ appears to have been made, revealing the influence of the decimal system, and this yielded a heavy manah of 1031·1 g. to 1035·3 g.

Finally, for the purposes of coinage, some deduction had to be made to defray the expense. This appears to have been calculated on a basis of two per cent., which yields a heavy manah of 1008 g. to 1010 g.

The raising of weights for the purpose of taxation is *a priori* probable, and the theory that weights were so raised is borne out by a weight of the time of Darius Hystaspes[1] with inscriptions in old Persian (the royal dialect), new Susic, and new Babylonian. The two latter inscriptions call the weight ⅓ mina 1 shekel; the royal inscription calls it 2 *karasha*. Now since the weight mina = 60 shekels, 1 shekel = $\frac{1}{20} \times \frac{1}{3}$ mina. Therefore 2 karasha = ⅓ mina + an addition of one-twentieth, or five per cent. The weight in question therefore is five per cent. in advance of the common ⅓ mina, and we have here an instance of the king's adding five per cent. to the common weight, and explaining the addition by inscription in the vernacular.

As regards the deduction for the mint, the evidence is not quite so clear[2]. But the usual weights of 8·40 g. for the daric (Pl. I. 11) and 5·60 g. for the siglos (Pl. I. 10) seem to have been obtained by some such deduction. The occurrence of higher weights, on the other hand, shows that the deduction was not always made. Again[3], the Ptolemaic drachm is

---

[1] Lehmann in *Verhandl. der Berl. Gesellsch. für Anthrop.* &c., 1889, p. 273.

[2] The daric, on which as weighing 8·57 g. Lehmann (op. cit. p. 279; Brandis, p. 66) bases one argument, weighs, according to Babelon (*Perses Achém.*, no. 124), only 8·25 g. The highest weight of any daric known to me is 8·46 g. (Babelon, no. 95); of any double daric, 17·002 g. (Brit. Mus.).

[3] Lehmann in *Hermes*, 1892, p. 535, note 2.

3·63 g. (the tetradrachm being a Phoenician stater of the common norm 14·55 g.); the maximum weight as found is 3·57 g. to 3·58 g. The Athenian gold drachm is never above 4·32 g. The reason is that the deduction for the cost of striking was made rigorously in consideration of the precious character of the metal. 'The measure in question,' as Lehmann points out, 'was a protective one. Metal which has already gone through the processes of smelting, refining, &c., is naturally the more valuable for the change. Ornaments made of such metal could obviously be placed on the market with more profit than if these laborious processes had to be performed. By keeping the intrinsic worth of a coin a little below its nominal value, the authorities made it more profitable to retain it as a coin than to put it into the crucible. The reduction could also be effected by alloying. In early times, in well-ordered states, where purity was an object, this method was avoided. And the occurrence of pieces of full weight, as in the Solonian coinage, was also due to a wish to win a reputation for the currency.'

The standard as thus reduced might be regarded as a new standard. Another state copying the standard in this reduced form, and making its own reduction, would bring about a further fall in the standard. This is probably one secret cause of the degradation to which coin-standards were subject.

The principle on which, for the purposes of coinage, the units within each norm were arrived at, may be explained by the following instance. Taking the light mina of the reduced royal norm at 505 g. we find that it contains sixty shekels or staters of 8·4 g. This was the unit employed for gold coinage on this norm. For monetary purposes, again, the weight-mina of sixty shekels was not used, but a money-mina of fifty shekels (420 g. in this case) was employed. This was the system for gold. But for silver another standard was required, because at this time the relation of gold to silver was of an inconvenient kind, being $13\frac{1}{3} : 1$ [1]. One gold shekel of 8·4 g. was therefore worth 111·72 g. of silver, or (a) ten pieces of silver of 11·172 g., or again (b) fifteen pieces of 7·44 g.

---

[1] Herod. iii. 95 τὸ δὲ χρυσίον τρισκαιδεκαστάσιον λογιζόμενον. This is only approximate, the truer relation being as in the text: Mommsen-Blacas, *Monn. Rom.* i. p. 407.

These weights could therefore be conveniently employed as units for silver coinage. We thus get the following system:—

Weight Mina.

Gold Shekel $= \dfrac{1}{60}$ of weight mina.

Gold Mina $= \dfrac{50}{60}$,, ,,

Silver Shekel (a) $= \dfrac{1}{10} \times \dfrac{13\frac{1}{2}}{60} = \dfrac{1}{45}$,, ,,

Silver Shekel (b) $= \dfrac{1}{15} \times \dfrac{13\frac{1}{2}}{60} = \dfrac{2}{135}$,, ,,

The shekel (a) is generally known as the Babylonian, Lydian or Persic, the shekel (b) as the Phoenician or Graeco-Asiatic. The Greeks appear to have obtained the former through the Lydians, the latter through the Phoenicians.

Calculated on this principle the gold and silver weights may be tabulated as follows:—

I. COMMON NORM.

Name of Weight.	Proportion of the Weight-Mina.	Heavy System. Weight in grammes.	Light System. Weight in grammes.
Weight Mina	$\frac{60}{60}$	982.4 to 985.8	491.2 to 492.9
Gold Mina	$\frac{50}{60}$	818.6 ,, 821.5	409.3 ,, 410.7
Gold Shekel	$\frac{1}{60}$	16.36 ,, 16.42	8.18 ,, 8.21
Babylonian Silver Shekel	$\frac{1}{45}$	21.82 ,, 21.90	10.91 ,, 10.95
Phoenician Silver Shekel	$\frac{2}{135}$	14.54 ,, 14.60	7.27 ,, 7.30

II. ROYAL NORM.

(a) *First full form* ($\frac{1}{24}$ higher than Common Norm).

Weight Mina	$\frac{60}{60}$	1023.3 to 1026.8	511.7 to 513.4
Gold Mina	$\frac{50}{60}$	852.8 ,, 855.7	426.4 ,, 427.8
Gold Shekel	$\frac{1}{60}$	17.04 ,, 17.10	8.52 ,, 8.55
Babylonian Silver Shekel	$\frac{1}{45}$	22.74 ,, 22.80	11.37 ,, 11.40
Phoenician Silver Shekel	$\frac{2}{135}$	15.16 ,, 15.20	7.58 ,, 7.60

(b) *Second full form* ($\frac{1}{20}$ higher than Common Norm).

Weight Mina	$\frac{60}{60}$	1031.5 to 1035.1	515.8 to 517.6
Gold Mina	$\frac{50}{60}$	859.6 ,, 862.6	429.8 ,, 431.3
Gold Shekel	$\frac{1}{60}$	17.18 ,, 17.24	8.59 ,, 8.62
Babylonian Silver Shekel	$\frac{1}{45}$	22.92 ,, 23.00	11.46 ,, 11.50
Phoenician Silver Shekel	$\frac{2}{135}$	15.28 ,, 15.34	7.64 ,, 7.67

		(c) Reduced form	b taxed at two per cent.).			
Weight Mina	84/85	10.08 to 10.10	504 to 505
Gold Mina	84/85	840 ,, 841.6	420 ,, 420.8
Gold Shekel	1/50	16.80 ,, 16.82	8.40 ,, 8.41
Babylonjan Silver Shekel	1/45	22.40 ,, 22.44	11.20 ,, 11.22
Phoenician Silver Shekel	1/67½	14.92 ,, 14.96	7.46 ,, 7.48

For the purpose of comparing the Babylonian with the Phoenician silver shekel, we may note that the heavy Phoenician silver shekel contains four times the unit which is contained three times in the light Babylonian silver shekel: thus, if we take the reduced royal norm, the light Babylonian silver shekel of 11·20 to 11·22 g. is ¾ of the heavy Phoenician silver shekel of 14·92 to 14·96.

§ 3. *Distribution of the Three Oriental Standards.*

The 'gold shekel' standard, as it may be called, was almost universally used for gold coins. The more important exceptions which occur, where gold is struck on different standards, will be noted in due place. Besides gold, electrum was occasionally issued according to this standard, or one closely resembling it. Thus we find the gold standard used for electrum at Cyzicus (16·328 to 16·005 g.), Lesbos (16·07 g.), Samos (8·618 g.). The famous early staters of Phocaea, weighing 16·516 to 16·458 g. (Pl. I. 2), are however not electrum, but gold. A high form of the gold standard was that in use in the Crimea (Pl. V. 4).

The Babylonian or Persian standard from Persia spread over the greater part of Asia Minor, passing along the southern and northern coasts, taking root sporadically on the west coast. Naturally, also, we find it in Cyprus, and perhaps hence, because of Cypriote trade, it passed to the Phoenician Aradus. From Asia Minor it passed across the Propontis to the southern coast of Thrace. And far away to the south-east we find it in later times, in the imitative coinage of Southern Arabia, although here some other standard may have accidentally assumed the Babylonian form.

The Phoenician standard prevailed less in Asia Minor than did the Babylonian. Still it was in use for the early electrum coins of Western Asia Minor. Most of the early coinage of Phoenicia is of course of the Phoenician standard; and even the dominion of the Syrian kings, who used another standard, failed to dislodge it. It held its ground at cities like Antioch even after they had fallen into the hands of Rome. The remarkable coins struck by the Jews in their first revolt (Fig. 7) are

Fig. 7.—Half-shekel of the First Revolt of the Jews. *Obv.* 'Half-shekel, year 3.' *Rev.* 'Jerusalem the Holy.' Weight: 7·11 g. [Slightly under actual size.]

of the Phoenician standard. Westward we find the Phoenician standard in some of the islands of the Aegean Sea, and farther north at Byzantium (where, however, it only obtained for a time), Abdera (whence it passed to the Bisaltian tribes in the interior), and Amphipolis. It was adopted by the early Macedonian kings, and made its way, after the failure of Athenian influence towards the end of the fifth century, into Thasos, Neapolis, and Chalcidice. In early times the Phocaeans had carried it to their colony of Velia in Southern Italy. Here it took firm root, producing the 'Campanian standard'; and still further west we find it in the Phocaean colony of Massalia. This was the progress of the Phoenician standard along the northern shores of the Mediterranean. Along the south coast it is equally wide-spread; Carthage naturally employs it, when at the end of the fifth century she begins to coin, not merely for silver but also to some extent for gold and electrum; in Cyrenaica it is found towards the close of the sixth century; and in Egypt, after a brief struggle with other standards in the time of Ptolemy Soter, it becomes the standard in use for both gold and silver.

§ 4. *The Aeginetic and Euboic-Attic Standards.*

The earliest coinage of Greece proper, of some of the Aegean islands, and of many other places scattered about the Greek world, is struck on a standard which cannot be identified with any of those just described. It is known, from the fact that its most famous representative is the currency of Aegina, as the Aeginetic standard. The highest weight reached by a coin of this class is 13·44 g. (a unique electrum stater at Paris)[1]. A few weigh 12·96 g. or a little more, but the normal weight is 12·57 g. If we except the Paris coin, and the iron pieces mentioned above (p. 17), the standard is confined to silver.

The usual explanation of this stater is that it is the stater of 14·5 g. in a degraded form[2]. Such a degradation at this early period (seventh century B.C.), face to face with the adoption of other standards in an unreduced form, is highly improbable. The standard has also been explained as a compromise between the Babylonian and the Phoenician standards, the old Aeginetic silver mina of 628·5 g. being equivalent to about six gold shekels of the royal weight (taking 13·4 g. as the normal weight of the Aeginetic stater, and the relation between gold and silver as 13·3 : 1). Mr. Ridgeway remarks[3] that this equation seems somewhat arbitrary. He himself supposes that the relation of gold to silver in Greece was not 13·3 : 1 as in Asia Minor, but 15 : 1. One gold piece of 8·4 g. would, therefore, be equivalent to ten silver pieces of 12·6 g., i.e. to ten Aeginetic staters of the normal weight[4].

It would be easy to multiply hypotheses of this kind. If, for instance, we assumed 16 : 1 as the relation of gold to silver, and reckoned from the gold shekel of the common norm, one gold piece of 8·18 g. would be equivalent to ten silver pieces of 13·08 g. This would explain the weight of all but the electrum stater, the exceptional weight of which might be explained as due to its material.

There is, however, a less arbitrary explanation[5]. The stater of 13·44 g. maximum gives a mina of 672 g. This is $\frac{2}{3}$ of the heavy, $\frac{4}{3}$ of the light Babylonian weight mina of the reduced royal norm, or $\frac{60}{50}$ of the light Babylonian silver mina of the same norm[6].

The later Aeginetic stater of 12·60 g. may be derived[7] with

[1] It is worthy of note that the reverse of this stater is of a character otherwise confined to the earliest coins of Rhodes. See Head, *Brit. Mus. Catal*, *Caria*, Pl. 34, nos. 7–10; Pl. 35, nos. 7–9. The attribution of the coin to Aegina is therefore doubtful.
[2] So Head, *H. N.* pp. xxxviii and 332. [3] Op. cit. p. 219.
[4] Mr. Ridgeway is, however, inconsistent with this explanation when he says (p. 217) that 'the weight of the heaviest specimens of any series must be regarded as the true index of the normal weight.'
[5] Lehmann, *Hermes*, 1892, p. 558.
[6] The Attic trade mina of 655 g. was derived in the same way from the common norm.
[7] Lehmann, *Verhandl. der Berl. Gesellsch. für Anthropologie*, &c. (1889), p. 278.

almost equal probability from the second full form of the royal norm. The stater in question implies a mina of 630 g. This is $\frac{6 0}{5 6}$ of the light Babylonian silver mina, $\frac{6 0}{5 6}$ of the light weight mina of this norm.

Whatever may have been the origin of the Aeginetic standard, its spread was, with the course of trade, towards the West. There are sporadic cases of its use as far east as Mallus and Celenderis in Cilicia, and Cyprus, but these are quite exceptional; it prevails largely, though not exclusively, in the Aegean islands. We find it also in Crete; and as far north as the western coast of the Euxine. But its chief home is on the Greek mainland, from Thessaly downwards, and in the Ionian islands (if the Corcyrean standard is a light form of the Aeginetic); Aegina itself counts as part of the mainland in this respect. Through the field occupied by the Aeginetic standard, the Euboic-Attic-Corinthian standard (to be described below) forced its way like a wedge, reaching across towards Italy and Sicily. The Aeginetic standard passed to Italy and Sicily with the earliest Chalcidian colonies, showing how great was the Aeginetic trade in this direction; for Chalcidian colonies, one would expect, would have used the standard of their mother-country [1].

The Euboic-Attic standard (stater of 8·72 g., mina of 436·6 g.) has generally been explained as derived from the Babylonian royal gold standard (stater of 8·42 g., mina of 421 g.). This derivation is open to the objections that a gold standard would be thus transferred to silver, and at the same time raised by a small amount [2]. Lehmann's suggestion [3] is again more plau-

---

[1] If, however, we accept the theory of Imhoof-Blumer, that the silver coins of Naxos, Zancle, Himera, and Rhegium were thirds and eighteenths of the Euboic-Attic tetradrachm (and this seems on the whole most probable), it is still noteworthy that these curious denominations must have been chosen because they fitted in with the Aeginetic standard. Mr. A. J. Evans notes (*Num. Chron.* 1898, p. 321) that the coins weighing about ·90 g. struck at these cities have no obvious relation to any but the Aeginetic system, of which they are obols; on the other hand, what appear to be Euboic-Attic obols were commonly struck at Zancle and Naxos. In any case, therefore, the system was a dual one.

[2] A principle to be observed in the explanation of standards is that when two standards resemble each other so closely, the resemblance may be due as well to coincidence as to relation. It should, however, be noted that this standard was actually used for electrum; see below, p. 38.

[3] *Hermes*, 1892, p. 549, note 1.

CH. II] THE COIN AS A MEDIUM OF EXCHANGE 37

sible. He supposes that Chalcis, the copper-city, where this standard probably originated, commanded the market in copper, and was able to put an unusually high price on that metal[1]. The relation of silver to copper in Ptolemaic times, and in all probability during many previous centuries, was 120 : 1. If we suppose that the people of Chalcis raised the price of copper one-fifth, the relation of silver to copper would now be 96 : 1. Now, when silver was to copper as 120 : 1, one light mina of silver was equivalent to 120 light minae of copper

$$= 2 \text{ light talents} \atop \text{or } 1 \text{ heavy talent} \Big\} \text{ of copper,}$$

and $\frac{1}{2}$ light mina of silver = 1 light talent of copper.

If the proportion were changed to 96 : 1, we should no longer have

but
    1 light silver mina = 1 heavy talent of copper
    $\frac{1}{2}$,, ,, ,, = 1 light ,, ,,
    $\frac{4}{5}$ light silver mina = 1 heavy talent of copper
    $\frac{2}{5}$,, ,, ,, = 1 light ,, ,,

Now $\frac{4}{5}$ of the light, or $\frac{2}{5}$ of the heavy, Babylonian silver mina of the common norm is exactly equivalent to the Euboic-Attic

FIG. 8.—Athenian Chalcūs. *Obv.* Head of Athena. *Rev.* Owl and Amphora.

mina of 436·6 gr. It is noticeable, in confirmation of this derivation on the basis of the ratio 96 : 1 for silver as compared with copper, that in the Euboic-Attic system the *chalcūs* (Fig. 8) was $\frac{1}{96}$ of the stater. The χαλκοῦς (στατήρ) was therefore, originally, a stater's weight of copper, and one stater of silver was worth ninety-six of copper.

[1] That is to say, it is supposed that Chalcis had a monopoly, if not in copper, yet in that kind of copper which was most in demand for bronze-work in the parts of the world with which Chalcis traded. It was therefore able to put up the price of the metal. The effect of abundance of gold in Panticapaeum (see below) was precisely the contrary; but this only means that no attempt was made to establish a monopoly. It must be admitted that Lehmann's theory is based on a conjecture, but it is a conjecture remarkably confirmed by the place of the χαλκοῦς in the scale of denominations.

The so-called Corinthian standard was the same as the Euboic-Attic, differing only in its divisional system. It will be discussed in greater detail below (§ 6).

This Euboic-Attic standard is met with occasionally on the west coast of Asia Minor in early times. The rude but remarkable pieces of electrum attributed by Babelon[1] to Samos are struck on this standard (17.42 g. to the stater). But its real home is in Euboea and Attica. Hence it spread northwards to Chalcidice, Aenus, and elsewhere. It passed westwards to Sicily, where, having ousted the Aeginetic standard (see above, p. 36, note 1), it became thoroughly established in the early years of the fifth century. From Sicily it went northwards to Etruria (see below, § 12). But the great triumph of the Attic standard was reserved for the Hellenistic age. Its adoption by Alexander the Great, and the enormous number of coins issued by him and his successors on this standard, changed the whole face of the Greek coinage. The innumerable copies of the tetradrachms of Alexander and Lysimachus, and the large showy 'spread' tetradrachms of Asia Minor, all of Attic weight, are evidence of the popularity of the standard. It penetrated even to Syria, and practically as far east as Alexander's civilizing influence was felt, until it lost itself in India.

These five ('Gold-shekel,' Babylonic, Phoenician, Aeginetic, Euboic-Attic-Corinthian) were the standards of Greece proper and the East. The most important of the peculiarly Western standards was of course the Roman. This was really a local standard, and did not spread over the civilized world in the natural course of commerce. Its adoption outside the Italian peninsula was due to the force of Roman domination. It may, therefore, be most suitably discussed when we reach Italy in the survey of the various countries in which standards were used other than the five great ones already described.

§ 5. *Local Standards of Asia Minor.*

On the western coast of Asia Minor, the great seaport of Miletus is credited with a large series of early electrum coins, the weight of the stater being 14.18 to 14.24 g. The standard

---

[1] *Rev. Num.* 1894, pp. 149 ff.

appears to be an adaptation of the Phoenician standard of the common norm, by a deduction of $\frac{1}{40}$ (for $14.18 = \frac{39}{40} \times 14.54$)[1]. This standard is also found in the electrum coinage of Chios (14.06 g.) and Samos (same weight, Pl. I. 12).

Chios itself employed a peculiar standard for its silver coinage. The earliest silver didrachms (Pl. I. 16) weigh 7.97 g., pointing to a tetradrachm of 15.94 g., the slightly later tetradrachms (still early in the fifth century), 15.29 g. The standard is explained by Mr. Head[2] as a raised form of the Phoenician, but the elevation was probably due to adjustment with the Aeginetic standard, since four silver staters of 15.5 g. = five Aeginetic silver staters of 12.4 g.[3].

When Rhodes, about 400 B.C., deserted the Attic standard, its silver (Pl. V. 5) was struck on a standard according to which the tetradrachms weigh 14.90 to 15.55 g.; probably the same as the Chian standard [4].

To Samos belongs a peculiar standard, according to which the silver tetradrachm weighed 13.3 g. This is roughly $\frac{5}{6}$ of the weight of the contemporary Chian tetradrachm of 15.94 g. ($13.3 \times \frac{6}{5} = 15.96$).

The cistophori, circulating in that part of Asia Minor which afterwards became the province of Asia, represent a peculiar standard. These coins were a quasi-federal currency, which originated probably at Ephesus about 200 B.C., and was adopted at Pergamum (Pl. X. 2) and spread by Pergamene influence. The tetradrachms weigh 12.73 g. normal. They were regarded by the Romans as equivalent to three denarii, and were worth rather less than $\frac{3}{4}$ of the Attic tetradrachm of 17.44 g. ($12.70 \times \frac{4}{3} = 16.93$) which circulated so widely at this time in the Eastern Mediterranean. Nevertheless, we frequently find on the staters of Side (Pl. VIII. 5), which are of Attic weight, the counter-marks of cistophoric mints, which would seem to show that these staters were tariffed as equivalent to cistophori. Cistophori were also issued in Crete.

An exceptional issue of gold by Ephesus during the Mithradatic war is represented by staters of the usual weight, and

---

[1] Lehmann, *Altb. Maass.* p. 264. [2] *H. N.* p. 513.
[3] This connexion is proved by the name τεσσαρακοστὴ Χία, the Chian silver stater being $\frac{1}{40}$ of the Aeginetic mina. Hultsch, *Metr.* p. 554.
[4] Head, *Brit. Mus. Catal., Caria*, p. civ.

smaller coins of 5·461 g. The latter are explained as being halves of the Roman aureus of 10·912 g.

The so-called 'medallions of Asia Minor,' struck under the early Empire (Pl. XII. 8) down to the time of Hadrian, were a continuation of the cistophori, and equivalent to three Roman denarii (normal 11·70 g. down to the time of Nero, thenceforward 10·23 g.).

§ 6. *Local Standards of European Greece.*

The most important city inhabited by Greeks in the Crimean district (Panticapaeum) struck gold staters of 9 072 g. (Pl. V. 4). This high standard was probably due to the cheapness of gold in this district, through which would pass great quantities of the metal from the gold-bearing regions of Central Asia [1].

In Greece proper, the Victoriate standard, which is of Italian origin, and will be discussed below, is found in Northern Greece after the 'liberation' by Flamininus in 196 B.C.

The most important state on the east coast of the Adriatic in early times was Corcyra, which employed a light form of the Aeginetic standard (stater from 11·87 to 11·01 g., Pl. II. 7). In the course of two and a half centuries the weight declined, so that by the end of the fourth century B.C. the stater weighed as little as 10·36 g. The drachm of about 5·18 g. could now be regarded as a didrachm of the Corinthian standard. The Corcyraean standard, used in various neighbouring places, such as Apollonia and Dyrrhachium, down to the fourth century, was finally ousted by its powerful rival, the Corinthian. But before this it had made its way across the Adriatic, and established itself as one of the two standards in use in Etruria.

The origin of the Attic standard has already been explained. The history of the Athenian coinage, however, contains one episode of great interest and historical importance. Before the time of Solon's introduction of the Attic standard a weight-standard known as the Pheidonian, from its founder Pheidon, king of Argos (see above, p. 6), was in use at Athens. Solon introduced a new and heavier system, in which the drachm weighed $\frac{1}{70}$ of the Pheidonian mina. The resultant stater (or didrachm) of this Solonian system weighed 17·46 g.

[1] Head, *H. N.* pp. 238, 239.

That 'didrachm' is what was afterwards called a tetradrachm; but Aristotle or his redactor[1] clearly tells us that the 'old struck coin' was a didrachm. The drachm was lowered to half its weight, in all probability by the tyrant Hippias[2].

The standard of Corinth, the earliest coins of which city belong probably to the time of Periander (B.C. 625–585) has the same unit as the Euboic, but differs in its divisional system. The stater (Pl. II. 5) at first weighed 8.40 g., later as much as 8.66 g.; but it was divided into three drachms (Pl. II. 6). These drachms weigh 2.91 g., a weight which implies a full stater of 8.73 g., i.e. nearly exactly the normal weight of the Attic didrachm. Thus two Corinthian drachms (5.82 g.) would be fairly equivalent to one Aeginetic drachm of about 6.30 g., at least for purposes of ordinary trade. The Corinthian standard was thus practically connected with both the Euboic-Attic and the Aeginetic standards. The Corinthian standard was the origin of the peculiar 'Italic' and 'Tarentine' standards.

§ 7. *The Western Mediterranean.*

We may now pass to the Western Mediterranean. In such parts as were colonized by the Greeks we find various Greek standards — Aeginetic (possibly), Phoenician, Euboic-Attic. But before the introduction of coinage there existed in these parts a medium of exchange in uncoined bronze, and the earliest standard of Italy at least is therefore a bronze standard. It can nevertheless be fitted into the Babylonian system. The old Italic pound of 273 g. is half the light Babylonian silver mina of the common norm (545 to 547 g.). The Roman pound of 327 to 328 g. is one-third of the heavy weight mina, or three-tenths of the heavy Babylonian silver mina, of the same norm. It is on this pound weight of bronze of 327.45 g. (*libra*, λίτρα) that the Roman currency is based, the bronze *as libralis* being the coin of the weight of the Roman pound. The silver equivalent of the pound weight of bronze was in

---

[1] 'Αθηναίων Πολιτεία, cap. 10 : ἦν δ' ὁ ἀρχαῖος χαρακτὴρ δίδραχμον.
[2] See below, ch. iii. § 2. For the theory of Solon's reform of the standard stated in the text, I have given reasons in *Num. Chron.* 1897, pp. 284 ff. The arguments of G. Gilbert (*Neue Jahrbücher f. Philologie*, 1896, p. 537), which I had not seen at the time, do not seem to me to establish the theory that the type of the Solonian coinage was an ox.

Rome a scruple (*scripulum*), of 1·137 g., and this was the basis of the Roman silver currency, the coin (*nummus*) of this weight representing in value the libral as.

The scripulum and the λίτρα are also the units of the gold coinage of this part of the world.

§ 8. *Sicily.*

The Euboic-Attic system, when introduced into Sicily early in the fifth century, was brought into connexion with the native Sicel system in a curious way. When the Sicel towns became Hellenized, they struck small silver coins of 0·87 g. being the equivalent in value of a litra of bronze, and therefore called litrae. This silver litra was, as we are told by Aristotle[1], one-tenth of the Corinthian or Euboic-Attic stater. The towns using the Attic standard thus worked the litra into their own system, in some cases distinguishing it from the obol by a different type. The litra was divisible into twelve parts. We thus find in Sicily an elaborate system of weights, some of which belong to the litra-system, some to the Attic system, and some to both[2].

Gold was first coined in Sicily towards the end of the fifth century B.C.[3]. The weights of the coins are not calculated according to the usual system, but depend on the relative value of gold and silver: any one gold piece being exchangeable for a round number of the ordinary pieces of silver (the Corinthian stater or the Attic tetradrachm). The first gold pieces of Syracuse, Gela, and Catana or Camarina appear to prove a ratio of 15 : 1. On this ratio we have pieces of

$$1\cdot75 \text{ g.} = 1\cdot75 \times 15 \text{ g. of silver} = 3 \text{ staters or 30 litrae.}$$
$$\left.\begin{array}{c}1\cdot17 \text{ g.}\\1\cdot15 \text{ g.}\end{array}\right\} = 2 \text{ staters or 20 litrae.}$$
$$0\cdot58 \text{ g.} = 1 \text{ stater or 10 litrae.}$$

A little later we have pieces of gold at Agrigentum of 1·33 g.,

---

[1] Pollux, 4. 175.
[2] See the table in App. I.
[3] According to Mr. Head between 415 and 405 B.C. (*H. N.* p. 153), according to M. Th. Reinach (*Sur la Valeur rel. des Métaux mon. dans la Sicile grecque, Rev. Num.* 1895, pp. 489 ff.) between 440 and 420 B.C.

CH. II] THE COIN AS A MEDIUM OF EXCHANGE 43

marked with two globules. On a ratio of 13 : 1, these would be equivalent to two staters of silver.

The ratio 12 : 1 comes in after 412 B.C. and lasts for a considerable time, but in the third century there seems to be evidence for a ratio of 10 : 1.

Thus we have at Syracuse—

B.C.	Weight of gold coin in grammes.	On Ratio 12 : 1 equivalent to	On Ratio 10 : 1 equivalent to
After 412	5.75–5.80	8 staters or 80 litrae	
	2.90	4 staters or 40 litrae	
Time of Timoleon	2.12–2.15 (one marked ∴)	3 staters or 30 litrae	
340–317	4.30–4.35	6 staters or 60 litrae	
	2.85–2.90	4 staters or 40 litrae	
	1.40–1.42	2 staters or 20 litrae	
310–289	8.70	12 staters or 120 litrae	
	5.70	8 staters or 80 litrae	
	4.20	6 staters or 60 litrae	
287–270	4.30	6 staters or 60 litrae	
270–212	8.47		96 litrae
	4.25		48 litrae
	4.20		48 litrae
	2.12		24 litrae
	2.72		32 litrae

Electrum was struck at Syracuse in the time of Timoleon or of Dion, of the following weights:—

Grammes.	At ratio of 10 : 1 equal in silver to
6.90	4 tetradrachms or 80 litrae
3.60	2 tetradrachms or 40 litrae
1.85	1 tetradrachm or 20 litrae
0.72	10 obols or 8 litrae.

This ratio of 10 : 1 was that which obtained between native electrum and silver in the East at the end of the fifth century, and was probably the ratio prevailing in the West.

Bronze in Sicily was coined as real money, after the time of Timoleon's expedition, at Syracuse and various Sicel towns such as Adranum, Agyrium, Herbessus, &c. Up till then bronze coins as a rule only represented value conventionally. Even now the bronze coins probably represented a somewhat greater value than was justified by their actual weight. The weights however, at any time, seem to be so irregular that it is impossible to arrive at any certainty as to the exact weight of the litra of bronze[1].

§ 9. *Roman Bronze.*

In the history of the coinage of the Italian peninsula there are two great factors, Greek and Roman influence. The spheres corresponding to these factors in early times are

Fig. 9.—*Aes rude* from Caere. (From Garrucci, *Le monete dell' Italia Antica*, I Pl. IV.)

practically Southern Italy and Etruria for Greek, Central and non-Etrurian Northern Italy for Roman. In spite of the order of treatment to which chronology points, it seems necessary to deal first with the standards in use in Rome and Central Italy.

It will be convenient to deal with the various standards of coinage employed at Rome according to the chronological order in which the three metals were introduced into the coinage-

---

[1] See Head, *H. N.*, under Agrigentum, Camarina, Himera, Panormus, Segesta. The nominal weight of the Sicilian litra of bronze was 218 g., the relation of silver to bronze being as 250 : 1. Hultsch, *Metr.* p. 660 f.

system. The oldest metallic medium of exchange employed by the Romans and Italians, the *aes rude* (Fig. 9), consisting of amorphous lumps of bronze [1], was not cast in pieces of fixed weight. Scales were continually employed in all transactions in which this medium passed. There is, however, a certain uniformity traceable in the weights; the heaviest pieces weigh about 5 Roman lbs. (1640 g.); others about 4¼ lbs. (1490 g.). The basis of the system of coins properly so called was, as

Fig. 10.—Reverse of Italian *aes signatum* (⅔ scale). Weight: 1790.23 grammes (27627 grains Troy).

already stated (§ 7), the pound (*libra*) of bronze (327.45 g.). The early heavy bronze coinage of Rome, which began about the middle of the fourth century [2], is consequently known as the libral *aes grave*.

The highest denomination of this early system of circular coins is the *as* of one lb. weight [3]; but not earlier than the introduction of this coinage are the large oblong bricks of

[1] With very little tin (one piece contained only 0.063 of that metal). Hultsch, *Metr.* p. 255.
[2] Not the fifth, as was formerly supposed. Samwer u. Bahrfeldt, *Gesch. des ält. röm. Münzwesens* (Wien, 1883), p. 14 ff.
[3] 'Scriptula CCLXXXVIII, quantum as antiquos noster ante bellum Punicum pendebat,' Varro, *de R. R.* 1. 10; Hultsch, p. 258.

bronze (Fig. 10), which were issued in Rome and other parts of Italy even in the third century. These probably passed as multiples of the libral *as*. The denominations from the *as* downwards were as follows:—

	Mark of value.
As of 12 unciae	I
Semis of 6 unciae	S
Triens of 4 unciae	• • • •
Quadrans of 3 unciae	• • •
Sextans of 2 unciae	• •
Uncia	•

Very few extant coins testify to the full libral weight of the *as*. A solitary specimen weighs the excessive amount

FIG. 11.—Roman *as* of 10½ oz. *Obv.* Head of Janus. *Rev.* Prow of galley, and mark of value I. ⅔ scale. Weight: 289.88 grammes (4473.5 grains Troy).

of 390.3 g., but it is probably under the influence of some non-Roman standard[1]. There exist however a

semis of 161.25 g. indicating an *as* of 322.50 g. (Vienna),
a *triens* of 110.44 g. indicating an *as* of 331.32 g. (Vienna),
and an *uncia* of 27.32 g. indicating an *as* of 327.84 g. (Collegium Romanum).

The heaviest *asses* (apart from the exceptional one just mentioned) weigh from 312.3 g. to 300 g., i.e. between 12 and 11 oz.

This high standard was not long maintained. Probably

[1] Kubitschek in Pauly-Wissowa, *Real-Enc.* ii. 1509.

before the end of the fourth century, the effective weight of the *as* was 10 oz. (Fig. 11). The Roman colony of Luceria (in Apulia), which was founded in 314 B.C., issued its first coins on the standard of 10 oz. Between this date and 268 B.C. the standard sinks rapidly, pausing, as it were, for a while, although without definite legal recognition, at 7½ oz., about the turn of the century. By 268 B.C. the as weighed from 3 to 2 oz.[1]. In this year[2] the silver coinage was introduced. The earliest silver of the highest denomination (*denarius*) weighs 4·63 g. to 4·45 g. (Pl. XI. 8), and the normal weight was 4 scruples or $\frac{1}{72}$ of the pound (4·55 g.). The *quinarius* (Pl. XI. 11) similarly weighed normally 2 scruples; the *sestertius* (Pl. XI. 10) 1 scruple. These denominations bear marks of value:—

X = 10 *asses*,
V = 5 *asses*,
IIS = 2½ *asses*.

The as in terms of which the value of these coins is expressed is not the old libral, but the new sextantal as. The ratio between silver and bronze shown by this system is 120 : 1. So low had silver fallen from the time when the scripulum ($\frac{1}{288}$ lb.) of silver was the equivalent of the pound of bronze.

Besides the three silver coins mentioned, the *victoriatus* (Pl. XI. 12) was also issued in or soon after 268. This coin was struck at a normal weight of 3 scruples (¾ denarius) or 3·41 g. Together with it appeared its half (with the mark of denomination S) and its double (a rare coin). The absence of marks of value showing the worth of these coins in *asses* may be explained by the statements of ancient authors that the victoriatus was treated *loco mercis*[3].

Between 268 and 241 B.C. silver of the standard described and bronze of the sextantal standard were issued by the same moneyers. The stress of the First Punic War caused a fall in the weight of the denarius, which, probably about the

---

[1] The system in which the *as* weighed but 2 oz. (the weight of the old *sextans*) is known as the sextantal system.

[2] The law introducing the silver coinage may have been introduced in 269, the coinage itself in 268. This would explain the discrepancy in the dates given by ancient authorities (Hultsch, p. 267).

[3] It was indeed struck to meet the demand of a trade with Northern Greece.

close of the war[1], was fixed by law at $\frac{1}{84}$ lb. (3·90 g.). At this weight it remained until the time of Nero. The sesterce was probably not issued after the end of this war; but the quinarius appears occasionally even after 217 B.C. The sesterce, however, remained the unit for reckoning sums of money. This it had been from its inception when, probably, the old libral *asses* which were in circulation were tariffed as equivalent to one sesterce[2]. For we find that in all calculations the (old libral) as and the sesterce are convertible terms.

The next great change in the coinage coincides with the

FIG. 12.—*As* of 1⅓ oz. Weight: 32·63 grammes (503·5 grains Troy).

crisis in the Hannibalian war. In 217 B.C., by the *lex Flaminia*, the *uncial* standard was legalized, the as now weighing no more than $\frac{1}{12}$ lb. Fig. 12 shows an as probably issued just before the fixing of this standard. At the same time the denarius was made equivalent to 16 asses instead of 10[3]. Silver thus stood to bronze in the relation of 112 : 1. About two years later the quinarius was issued for the last time, and shortly afterwards (about 211 B.C.) the victoriate coinage came to an end. From about 160 to 110 B.C. only the lower denomina-

---

[1] Bahrfeldt in *Z. f. N.* v. p. 43.
[2] By such an arrangement all possessors of *asses* of more than 5 (old) oz. would suffer considerably.
[3] The sign XVI, or its equivalent ✳, accordingly appears on the denarii, but not to the exclusion of the old X. In the case of soldiers' pay, *semper denarius pro decem assibus datus est* (Plin. *N. H.* xxxiii. 45). This meant that the legionary continued as before to receive an annual *stipendium* of 1200 old-standard asses or 120 denarii. Caesar raised this to 225 denarii, by giving 3600 asses of the new standard for 1200 of the old standard. The legionary thus got 10 new-standard asses per day (Tac. *Ann.* i. 17).

tions of the bronze coinage were issued. In 89 B.C. the *lex Papiria* fixed the weight of the as at half an ounce, thus establishing the *semuncial* standard[1].

After the reductions had begun, the small size of the as permitted of the issue of larger denominations of a circular form. A single *decussis*, weighing in its present condition 1105·900 g.[2], seven *dupondii* (from 220·25 g. to 151·70 g.), and six *tresses* (from 313 g. to 208 g.) are known. They all have the same types: on obv. head of Minerva, on rev. prow to the left. The marks of value are X, III and II. *Dupondius* is of course an erroneous, if intelligible, name for a coin which no longer came near a single pound in weight. These high denominations, however, disappeared soon after the uncial reduction, while the sextans and uncia were rarely issued. The Roman bronze issues ceased between 84 and 74 B.C., not to be revived in Rome until Imperial times. Roman

---

[1] This sketch of the reduction of the Roman as and denarius is founded on the work of Samwer-Bahrfeldt, *Gesch. des ält. röm. Münzwesens*. This treatise has made it necessary to considerably modify the hitherto almost universally accepted theory of Mommsen, which assumes (1) an original 10 oz. as, only *de jure* libral; (2) a triental instead of a sextantal standard in association with the denarius of 268 B.C.; (3) the year 217 B.C. as the date of the reduction of the denarius. The facts are by no means certain. In favour of Mommsen's theory are certain minor circumstances. Thus the colony of Brundisium, founded in 244 B.C., issued its first coins on the triental standard. But no safe inference can be drawn from distant colonies, whose standards were subject to local influence. Thus Ariminum, colonized in 268 B.C., used a standard in which the *as* weighed more than 388 g. Mommsen argues from this that the libral standard was in use in Rome (at least, legally recognized) down to 268 B.C. But the weight is much in excess of the Roman pound, and evidently due to local circumstances. Logically, Mommsen should have argued from this weight not to a libral, but to a plusquam-libral standard at Rome. Mommsen's theory that 2½ triental asses were equivalent to one original as of 10 ounces is true, but for the important exception that the 10 ounce as was not the original one. The sestertius (valued at 2½ new asses) was therefore not really equivalent to the original as, even if the new asses were triental, instead of being, as they were, sextantal. Finally, there is literary testimony to the fact that between the libral and sextantal standards there was no legal definition of any other standard (Samwer-Bahrfeldt, pp. 176, 177). These questions cannot of course be finally dismissed in a footnote; and the rival arguments, as stated by their formulators, must be weighed by those who wish to come to a definite opinion.

[2] Prof. Luigi Pigorini has been good enough to furnish me with the exact weight. But the coin is perforated by a hole 8 mm. in diameter, causing a loss of weight which he estimates at about 4·500 g. The full weight of the piece may therefore be put at about 1110·400 g.

generals occasionally issued bronze coins bearing their names: pieces of 4, 3, 2 *asses*, and 1, ½, and ⅛ (or perhaps ¼) *as*; the bronze 'sesterce' of 4 asses, which now appears for the first time, bears the mark HS or sometimes Δ (= 4).

In 15 B.C. the Senate received authority to strike coins in the baser metal, with the letters S C (*Senatus Consulto*).

Fig. 13.—*As* of Augustus, struck by T. CRISPINVS·SVLPICIANVS IIIVIR. A. A. A. F. F. S. C. 15 B.C. Weight: 10·89 grammes.

The denominations were the *sestertius* (Pl. XII. 11) of 4 asses (τετρασσάριον), the *dupondius* (Pl. XII. 9) of 2 asses, the *as* (Fig. 13), and the *semis* (Fig. 14). The last is found until the time of Caracalla, and subsequently under Trajan Decius. *Quadrantes* appear also to have been issued, though

Fig. 14.—*Semis* of Q. *Aelius* LAMIA, C. SILIVS and ANNIVS, IIIVIRi A. A. A. F. F. S. C. Simpulum and lituus. 13 B.C. Weight: 3·04 grammes.

not after Trajan's time. *Sestertius* and *dupondius* were made of brass, *as* and *semis* of copper; the sestertius had the weight of 8 denarii (1 ounce, 27·29 g.), the dupondius and the as were equal in weight (4 denarii). The semis and quadrans weighed ⅛ and 1/16 oz. respectively. Under Nero some of these coins were for a time given marks of value (II, I, S for dupondius, as, and semis); afterwards the head of the emperor was represented radiate on the dupondius, and laureate or bare on the as. Other obvious distinctions of denomination there were none. The values of the baser metals in relation to gold and silver at this time need not concern us.

The degradation[1] of the silver coinage in the third century caused it to become indistinguishable from the bronze, but for a slight silvery tinge, given by an admixture of silver, and the absence of the letters S C. Probably the denarius became mere bronze change, while the *antoninianus* (Pl. XV. 4), introduced by M. Aurelius Antoninus (Caracalla), retained as long as possible a legal value above its intrinsic worth. The continued degradation caused the bronze of the earlier senatorial issues and of the provinces, and perhaps also the denarius (as opposed to the antoninianus) to have a value as coins, properly speaking, and not as mere tokens. The bronze coinage proper came to an end shortly before the time of Diocletian.

The bronze coins of Diocletian[2] and his co-regents fall into two classes, 'middle' and 'small' (to use the parlance of collectors). Both contain a little silver which is driven on to the surface of the coin by chemical treatment. The smaller kind have the radiate head; these ceased to be issued when Diocletian reformed the currency in 296 A.D. The larger coins (Pl. XV. 9), struck after the reform, bear marks of value XX, XX·I, XXI or I (K, KA, AK or A)[3]. The XX or K must signify that the coin is the double denarius or *follis*[4] of the time; the I or A that it is the unit of reckoning. XX·I, probably, is meant for an equation (2 denarii = 1 unit). Diocletian did not strike denarii, but a small bronze coin, probably the half-

---

[1] For the state of affairs at the beginning of the third century, see the inscription of Mylasa in Caria, published by Th. Reinach, *Bull. Corr. Hellén.* 1897, pp. 523 ff.; *Nouv. Rev. hist. de Droit*, 1898, pp. 5 ff.

[2] For this period see especially O. Seeck (*Die Münzpolitik Diocletians u. sein. Nachfolger*, *Z. f. N.* 1890, pp. 36 ff.) from which article the following details are taken.

[3] Some of these marks appear on the coins as early as the time of Aurelian.

[4] Follis means (1) a purse; (2) a purse of bronze coins ('collective follis'); (3) a small bronze coin ('coin-follis'), which, with a number of its fellows, went to make up a follis in the second sense. The coin-follis was equivalent to 2 denarii and $\frac{1}{12}$ or more probably $\frac{1}{25}$ of the siliqua (see below). The so-called silver follis was merely the silver value of the collective follis. Seeck (*Num. Zt.* xxviii. p. 178 f.) identifies the *follis* and *sestertius*.

denarius or *centenionalis*, measuring about 13 mm. Constantius, Severus, Maximinus II, and Galerius also struck this denomination, but with a larger diameter (18 to 19 mm.) and only at Siscia. All these centenionales weigh from 1·1 g. to 2·55 g. Centenionales with the heads of Divus Maximianus and Divus Romulus were also issued by Maxentius.

The follis introduced by Diocletian soon began to lose weight. In 313 Constantine set it aside in his part of the Empire, striking instead the denarius (marked X and weighing 2·5 to 3·5 g.). This denarius was in its turn driven out by the degradation of the coinage which set in about 330. Towards 348 came a new reform, whereby Constantius established the *pecunia maiorina*, measuring 20 to 24 mm., weighing about 7·5 g., and the *centenionalis*, measuring 17 to 19 mm. and

FIG. 15.—*Follis* of Anastasius I (A.D. 491-518): D(ominus) N(oster) ANASTASIVS P(er,P(etuus) AVG(ustus).

weighing about 3·5 g. The figures LXXII, which are found sometimes on the former, suggest that it was regarded as worth $\frac{1}{72}$ of the *miliarense* (see below). Constantius' system was short-lived, being superseded about 360 by the following:—

	mm.	grammes.	type.
Follis	28	8·50 to 9	head of emperor.
Denarius	23 to 25	2·3 to 3·3	,, ,,
Centenionalis	15 to 18	about 1·5	head of a deity.
Half Centenionalis	11 to 14	about 1·0	,, ,,

The smallest of these soon disappeared, and in 395 Honorius abolished two others, leaving only the centenionalis. From this time bronze coinage became rare in the West. In the

CH. II] THE COIN AS A MEDIUM OF EXCHANGE 53

East also it was limited, until Anastasius revived it in quite a new form :—

	mm.	grammes.	mark of value.
Follis (Fig. 15)	33 to 37 23 to 24	14.2 to 17.8 6.8 to 9.0	M = 40
Denarius	25 to 27 19 to 20	7.8 to 9.2 3.9 to 4.6	K = 20
Centenionalis	15 to 16	1.9 to 3.3	I = 10
Nummus (Fig. 16)	14 to 15	1.65 to 2.55	Є = 5
(Unit)	8 to 12	0.45 to 0.85	(none).

FIG. 16.—Reverse of *Nummus* of Anastasius I (A. D. 491–518).

§ 10. *Roman Silver*.

The earliest Roman denarii (Pl. XI. 8) weigh, as we have seen, 4.55 g., i.e. 4 scripula or $\frac{1}{72}$ of the Roman pound of 327.45 g. The later, reduced denarius was fixed at $\frac{1}{84}$ lb., i.e. 3.90 g., and at this weight it remained till the time of Nero, who further reduced it to $\frac{1}{96}$ lb. (3.41 g.). Caracalla introduced the argenteus antoninianus (Pl. XV. 4), fixing its weight, probably, at $\frac{1}{64}$ lb., i.e. 5.12 g. The quality of these coins became rapidly worse. Pure silver was reintroduced by Diocletian[1] who, at least as early as 290, if not in 286 A.D., struck a silver coin (Pl. XV. 8) of $\frac{1}{96}$ lb. (the Neronian denarius revived, but now called the *miliarense*). The name miliarense implies that the coin was worth $\frac{1}{1000}$ lb. of gold. This harmonized well with the system established by Diocletian in 301 A.D., in which, accordingly, 1 pound of gold = 50 aurei = 1000 miliarensia = 50,000 denarii, the denarius thus having the same relation to the miliarense as the aureus to the pound of gold. But when in 303 a change was made in the gold-system (see below), the harmony was destroyed, although the name miliarense was retained. Of Diocletian's successors only Maxentius coined

[1] See Seeck, *Z. f. N.* 1890, p. 57 ff.

miliarensia in any quantity. Under Constantius and Julian we find a new silver coin (Pl. XV. 13), the siliqua ($\kappa\epsilon\rho\acute{a}\tau\iota\circ\nu$) $=\frac{1}{24}$ solidus (weight 2·72 g. maximum). This in Julian's time ousted the miliarense as current coin, although the latter was still issued as a 'medallion,' and is mentioned by name as late as the sixth century.

The siliqua was followed in the time of Honorius by the decargyrus (=10 denarii?) of 1·13 g. maximum. A similar piece prevails under the following emperors; while under Justin and his successors we find pieces which were probably equivalent to half and quarter siliquae.

§ 11. *Roman Gold.*

The earliest Roman gold coinage (Pl. XI. 9) consists of pieces of 1, 2, and 3 scripula ($\frac{1}{288}$, $\frac{1}{144}$, $\frac{1}{96}$ of the pound). The aurei of Sulla (Pl. XII. 2) weighed $\frac{1}{30}$, less commonly $\frac{1}{36}$; those of Pompeius $\frac{1}{36}$; those of Caesar $\frac{1}{40}$ of the pound[1]. The last weight harmonized with that of the Greek gold stater of 8·18 g. The pieces struck after Caesar's death follow the same standard, but the weight gradually falls to $\frac{1}{42}$ of the pound (7·80 g.) under Augustus (Pl. XII. 10). This remained the normal (though by no means always the actual) weight until the time of Caracalla, towards the end of whose reign the weight fell to $\frac{1}{50}$ lb. (6·55 g). In spite of an attempt on the part of Macrinus to return to the earlier standard, this weight recurs under Elagabalus and Severus Alexander. Then begins a hopeless confusion, such that the scales must have been necessary in all transactions in which gold passed. Diocletian's earliest gold coins belong to the period of chaos, but they are followed by four classes of coins which show that he attempted (without much success) to arrive at a more satisfactory state of things.

Aureus $= \frac{1}{70}$ lb., 4·68 g. normal, bearing mark of value O = 70.

Aureus $= \frac{1}{60}$ lb., 5·45 g. normal (Ξ = 60).

Aureus $= \frac{1}{50}$ lb., 6·55 g. normal, without mark of value; this system is presumably connected with the rating of the pound of gold at 50,000 denarii in 301 A.D.

---

[1] Hultsch, *Metr.* p. 302.

Aureus = $\frac{1}{60}$ lb., 5·45 g. normal ($\mathbf{Z}$ = 60, Pl. XV. 7). This system began in 303 A.D. and lasted in the East probably till 324 A.D., in Italy and Africa till 312, in Illyria till 314.

From the time of Constantine the weight of the gold coin (now called *solidus*, Pl. XV. 10) was fixed at $\frac{1}{72}$ lb. (4·55 g., normal), marked (at a later period) LXXII or OB. There appears to be some reason for supposing that this weight was actually in use before the year 312, to which date its introduction is usually assigned; it may have been first employed by Constantius Chlorus. The solidus and its third (triens, tremissis), whenever introduced, remained thenceforward the denominations of the gold currency in use down to the fall of the Roman Empire.

§ 12. *Etruria.*

Gold.—The Etruscan gold falls into two series, the unit of one being four times the unit of the other.

(α) Coins marked X = 10, weighing 0·582 g.   ⎫
  „   „   XII〈 = 12½, „   0·72 „   ⎬ yielding a
  „   „   ΛXX = 25,   „   1·45 „   ⎬ unit of
  „   „   ↑ = 50,   „   2·85 „   ⎭ 0·0582 g.
            (normally 2·91 „)

(β) Coins marked Λ = 5. weighing 1·15 g. ⎫ yielding a unit
  „   „   XX = 20,   „   4·67 „ ⎭ of 0·2335 g.

According to Deecke and Hultsch[1] the series (β) belongs to the fifth century; but it is difficult to understand how coins of this style could have been struck so early. If, for instance, the gold coin illustrated in Pl. XI. 3 belongs to the fifth century, then Etruria was a long distance ahead of Greece in artistic development. In any case this series corresponds to a silver series (β) in the list given below. The series (α), with a plain reverse, similarly corresponds to the (α) series of silver described below. Judging by style these are somewhat earlier than the series (β), although by Deecke they are placed later.

Silver.—The silver of Etruria is struck on no less than four standards, which fall into two groups.

[1] Hultsch, p. 687.

(a) **Euboic-Syracusan.**

Unit, *litra* of 0·87 g.

Denomination.	Actual weight in grammes.	Normal weight in grammes.	Mark of value.
20 units	16·653	17·40	X
10 ,,	8·424 [1]	8·70	·Λ
5 ,,	4·146	4·35	ΙΙΙ
2½ ,,	2·073	2·17	Ι
1 ,,	0·907 to 0·842	0·87	

(a_2) The same standard reduced by one-half.

20 units	8·488	8·70	XX
10 ,,	4·310	4 35	X
5 ,,	2·073	2·17	Λ
2½ ,, [2]	1·200	1·09	ΛΙΙ
1 ,,	0·427	0·437	none.

(β) **Corcyrean (?) or Persic standard.**

5 units	11·339	11·37	Λ
2½ ,,	5·442	5·68	none.

($β_2$) The same standard reduced by one-half.

20 units	22·67	22·74	XX
10 ,,	11·534	11·37	X
5 ,,	5·378	5·68	Λ

The unit of (a) is a silver coin equivalent to the Syracusan litra of 0·87 g. That of (a_2) is just half the litra. The unit of (β) is double the weight of the Roman scripulum of 1·137 g., and the unit of ($β_2$) is accordingly equivalent to the scripulum. The coin in series (a_2) which bears the mark ΛΙΙ, corresponding to the ΙΙS of the Roman sestertius, is nearly equivalent in weight to that coin. Now the silver sestertius was introduced into Rome in 269-8 B.C. Hultsch would suppose that the Etruscan system was modelled on the Roman. The analogy of Roman history would rather point to the Etruscan system being adopted by Rome. We may therefore safely say with Head that the Etruscan silver of the classes

---

[1] Cf. Pl. III. 1.
[2] This weight, which is reached by two coins, Deecke, *Etrusk. Forsch.* ii. p. 18, nos. 32a, 32b, is considerably over the normal.

a_2 and β_2 had been in existence for some time when it was superseded by the Roman silver coined for the first time in 269-8 B.C.

The unit of the silver class a (0·87 g.) is fifteen times as heavy as the unit of the gold class a (0·0582 g.). The analogy of Sicily, where in early times a similar relation prevailed between gold and silver, and the same silver unit existed, would lead us to expect the relation between silver and bronze here also to be 250 : 1, giving a bronze litra of 218 g.[1] We find the following denominations issued on this basis:—

Denomination.	Actual weight in grammes.	Normal weight in grammes.	Mark of value.
As	206	218·288	12 globules or |.
Semis	106 (one of 113)	109·144	6 globules.
Triens	67 (one of 78)	72·764	4 ,,
Quadrans	54·5	54·572	3 ,,
Sextans	36	36·382	2 ,,
Uncia	18 (one of 21 and one of 19)	18·191	

Taking the β classes of gold and silver, we find that the silver unit is roughly ten times the weight of the gold unit (0·2335 g.[2]). If gold be to silver as 10 : 1, and silver to bronze as 288 : 1, we obtain the following bronze units, according as we calculate from the gold unit or from the silver unit:—

(1) 0·2335 g. × 10 × 288 = 672·48 g.,
(2) 2·274 g. × 288 = 654·9 g.

The former is equivalent to the Aeginetic monetary mina, the latter to the Attic trade mina.

The bronze coinage of Etruria went through a process of reduction, the stages of which are described by Deecke[3] as follows:—

(1) Reduction by $\frac{1}{8}$.

Denomination.	Actual weight in grammes.	Normal weight in grammes.	Mark of value.
Semis	88	90·9	⌒
Quadrans	45	45·5	3 globules.
Uncia	15	15·16	1 globule.

[1] See above, p. 44, note 1.
[2] This rate at one time prevailed in the West. See above, p. 47, and ch. iii. § 6.
[3] *Etruskische Forschungen*, ii.

(2) Reduction by ⅓.

Denomination.	Actual weight in grammes.	Normal weight in grammes.	Mark of value.
Triens	53	54·5	
Quadrans	43·1 to 42	40·9	
Sextans	28	27·3	

To this stage appear to belong also the

| Quincussis | 736 to 730 | 818·580 | Λ |

and

| Dupondius | 327 to 285 | 327·432 | II |

(3) Reduction by ⅙.

Dupondius	276	291	II
As	129	145	I
Quadrans	32	36	3 globules.
Sextans	21	24	2 globules.
Uncia	12 to 11	12	

(4) Reduction by ½.

Dupondius	231	218	
As	111·4 to 91	109	
Semis	52 to 40·2	54·5	
Triens	39 to 37	36·4	
Quadrans	28 to 26	27·3	
Sextans	20·8 to 13	18·2	
Uncia	10 to 7·1	9·1	

During the second century the weights of the bronze coinage sank as low as the weights of the Roman sextantal coins, and even lower. We find coins calculated according to a unit which is equivalent to $\frac{1}{100}$ of the Roman sextantal as. The denominations are as follows:—

Denomination.	Actual weight in grammes.	Normal weight in grammes.	Mark of value.
100 units	40·6 to 32	54·57	)IC
50 ,,	26·38 to 19·12	27·28	↑
30 ,,	14·04 to 13·45	16·37	XXX
25 ,,	11·6 to 10·72	13·64	ΛXX
20 ,,	10·7	10·91	XX
12½ ,,	6·40	6·82	>IIX
10 ,,	(?)	5·45	X (?)
5 ,,	2·49	2·73	Λ
1 [presupposed]	—	0·54	

§ 13. *Northern and Central Italy.*

The silver of Central Italy is limited to three Latian towns, Alba Fucentis, Cora, and Signia; and the coins attributed to the second town are Campanian in fabric. They weigh 6·02 g.[1] At Alba and at Signia, on the other hand, we have coins dating between B.C. 303 and 268, weighing 1·18 g. and ·583 to ·537 g. These are *nummi* and half-*nummi*, the nummus corresponding, at the rate of 250:1, to an *as* of about 10 Roman ounces.

The average *as* of Central Italy[2] was as a matter of fact equivalent in weight to about 10·43 Roman ounces[3]. The extant *asses* of Hatria (Fig. 17),

FIG. 17.—*As* of Hatria. *Obv.* ⌊ Head of Silenus. *Rev.* HAT Dog sleeping. ⅔ scale. Weight: 395·8 grammes (6108 grains Troy).

however, have an average weight of 15·32 Roman ounces. The

[1] Mommsen, i. p. 259.   [2] Ibid. i. pp. 332-343.   [3] Hultsch, p. 683.

normal Hatrian pound was probably[1] the 'Italian mina' of 492·9 to 491·2 g., i. e. 18 Roman ounces. The heavier standards belong as a rule to the eastern side of the peninsula (e.g. Hatria and Ariminum).

The marks of value found on the bronze of this district are:—

Tressis	❘❘❘ (Alba Fucentis ?)
Dupondius	❘❘ (Alba Fucentis ?)
As	❘ or ⌊ (Hatria)
Semis	) (Iguvium), ⌒ (Tuder), S, ? or ∞, or ••••••
Quincunx	•••••
Triens	••••
Quadrans	•••
Sextans	••
Sescuncia	C• (Asculum ?)
Uncia	•
Semuncia	Σ or Ƶ, also Ƽ or Ɛ (series with helmeted head).

The methods of division vary; thus the semis is unknown in the East, the quincunx in the West.

§ 14. *Southern Italy.*

The earliest gold coinage of Southern Italy consists of small pieces of 0·35 g. struck at Cumae in the first years of the fifth century. These are $\frac{1}{24}$ of the ordinary gold stater of 8·4 g., and at the rate of 15 : 1 would have been nearly equivalent in value to one Aeginetic drachm of 5·44 g., which is the weight of the silver coins of Cumae at that time. This gold coinage is however exceptional, and the chief gold coins of Southern Italy are those of Tarentum (Pl. XI. 2) in the fourth and third centuries. Here we have gold staters of the weight of 8·74 g. maximum, 8·62 g. normal, with drachms and smaller divisions down to $\frac{1}{10}$ (litra), $\frac{1}{12}$ (obol), and $\frac{1}{20}$ (hemilitron). At Heraclea at the same time we find a quarter-stater of 2·138 g.; and at Metapontum in the fourth century a tetrobol of 2·85 g.

Towards the end of the fourth century, Capua, under Roman rule, issued gold coins on the local (Campanian) standard, viz. staters of 6·86 g. maximum and drachms (Pl. XI. 7) of 3·41 g. maximum[2], or 6 and 3 Roman scruples respectively.

---

[1] Hultsch, pp. 673 (no. II), 683, compared with table of weights, above, p. 32.

[2] Pieces of 4·52 to 4·46 g. or 4 Roman scruples are marked XXX (*scil.* Roman asses), which would show that the Romans tariffed Capuan money unfavourably, since the piece of 4 scruples should have been equivalent

The only other gold coinage of Southern Italy is that of the Bruttians, who during the third century issued gold staters of the normal Attic weight.

The Capuan electrum coins were probably issued in the Hannibalian war, B.C. 216–211[1]. These coins weigh from 3·10 g. to 2·6 g., and are simply adulterated gold. The electrum coins weighing 2·82 to 2·77 g. (2½ scruples) on the other hand are probably frank electrum and circulated for the value of 2 scruples of gold[2]. They contain twenty per cent. of alloy. These coins are contemporary with the Roman gold coins struck for Campania.

The silver standards of Southern Italy are complicated and peculiar. They may best be considered in connexion with the Eastern standards from which they were derived.

(a) Derived from the Phoenician standard was that which is known as the *Campanian*. It appears to be a raised form of the Phoenician standard, and the elevation was perhaps meant, as at Chios, to effect an adjustment with the Aeginetic standard. The standard had its origin, so far as Italy was concerned, in the Phocaean colony of Velia in Lucania, where we find a drachm (Pl. III. 10) of 3·98 to 3·75 g., pointing to a didrachm of 7·96 g. maximum (the highest form of the light Phoenician silver shekel is only 7·67 g.). On the other hand, in most of the Campanian cities a somewhat lower form was in use, the didrachm weighing 7·41 g. maximum, which is very near the Phoenician shekel of the reduced royal norm (7·46 to 7·48 g.). Outside Campania we find the Campanian standard at Velia and Poseidonia in Lucania, at Arpi and Teate in Apulia (didrachm of 7·128 g.), in Calabria at Baletium and even at Tarentum (although the Tarentine coins on this standard were probably meant for Campanian circulation only). Roman influence about 318 B.C. caused the reduction of the standard, the didrachm being made equivalent to 6 Roman scruples (6·82 g.).

(β) Two important standards were derived from the Corinthian :—

(i) The *Italic* standard. This is a reduced form of the

to XL asses. But the specimen in the British Museum, and probably also that in the Vatican, are false (Babelon, *Monn. de la Rép. rom.* i. p. 24; Head, *H. N.* p. 29).

[1] See P. Gardner, *Num. Chron.* 1884, p. 220 f.
[2] Mommsen, *M. R.* i. p 264.

Corinthian standard, the stater weighing about 8·164 g. maximum. It is found at Sybaris, Siris, Pyxus, Croton and dependencies, Caulonia, Laus, Pandosia, Thurium, and other places; and the coins of Poseidonia, Metapontum, and Locri were partly issued on this standard. The ternary system of division distinguishes it from the other derivative of the Corinthian standard.

(ii) The *Tarentine* standard, in which the stater (Pl. XI. 1), weighing about the same amount (8·16 g.), underwent a binary division. The Tarentine standard is important both because of the great quantities of coins issued by Tarentum, and because of a question as to the value of the τοῦμμος or νόμος which is connected with it. According to Aristotle[1] the name νοῦμμος was at Tarentum given to a coin with the type of Taras riding on a dolphin. This was the regular type of the stater, which we might therefore suppose to be the νοῦμμος. But there is a possibility that the νοῖμμος was a smaller coin, viz. the diobol of 1·48 g. maximum. For, in the first place, the type of Taras on the dolphin does occasionally occur on coins of this weight. Further, the Romans gave the name *nummus* to a coin of nearly this weight. Finally, the obol is marked ·····; the diobol therefore was equivalent to ten units, presumably of bronze. Now at Teate and Venusia in Apulia the largest bronze coins are marked N and N I (one nummus); these are *dextantes*; and as the silver coins of the former place are struck on the Tarentine standard, it may be presumed that the bronze dextans or nummus was equivalent to the silver diobol. From these facts it would appear that the nummus was the diobol.

Another important division of the stater was the litra or one-tenth, weighing ·87 g. maximum, and bearing the type of the pecten-shell, with its half of ·433 g. On a coin of ·907 g. we have ···; it is therefore presumably a trias, or fourth. 4 × ·907 g. gives a weight of 3·628 g. which is just the weight of the Tarentine drachms issued from the fourth century onwards.

Outside Tarentum itself we find the Tarentine standard in use in

---

[1] Poll. ix. 80 Ἀριστοτέλης ἐν τῇ Ταραντίνων πολιτείᾳ καλεῖσθαί φησι νόμισμα παρ' αὐτοῖς νοῦμμον ἐφ' οὗ ἐντετυπῶσθαι Τάραντα τὸν Ποσειδῶνος δελφῖνι ἐποχούμενον.

Apulia—where the earliest coinage consists of silver diobols and didrachms of Tarentine standard; while after 300 B.C. the smaller divisions only are Tarentine.

Lucania—at Heraclea, and Velia.

No more than the other standards did the Tarentine maintain its full weight. In the third century the weight of the stater seems to have been reduced to about 6·609 g.; although a certain number of coins dating about B.C. 212 to 209 belong to the higher standard, with the stater of 7·77 g.

Most of the bronze coinage of Southern Italy, until about the middle of the third century, is, like most Greek bronze, merely token money; it very seldom bears marks of value[1]. Before this period, however, we find in Apulia a bronze coinage apparently based on the bronze equivalent of the Tarentine silver diobol (which, if the ratio of silver to bronze be taken as 250 : 1 yields a weight of about 324 g.). Thus we have at Luceria and Venusia, about B.C. 314 to 250, a libral *as* (sometimes marked I) and smaller denominations from the quincunx to uncia, marked with five pellets down to one, as well as a semuncia (?) with no mark. About 250 B.C. at Atella and Calatia in Campania, at Luceria, Mateola, and Venusia in Apulia, at Brundusium in Calabria, we find bronze issued on the triental system. The marks of value in these places are:—

•••••	quincunx,
••••	triens,
•••	quadrans,
••	sextans,
•	uncia,
Σ	semuncia,
C	quarter-uncia,
Ⱡ	one-eighth uncia,

although all these denominations are not found at all the cities mentioned.

About 217 to 200 B.C. we find first the sextantal, then the uncial standard, a larger number of cities falling into line. To the marks of value in use in the previous period must be added N or N . I for the nummus (= dextans), N . II (2 nummi), and • S for the sescuncia. From about B.C. 200 to B.C. 89 the

[1] At Metapontum there are bronze coins (about B.C. 350 to 272) with the inscriptions ΟΒΟΛΟΣ, ΤΕ ($\tau\epsilon\tau\alpha\rho\tau\eta\mu\delta\rho\iota\text{o}\nu$?), and ΗΕ ($\dot\eta\mu\iota\tau\epsilon\tau\alpha\rho\tau\eta\mu\delta\rho\iota\text{o}\nu$?): Head, *H. N.* p. 66.

semuncial standard prevails (I = as, S = semis, • or * = uncia, and the other usual marks of value). The independent coinage of this part of Italy ceases altogether in B.C. 89.

The standards in use in Gaul and Spain, and along the southern shores of the Mediterranean, either fall in with one or other of the important standards already described, or else (as for instance in the case of Carthage) offer such difficulty, and have received such inadequate attention, that it would be unwise to attempt to describe them here.

§ 15. *Coin-Denominations.*

In describing the various standards, we have neglected, except in a few cases, to note the divisional systems employed. These are very various. The minuteness of the divisions may be understood from a list of the denominations of silver coins struck at Athens. These are:—

	Normal weight in grammes.	Expressed in didr.
Decadrachmon	43.66	5
Tetradrachmon	17.44	2
Didrachmon	8.72	1
Drachme	4.36	$\frac{1}{2}$
Pentobolon	3.63	$\frac{5}{12}$
Tetrobolon	2.90	$\frac{1}{3}$
Triobolon	2.18	$\frac{1}{4}$
Diobolon	1.45	$\frac{1}{6}$
Trihemiobolion	1.09	$\frac{1}{8}$
Obolos	.72	$\frac{1}{12}$
Tritemorion	.54	$\frac{1}{16}$
Hemiobolion	.36	$\frac{1}{24}$
Trihemitetartemorion	.27	$\frac{3}{32}$
Tetartemorion	.18	$\frac{1}{48}$
Hemitetartemorion = bronze *chalcūs* (Fig. 8, p. 37)	.09	$\frac{1}{96}$

The κόλλυβος was probably a still smaller denomination (perhaps a quarter of the chalcus, as we hear of a dikollybon and trikollybon). There existed also a πεντέχαλκον and a δίχαλκον. All these were issued in bronze.

A divisional system characteristic of some of the Asiatic standards is that in which the stater is divided into thirds and sixths. Here again the division was carried down to very minute weights, as low as $\frac{1}{96}$ of the stater. This we find in the early electrum coinage of Asia Minor [1]. Some of the most important electrum currencies of the fifth and fourth centuries B. C., those of Cyzicus, Phocaea, and Lesbos for instance, consisted entirely of staters and sixths [2]. Many other places using the Babylonic standard practically confined their denominations to staters and thirds (tetrobols).

The multiples of the drachm could naturally be carried to any height that convenience or, more usually, love of magnificence might dictate. Besides the tetradrachms and decadrachms already mentioned, we find tridrachms, pentadrachms, hexadrachms, octadrachms, and dodecadrachms. The large gold octadrachms of Ptolemy Philadelphus and Arsinoe II (Pl. VII. 8) and their successors are among the most pretentious products of ancient art. The use of these heavy denominations was on the whole rare in Greece. Athens in early times produced a decadrachm; there are also a few decadrachms of Alexander the Great, probably struck at Babylon either by Alexander himself or his generals. Large silver octadrachms are characteristic of some of the Thraco-Macedonian tribes (Bisaltae, Edoni, &c., Pl. II. 9) and Thracian cities (as Abdera) in the period before the Persian wars. The Syracusan decadrachms, both the early Demareteia (Pl. III. 6), and the later 'medallions' of Cimon (Pl. VI. 6) and Evaenetus (Pl. VI. 4), are, with the rare decadrachms of Agrigentum, the only high denominations, though in themselves a host, from Sicily. Carthage produced a few octadrachms and decadrachms, and the Syrian kings, like the Ptolemies, were fond of this form of extravagance. But the palm was borne away by the Bactrian Eucratides, whose gold 'medallion,' now in the Bibliothèque Nationale, is equal in weight to twenty staters.

The indication of denomination by any other means than weight is a comparatively rare thing in Greek coinage. The use of numerals is common in the West, but there are instances of the actual name (δραχμή, ἀσσάριον and the like) being written in full on the coin, although these are mostly confined to Imperial times [3]. The distinction by means of types appears to follow no fixed rule. An interesting instance of

[1] Head, *Brit. Mus. Catal., Ionia*, pp. 3 ff.
[2] See above, pp. 14, 15.   [3] See below, ch. viii. § 5.

such a distinction is furnished by a series of coins belonging to Euboea[1], and dating about 520-460 B. C. The series is as follows:—

Tetradrachms	16.77. 15.68 g.	Quadriga facing.
Octobols	5.60, 5.56 g.	Rider facing, leading a second horse.
Tetrobols	2.79, 2.63, 2.46 g.	Rider facing.

Better known than this group is that with a similar scheme found in the coinage of Syracuse in the time of Gelon:—

Denomination.	Type of Reverse
Tetradrachm	Quadriga.
Didrachm	Horseman leading a second horse.
Drachm	Horseman.
Obol	Wheel.

[1] *Journ. Hellen. Stud.* 1897, p. 80.

CHAPTER III

MONETARY THEORY AND PRACTICE

§ 1. *Aristotle's Conception of Money.*

The considerations to which the preceding chapter has been devoted may help to throw light on the attitude assumed by the ancients towards various economic problems.

Any attempt to ascertain the nature of ancient theories of money must be based on the definition given by Aristotle[1]. 'For the purpose of exchange men agreed to give and take mutually something, which, itself belonging to the class of things useful, was easily made to do service in ordinary life. Such were iron and silver, and the like. At first these metals were used in pieces having a definite size and weight only, but finally they also received a type, in order to save the trouble of measuring; for the type was impressed in order to show that the coin possessed a given value[2].' Nevertheless, Aristotle carefully guards against the confusion between wealth and plenty of money; 'it were odd that wealth should be a thing, the possession of plenty of which could not prevent one from dying of hunger, as did Midas in the myth.' The instance is a bad one, since the sphere of political economy is of course not mythological; the science deals with ordinary circumstances in which the possession of plenty of money does as a rule prevent death by hunger. The point to be realized,

---

[1] *Pol.* i. 9. 14 ff. 1257 a 35.
[2] ὁ χαρακτὴρ ἐτέθη τοῦ ποσοῦ σημεῖον. This does not imply that the type was an indication of how great the value was, but only a token that the full value, whatever it might be, was present. The importance of this apparently subtle distinction lies in its bearing on the significance of types (see ch. vii. § 2).

the basis of the sound theory of money, is simply this, that money must be a real equivalent, not a merely conventional token which does not truly represent value. Of this point Aristotle seems aware when he says that money must belong to the class of useful things. But he appears to contradict himself subsequently when he says: 'Sometimes money seems to be a mere futility; a universally accepted convention, but, so far as its nature goes, a mere nothing; since if those who use it give up one currency for another, it becomes worthless, and of no use for any of the necessities of life.' Now, money being αὐτὸ τῶν χρησίμων, this is absurd; good money will always have its value, even if being demonetized it is to a certain extent depreciated. The story of Midas is not to the point, since, as he could not change his gold for anything else, his gold had no value. A government cannot give value to a currency which has none, without being found out in a very short time and becoming bankrupt[1].

Money therefore does not constitute wealth, but is only the potentiality of wealth when it is good money, that is to say, is not adulterated or a mere token. Whatever may have been the theories of the Greeks on this point, their practice shows a certain diversity of opinion.

§ 2. *The Quality of Ancient Money.*

It is usual to praise the ancients highly for the quality of their metal. As a matter of fact, there was no lack of bad money in circulation[2]. It is too much to expect that the Greeks, understanding as they did the art of alloying, should not occasionally have been guilty of fraudulent adulteration. There are, of course, economic excuses for a slight adulteration or deduction from the nominal weight of a coin, in order to defray the cost of striking[3].

The Athenian coinage was on the whole excellent. Demosthenes[4] records a remark of Solon that, while nearly all states punished with death the adulteration of money (ἐάν τις τὸ νόμισμα

---

[1] A paper or similar currency is of course justifiable only when bullion to the amount of notes issued is possessed by the bank which issues them.
[2] See ch. i.   [3] See above, p. 31.
[4] 24 *In Timocr.* 212-214.

διαφθείρῃ), many states, nevertheless, openly used silver money which was alloyed with copper and lead. It is implied, of course, that the Athenian coinage was pure, and analysis has proved this to be true. Xenophon[1] also testifies to the character of the Athenian money, which was as gladly accepted, and as profitably disposed of, outside Athens as is English gold abroad at the present time. The abuse which in a well-known passage of Aristophanes is bestowed on the coinage of the end of the fifth century B. C. is difficult to understand[2]. In any case it is clear that the new gold coins of the end of the fifth or beginning of the fourth century, which are of excellent quality, cannot be meant by Aristophanes. The reference is presumably to the new bronze coinage of the time, which may possibly have been given a somewhat arbitrarily high value[3].

There was one occasion on which the Athenian government dealt fraudulently with its creditors in the matter of the currency[4]. The tyrant Hippias, however, did not alter the quality of the coinage, but merely swindled his creditors by commanding them to call their old coins by a new name. The unit of the coinage had previously been a didrachm. Hippias, pretending that he was about to issue a new coinage, called in the current coins. As a matter of fact he reissued the same coins, but called them tetradrachms, and thus made a profit of cent. per cent. on his transaction. It was, however, in accordance with the sound foreign policy of the Peisistratids that Hippias played a trick which, while profiting himself, could not damage the credit of Athens in the outside market, as the ordinary process of adulteration would have done. It was

---

[1] *De Vect.* iii. 2.
[2] *Ran.* 720. See the discussion in Head, *Brit. Mus. Catal., Attica,* &c., p. xxvii.
[3] The introduction of bronze coinage seems occasionally to have been as unpopular as was, for instance, the change from copper to bronze in the English coinage in 1860. At Gortyna, as we learn from an inscription, the state had to enforce the acceptance of bronze money (νόμισμα τὸ καυχόν) instead of silver obols by a penalty of five staters of silver (F. Halbherr, *Amer. Journ. of Arch.* 1897, p. 191, and *Journ. Internat.* 1898, p. 165). As M. Svoronos shows, ibid., p. 173, the inscription in question cannot belong to the period of the first introduction of bronze in Gortyna.
[4] The account given in the text of Hippias' measure is based on the remarks of M. J. P. Six, *Num. Chron.* 1895, p. 178, and is to a certain extent conjectural.

only the individual Athenians who suffered by this measure; the Athenian money still passed outside Athens for the same amount as before.

It has been said that such debased coinage as we do find among the Greeks is mostly confined to necessitous tyrants. It is true that public opinion to a certain extent insisted, in the free states, on the purity of the coinage. And the debased coins of Dionysius of Syracuse are perhaps the most famous instance of the fraudulent coinage of antiquity[1]. But it is necessary to realize that the operation of arbitrarily placing an excessive value on coins was undertaken by several free states. The greater part of the electrum coinage of Asia Minor is indeed an illustration of the tendency to debase coinage. The Phocaean 'gold,' we are told, had the worst reputation in antiquity (τὸ κάκιστον χρυσίον)[2]. This must refer to the Phocaean coinage of the electrum union with Lesbos, not to the nearly pure gold coins of the time of the Phocaean thalassocracy. The quality of the Lesbian electrum of the same time is no better than that of the Phocaean. Probably only a small proportion of the electrum coins possessed the value conventionally assigned to them. The value of the original gold Phocaic stater was twenty Babylonian silver staters, and this value remained the nominal one long after the Phocaic staters were of electrum instead of gold. Naturally such coins were subjected to a discount in markets outside the district within which they were legal tender for a fixed sum[3]. This was the case with the electrum coins of Cyzicus and Lampsacus as well as with those of Phocaea and Lesbos. The latter state in quite early times carried the adulteration of silver so far as to produce money (Pl. I. 13) of a horrible metal containing only about forty per cent. of silver[4].

In addition to Asia Minor both Italy and Carthage suffered from the frauds to which the possession of electrum seems to have tempted ancient governments. The electrum money struck by the Romans for circulation in Campania contained

---

[1] See above, pp. 16, 17.   [2] Hesych. s. v. Φωκαεῖς.
[3] The poet Persinus found that he could get better exchange for his Φωκαΐδες in Mytilene than in Atarne (Pollux, ix. 93 ad fin.).
[4] This billon coinage ceases about 440 B. C. (Wroth, *Brit. Mus. Catal., Troas*, &c., p. lxiv).

twenty per cent. of alloy, and though weighing only $2\frac{1}{3}$ scruples circulated at a value of $2\frac{1}{2}$ scruples of gold. The electrum of Carthage was evidently meant to pass as gold, since the coins were so treated that their exterior had the appearance of the nobler metal.

The most extensive frauds, however, in connexion with money were perpetrated by the Romans under the Empire. The silver, which at first contained from one per cent. to two per cent. of alloy, underwent a speedy degradation. Nero's silver contains from five per cent. to ten per cent. of alloy; under Vitellius, the proportion is nearly twenty per cent. The Flavians improved the coinage, lowering the proportion to ten per cent. From the end of Trajan's reign to that of Antoninus Pius it is again nearly twenty per cent.; twenty-five per cent. under Marcus Aurelius, nearly thirty per cent. under Commodus. Thus it gradually rises to fifty per cent. or sixty per cent. under Septimius Severus[1]. Caracalla, besides his billon coins, issued pieces of lead plated with silver, and mingled with his aurei copper plated with gold. Under Gordian III the alloy in the silver amounts to about sixty-seven per cent. Gallienus began by improving the coinage, and then proceeded to the opposite extreme, some of his coins being only twenty per cent. or even five per cent. fine. Exceptionally, however, we find a few pure silver coins of this time; but the *argentei antoniniani*, by far the commonest class of 'silver' coins, are nearly all of the quality above described. Thus Diocletian on his accession found practically nothing but a bronze and a gold coinage in existence. He revived the use of silver, which from this time onward was usually of very fair quality[2].

§ 3. *Plated Coin.*

More disgraceful if possible than the adulterating of the metal was the practice of plating. It is not uncommon to find plated Greek coins[3], but the practice of issuing them

[1] These details are taken from Mommsen, *M. R.* iii. p. 29.
[2] Mommsen, *M. R.* iii. p. 86 ff.
[3] Among the most interesting of these is the British Museum specimen of the coin issued by Themistocles at Magnesia (Head, *Brit. Mus. Catal., Ionia*, p. 158). The Paris specimen (Pl. IV. 1) is solid.

can hardly be called general, and as a state measure, was probably very rare. Among the Romans, however, plated money occurs in great quantities, and the practice of issuing a certain number of plated coins from time to time was recognized by the Romans as a legal source of state profit. The Greeks had from early times issued (though seldom openly) coins consisting of bronze or lead plated with silver or gold; the Romans introduced an iron core [2]. The vast majority of the Roman plated coins are proved not only by literary tradition, but by the skill with which they are executed, as well as by their numbers, to be state issues [3], and not the products of private forgers. The first state issue of plated coins is said to have taken place during the Hannibalian war [4]. In spite of enactments compelling the acceptance of this bad coin, it was avoided when possible, and in 84 B.C. the popular praetor M. Marius Gratidianus recalled all such pieces. The reactionary Sulla, however, put the praetor to death and cancelled his wise measure. Plated pieces continued to be issued until the time of the Empire, but it would appear that Augustus called in the plated pieces, when he made his monetary reform in 15 B.C.[5] Even then, however, plated pieces were issued by the state for exportation, and the practice was soon revived in Rome itself, although the gradual adulteration of the unplated money made it less worth while to issue plated pieces.

§ 4. *Precautions against Forgery.*

Our information as to the legal precautions taken by the state against false coining is very scanty [6]. The statement of Solon,

---

[1] Herod. iii. 56; Polyaen. *Strat.* iv. 10. 2; Arist. *Ran.* 720 ff. and Schol.

[2] Pseudo-Aristot. however, *Oecon.* ii. 2, says that the people of Clazomenae in a time of necessity issued iron instead of silver. These pieces they gave to the wealthiest citizens, and received a corresponding amount of silver in return. Some have supposed that these coins were plated. But the transaction has the appearance of a loan, and it is possible that the iron pieces were not plated, and were meant to be redeemed by the State when the crisis should be past; in fact they were certificates.

[3] The technical phrase was *miscere monetam*, or *aes*, or *ferrum argento miscere*, which does not, except in late times, mean to alloy, but to plate. The legal term for plating with gold was *tingere* or *inficere*.

[4] Zonaras, *Ann.* viii. 26 s. fin.   [5] Lenormant, i. p. 234.

[6] See Eckhel, *Doctr. Num.* i. p cxiii f.

that the crime was in most states a capital one, has already been mentioned. The false moneyer, whether a private person or the state official, was subject to the same penalty. The death penalty is mentioned in the inscription relating to the Lesbio-Phocaean electrum union [1]. In Rome, the adulteration of gold or silver was regarded as equivalent to forgery [2]. The *lex Iulia peculatus* of Augustus [3] provided against the adulteration of the public gold, silver, or bronze. Of the enactments of the later emperors, that of Tacitus is worthy of notice, making it a capital offence (involving confiscation of the offender's property) to alloy gold with silver, silver with bronze, or bronze with lead [4]. And there are numerous provisions against the issue from the mint of cast instead of struck coins.

§ 5. *Protection by Tariff.*

As we have said, money to which the law gave an arbitrarily high value within the district subject to that law, fell to its proper value outside the limits of the jurisdiction concerned. Similarly money which was thoroughly sound was, it might be supposed, always worth carrying with one [5]. In the autonomous period of Greek history this was probably always the case. But when the Greek world became subject to Rome, certain measures were taken by the mistress of the world towards protecting her own money; the money, i.e. of the Roman state, and that issued by Rome for provincial purposes. The denarius being in Imperial times made the official money of account all over the world, all forms of money were brought into rough and ready relations with the denarius, and always to their disadvantage. Before Imperial times we see a similar measure adopted to the disadvantage of the tetradrachms of the Attic standard still in circulation, which were assimilated in value, though not in weight, to the lighter cistophoric

---

[1] See below, ch. iv. § 13.
[2] 'Lege Cornelia cavetur, ut qui in aurum vitii quid addiderit, qui argenteos nummos adulterinos flaverit, falsi crimine teneri' (Ulpian, Dig. xlviii. 10. 9). Notice the distinction between the gold, which was in bars, and the silver, which was coined.
[3] Mommsen, iii. p. 37; Dig. xlviii. 13. 1.
[4] *Scr. Hist. Aug.* Tacit. 9.   [5] Xen. *De Vect.* iii. 2.

standard[1]. In Imperial times, the silver tetradrachms issued from the mint of Antioch were tariffed at three denarii, whereas four would have been a fairer estimate. Similarly the last drachms issued from the Rhodian mint (after B. C. 88) were probably made to exchange against Roman denarii, considerably to the advantage of the latter, which weighed only about 3·88 g. as against 4·21 to 4·53 g.[2]

§ 6. *Relative Values of the Metals.*

Closely connected with the question of the adulteration of money by the state is a problem which in the present day has assumed remarkable proportions. This problem is concerned with the relation of the various metals to each other. So long as the coinage of Greece was confined to a single metal, the others circulating merely in uncoined form, no difficulty could have arisen. The state of things must have been parallel to that in Mediaeval Europe, from the disappearance of gold in the seventh century down to its reappearance in the middle of the thirteenth. But in so far as gold, electrum or bronze circulated beside silver, a very natural attempt was made to fix the relation between the metals. Some states, such as Athens, seem to have been content to leave the matter to the market; they struck their gold coins of a certain weight, their silver also of a certain weight, but made no attempt, so far as we can judge from the coins, to fix a rate of exchange. But other states, such as Syracuse, were continually altering the weights in their gold coins, in order to bring them into satisfactory relation with the silver. The frequency of such alterations is sufficient to show that the system was a failure. The extraordinary complications of the standards of weight in the Greek world are mainly due to the attempt to adjust the weights of the coins to the relative value of the two metals[3].

In regard to the relative values of the three chief metals, a brief summary of the results arrived at by various investigators must suffice[4]. Throughout, we have to remember that

---

[1] See above, p. 39.
[2] Head, *Brit. Mus. Catal., Caria,* &c., p. cxiii.
[3] The evidence for this will be found in ch. ii.
[4] See especially Hultsch, *Metrologie* (1882), *Index,* s. v. Werthverhältniss; Lenormant, *La Monnaie,* i. pp. 145 ff.

there is often a distinction between the actual rate of exchange and the rate, often arbitrary, assumed for the purposes of coinage.

Relation of gold to silver.—At and long before the time of the introduction of money, the normal rate of exchange between gold and silver was $13\frac{1}{3}$: 1 in Babylonia and in the nations commercially dependent on it. The early coins of Chios give a rate of 13·84 : 1. According to Herodotus [1], the rate prevailing in the Persian kingdom was 13 : 1. So far as Athens was concerned the rate was not legally fixed, and we find that it fluctuates from $11\frac{1}{2}$: 1 up to 14 : 1 during the fifth and fourth centuries B.C. The metals were allowed to find their own levels, and such too was the case in Macedon, where Alexander's coinage shows that no rate was fixed. There was a popular idea that gold might be regarded as roughly ten times as valuable as silver, and many calculations seem to have been made on this basis. In one case we find a rate of 10 : 1 fixed by law, viz. in the treaty of Rome with the Aetolians in 189 B.C. And this was the rate in the Cimmerian Bosporus before the days of Alexander. It is safe to regard 12 : 1 or $12\frac{1}{2}$: 1 as the most usual rate in the Mediterranean basin under ordinary circumstances. But there are frequent exceptions. Thus the earliest coinage of Etruria proves a decimal relation; the coinage of the same district in the fourth century a ratio of 15 : 1. The rate at Carthage in 306 B.C. was also 10 : 1, owing probably to the adulteration of the gold coinage. The earliest Roman gold coinage (217 B.C.) is evidence for the extraordinary high rate of $17\frac{1}{7}$: 1 [2]. During the last two centuries of the Roman Republic the legal rate was probably 11·90 : 1. But the discovery of gold in Noricum in the middle of the second century B.C. sent the price of gold down by one-third, and although it recovered, it suffered a similar shock from Caesar's Gallic victories a century later. Under the Early Empire the rate is 12·5 : 1. Nero's adulteration of the coinage, owing to which the silver coins became merely a money of account, gave gold an arbitrarily low value (10·31 : 1, and in the next century 9·375 : 1), from which it only really recovered under Diocletian, who fixed the ratio at 13·67 : 1. From Constantine I to

[1] iii. 95.
[2] But the circumstances were special. See below, ch. iv. § 11.

Theodosius the rate ranges from 13·89 to 14·40 : 1 [1]. About the year 400 the rate is as high as 15·18 : 1.

In Sicily the relation between gold and silver was, as we have seen (pp. 42, 43), subject to considerable fluctuations, ranging from 15 : 1, on which ratio the first gold coins were issued, down to 10 : 1.

Relation of silver to copper.—In countries where a copper standard was in vogue, this relation was of course important; but where, as in the greater part of Greece, and in Italy after the introduction of a silver coinage, silver was the standard metal, copper coins were merely a money of account, and the relation of silver to copper is unimportant for our purposes.

The rate 120 : 1 was that prevailing in Ptolemaic times [2], and it is probable that it also prevailed in the Aegean in very early days, long before the coinage of copper. We have seen (p. 37) that to explain the origin of the Euboic standard it is necessary to suppose that the great copper-city, Chalcis, put an unusually high value on copper, making the rate 96 : 1, a difference of one-fifth; but this was of course an exceptional rate. Lenormant arrives at a rate varying between 120 : 1 and 100 : 1 as the most probable one, both for commercial and monetary purposes, in the Greek world. The rate 105 : 1 can be fixed for the district north of the Euxine from the *aes grave* of the great commercial city of Olbia. For the rest of Greece, after the time of Alexander, the actual value of copper is in no way to be ascertained from the coinage in that metal, which is purely a token-money.

In the West, if we exclude Carthage, the relation between the two metals was very different. The original rate appears to have been 288 : 1, but with increasing commerce, and the consequently increasing influx of silver, the rate gradually sank. The gradual fall in the value of silver, as compared with bronze, keeps pace with, or rather is the chief cause of, the fall in the weight of the bronze coins of the Republic. The monetary exchange value (56 : 1) established in 89 B. C. (the

---

[1] Under Julian the actual rate was 14·25 : 1, the rate fixed for coinage 12 : 1.

[2] The latest discussion of the most difficult problem of the silver and copper coinage of the Ptolemies is by B. P. Grenfell (*Revenue-Laws of Ptolemy Philadelphus*, pp. 193 ff.).

date of the introduction of the semuncial *as*) does not however express the real commercial value of bronze. The same is true of the rates fixed under Augustus (56 : 1), Nero (71·11 : 1), and Trajan (80 : 1). Brass, which was largely employed for coinage under the Empire, was also fixed at an arbitrary value, and retained a constant relation to copper of 2 : 1.

Electrum, which was regarded for the purpose of coinage as a distinct metal, was rated at ten times the value of silver, both in Asia Minor and in Greece Proper. Gold being to silver as $13\frac{1}{3}$: 1, the rate of 10 : 1 would be true of a mixture in which seventy-three per cent. of gold and twenty-seven per cent. of silver were combined. It has already been remarked that as a matter of fact the ingredients varied very considerably from this standard.

CHAPTER IV

THE COINAGE AND THE STATE

§ 1. *Private Coinage.*

THE most primitive stage of commerce, in which exchange was conducted by means of barter, was no sooner succeeded by the stage in which a definite medium of exchange was adopted, than it became necessary for the state to regulate the conditions under which that medium was produced. It was possible no doubt for a private person to place his stamp on a piece of metal in order to relieve others of the trouble of constantly weighing it; but his guarantee would be accepted only within a small circle in which his credit was established. With the extension of commerce it became necessary that coins should be marked by some better known authority, and that authority was naturally the state. Outside the bounds of the state, it depended on its credit whether its coinage would be accepted without weighing; whether, that is, it would be accepted as a medium of exchange or treated as merchandize. In ancient times the credit of many states stood so high that their coins were always accepted at a fixed value; that of others was regarded *loco mercis*.

The history of ancient coinage is thus bound up intimately with the political history of ancient states and rulers, and it is therefore necessary to inquire in some detail into the conditions attached to the prerogative of coinage.

A private coinage implies the absence of a state coinage, for the guarantee of the state is more secure than the guarantee of the individual, and only when the better guarantee is not to

THE COINAGE AND THE STATE 79

be had will the worse be accepted. It has been suggested [1] that a large number of the earliest coins which it is customary to attribute to various Asiatic cities are in reality private money, and that the types thereon are the private badges of influential bankers. Nevertheless it is doubtful whether any of the instances which the author of this theory adduces are really conclusive. The great stores of staters which we are told were in the possession of wealthy bankers like Sadyattes or Pythes, may well have been state issues. In all probability the marks which were placed by such bankers on coins were subsidiary countermarks, which served to give a further guarantee to state issues which they had tested and found satisfactory. The minor types which are occasionally found on the reverses of the early electrum coins, inside the incuse [2] impressions, can hardly be explained as the badges of individual bankers ; or, if they are to be so explained, they can only have served as a secondary guarantee of genuineness, the primary one being afforded by the main type of the obverse. The comparative regularity with which the 'incuses' are disposed on the reverses of all these coins shows that, where two or three incuses appear on one coin, they must all have been impressed at one and the same time. When they do contain designs (and this in early times is by no means the rule), those designs very possibly belong to the officials appointed to superintend the striking of the coin, and are analogous to the symbols which at a later time appear in the field beside the main type. Finally, the electrum stater of 'Phanes' (Pl. I. 4), on which so many questions seem to depend for their answers, does not by any means enable us to decide this one with certainty. Babelon recognizes in Phanes a banker or merchant who stamped his pieces of gold with his badge and name. But Phanes may well have been a potentate of whom there is no other record [3].

---

[1] E. Babelon, *Les Origines de la Monnaie*, p. 91 ff.
[2] The origin of these incuse or sunk rectangles is explained in ch. vi.
[3] So far I assume that the name on the coin is rightly explained as the genitive of a name Φάννης, Φαίνης, or Φαένης. If so, the badge is definitely stated to be that of Phanes. There is, therefore, no reason to attribute the coin to Ephesus, simply because the stag (the symbol of Artemis) appears on this coin as on the coinage of that city. Indeed Phanes would be less likely to adopt the stag as his σῆμα in Ephesus than elsewhere. There is

Whether there ever existed in ancient times a subsidiary private coinage corresponding to the token coinage of modern times (such as the tradesmen's, civic, and bank tokens of England during the seventeenth, eighteenth, and early nineteenth centuries), it is impossible to say with certainty. At least, no recognizable specimens have come down to us. These token coinages differ from the private coinage, the existence of which M. Babelon has tried to establish for early times, in that they attempt not to rival the state issue, but only to supply the gaps which it leaves unfilled; that is to say, when the state issues only the more valuable kind of coin, private money in small denominations is issued to facilitate small transactions. The series of many ancient states are notably deficient in small denominations; but it would seem that the want was supplied by the use of uncoined blocks or bars of the meaner metals, such as had been in use before the introduction of coined money.

§ 2. *Nature of 'Temple coinage.'*

There is, then, no certain instance in ancient history of anything which can properly be called a private coinage. The prerogative invariably, so far as we are informed, belonged to the state. Whenever in Hellas coins were issued by individuals, those individuals were rulers, whether constitutional kings or tyrants. Even what are known as temple coinages are probably merely a variety of state coinage. The temple at Didyma issued coins (drachms or hemidrachms) of the same types as those of the Milesian coinage, but with the inscription ΕΓ ΔΙΔΥΜΩΝ ΙΕΡΗ (*scil.* δραχμή). The inscription proves that the coins were issued from the temple; but, taken in conjunction with the type, it also proves that they

---

much more to be said for the attribution to Halicarnassus, where the coin was actually found, and where we have, in later times, a record of a certain Phanes, who acted as an auxiliary of Cambyses in Egypt. But as Fränkel has pointed out (*Arch. Zeit.* 1879, pp. 27-30; Weil, in *Berl. Phil. Woch.* 1898, p. 1337), the form Φαινος, which appears to be the correct reading of the name, is the genitive, not of Φαίνης (which would give the uncontracted form Φαίνεος in the third, and Φαινέω in the first declension), but of Φαινώ, an epithet of Artemis. This being so, the attribution to Ephesus is made more probable.

were issued with the authority of Miletus. This was, in other words, a special Milesian issue meant for religious purposes. On the other hand, the Arcadian coins (Pl. II. 8) reading Ἀρκαδικόν, although very possibly issued from a great common sanctuary, are not a mere temple issue, as we shall have reason to see (below, § 14). The stater of Olympia with the legend Ὀλυμπικόν belongs to a special issue of the coinage of Elis associated with the Olympic festival. The coinage of the Delphic Amphictiones may most properly be classed with federal coinages, which will be dealt with below. Another sanctuary coinage is probably that of Eleusis (Pl. IV. 5), issued during the latter half of the fourth century B.C. 'to meet the requirements of the Festival of the Thesmophoria to which the types refer [1].'

§ 3. *Coinage of Monarchs.*

In the case of individual rulers, the custom most prevalent in Greece Proper and in Western Greece, until the period after Alexander the Great, was for the ruler to conceal his identity, so far as the coinage was concerned, under the name of the state which he governed. Thus Peisistratus and his sons, the tyrants of Athens, Anaxilas of Rhegium, Gelo, Hiero I and the two Dionysii of Syracuse, Thero of Acragas, the Battiadae of Cyrene, and others all employed on their coinage not their own names but the names of the subject states. No doubt this practice was dictated by motives of policy. In outlying districts where monarchy was constitutional, or tyrants more audacious, owing to the lower grade of civilization of their subjects, personal names appear, as at Termera in Caria (where the tyrant Tymnes, in the fifth century, issued coins bearing the legends TYMNO and TEPMEPIKON [2]), among the Edonians (King Getas, about B.C. 500, Pl. II. 9), and the Macedonians (King Alexander I and his successors). Alexander and Teisiphonus,

---

[1] Head, *Brit. Mus. Catal., Attica*, p. lx.
[2] It would be natural to explain this as a case of a Persian vassal issuing coins; but we find that the Κᾶρες ὧν Τύμνης ἄρχει paid tribute to Athens in B.C. 440 (*C. I. A.* i. 240, col. ii. v. 76). The coins in question are, it is true, usually placed in the first half of the fifth century B.C. And it must also be remembered that the Lycians were at once vassals of Persia and tributaries of Athens.

tyrants of Pherae in Thessaly, placed their names on their coins, but the coins of their predecessors, Lycophron and the famous Jason, read simply ΦΕΡΑΙΟΝ. In this connexion it would have been interesting had the Spartans, with their constitutional double monarchy, possessed an early coinage other than the (doubtless anonymous) ὀβελοί.

The breaking down of the old Greek traditions of autonomy by Alexander the Great brought about the frank declaration of the royal prerogative on the coinage of most monarchic states. Alexander's name naturally appeared on his own coins in continuation of the old Macedonian custom. That custom was eventually adopted, though with some hesitation, by his successors: and from them it was copied by Agathocles at Syracuse. Even Sparta at this time followed the fashion, for a tetradrachm of Alexandrine types reading ΒΑΣΙΛΕΟΣ ΑΡΕΟΣ is known[1]. And from this time onwards it is the rule that the name of the monarch should appear on his coinage, although some of the more conservative states offer exceptions[2].

§ 4. *The Coinage and the Sovereign Power.*

'In antiquity, as in modern times, the right of striking money was generally an exclusive attribute of sovereignty[3].' The independent right of coinage being but a sign of political independence, it was inevitable that the ancient Greeks, so far as their history is that of a number of small independent states, should produce an extraordinary variety of independent issues. The history of Rome, on the other hand, and that of Persia, are histories of sovereign states, with subjects grouped under them; and in the coinage of these empires we are therefore concerned with series partly imperial, partly delegated to subordinate authorities. The distinction between

---

[1] Areus reigned from B.C. 310-266. On coins not much later than this period appears the diademed head of a king who is not named. The tyrant Nabis (B.C. 207-192) is named and portrayed on a unique tetradrachm in the British Museum, reading ΒΑΙΛΕΟΣ (= Βα'ιλέος) ΝΑΒΙΟΣ (*Num. Chr.* 1897, p. 107 ff.; 1898, p. 1). But as a rule the Spartan coinage was civic. Nabis himself on his earlier coinage placed his name alone without the title of king.

[2] Gardner, *Types*, pp. 29, 30.   [3] Lenormant, ii. p. 3.

imperial and autonomous coinage obtains broadly throughout the ancient world, although there are in the course of history instances of the small state or individual ruler becoming an imperial authority with subjects whose coinage required control, or joining with other states in a political or commercial federation which was appropriately accompanied by a monetary union.

In so far as the relation of ruler to subject was clearly understood in the political world, this relation may be found reflected in the coinage. The relation of Athens to her subject-allies in the fifth century, for instance, was one of disguised empire. Consequently we find that the imperial city was unable to interfere openly with the coinage of the allied states. Nevertheless, as Holm has pointed out[1], those districts, such as the Cyclades, which were in closest dependence on Athens, were most restricted in their coinage. The close relations between Miletus and Athens account for the fact that hardly any coins can be attributed to the former city at this period. Cities like Cnidus and Phaselis show at the same time a considerable restriction if not a complete cessation of coinage. But it is possible that this feature may be explained rather by exhaustion on the part of the tributary states than by an actual interference by Athens with their right of coinage[2].

The coinage of the kings of Macedon is an illustration of the way in which a Greek ruler controlled the coinage of his dominions. When Philip in 358 B.C. founded the town which bore his name, he gave it permission to strike coins in all three metals bearing the autonomous legend Φιλίππων (Pl. VII. 3); but before his reign was over the grant was withdrawn, and Philippi was placed on a level with other Macedonian cities, used as regal mints, but only to be identified by subsidiary

---

[1] *Gr. Gesch.* ii. p. 267; Eng. transl. ii. p. 233.
[2] In the *Beiblatt* of the *Oesterreich. Jahreshefte*, i. (1898), p. 43, Dr. Wilhelm now announces the discovery on Siphnos of an inscription showing that the Athenians interfered to regulate the coinage, weights and measures of her allies. Another copy of the same document was seen at Smyrna and published by Baumeister in the *Berichte der Berliner Akademie*, 1855, p. 197, but has since been lost and forgotten. Both texts are much damaged. Pending the fuller publication and discussion of the new inscription, I must be content to note that the passage in the text will probably require considerable modification in the sense indicated.

mint marks. Alexander the Great continued the system; but in his character of liberator he accorded the right of independent coinage to all those states which freely accepted his suzerainty. Even the issue of gold was permitted to them, a liberty which they had not enjoyed under the Persian domination.

For the Great King had reserved to himself most strictly all rights connected with the issue of the imperial metal. When we find gold issued by some of the dynasts under Persian rule (thus Pixodarus, dynast of Caria, B.C. 340 to 334, issued a gold coinage), it is 'a sign of a general relaxation of direct Persian control[1].' The difficulty of controlling the outlying island of Cyprus also accounts for the issues of gold coins by the kings of Citium, Marium, Paphos, and Salamis. In the great body of his own dominions the Persian king was able to prevent the coinage even of silver except by his own authority. Where, however, the king's authority was represented by satraps or tributary dynasts, we find large series of silver coins, issued partly by the cities, partly by his generals and in their own name.

Thus practically the whole of the coasts of Asia Minor and Syria are represented by a silver coinage. We even hear of a satrap of Egypt, Aryandes, issuing silver coins[2]. At Tarsus we find issues of silver bearing the legends ΤΕΡΣΙΚΟΝ and ΚΙΛΙΚΙΟΝ and their Aramaic equivalents. These and similar adjectives, like ΝΑΓΙΔΙΚΟΝ, ΣΟΛΙΚΟΝ at other Cilician mints, have been explained as showing that the coins are not properly autonomous issues (which would require the form ΤΑΡΣΕΩΝ, &c.)[3]. Parallel with these issues are those bearing the names of satraps such as Datames, Mazaeus, Pharnabazus, and tributary tyrants and dynasts such as Maussollus and his successors in Caria, or Dionysius and Timotheus at Heraclea in Pontus. The most interesting coin of the kind

---

[1] Head, *Brit. Mus. Catal.*, *Caria*, &c., p. lxxxiv.
[2] Herodotus, iv. 166. Darius, from Herodotus' account, would appear to have been angry with Aryandes for issuing silver of excessive purity. There are no extant coins which can be attributed to this satrap. It may be that he coined sigli with the royal types which should only have been issued by the royal mint, and that this was the real reason of his fall.
[3] But there seems to be insufficient foundation for this view; see Babelon, *Perses Achém.* pp. xxvii. f.

is that struck by Themistocles (Pl. IV. 1) when in exile at Magnesia[1].

Ptolemy Soter allowed to the province of Cyrenaica considerable privileges in the matter of coinage. Thus, under his rule (B. C. 321-308) there seems to have been no limitation of the coinage, which is found in all three metals. From the time of Ptolemy IV, Philopator, down to the acquisition of Cyrenaica by the Romans in B. C. 96, there is, however, no autonomous coinage, Cyrene being used as a royal mint.

The letter of Antiochus VII to Simon Maccabaeus[2] is an interesting record of a grant of the right of coinage made by a ruler to his vassal. The tenor of the letter shows that it was only when Antiochus was in need of help that he thought fit to grant this privilege, which he retracted as soon as he could safely break with the Jewish prince[3].

The grant of the right of coinage was occasionally accompanied by the condition that the head of the sovereign should appear on the coins. Such was the case with the autonomous coinage of several cities of Cilicia and Northern Syria under Antiochus IV[4]. But the reason for the appearance of regal portrait-heads on autonomous coins is often merely complimentary: such is the case with the head of Cleopatra on the coins of Patrae (where M. Antonius stayed the winter B. C. 32-31).

§ 5. *Rome and her Subjects. Restriction of Gold.*

The regulation by Rome, from the time that she became an extra-Italian power, of the coinage of her subjects, is a matter which can only be briefly touched upon here. In this respect, a more or less definite line may be drawn between the western

---

[1] Waddington, *Mélanges*, i. Pl. I. 2; Head. *Brit. Mus. Catal., Ionia*, p. 158 (the latter a plated specimen ; the Berlin Museum has recently acquired a third specimen (*Zeitschr. f. Num.* xxi. p. 73 note).

[2] 1 Macc. xv. 5 νῦν οὖν ἵστη. ἱ σοι πάντα τὰ ἀφαιρέματα, ἃ ἀφῆκάν σοι οἱ πρὸ ἐμοῦ βασιλεῖς, καὶ ὅσα ἄλλα ἀφαιρέματα ἀφῆκάν σοι, ποιῆσαι κόμμα ἴδιον νόμισμα τῆς χώρας σου.

[3] The correctness of the attribution to this period of the well-known Jewish shekels and half-shekels (Fig. 7, p. 34) has rightly been doubted. They are rather to be given to the first revolt of the Jews under Nero (see the references to recent literature on this subject in *Num. Chr.* 1893, p. 75).

[4] Lenormant, ii. 34 ; Babelon, *Rois de Syr.* p. ci. ff.

and the eastern provinces. In the former (with which the Adriatic district must be classed) the denarius was the basis of all the coinage; all coins belonging to any other standard were demonetized. Thus the coinage of silver was either stopped, or limited to issues on the denarius standard. There was of course no legal gold coinage except that of Rome herself or her direct representatives. The striking of a gold piece by the allies in the Social War [1] was even more treasonable than their issue of denarii. The local issues—both provincial and municipal—lasted to the time of the Empire, the provincial coinages of Spain, Africa, and Gaul (the last centring round the altar of Rome and Augustus at Lyons), being most important. But by the time of Nero all these local issues had been entirely superseded by imperial coins. Sicily throughout was placed under the same system as Italy, a bronze coinage alone being allowed, and that only to certain favoured cities like Panormus, which were free and 'immune.'

The coinage of the East was more complex. Here also the general rule prevailed limiting the coinage of gold to Rome. There are, however, one or two exceptions. Most important is the large issue of gold coins (gradually degenerating into electrum) which belongs to the kings of the Cimmerian Bosporus (Pl. XIII. 3). Electrum continued to be coined by these rulers as late as the second half of the third century A. D., but by this time the material of the money is more properly to be called bronze with a wash of gold. From the time of Domitian onwards the head of the emperor always occupies one side of the coin, the head of the vassal king the other.

Certain gold coins reading ΚΟΣΩΝ are often attributed to a Thracian prince who supplied Brutus with gold before the battle of Philippi [2]. On these coins Brutus is represented marching between two lictors. But it is not very probable that the name of such a person should have been placed in the nominative on these coins, which are really a Roman issue.

---

[1] Friedländer, *Osk. Münz.* p. 73; Pinder u. Friedländer, *Beiträge*, i. p. 176; Mommsen, *M. R.* ii. p. 426, no. 225.

[2] Mommsen (*M. R.* iii. p. 283) speaks definitely of 'Coson, prince de Thrace.' The passage of Appian, on which alone the theory is based, does not mention the name of the king *whose widow* brought gold to Brutus.

The word Κόσων may be a genitive plural, and the name of a people[1].

The gold pieces belonging to the time of Caracalla and bearing types relating to Alexander the Great are of course not coins, and therefore do not concern us[2].

The result of this restriction of the coinage of gold was a gradual disappearance of this metal from the coinages of the outskirts of the Roman dominion in proportion as that dominion made itself felt. Thus both in Gaul and Britain the advance of Roman influence caused the gradual disappearance of the gold coinage. And independent rulers, as the Roman power threatened their existence, abstained more and more from employing this metal. The issue of a gold stater at Athens in the name of Mithradates the Great (Pl. IX. 7) was of course an act of war. There is a curious exception to this rule in the gold decadrachm struck at Tyre in 102 B. C.[3] The issue of a gold coinage by Ephesus and Pergamum in B. C. 87-84 was a 'declaration of independence[4].'

§ 6. *Restriction of Silver.*

As regards silver, the regulations were more lax. In the first place the denarius standard was not imposed; but at the same time an unfair tariff was established in accordance with which the silver coins in circulation were valued at a discount in terms of denarii. In the province of Asia the issue of Attic tetradrachms ceased, and the cistophori were the only silver coins which under ordinary circumstances were legal tender. The Attic tetradrachms of Side were, however, admitted to the province, but only when assimilated in value to the cistophori. The issue of Phoenician tetradrachms in

---

[1] The people of *Cossea* has been suggested. Babelon, *Monn. de la Rép. rom.* ii. p. 114.

[2] Longpérier, *Rev. Num.* 1868, Pl. 10-13. The little gold coins of Alexandria Troas belong to the same class (Wroth, *Brit. Mus. Catal., Troas,* &c., p. 12, note). Of the gold coins of Amyntas, it may be said that the evidence against their genuineness is too strong to allow of their being admitted to the text. The stater at Paris is certainly false; some of the sixths appear to be of better style than others, but the resemblance is too close to allow of a satisfactory distinction between false and true (see Wroth, *Brit. Mus. Catal., Galatia,* &c., p. xviii).

[3] At Berlin, *Z. f. N.* iv. p. 6.

[4] Head, *H. N.* p. 497.

Phoenicia was interfered with and partially stopped. Still most of the Greek cities that possessed the title of 'free' or 'autonomous' retained the right of silver coinage; and certain confederations created or patronized by the Romans enjoyed the same privilege. Thus we have silver coins of the Lycian league (Pl. IX. 5) certainly as late as the time of Augustus; we have the federal coinage of the Regions of Macedon, during the short period 158-146 B.C., those of the Magnetes, Thessalians, &c., and that of Hispania Citerior down to the war of Numantia. It was natural that in mining districts such as the last-mentioned a silver coinage should be permitted.

In Greece, after the formation of the provinces of Achaea and Macedonia in 146 B.C., the various federal coinages come to an end. We now have a provincial coinage in Macedonia in both silver and bronze. The earliest pieces, while resembling in types the earlier regional coinage, now bear the word LEG(atus) (Pl. X. 5); the later pieces, on which the quaestorial insignia occupy the reverse, are marked with the names of the praetor, quaestor, or legatus pro quaestore[1]. Bronze coins were also issued by at least two quaestors. On these the whole legend is in Greek, while on the silver the Greek lettering is confined to the word ΜΑΚΕΔΟΝΩΝ.

In the Province of Asia the cistophori were taken up by the Romans, and on the later of them appear the names of Roman proconsuls of the Province of Asia, as *T. Ampi(us) T. f. pro co(n)s(ule)*. On the Phrygian cistophori, since the Phrygian cities were at times within the jurisdiction of the governor of Cilicia, the names of Cilician proconsuls (P. Lentulus, Pl. X. 6, and M. Tullius Cicero) occur, as well as those of the Asiatic governors.

Generally speaking, down to the time of the Empire the coinage of silver in the eastern provinces was limited to the Romano-provincial coinage, and to the issues of a few cities or rulers specially favoured (such as Alexandria Troas, Tyre, Side in Pamphylia, Amyntas, the kings of Cappadocia, &c.). Other states and monarchs received the right of coinage, but were limited to bronze. And that a distinct grant was necessary is shown by the curious way in which some of the most important cities are ill represented, or entirely unrepresented, by coinage

---

[1] *Aesillas q(uaestor), Suura leg(atus) pro q(uaestore).*

after they come under the power of Rome. The scantiness of the Rhodian coinage under the Empire is doubtless due to the sufferings of the island state in the civil war.

§ 7. *The Eastern Provinces under the Empire.*

The advent of the Empire caused considerable changes in the provincial administration. In the first place, although local money was not suppressed, Augustus made Roman coins, weights, and measures obligatory in all parts, in so far as they were to be legal in all transactions, and all public accounts and tariffs were to be based on the denarius [1]. If the drachm is mentioned, it is regarded as equivalent to the denarius, unless a special tariff was arranged [2].

It took, however, some three centuries, before the Roman coinage actually expelled the local coinage from all parts, and then the cessation of the local coinage may have been due rather to exhaustion and disorganization than to other causes.

The silver money of the East in Imperial times is designed to meet the want of the provinces for a silver coinage which could not be supplied in sufficient quantity by the Roman mint. In the first place, the cistophori were continued by the so-called 'silver medallions' of Asia Minor (Pl. XII. 8). Farther East, the great mint of Caesarea in Cappadocia issued enormous quantities of silver coins, mostly with a local type, the Mons Argaeus (Pl. XIV. 2). Syria and the further East were served by Antiochia on the Orontes (Pl. XIV. 7) and its subordinate mints (Tyre, Heliopolis, Emesa, and others; even places like Seleucia ad Calycadnum struck an occasional billon coin which is evidently to be classed with the Antiochene series). The third important coinage of this kind is that of Alexandria in Egypt, which extends down to the end of the third century A.D.[3] These coins do not bear the name of the mint, but are distinguished by their fabric and by the careful system of dating

---

[1] Egypt, however, seems to have been excepted; not till Diocletian's time did drachms and obols go out of use in accounts.

[2] Thus we hear of the Rhodian drachms current in A.D. 71, that they were tariffed at 10 assaria, or ⅝ of the denarius (inscription of Cibyra, C. I. G. 4380 a, vol. iii. p. 1167).

[3] As Pick has pointed out (*Z. f. N.* xiv. p. 300 f.; *Journ. Internat.* 1898, p. 462), the coinage of Alexandria under the Empire is not the coinage of the city, but of the provincial government.

according to the regnal years, the symbol L being employed, as a rule, instead of ЄTOVC (Pl. XIV. 5, 8). The character of these coinages is by no means high, and the silver rapidly becomes billon, and the billon bronze.

Besides these important issues, we may mention some of a more sporadic character. After the dissolution of the Lycian league and the constitution of the imperial province of Lycia-Pamphylia by Claudius in 43 A.D., a series of denarii were issued until the time of Trajan. This coinage ceases with the transference of the province to the Senate. Less important are the casual issues of silver at Byzantium[1] and at Ephesus[2]. There are also silver coins struck in Imperial times at Stratonicea, Aphrodisias, and Tabae in Caria, in the first case as late as the time of Antoninus Pius. The silver coins struck in Cyprus during the last three years of Vespasian's reign (in the names of Titus and Domitian) are of the same exceptional character. Crete has a series of silver coins from Augustus to Trajan. The little silver coins struck at Nicopolis in Epirus with the head of Faustina Senior (ΘЄΑ ΦΑVCTЄΙΝΑ)[3] were issued in connexion with the Actian games. Tarsus occasionally issued silver. The silver coinage of Tyre lasts down to 57 A.D.; and this city, as we have already noticed, was one of the mints of the Antiochene series. The source of a peculiar series of silver coins struck in the time of Marcus Aurelius and his family, and reading ὑπὲρ νίκης Ῥωμαίων or ὑπὲρ νίκης τῶν κυρίων Σεβ(αστῶν), was probably Edessa in Mesopotamia.

The irregular and scattered character of this silver coinage shows how much the right of coinage depended on the will of the provincial governors. It seems impossible to elicit from the known facts any kind of rule governing the distribution of silver mints. That they were kept under strict control is shown by the fact that a governor in the time of Marcus Aurelius is known to have demonetized the silver of a mint (unknown) owing to its debased condition[4].

[1] With the heads of the deified Augustus and Livia, therefore presumably struck by Tiberius.
[2] Under Nero, with the inscriptions ΔΙΔΡΑΧΜΟΝ and ΔΡΑΧΜΗ.
[3] Wroth in *Num. Chr.* 1897, p. 104, no. 19.
[4] *Digest.* xlvi. 3. 102, pecunia, qua illa res publica utebatur, quasi aerosa iussu praesidis sublata est. After the time of Augustus the number of

The coinage of bronze was permitted in enormous quantities. The right was, even so, strictly controlled by the home government. There were only two senatorial[1] mints (Rome and Antioch), and local issues supplied the remainder of the bronze coinage. The bronze coins issued by Roman procurators in Judaea (of which later) may perhaps form another class. The local issues are of two kinds, those bearing the heads of emperors or personages of the Imperial family, mostly empresses, and those with a quasi-autonomous type. The emperors or empresses are occasionally identified with deities; Plautilla appears as ΝΕΑ ΘΕΑ ΗΡΑ, Commodus as ΗΡΑΚΛΗϹ ΡΩΜΑΙΟϹ (Pl. XIII. 2). Similarly even on Roman coins we find Livia in the character of PIETAS.

Next to the heads of emperors, and forming a transition to the more frankly autonomous types, come the personifications of the Roman Senate (ΙΕΡΑ ϹΥΝΚΛΗΤΟϹ, ΘΕΟΝ ϹΥΝΚΛΗΤΟΝ, Pl. XIII. 6) and of Roma herself (ΘΕΑ ΡΩΜΗ, ΘΕΑΝ ΡΩΜΗΝ, Pl. XIII. 6). These are limited to senatorial provinces, or rather, one may say, to the province of Asia[2].

The individual city is represented on its coins by its ΔΗΜΟϹ (Pl. XIV. 9, 10), ΒΟΥΛΗ (ΙΕΡΑ ΒΟΥΛΗ, Pl. XIV. 11), ΓΕΡΟΥϹΙΑ (ΙΕΡΑ ΓΕΡΟΥϹΙΑ), or personified, in which case the name of the city, or simply ΠΟΛΙϹ, is inscribed beside the bust. A fine coin of Sardes (Pl. XIII. 1) has a representation of the Μητρόπολις Σάρδις Ἀσίας Λυδίας Ἑλλάδος α΄. But the greater number of these quasi-autonomous coins bear representations of deities or heroes locally important, such as Zeus Poteos at Dionysopolis (Pl. XIV. 12).

The right of coinage gradually became more and more an empty honour. The greater part of the later bronze coinage of Asia Minor seems to have been connected with local festivals and games, and coins were probably issued in vast numbers on these occasions in order to supply the wants of the unusual

---

mints from which silver was issued was considerably reduced. Again, under Hadrian and Antoninus Pius there were numerous changes, some mints being closed, other new ones opened, many only for a few years.

[1] See p. 50, for the authority of the Senate in the matter of coinage.

[2] ΡΩΜΗ occurs outside the province, as at Amisus and Alexandria. The interference of the Roman Senate in local affairs is evidenced at Laodicea in Phrygia by the phrase Δόγματι Συνκλήτου, which is equivalent to *Senatus Consulto*.

concourse of spectators. After the time of Gallienus, Greek Imperial coins were rarely struck; the Emperors Claudius II, Aurelian, and even Tacitus are, however, represented (the last only at Alexandria and Perga). At Alexandria the coinage went on (long after the billon had degenerated into bronze) until the time of Diocletian, who established there one of his Roman mints.

The treatment of vassal rulers seems to have varied as much as that of subject cities. The gold coinage of the Crimean kings has already been mentioned. In the closing days of the Republic and the beginning of the Empire the kings of Mauretania, of Cappadocia, of Pontus (that is·to say, the Zenonid family), the kings of Nabathaea, and Amyntas of Galatia are all represented by silver. On the other hand, the kings of Thrace (with the possible exception of a Cotys in the first century B.C.), the Jewish rulers, the kings of Commagene, the dynasts of Olba, the kings of Cilicia, and (from the time of Trajan downwards) the princes of Edessa were limited to bronze. The usage as to putting on the coins the head of the emperor seems to have varied in different places, and under different rulers in the same place.

The Roman governors and their subordinate officers, having authority over the various provinces, naturally appear on the coins of places under their control; in these cases the inscriptions are in Greek [1].

§ 8. *Roman Colonies.*

A peculiar position in the monetary system of the Roman dominions was occupied by the Roman colonies. Strictly speaking, that colonies of Roman citizens should ever have had a coinage other than the state coinage was an anomaly. That colonies with limited citizenship should have had certain rights of coinage was, on the other hand, only to be expected. Accordingly we find in the earliest period that cities like Caere and Capua (which possessed the 'Caeretan right'), and colonies with the 'Latin right,' standing in the same position as allied states, did possess a coinage of their own. Until 268 B.C., when the Roman silver coinage was introduced, the

---

[1] See below, ch. v. § 8.

right of coinage in these colonies was unrestricted. At this date, however, the issue of silver by the colonies was stopped, and a similar measure was adopted with the allies (the Brettians alone excepted). About four years later, all mints, colonial or other, were closed in Central Italy, and at the same time the system of the *as* was imposed on the southern part of the peninsula. The bronze now issued was, however, of a lower standard than the Roman; and after a time none but the smaller divisions were allowed. The admission of all Italians to the citizenship by the *leges Julia* and *Plautia-Papiria* (B. C. 90–89) naturally carried with it the abolition of the independent coinage of Italian colonies and allies, excepting only Paestum. The coinage of Sicily and Spain, however, continued; but here again, as earlier in Italy, the weights were kept below the Roman standard.

In the period of transition to the Empire, the old rule was broken, notably in the case of Corinth, which, though a colony of Roman citizens, issued coins. Gades is another instance of the same breaking down of the old distinction. About this time also we find a number of municipia striking money, some of them even placing their title on it [1]. Some of these may, however, have been municipia with the Latin right only. We have also in the coins of Vienna and Lugdunum (under the name of COPIA) further instances of the same relaxation of the rule; and Nemausus and Cabellio (with the Latin right) and Lugdunum (with the Roman right) even issued silver *quinarii*.

Augustus removed the anomaly by abolishing the distinction between the two forms of right, and making it possible for all colonies outside Italy alike to issue bronze. The right, however, had to be specially granted in each case, and the circumstance of the grant is noted on many coins. As it was at first made by the emperor directly, we find the formulae *Perm(issu) Augusti*, *Permissu Caesaris Aug(usti)*, *Per(missu) Imp(eratoris) Caesaris Augusti*, *Indulgentiae Aug(usti) Moneta impetrata* (this at Patrae), and even *Perm(issu) Divi Aug(usti)*. But after the reorganization of 15 B. C. the proconsuls were competent to make the grant, and thus we meet with the names of legates and proconsuls in formulae such as: *Perm(issu)*

[1] As at Emporiae, EMPOR—MVNIC.

Silani (at Berytus), *Permissu L. Aproni procos. III* (at Clypea). The mention of these permissions ceases in the time of Tiberius[1]. The most abbreviated form in which they are found is PPDD (*Permissu Proconsulis, Decurionum Decreto*).

Colonial coinage in the West has but a brief duration. In Sicily, it ends with Augustus; in Africa and Numidia, with Tiberius; in Spain, with Caligula; in Gaul, about the time of Nero: Babba in Mauretania, curiously, strikes as late as Galba's reign. The exceptions are only apparent. When Commodus perpetrated his freak of colonizing Rome, the new colony struck coins with the title *Col(onia) L(ucia) An(toniniana) Com(modiana)* (Fig. 18). The coins of the fourth consulate of

FIG. 18.—Reverse of *as* of Commodus (A. D. 190): COL(onia) L(ucia) AN(toniniana) COM(mcdiana). P(ontifex) M(aximus), TR(ibunicia) P(otestate) XV, IMP(erator) VIII, CO(n)S(ul) VI. S. C. Priest ploughing.

Postumus (A. D. 265-266) struck at Cologne, reading *Col(onia) Cl(audia) Agrip(pina)* or *C(olonia) C(laudia) A(ugusta) A(grippina)*, are really imperial, not colonial coins. In the East the colonial coinage lasted down to the time of Aurelian.

The official language of these colonies was of course Latin. Still we find Greek in some of the colonies of late foundation, as Thessalonica, and Philippopolis in Arabia. Greek in fact is the rule in the remote East, where it must have been difficult to inculcate Latin. And even in Asia Minor the Latin legends are often sadly blundered[2]. The later coins of Antiochia on the Orontes reading S C and Μητρο. Κολωνία have been explained, on

---

[1] But Corinth, which received again from Domitian the right which it had lost under Vespasian, records the fact in the legend *Perm(issu) Imp(eratoris)*.

[2] For instance, the title of Volusian appears (in the dative) on coins of Pisidian Antioch as IMPCVIRAPCALVSSIANOAVG.

the ground of the two Latin letters, as really senatorial coins[1]. The letters **S R** on the coins of Antioch in Pisidia point to some interference on the part of the Roman Senate with the coinage of the colony (Pl. XIV. 3)[2].

The obverse type of colonial coins under the Empire is almost universally the emperor's head. In the earlier period it is not unusual to find mention of the Roman patrons of the city. At Gades we find Agrippa as *Municipi Patronus et Parens*; earlier at Paestum *Cn. Corn(elius) M. Tuc(cius) Patr(oni)*. Agrippa's third consulate is commemorated on coins struck at Caesaraugusta (Tarraconensis) as late as the reign of Caligula.

The types of the colonial coins are as a rule somewhat uninteresting. The most common are:—

A priest tracing the pomoerium with a plough drawn by a yoke of oxen.

The Wolf and Twins.

Marsyas (a copy of the Silenus-statue in the Roman forum, popularly called Marsyas and supposed to be a type of the Latin right)[3].

Military standards (denoting a *deductio* of veterans) sometimes accompanied by an indication of the legion concerned.

But besides these and other stock types (such as Victory, the emperor performing various functions, the Roman eagle, &c.), there occur interesting local representations, such as Apollo Smintheus at Alexandria Troas, Mên at Antioch in Pisidia (Pl. XIV. 3), or the types relating to the myths of Bellerophon and of Melicertes at Corinth.

§ 9. *Delegated Coinage: the Satraps.*

We have already mentioned the subsidiary coinages of the Persian Empire: those coinages which, to meet the military necessities of the outskirts of the Empire, were by the Great King's permission issued by his generals or satraps, and by

---

[1] **SC** occurs elsewhere, e.g. at Philippopolis in Arabia and at the colony of Mallus in Cilicia.

[2] An interference limited at first (from Septimius Severus to Gordian III) to the sestertii, and then extended to all the coins. The meaning of the abbreviation is, however, by no means certain. The letters also occur at the colony of Parlais in Lycaonia.

[3] Serv. ad Aen. iii. 20; iv. 58.

the dynasts who owned allegiance to him. From one point of view (*de facto*) the coinage of these last was simply the outcome of a privilege granted to subjects (from whom it could hardly be withheld); from another (*de jure*), the right of coinage may be looked upon as delegated to them by the Great King. The coinage of the satraps and generals, on the other hand, is a purely delegated coinage without any of the character of autonomy. In Paphlagonia, Ionia, and Cilicia the satrapal coinage is especially important. In the northern province, the mint of Sinope was used by Datames, by his son Abd Susin(?)[1], and by Ariarathes; the last-named struck coins also at Gaziura in Pontus. The legends on all these coins, except those of Datames, are in Aramaic. Besides the satraps themselves, however, it is possible to recover from these coins the names of a certain number of their subordinates, such as those which M. Six has read on coins of the series of Datames[2].

As satrap of Dascylium, Pharnabazus issued staters bearing a fine portrait of himself (Pl. V. 6), perhaps from the mint of Cyzicus, on the occasion of the loss of that city by the Athenians[3]. These coins bear the satrap's name in Greek letters. More than thirty years later, when he was preparing his expedition against Egypt (B.C. 378-372), it is probable that Pharnabazus issued from Tarsus coins bearing in Aramaic characters his name and the supplementary legend *hlk* or KIΛIKION, showing that the coinage was meant to defray the expense of his military preparations in Cilicia. These satrapal coins, therefore, were probably nothing but a military issue[4].

---

[1] *Num. Chr.* 1894, p. 302. In the pseudo-Aristotelian second book of the Oeconomics (c. 24) is an interesting story of Datames and the plundering of a temple for plate which he carried to Amisus and converted into money to pay his troops.

[2] Vararanes, Tir..... Orontobates (perhaps identical with the last dynast of Caria).

[3] B.C. 410. Wrath, *Num. Chr.* 1893, pp. 11-13.

[4] ' C'est comme généraux placés à la tête d'armées en campagne et non comme satrapes, exerçant les pouvoirs réguliers de cette charge, que les personnages en question les ont fabriquées et y ont inscrit leurs noms ' (Lenormant). Probably also the representation of the satrap's own features which we find at Cyzicus would not have been permitted in the province of Cilicia, which was nearer home.

The word *mzdy*, which occurs on a large number of Cilician coins of later date than those of Pharnabazus, was once interpreted as equivalent to the Greek μισθός [1]; but it is now generally agreed that the letters represent the name of Mazaeus, whose career as satrap in Cilicia, in Eber-nahara (i.e. northern Syria, 'across the river' Euphrates), and finally in Babylon under Alexander, lasted from 362 to 328 B C. He issued coins for all three satrapies, the most remarkable piece being that (Pl. IV. 12) which describes him as 'Mazaeus, who is over Eber-nahara and Cilicia.'

In considerably later times the Parthian king Phraates II (B.C. 136-127) in order to pay his troops in the war against the Scythians, issued drachms which bear the word καταστρατεία ('campaign').

§ 10. *Military Coinage in the West.*

Examples of a military coinage are by no means wanting when we pass from the East to the Greeks of Greece Proper. The enigmatic 'Thibronian money' mentioned by Photius [2] was presumably that struck by one of the two men named Thibron, probably the Spartan harmost, to pay the Greek troops which he organized against Tissaphernes [3]. The coins have not been identified with any degree of certainty [4]. An instance of a military coinage issued in common by a number of Sicilian towns will occupy us subsequently [5].

But the most important instance (outside Rome) of the issue of coins for purely military purposes is found in the Western Mediterranean. The Carthaginians, who did not possess a citizen army, were obliged to spend large sums in payment of their mercenary troops. The earliest Carthaginian coins are those struck in Sicily for this purpose at the time of the great invasion of 410 B.C. (Pl. XI. 5). The workmanship

---

[1] Lenormant, ii. p. 262.
[2] Θιβράνειον νόμισμα : ἐδόκει ἀπὸ Θίβρωνος τοῦ χαράξαντος εἰρῆσθαι, Lenormant, ii. p. 258.
[3] Xen. *Exp. Cyr.* vii. 6. 1.
[4] See Willers, *Z. f. N.* xxi. p. 66 f. It appears that the coins were not of good quality.
[5] For the coin supposed to have been struck by the Athenian army in Samos (Lenormant, ii. p. 260), see Gardner, *Samos*, pp. 45, 46.

of these coins is thoroughly Greek; but the inscription in Punic characters, an occasional Punic symbol, and types such as the date-palm, the head of a queen (Dido?), and others proper to Carthage distinguish them from the issues of the Greek cities of Sicily. At the same time the head of Persephone surrounded by dolphins, which often occurs, is an obvious imitation of the head on the Syracusan coinage. The inscriptions fall into two classes. The one includes the names of cities occupied by the Carthaginians, such as Heraclea Minoa, Motya, Panormus (?), Eryx, Solus. Of the others one is the name of Carthage ('New city of Carthage'), which does not imply that the coins were struck there, as the analogy of ROMA on coins struck at Capua and other places suffices to prove. We find also *Am Machanat* and similar forms, meaning 'the people of the camp' or 'army.' Finally, *Mechasbim* appears to denote the quaestors or paymasters in attendance on the commanders.

This camp coinage of the Carthaginians in Sicily probably terminated in the time of Agathocles, having lasted about a century.

§ 11. *Roman Military Coinage.*

The military issues were, as has been already indicated, an exceedingly important part of the Roman coinage, both in their bulk and by the historical fact that[1] the process by which the coinage of the Republican state became the coinage of the emperor was entirely conditioned by the laws relating to the military coinage. In accordance with the whole constitution of the Empire, Julius and Augustus applied the principles of the military coinage, up till then confined to the provinces, to the coinage of the city; the right of coinage belonging to the *Imperator*, which included the right of portraiture, was thus assumed by the head of the State in civil as well as in military affairs. The military commander in virtue of his *imperium* struck coins either in his own name, or through his financial officers (*quaestor*, *legatus*, or *pro*

---

[1] As Lenormant has said in a passage (ii. pp. 272, 273) the gist of which I have tried to reproduce. See also Mommsen, *Monn. Rom.* ii. pp. 57-63.

quaestore[1]). The authority of the Senate was not needed and is only exceptionally mentioned[2]. The coinage thus issued by the military commanders was part of and conformed to the system of Roman state coinage; its circulation was not confined to any one part of the Roman dominions. But the governors of provinces also issued local coinages of a limited character and conforming to local standards and types (such as the Macedonian series or the cistophori[3]), which must not be confounded with the military coinage proper, although the *imperium* in virtue of which the two classes of coins were issued was one and the same[4].

The first coins certainly of a military character issued by the Roman Republic are small gold pieces of 60, 40, and 20 sesterces (Pl. XI. 9). The obverse bears the helmeted head of Ares and the mark of value; the reverse an eagle on a thunderbolt, and the inscription ROMA. The work is Greek. These pieces were issued during the Hannibalian war, beginning in 217 B.C. The extraordinary value attributed to them (giving a ratio of $17\frac{1}{7}$: 1 between gold and silver[5]) shows that they were issued under stress of circumstances.

The 'liberator' of Greece, T. Quinctius Flamininus, issued during or after the Second Macedonian war (B.C. 200-197) a gold stater with his portrait and name (T. QVINCTI). In some respects this rare coin[6] is an exception to the rule that Roman military coinage conformed to the general Roman system; for it is a stater of Attic weight, and the reverse type is that of the gold staters of Alexander the Great (Nike with wreath and palm-branch). But, as Lenormant has remarked, at this early period a coin of Roman weight would have puzzled the Greeks.

The Social War saw the issue of a large military coinage by the revolted allies (Pl. XI. 13, 14). This records the names

---

[1] Other officers were occasionally, but only in special circumstances, granted the right; e. g. *legati pro consule* or *pro praetore*, and in the civil wars the urban quaestors and the *triumviri monetales* replace the military quaestors.
[2] On coins of Sulla's two lieutenants C. Annius, C. Valerius Flaccus; of L. and C. Memmius, quaestors during the Sertorian war; and the praetor C. Coponius in the war between Caesar and Pompeius.
[3] See above, p. 88.
[4] A list of these provincial issues in Lenormant, ii. pp. 277-287.
[5] Hultsch, p. 302.   [6] See Head, *H. N.* p. 205.

of their generals (and perhaps also their military quaestors), and C. Papius Mutilus is sometimes actually called (in Oscan characters) *Embratur* (i.e. *Imperator*)[1].

The great series of Roman military issues begins, however, with Sulla. His quaestor in the Mithradatic war, Lucullus, issued for the payment of the troops coins which were actually known as 'Lucullan.' These are probably the pieces of somewhat hasty execution reading *L. Sulla* on the obverse, and *Imper. iterum* on the reverse. The obverse bears a head of Venus, before it Cupid with a palm-branch; the reverse, a sacrificial ewer and a lituus between two trophies (Pl. XII. 2). Two peculiarities may be noticed: exactly the same types occur in both gold and silver; and the gold pieces are struck at thirty to the pound[2].

The example set by Sulla was followed by Pompeius, by Julius Caesar, and by the minor combatants in the civil war. In 49 B.C., for instance, the praetor C. Coponius, in command of the fleet at Rhodes, struck denarii with his own name: *C. Coponius Pr(aetor)*, and that of the monetary triumvir Q. Sicinius: *Sicinius IIIvir*. The fact that both these men were holding 'home' magistracies, and therefore had no real right to strike military coins, made it necessary for them to mention the Senate (*S. C.*) as authorizing the issue. These coins well illustrate the disturbed condition of the political world at the time.

Caesar, once in possession of the city of Rome, made it the mint of his imperatorial coinage, while the urban officers, as we have seen, struck outside the city the coins which should have been issued at home. In 44 B.C. an order was made by the Senate that the portrait of Caesar should be placed on the coins. This was done in the case of the urban silver coinage which was issued by the monetary magistrates instituted by Caesar (Pl. XII. 7). But the order did not apply to the gold coins, which did not come within the Senate's control. For the issue of money by the urban officials was still strictly limited to the baser metals, except in the case

---

[1] Friedl. *Osk. Münzen*, Pl. IX. 6 and 9. See also below, § 14; Conway, *Italic Dialects*, i. pp. 216 ff.

[2] Sulla occasionally issued gold at thirty-six to the pound; Hultsch, p. 302. The weight of the Roman aureus gradually fell (see above, p. 54).

of military coinage; and the aurei of Caesar were all issued in virtue of his military office. Not till the year after Caesar's death was an urban gold coinage instituted. A single gold coin of Julius Caesar (if indeed it is not a coin of Hirtius which has been tooled) bears his portrait [1]; but in placing his portrait on this gold piece he was not conforming to any decree of the Senate, but to the example set long before by Flamininus. The right of portraiture was not actually a prerogative of monarchy at this time; witness the fact that not only M. Antonius and Octavius, but also the most eminent republicans (Cassius excepted), followed Caesar's example after his death. The privilege was extended by the triumvirs to their families (thus we find the heads of Octavia, of Marcus Antonius Junior, even of Cleopatra, on coins of Marcus Antonius). The right of portraiture was retained by the governors of senatorial provinces even under the Empire, but only until the year 6 A.D. From that time onwards it was an imperial prerogative [2].

We have traced the process by which the military coinage of the Republic became the chief state issue of the Empire. This coinage now passes out of the limits of this section, as being no longer an issue delegated or permitted by the state to its military representatives. Before leaving this subject, however, we may take notice of the coins struck by the propraetor P. Carisius in Spain (23-22 B.C.), the last on which a general was allowed to place his name [3]. Henceforward the military coinage is absorbed in the general imperial system. Certain classes of coins may, however, be distinguished by type or legend as having a closer connexion with the army than the rest; such are the coins with the legends FIDES MILITVM, CONCORDIA MILITVM, &c., or with the names of the legions, such as LEGio XIII GEMina Martia Victrix [4].

[1] Lenormant, ii. 328. The portrait is, however, disguised as a head of Pietas. As to the genuineness of the coin see Bahrfeldt, *Nachträge u. Berichtigungen*, p. 140. The specimen in the British Museum is certainly of very doubtful authenticity.

[2] But it was not recognized as such by Clodius Macer, who, while attempting to revive the republican constitution after the fall of Nero, and without calling himself *imperator*, nevertheless placed his portrait on his coins.

[3] Lenormant, ii. p. 362; Babelon, *Monn. de la Rép.* i. p. 317 f.

[4] These legionary coins occur under M. Antonius and again in the third century under S. Severus, Gallienus, &c.

§ 12. *Combined Coinages: Real and Complimentary Alliances.*

Besides the exercise of the right of coinage by the single state, Greek history presents several instances of its being exercised by more than one state in common. It is necessary at the outset to distinguish the apparent from the real alliance coinages. A complimentary understanding (ὁμόνοια) between two states was often, under the Roman Empire, accompanied by what are called 'alliance coins' on which the names of the two states were coupled. Thus we have a coin of Valerian I. struck at Side with CIΔHTΩN ΔΕΛΦΩN OMONOIA (Fig. 19), commemorating doubtless an understanding with Delphi at a time when Pythian games were celebrated at Side. There are coins of Apollonia in Pisidia in 'alliance' with the Lycians, from whose land the Apolloniates claimed to have come. The states are usually represented by their deities, and also named, but occasionally the types are regarded as sufficient to identify the states concerned [1].

FIG. 19.—Reverse of bronze 'Alliance-Coin' of Side and Delphi. Two Victories holding prize vase with palm - branches. [*Obv.* Bust of Valerian I.]

These coins, which are especially common in Asia Minor, cannot be regarded as expressing alliances either political or monetary, considering the conditions of the Roman rule under which they were issued.

The real alliance coinages of Greek antiquity are either primarily political or primarily commercial. A third class, however, in which the coinages centre round a religious point, may perhaps be distinguished. As a rule, coinages originating out of purely commercial reasons have the characteristic that the states concerned retain their own types, but conform to a certain standard and fabric. The coinages of alliances

---

[1] Mionnet (vol. iii. p. 47, no. 114) describes a coin reading merely OMONOIA MYTIΛHNAIΩN on which the divinities represented show that the alliance was between Mytilene, Pergamum, Ephesus, and Smyrna.

that are primarily political range between two extremes; one, in which the individuality of the various states is so completely sunk in the federation that they all use coins exactly alike and struck at one mint; the other, in which a certain type and standard are common to all, while the various states distinguish their own issues by mint marks, subsidiary types, or inscriptions. Between these two extremes there is much variation; frequently we find states supplementing the federal coinage by means of a coinage of their own. And usually it may be taken for granted that where the former extreme of an absolutely uniform coinage is found, its existence is owing to the undue predominance of a single state. In these cases the federal name ΧΑΛΚΙΔΕΩΝ (Pl. V. 11) or ΒΟΙΩΤΩΝ or the like is placed on the coinage for reasons of policy. The true federal coinage, in which the equality of the various members of the state is properly expressed, is one in which those members have their own distinctive issues.

§ 13. *Commercial Unions.*

Of the commercial unions leading to the adoption of a coinage uniform in essential particulars, there are two great instances, the union of Southern Italy, and that between Phocaea and Mytilene. The peculiar fabric of the early coinage of a part of Southern Italy will occupy us later [1]. The states which issued these remarkable coins were in the main Achaean colonies or their dependencies; but the Dorian Tarentum was drawn into the system for a time. It is a noteworthy fact, recently discovered by Mr. A. J. Evans, that the Chalcidian city of Zancle across the Sicilian strait also had an early coinage of a fabric similar to that of the Achaean cities. The federal coinage which began in the middle of the sixth century, and lasted until about 480 B. C., was perhaps partly the outcome of the political projects of the Pythagorean brotherhood [2]. As the federation was never very firmly established, we find considerable laxity in the system of the coinage. Croton, Sybaris, Metapontum, Caulonia (Pl. III. 3), Laüs, Siris, Pyxus and

---

[1] Ch. vi. § 4.
[2] Head, *H. N.* p. li. In so far as this is true, the union cannot have been founded on a purely commercial basis.

a few other cities conform in all respects to the federal fabric and weight (staters of 8·16 g., thirds of 2·72 g.). Poseidonia (Pl. III. 2) conforms in fabric, but in standard and mode of division it follows the Campanian system (staters of 7·64 g., drachms of 3·82 g.). Tarentum observes the rule of fabric at first, but about 500 B. C. places a new type in relief on the reverse; and the stater is throughout divided into halves. Finally, Zancle, in the earliest period of its numismatic history, struck drachms of 5·68 to 5·12 g.[1]. A peculiarity to be noticed is that a large number of the cities place their names side by side on the coins. We find the following combinations:—

Παλ ... and Μολ ... (both retrograde)	Pal ... and Mol ...
Σιρινος (retrogr.) and Πυξοες	Siris and Pyxus.
Ποσ ... and ƒυs ...	Poseidonia and Phistelia?
Ϙρο ... and Συ ... (retrogr.)	Croton and Sybaris.
Ϙρο ... and Τε ...	Croton and Temesa.

In some cases of alliance the type on the reverse is varied, although still incuse (thus the coin of Croton and Temesa has on the obverse a tripod—type of Croton—on the reverse a helmet incuse—type of Temesa). But equally often the same type does duty for both cities.

No less important than the union just described, but of a later date, was the monetary union between Phocaea and Mytilene which is attested by an inscription dating about 400 B.C.[2]. This inscription records an agreement between Phocaea and Mytilene to issue a common coinage in electrum, the quality and weight of which is fixed; the mints were to work alternately for a year, the lot falling upon the Mytilenaean mint to begin. Omitting the mutilated beginning of the inscription, we read:—

Τ[ὸν δὲ κερνάντα τὸ] χρυσίον ὑπόδικον ἔ[μμεναι ἀμφοτέρ]αισι αἶς πολίεσσι· δι[κασταὶς δὲ ἔμ]μεναι τῶι μὲν ἐμ Μυτιλήναι [κερνάντι] ταὶς ἀρχαὶς παίσαις ταὶς ἐμ Μ[υτιλή]ναι πλέας τῶν αἰμίσεων, ἐμ Φώκαι δ[ὲ τ]αὶς ἀρχαὶς παίσαις ταὶς ἐμ Φώκαι πλ[έ]ας τῶν αἰμίσεω[ν]· τὰν δὲ δίκαν ἔμμεναι ἐπεί κε ὠνιαυτὸς ἐξέλθηι ἐν ἐξ μήννε(σ)σι. αἰ δέ κε καταγ[ρε]θῆι τὸ χρυσίον κερνᾶν ὑδαρέστε[ρ]ο[ν] θέλων, θανάτωι ζαμιώσθω· αἰ δέ κε ἀποφ[ύ]γηι μ[ὴ]

---

[1] *Num. Chr.* 1896, p. 101. Thirds of the Euboic tetradrachm? or Aeginetic drachms? See above, p. 36.

[2] The latest account in Wroth, *Brit. Mus. Catal., Troas,* &c., p. lxv. The text is given in Michel, *Recueil d'Inscriptions grecques,* no. 8.

θέλω[ν] ἀμβ[ρυ]τὴν, τιμάτω τ[ὸ] δικαστήριον, ὅττι χρὴ αὐτ(ο)ν παθῆν ἢ κατθέ[μ]εναι. ἀ δὲ πόλις ἀναίτιος καὶ ἀζάμιος [ἔσ]τω. ἔλαχον Μυτιληνᾶοι πρόσθε κόπτην. ἄρχει πρύτανις ὁ πεδὰ Κόλωνον, ἐ[μ Φ]ώκαι δὲ ὁ πεδὰ Ἀρίσ[τ]αρχον.

By this convention the official who makes the alloy of gold and silver (i e. the electrum of which the coinage of the two cities is composed) is responsible to the government of his state, the trial to take place within six months after the expiry of his term of office. The punishment for wilfully making the alloy too base (ὑδαρέστερον) was death. In any case the official, and not his city, was alone responsible.

The electrum coins of Phocaea (Pl. IV. 8) are distinguished by the canting symbol of the city, a seal (φώκη); a certain number of Mytilenaean sixths are distinguishable by the letters Μ or ΛΕ (Lesbos), but the greater number (Pl. IV. 9) are uninscribed. The strong resemblance to each other of these sixths proves that they were issued from a single mint; probably for use in the various Lesbian cities (as the inscription ΛΕ would seem to show). The Phocaic staters and sixths were accepted in Lesbos as legal tender, and the Lesbian in Phocaea. In the neighbouring Atarne, on the other hand, Phocaean coins were at a discount [1].

The convention between Phocaea and Mytilene is the nearest parallel afforded by antiquity to such a union as the Latin Union of our day. The essential element in such unions is that they are purely commercial, and no political union is implied. With the convention between Phocaea and Mytilene may be compared other conventions on a smaller scale, the evidence for which rests entirely on a numismatic basis. Such is the agreement which seems to have subsisted in the fifth century B.C. between the cities of Side in Pamphylia and Holmi in Cilicia [2]. The earliest coins attributed to the former city bear a pomegranate and a dolphin combined. In the fourth century both Side and Holmi issued staters with the types of Athena and Apollo which they distinguished by symbols in the field, Side using a pomegranate, Holmi a dolphin. In all probability, therefore, the early coins just mentioned were struck by Side and Holmi in alliance.

[1] See above, p. 70, note 2.
[2] *Brit. Mus. Catal., Lycia*, &c., p. lxxxi.

Byzantium and Chalcedon, the two cities which shared the control of the trade which passed through the Bosporus, struck from 400 B.C. onwards coins, a comparison of which shows that some sort of convention must have been in force.

	BYZANTIUM.	CHALCEDON.
B. C. 400-350	ϒΠΥ Bull on dolphin. *Rev.* Mill-sail incuse square. Persic drachms.	ΚΑΛΧ Bull on corn-ear. *Rev.* Mill-sail incuse square. Persic drachms.
B. C. 350-280	Similar types. Phoenician tetradrachms, drachms, and tetrobols.	Similar types. Phoenician tetradrachms, drachms, tetrobols, and diobols.
B. C. 280-277	Foreign coins countermarked ϒΠΥ.	
B. C. 277-270	Head of veiled Demeter. *Rev.* Seated Poseidon ϒΠΥ, monogram and magistrate's name (Pl. IX. 3). Phoenician tetradrachms and Attic octobols.	Head of veiled Demeter. *Rev.* Apollo seated ΚΑΛΧ (Pl. IX. 4). Phoenician tetradrachms and Attic octobols.

The cities of Aspendus in Pamphylia and Selge in Pisidia, both on the river Eurymedon, seem also to have issued coins according to some convention[1] similar to that between Byzantium and Chalcedon. There is in fact great difficulty in distinguishing the coins of these cities in the fourth and third centuries, except in the case of the staters which bear their names. It is indeed possible that the resemblance may be due to imitation on the part of Selge.

§ 14. *Political Unions.*

In the great majority of cases the combined coinages of Greek states are merely the outcome and expression of a political combination. From these political combinations we should perhaps exclude those unions consisting of a number of villages allied by tribal relationship, such as the Odomanti, Derrones, Bisalti, and others, which produced a coinage bearing the name of the tribe. Still the difference between these coinages and the issues of such unions as the Boeotian league is merely one of degree of civilization; the former were the issues of a group of villages, the latter of a group of more highly organized cities. It is with the unions of πόλεις and not

---

[1] *Brit. Mus. Catal.*, *Lycia*, &c., p. cxiv.

of κῶμαι that we have to deal. Such unions of κῶμαι were not unknown even in imperial times, an instance being the κοινόν of the Hyrgalean plain in Phrygia, which issued coins reading Ὑργαλέων or Ὑργαλέων ὁμόνοια.

As early as the fifth century B.C., and probably even before that time, Arcadia was provided with a coinage consisting of silver triobols and obols with the legend 'Αρ..., 'Αρκα..., 'Αρκα²ιϘόν, and later 'Αρκαδικόν. (Pl. II. 8). The types are Zeus Aphesius with his eagle, and the head of Artemis. It has been maintained [1] that these coins are not a federal issue, since we know of no federation of the Arcadian cities prior to that founded after the battle of Leuctra in 371 B.C. The coins must, therefore, be a temple issue, and are to be associated with the sanctuary of Zeus Lycaeus near Lycosura, and the periodical festivals (Lycaea) there celebrated. Nevertheless it is difficult to understand how in this case the inscription could justifiably be placed on the coin. The issuing of coins with such an inscription must have been authorized by the Arcadian cities in common; and it is clear from the extant coinage that some sort of federation existed. That the federation was to some extent political is further clear, from the political significance of the inscription. In any case, the attribution of this coinage to the sanctuary on Mount Lycaeum is not certainly established, and there are reasons for supposing that it was issued from the city of Heraea [2]. If so, the parallel with other federal coinages, such as that of Chalcidice, is exact.

Euboea offers a curious variety of federal coinage. When delivered from the power of Athens in 411 B.C. the cities combined to use a coinage with the legend Εὐβοι.., Εὐβ.., Εὐ.., and the like, but with types that prove the coins to have been issued from the mint of Eretria. At the time of the Macedonian conquest the coinage ceases; but it revives again with the 'liberation' of Greece in 197 B.C. Now, however, the silver coins read Ἐρετριέων; but the federal legend Εὐβοιέων appears on the bronze. These federal coins, therefore, throughout proclaim the predominance of Eretria in the federation.

The coinage of Boeotia was from the earliest times largely a federal currency. Until the fourth century B.C. the coins of

[1] Lenormant, *La Monn.* ii. pp. 80, 81.
[2] Imhoof-Blumer, *Monn. Gr.* p. 196.

the various cities were distinguished by legends, the types being uniform; but about 378 B.C. a new currency was instituted, bearing the names not of the cities, but of the magistrates who issued it (Pl. IV. 10). After the battle of Chaeronea (B.C. 338) even these are abolished and replaced by the name of the Boeotians, which is retained (except for a short period, from 315 to 288 B.C. when coins were struck in the name of Thebes) until B.C. 146, when Greece fell under the power of Rome. The regular type of the earlier coinage is the Boeotian shield (possibly the shield of Athena Itonia) but it disappears after B.C. 288, when types relating to Zeus, Poseidon, Athena, Dionysus, &c., prevail in great variety.

In 392 B.C. the cities of Chalcidice formed a league, with Olynthus as headquarters. This league is represented by a uniform coinage with types relating to Apollo, with the inscription Χαλκιδέων (Pl. V. 11). In one case, on a silver tetrobol, the name of Olynthus is also given. The names of magistrates are given on the gold staters and silver tetradrachms, as well as on some silver tetrobols. There are also bronze coins. This coinage lasted probably until 358 B.C., when Philip II captured Chalcidice.

The types of the Epirote federal coinage (which probably began even before the definite constitution of the Republic in 238 B.C., and lasted to 168 B.C.) relate chiefly to Zeus Dodonaeus and Dione. The coins were probably struck at Phoenice.

The federal coinage of Acarnania begins as early as 400 and lasts till 168 B.C. The mint from which the coins were issued was shifted from town to town, Stratus, Leucas, and Thyrrheum all enjoying the privilege at various times. The dominant type is the head of the river god Acheloüs.

The Aetolian federal coinage begins with the period succeeding the invasions of the Macedonians (B.C. 314-311) and Gauls (B.C. 279). The reverse type of the gold coins and the higher denominations of silver (Pl. VIII. 6) is a figure of Aetolia, copied from a statue dedicated at Delphi[1]. She is seated on shields, some Gaulish, others Macedonian. This federal coinage is the only issue produced by the Aetolian cities.

In Thessaly, between B.C. 196 and 146, the Thessalians, the Perrhaebi, and the Magnetes struck federal coins, the mints

---

[1] Paus. x. 18. 7 γυναικὸς ἄγαλμα ὡπλισμένης, ἡ Αἰτωλία δῆθ.v.

being probably Larissa, Demetrias, and Oloösson. The coinage of the Perrhaebi in this period is limited to bronze. To the later part of the same period belong the coins of the Aenianes, struck presumably at their capital Hypata.

The coinage of the Bruttians in the third century B.C. has been explained as a federal coinage[1]. It is true that none of the pure Greek towns in the peninsula were allowed to strike anything but bronze after B.C. 272 (with the exception of some rare silver coins of Rhegium meant for Sicilian trade). But it is doubtful if the coins reading Βρεττίων were issued by the common authority of several states, and not rather in and by some one of the cities of which the Bruttians had gained possession.

In the first third of the second century B.C. (B.C. 185-168) the Macedonian subjects of Philip V and Perseus were allowed to issue an autonomous federal coinage of silver (tetrobols and diobols) and bronze, with a variety of types and the legend Μακεδόνων (sometimes abbreviated, the silver having as a rule merely Μακε.)[2]. This fact shows how weak was the authority of the kings over the Macedonian cities. These coins were probably struck at Amphipolis, and partly, at any rate, by the same officials as the regal coins (a fact proved by the appearance on both series of the same monograms). At the same time the districts of Amphaxitis and Bottiaea issued similar coins reading Ἀμφαξίων or Μακεδόνων Ἀμφαξίων and Βοττεατῶν or Μακεδόνων Βοττεατῶν (the defining names being sometimes expressed in monograms). The mint of Amphaxitis was probably Thessalonica; that of Bottiaea, Pella.

When the Romans in 168 B.C. took over Macedonia, they divided it into four *regiones*, at least three of which received in 158 B.C. the right of coining silver tetradrachms, tetrobols, and bronze. The coins bear the legends Μακεδόνων πρώτης, δευτέρας, τετάρτης (coins of the third region are at present unknown).

The federal coinages of the leagues of Lycia and Achaea, and of other unions to which we now proceed, differ from most of those already described, in that the cities composing the federations exercised a greater freedom in the matter of their coinage,

---

[1] Lenormant, ii. p. 86, after Mommsen, i. p. 127 f.
[2] Collected by H. Gaebler, *Z. f. N.* xx. pp. 179 ff. I have followed his views in this paragraph.

which was issued not at one special mint, but at each city. Nothing more than conformity in type and standard was required. We have already seen that a currency of this kind existed in Boeotia until the time when the power of Thebes became so predominant that all the coins of the federation were issued from that city alone. The type of coinage with which we have now to deal thus belongs to a federation in which no one member has a very marked predominance over the others.

The early coinage of Lycia, previous to the age of Alexander, has been placed in the category of federal coinages. In all probability some sort of political union existed in Lycia in the fifth century. Apart from the fact that the Λύκιοι καὶ συντελεῖς pay tribute to Athens [1], the homogeneity of the coinage is sufficient to prove this. The majority of the coins are, however, dynastic, and the federation probably consisted of an alliance (or rather, a number of alliances) between the rulers of the various Lycian cities. The prevailing type is the symbol consisting of a central ring with three (or sometimes four) curved branches radiating from it; a symbol which is associated with solar worship, and therefore doubtless with Apollo, the tutelary deity of the Lycians [2]. There is, however, in the early Lycian coinage so much variety within certain limits that it would be rash to assume from it the existence of a highly organized federation such as that known in later times as the Lycian League.

This was founded in 168 B.C. at the time when the Romans delivered Lycia from the Rhodian domination, and lasted until Claudius organized Lycia with Pamphylia as a province in A.D. 43. The coinage consists of silver and bronze. The silver is modelled in fabric and standard on the coinage of Rhodes, in that the reverse type is placed in a shallow incuse square. The drachms bear the head of the national deity, Apollo (as often as not between the letters Λ Υ), with his lyre [3] on the reverse (legend: ΛΥΚΙ or ΛΥΚΙΩΝ, and the initials of

---

[1] *C. I. A.* i. 234, col. iii. l. 31.
[2] The explanation of the triskeles (tetraskeles) symbol as symbolizing a political union of three (four) members is fanciful. For the various explanations, see Babelon, *Les Perses Achéménides*, p. xc.
[3] From which they were known as κιθαρηφόροι.

the city, as ΠΑταρα, ΠΙναρα, ΑΙμυρα)[1]. There are a few specimens without a city name, and these were probably struck at Xanthus. The hemi-drachms were only issued in the names of Cragus and Masicytes (of which below), and bear on the obverse the head of Artemis, on the reverse her quiver and the name ΚΡΑΓ or ΜΑΣΙ. The regular federal bronze has in some cases an incuse square similar to that of the silver, but towards the end of the period of the league this goes out, and a considerable variety of types and sizes is found, although types relating to Apollo and Artemis still prevail. On the silver, and on some of the bronze, the mint officials are represented by symbols (only in one case is a certain ΙΠΠΟΛΟ$\chi o s$(?) named). A peculiarity of this federal coinage is the existence of two large subdivisions, comprised in the districts of Cragus (which took in, for this purpose, the banks of the Xanthus and the district west of that river) and Masicytes, which, again for this purpose, comprised the whole district east of the Xanthus valley (the eastern coast and various outlying parts being probably excluded). The chief mint of Masicytes was Myra, that of Cragus probably Xanthus. There are large series of coins with the names of Cragus and Masicytes (Pl. IX. 5), and in many cases the names of cities such as Telmessus, Tlos, Xanthus, Myra are combined on the coins with the letters ΚΡ or ΜΑ. That the issues of Cragus and Masicytes do not belong to towns of that name, but to sub-federal districts, is probable for a number of reasons which I have given elsewhere[2]. From the time of Augustus the coinage of the league is practically limited to these two district issues, which are represented both by silver coins bearing the emperor's head on the obverse, and two lyres on the reverse, and by bronze of a variety of types.

The Lycian league was celebrated in ancient times, and apparently favoured by the Romans; but of far greater historic importance and of earlier date was the Achaean league, the most ambitious attempt made by the Greeks towards federal unity.

The earliest coinage of the Achaean league is prior to the Macedonian conquest. The silver coin (a hemidrachm of

[1] Occasionally the wider ethnic is omitted, and the name of the city written in its place, as ΦΑΣΗΛΙ, ΟΛΥΜΠΗ.
[2] *Brit. Mus. Catal., Lycia*, &c., pp. xlvii, lii.

the Aeginetic standard) bears on the obverse the head of Zeus Homagyrius, on the reverse the letters AX in monogram. The types of the bronze are similar. About 280 B.C. begins the more plentiful coinage on which the various mints are distinguished. The coinage is throughout uniform; for it was a part of the constitution that all members of the league should employ the same weights and measures and coins[1]. The silver coins (of 2·59 to 2·20 g.) bore on the obverse the head of Zeus Homagyrius, on the reverse, within a laurel-wreath, the Achaean monogram with the names, symbols, or monograms of the mints and mint officials (Pl. IX. 1). On the bronze is a full-length figure of the same Zeus, holding Nike and sceptre, with, on the reverse, a seated figure (possibly Demeter Panachaia, whose temple stood beside that of Zeus Homagyrius at Aegium, the centre of the league). On this metal the name of the city is written at length, accompanied by the word AXAIΩN. The league included not merely Achaean cities, but a very large number of cities in Argolis, Arcadia, Elis, Messenia, and even Lacedaemon itself. Many of the lesser cities were naturally only represented by bronze (and this was also the case in Lycia). The constitution of the Achaean league was stricter in the matter of the coinage than that of the Lycian, in that the bronze coinage was no less uniform than the silver. The federal coinage ceases with the constitution of the Roman Province in 146 B.C.

The federal coinage issued immediately after 394 B.C., when Conon's victories over the Spartans freed many of the Asiatic cities from oligarchic rule, is perhaps the most interesting, historically, of all such issues. Ephesus, Samos (Pl. IV. 13), Iasus, Cnidus and Rhodes all issued coins bearing the type of the infant Heracles strangling the snakes, and the legend ΣYN, i.e. συμμαχικὸν (νόμισμα). The same type, but without the inscription ΣYN, occurs on gold and silver coins at Thebes at this time, and it was from Thebes that the type was borrowed. The type also occurs at Lampsacus on gold and at Cyzicus on electrum. The silver coins are equivalent at once to three Rhodian drachms and to one Aeginetic stater. The connexion of the Asiatic cities with Thebes, already seen in the type, is sufficient to explain this peculiar standard. The

[1] Polyb. ii. 37.

sole evidence of the existence of this political combination is found in the coins of the cities concerned [1].

Cyrenaica during the reign of Ptolemy III, Euergetes (B.C. 247-222), was organized on a federal principle. The coins of this period, of silver and bronze, bear the usual types of the district (head of Zeus Ammon and silphium-plant) but read **KOINON** [2].

The combination of the Sicel towns in support of the Corinthian Timoleon, when he visited Sicily in 345 B.C. to deliver it from the Carthaginians, was accompanied by a new currency of a federal character. The metal (appropriately to the native states, for which bronze had always furnished the standard of value) was bronze. Many, but not all, of the coins were issued from Alaesa. The types are sufficiently suitable to the circumstances: the heads of Ζεὺς Ἐλευθέριος, of Sicily (Σικελία), of Apollo, the leader of colonists (Ἀρχαγέτας); the free horse (symbol of liberty), &c. The legends are Συμμαχικόν and Καινόν (i.e. 'moneta nova'), and in the case of Alaesa the name of the people is also given (Ἀλαισίνων).

The later Sicilian coins, reading Σικελιωτᾶν, were not a federal currency, but were struck at Syracuse under Hiero II, who was practically supreme over such parts of Sicily as did not belong to the Carthaginians.

The list of federal coinages proper may be closed with that of the Italians in the Social War of 90-89 B.C. (Pl. XI. 13, 14). Chiefly from Corfinium, the name of which they altered to Italia, the allies issued denarii imitated from the Roman coinage. The inscriptions are usually in Oscan characters, but one group (Pl. XI. 13) has the inscription **ITALIA** under a helmeted head modelled on the well-known representation of Roma. On the reverse of this denarius are the Dioscuri and the name (in Oscan letters) of **C. PAAPI. C.** (C. Papius Caii filius [3]).

In the second century B.C. the four cities of Antiochia, Seleucia, Apamea, and Laodicea in Syria issued a kind of

---

[1] See especially the valuable remarks of Holm, *Gr. Gesch.* iii. pp. 54 ff. Eng. transl. pp. 48 ff. The coins of Zacynthus and Croton with similar types may belong to 377 B.C.

[2] Lenormant (ii. p. 118) attributes these coins to the period B.C. 96-66.

[3] This and other varieties are illustrated in Head, *Coins of the Ancients*, Pl. 68. 12-15. See also above, pp. 99, 100; Lenormant, ii. pp. 291, 292; Conway, *Italic Dialects*, i. p. 216.

I

federal coinage of bronze. The legend ΑΔΕΛΦΩΝ ΔΗΜΩΝ is appropriate to places which all owed their foundation to one king, Seleucus I[1]. The coins bear dates, which show that they were issued between 149 and 128 B.C. As the four cities were subject to the reigning kings of Syria, they were not allowed to coin silver, and the confederation of the cities was of course of no importance except from a municipal standpoint.

§ 15. *Other Alliances.*

In the case of the coinages which have been dealt with so far it is as a rule comparatively easy to say what is the character of the federation which produced them:—political, commercial, or religious. There exist in addition a very large number of alliance coins between pairs of states which it is not always so easy to assign to any one class. On these the names of the participating states are indicated (instead of their being included under a federal title) either directly or by means of types. Perhaps the most remarkable instance of this kind of alliance is that commemorated on a silver tetradrachm of Cyrene (Pl. I. 15) struck in the time of Arcesilaus III (soon after B.C. 530). That king was restored to his kingdom, from which he had been expelled, by the help of Samian and Rhodian allies. The coin in question bears on the obverse the silphium plant and its fruit (types of Cyrene) and a lion's head (type of Samos or Lindus); on the reverse, in an incuse square, is an eagle's head holding a serpent in its beak (type of Ialysus). In this case it is easy to assign a political reason for the issue of the coinage[2].

In all probability political combinations were the cause of most of the alliance coins which are so characteristic of the coinage of Sicily and Magna Graecia. We have already enumerated some of these alliances which fall within the epoch of the commercial union of Magna Graecia. Of a later

---

[1] Αἵπερ καὶ ἐλέγοντο ἀλλήλων ἀδελφαὶ διὰ τὴν ὁμόνοιαν, Σελεύκου τοῦ Νικάτορος κτίσματα. Strabo, xvi. 749.

[2] It is the coinage, however, not of the states of Cyrene, Lindus (Samos), and Ialysus in alliance, but rather of allied groups of individuals from these cities.

date are several alliances between the various cities of this district :—

>   Croton and Temesa (types, tripod and ϘPO for Croton, helmet and TE for Temesa).
>   Croton and uncertain towns (Γ, IA, PA, tripod on both sides).
>   Croton and Pandosia (*obv.* ϘPO tripod, *rev.* ΓANΔO bull).
>   Poseidonia and Sybaris (*obv.* VM Poseidon, *rev.* MOꞀ bull). (Pl. III. 8.)
>   Mystia and Hyporon (*obv.* head of Apollo, *rev.* MY YΓΩP and tripod).

This last coin, which is of bronze, is considerably later than the others, being struck about 300 B.C. The others all belong to the fifth century.

To these must be added two alliance coins recently published by Mr. Arthur Evans[1]; one of Croton and Zancle, earlier than 493 B.C., but with both types in relief (ϘPO and DA, tripod on both sides), and one of Locri and Messana, of the second quarter of the century. (*Obv.* ΛO and MEΣΣANION, hare; *Rev.* biga of mules.) The latter coin shows the same exceptional arrangement of the names of both towns on the same side of the coin as is found on the Mystia-Hyporon piece. More peculiar, however, is the arrangement found on a Croton-Temesa piece, where TE is placed beside the Crotonian tripod, and ϘPO beside the helmet of Temesa, and on the coin of Poseidonia and Sybaris already described.

To the fifth century also belong the alliance coins of Leontini and Catana[2], and of Eryx and Segesta (which have a dog as a common reverse type). A small coin, struck probably by two or more towns of Western Sicily towards the end of the fourth century, has on the obverse a head of Homonoia, on the reverse an altar dedicated to the river Crimissus[3]. Certain coins struck by Theron of Acragas when in possession of Himera (*obv.* cock; *rev.* crab) have been called coins of alliance between these two cities; but the union they indicate is of course that of ruler and subject.

Alliances of the kind described, although commonest in

---

[1] *Num. Chr.* 1896, p. 106 f.   [2] A. J. Evans, *Num. Chr.* 1896, p. 129.
[3] A. J. Evans, l. c. p. 140.

Western Hellas, are also found in the East. The coins apparently representing an alliance between Holmi and Side have been discussed above (p. 105). A coin has been described bearing on the obverse the name and type (griffin) of Abdera, on the reverse the name of Amphipolis with a fish [1]. More than considerable doubt may be expressed as to whether the so-called alliance coins of Abdera and Dicaea, Maronea and Samothrace, Rhodes and Cnidus [2], are really anything of the kind. The head of the Rhodian Helios on the last is probably due to imitation merely. The Cilician coins with constant types, and the varying mint letters M, Σ, I, T (apparently for Mallus, Soli, Issus, Tarsus), are not alliance coins, but satrapal issues, and the uniformity of type is due to their being issued under the same authority.

§ 16. *Greek Colonies.*

The relation between Greek colonies [3] and the cities to which they owed their foundation seems seldom, especially in early times, to have been of the fixed character which is found, for instance, in the case of Roman colonies. In cases like those of the Athenian cleruchies, we find, it is true, a definite regulation of the duties of the colony to the mother-city [4]; but these were exceptional. In ordinary circumstances the relation may be regarded as moral rather than legal. There is, accordingly, no fixed rule affecting the coinage of Greek colonies in respect to their mother-cities. But their coinage nevertheless often bears evidence of the connexion. Since the colonies were usually founded on the line of trade, it resulted that they continued to use the standards current in their old home. But whether colonies were founded or not, standards were carried in this way all over the Greek world; and the presence of Asiatic standards or their derivatives in Southern Italy or Gaul is evidence only of the course of trade, and not of the establishment of colonies. The same is true, though to a much smaller degree, in regard to the retention by the colony of the coin-

---

[1] Lenormant, ii. p. 63, after *Catal. Wellenheim*, no. 1964.
[2] Lenormant, l. c. [3] Gardner, *Types*, pp. 36 ff.
[4] See especially the inscription relating to the colony of Brea, Dittenberger, *Sylloge*², no. 18; Hicks, *Gk. Hist. Inscr.*, no. 29.

types of its mother-city. Since colonists generally carried with them the gods whom they had worshipped at home, it was only to be expected that the old types, more or less modified, would appear on the coins of the new foundation. This is the explanation of the recurrence of Dionysiac types on coins of Naxos in Sicily, a foundation of the island Naxos in the Aegean Sea. So, too, the griffin of Apollo at Abdera is taken from the griffin of the mother-city of Teos. Other instances of the same phenomenon are found at Rhegium (the Samian type of a lion's scalp introduced by the Samian immigrants early in the fifth century), or at Thurium (an improvement on the Athenian head of Athena, Pl. VI. 5). What may be called a negative illustration is found at Corcyra, whose hatred of her mother city Corinth is signalized by the adoption of a type (Pl. II. 7) proper to Euboea, and of a standard which, whatever its origin, has nothing to do with Corinth[1]. The great commercial state was, however, more fortunate with other cities which, being either founded by her, or entering into friendly relations, adopted, in the fourth century, and in some cases earlier[2], the well-known types of the head of Athena and Pegasus. Even Apollonia and Dyrrhachium, although they took their origin from Corcyra, at one time broke through their connexion with their mother-city, and produced 'Pegasi' like most of the other cities in this part of the world[3].

§ 17. *Religious Combinations.*

With the issues of single religious centres such as Olympia and the temple at Didyma we have already dealt. To a certain extent these may be regarded as federal issues, since the importance of these centres was largely due to a combination of the various states interested in them. In the case of the Delphic issue of the Amphictiones we have a clear case of coins being struck by the authority of the representatives of a number of Greek states on the Amphictionic Council. These fine coins (which read 'Αμφικτιόνων, and bear on the

---

[1] Gardner, *Types*, p. 39, Pl. XVI. 24.
[2] 'Pegasi' were struck at Ambracia as early as 480 B.C. Head, *Brit. Mus. Catal.*, *Corinth*, &c., p. 104.
[3] Head, *Brit. Mus. Catal.*, *Corinth*, &c., p. 100.

obverse a head of the Demeter of Anthela, on the reverse types relating to the Pythian Apollo, Pl. V. 7) are probably to be associated with the festival of B.C. 346, after the deliverance of Delphi from the Phocians. During the revival in the time of the Antonines we meet with another similar issue, but in bronze instead of silver.

In imperial times the religious festivals which almost every city celebrated gave rise to an enormous coinage in bronze. Among these festivals were many which had a federal character, being celebrated in common by the various cities of a district, under direction of a chief magistrate. The right to organize common festivals and cults (especially the cultus of the Emperor) was granted by Rome as a slight compensation for the loss of political autonomy. The union of the cities for this purpose was known as a Κοινόν; thus we have the ΚΟΙΝΟΝ ΒΕΙΘΥΝΙΑC, which received the right of coinage under Hadrian (Pl. XIII. 4), the ΚΟΙΝΟΝ ΑCΙΑC, ΚΟΙΝΟΝ ΙΩΝΩΝ, ΚΟΙΝΟΝ ΙΓ ΠΟΛΕΩΝ in Ionia. The coins of this last union, which flourished under Antoninus Pius and Marcus Aurelius, bear the name of Claudius Fronto, who was Asiarch and Archiereus of the thirteen cities. The ΚΟΙΝΟΝ ΜΑΚΕΔΟΝΩΝ ΝΕΩΚΟΡΩΝ, the ΚΟΙΝΟΝ ΚΡΗΤΩΝ (sometimes abbreviated ΚΚ), and the ΚΟΙΝΟΝ ΚΥΠΡΙΩΝ are other well-known instances of this class of union [1].

Combinations of cities of this kind are in the West only known in the province of Africa, where the cities of Oea, Zitha and Zuchis issued a common coinage [2].

---

[1] A list in Head, *H. N.* p. lxxii. The term ΚΟΙΝΟΝ seems sometimes to imply no more than ΟΜΟΝΟΙΑ as on the coin of Mytilene and Perga (Wroth, *Brit. Mus. Catal.*, *Troas*, p. 215, no. 235).

[2] To these may perhaps be added Macaraea with Bilan (?), and again Oea with the same two cities. Much uncertainty, it must be remembered, still involves the numismatics of this part of Africa.

CHAPTER V

MONETARY OFFICIALS

A. AMONG THE GREEKS.

§ 1. *Magistrates' Signatures and Symbols.*

OUR knowledge of the offices held by those responsible for the issue of money among the Greeks is extremely obscure, and depends almost entirely on the coins themselves. What we do know is due to the fact that, in order to fix the responsibility for the quality of the coin, it was necessary to indicate directly or indirectly the person or persons by whom their issue was superintended. Directly, this could be effected by making the person place on the coin, in the field beside the type, either his own private signet or symbol, or his name (written monogrammatically, otherwise abbreviated, or at full length). Indirectly, it could be done by similarly indicating on the coin the eponymous magistrate of the time. A reference to the registers of the state would then, in case of need, be sufficient to bring home to the moneyer any fraud. The indication by symbol may be said, as a rule, to precede chronologically the indication by name, just as the earliest coinage of most Greek cities bears merely a type and not the name of the city. At the same time, not all symbols on early coins must be interpreted as magistrates' marks; and again, the representations by symbols and name often continue side by side.

A peculiar development of the symbol is found at two or three cities, where it becomes so important as to quite overshadow the type. At Cyzicus (Pl. I. 5, V. 8) and Phocaea (Pl. IV. 8) the city types (a tunny and a seal respectively) are reduced to the size ordinarily assumed by the symbol, while the greater part of the field is occupied by the symbol. The scope which this gave to variety of artistic display is obvious. At Lesbos this system was carried so far that on the electrum hectae (Pl. IV. 9) we look in vain for any state-type. At Lampsacus (Pl. V. 10) the obverse is occupied by changing types (some of them among the most beautiful of Greek coin-types) while the arms of the city (the forepart of a winged sea-horse) appear constantly on the reverse. At Abdera during a certain period (the last third of the fifth century) a changing type appears on the reverse; the occasional punning nature of these types justifies our supposing that they are magistrates' emblems. Thus we have a dancing-girl accompanying the signature ἐπὶ Μολπαγόρεω. It is true that the name Μολπαγόρης also occurs with the type of a young Dionysiac head. But such types as a warrior associated with Νικόστρατος, or a tripod with Πύθων, seem to be clear instances of puns. Or it may be that both name and symbol had a common source— such, e.g., as a military success on the part of Nikostratos' father, leading to the adoption of the name for his child and the symbol as a family signet; or, again, a vow to the Pythian Apollo in the case of Python. In this case[1] the types would not be punning types. But the former explanation is simpler, and in accordance with a very natural tendency, which was probably as characteristic of Greek heraldry as it was of mediaeval. Either alternative suits our argument.

At the same time, where we find name and symbol side by side, two possibilities have to be considered. Either the two belong to the same person, or else the symbol is the mark of some other official whose connexion with the coinage is not otherwise indicated. Thus, for instance, at Rhodes (in the period B.C. 166-88) we find the symbol of a right hand associated with the name Δεξικράτης[2]. Here we might be inclined to regard the symbol as a 'canting' device. But the same name occurs with at least three other symbols in the same period. Again, in the same period, the head-dress of Isis occurs as a symbol in conjunction with at least five names (Ἀρτέμων, Εὐφάνης, Ζήνων, Θρασυμήδης, Μάης). In all probability,

---

[1] I owe this suggestion to Professor Percy Gardner.
[2] Head, Brit. Mus. Catal., Caria, p. 254, no. 259, Pl. XL. 4.

therefore, the symbols which occur on the reverses of these Rhodian coins belong, not to the actual responsible official who signs his name, but to the eponymous magistrate [1], whose name does not occur. This theory is suggested by the arrangement of names and symbols on the coins of Apollonia and Dyrrhachium (Pl. IX. 6) in Illyria, where two magistrates' names occur on each coin. On one side the name is in the nominative. It is accompanied by a symbol which varies with the name on the other side. Lenormant has formulated the rule that a man's name in the genitive, whether accompanied or not by the preposition ἐπί, generally signifies that the coin was issued during the period of office held by that man, whereas a name in the nominative signifies responsibility. The difference, in fact, is that between Ἀγωνίππου (ἄρχοντος ἐχαράχθη τὸ νόμισμα) and Δινοκράτης (ἐχάραξε τὸ νόμισμα). The name in the genitive, then, is probably that of the eponymous magistrate. The names on the two sides are combined in a great many different groups which would seem to show that in each term of office of the eponymous magistrate, i. e. probably in each year, there were nine or ten moneyers at least, and, at the same time, that the moneyers remained in office during a number of years [2]. That being the case, it was necessary to inscribe on the coins both names, and also, in case of a re-election on the part of the eponym, the symbol used by the latter as his private mark. This, then, is the most probable explanation of the variation of symbols with the same name on series like that of Rhodes already mentioned [3].

§ 2. *The Athenian Monetary Officials.*

One of the most important series of magistrates is furnished by the Athenian coins of the 'new style,' from B. C. 220 onwards. The names on these coins are at first (B. C. 220-197) written in monogram (in two exceptions partially resolved);

[1] Namely, the priest of Helios.
[2] See the list given by Brandis, *Z. f. N.* i. p. 59 f.
[3] The names which occur in the nominative on the coins of Corcyra are those of the eponymous prytaneis (Lenormant, iii. 62, 63). In this and similar instances the responsibility for the coinage, if Lenormant's rule of the cases holds, rested with the eponymous magistrate of the state. But the rule is hardly universal.

from 196–187 we find the names of two magistrates written more or less fully; then follow series of three names. In nearly all cases we find symbols in the field in addition to these names; also letters on the amphora denoting the prytany or month in which the coin was issued [1], and certain letters beneath the amphora, supposed to indicate the various workshops in the mint. The system by which any fraud could be brought home to the perpetrator was exquisitely complete, and worthy of the Athenian democracy at this period. The question arises: to which of the two or three magistrates does the symbol belong? One would naturally suppose that it belonged to the first-named magistrate; and in one or two cases (some of historical importance) this is true. Thus, in the period B.C. 186–146, we have:—

Magistrates.	Symbols.
(a) { Ἀντίοχος—Νικογ.	Elephant.
Ἀντίοχος—Καραϊχος (Pl. IX. 8)	Elephant.
(b) { Μητρόδωρος—Μιλτιάδης	Grapes.
Μητρόδωρος—Δημοσθέν.	Grapes.

In the next period (B.C. 146–middle of first century, B.C.)

(c) { Εὐμαρείδης—'Αλκιδάμας	Triptolemus.
Εὐμαρείδης—Κλεομέν.	Triptolemus.
(d) Βασιλε. Μιθραδάτης—'Αριστίων (cf. Pl. IX. 7)	Sun and crescents.

The Antiochus of (a) is the man who afterwards became Antiochus IV, Epiphanes. This in itself would suffice to suggest that the elephant is his symbol, and not that of the second magistrate. Apart from this fact, since in (a), (b), and (c) the symbol does not vary while the first magistrate remains in office, the symbol must belong to the first magistrate. The King Mithradates of (d) is of course Mithradates the Great, and the sun and crescents his particular symbol.

[1] On certain series of the first period these letters run up to M (=12); hence, if we assume that the letters represent prytanies, these series are later than the foundation of the Attalis tribe about B.C. 200. M of course recurs on most of the later series. The letter N which occurs on some has been connected by Th. Reinach (Rev. des Ét. gr. 1888, p. 397) with the fact that there was a time before 200 B.C.) when there were thirteen prytanies (inscription from Eleusis, Ἐφ. ἀρχ. 1887, 177 ff.). But to transfer all series with N before 200 B.C. is impossible (Num. Chr. 1889, pp. 229 ff.). If, as is probable, the letters refer to months, N represents the μὴν ἐμβόλιμος.

The combinations which point to the symbol belonging to the second magistrate are the following:—

Period B.C. 186–146.

(a) { 'Αφροδίσι.—'Απόληξι.   Nike with wreath.
     { 'Αφροδίσι.—Διογέ.   Double cornucopiae.

Period B.C. 146–middle of first century B.C.

(b) { Κόιντος—Κλέας   Nike crowning Metellus?
    { Κόιντος—Χαρίας   Two ears of corn.
(c) { 'Αρχίτιμος—Δημήτρι.   Isis(?) holding flower.
    { 'Αρχίτιμος—Παμμένης   Thyrsus.
    { Διοκλῆς—Δεωνίδης   Asclepius.
(d) { Διοκλῆς τὸ δεύ.—Μήδειος Hygieia.
    { Διοκλῆς τὸ τρί.—Διόδωρος Dionysus.
(e) { Φιλοκράτης—'Ηρώδης   Dionysus.
    { Φιλοκράτης—Καλλίφρων   Nike.

From the above it would seem to be clear that the symbol belongs to the second magistrate. It might, however, be argued that, for instance, Architimos came into office a second time and therefore changed his symbol. If so, why is Diokles the only one who enumerates his successive tenures of office?

Finally, it may be noticed that we find some combinations which fall in with neither of the alternatives suggested.

These are:—

Period B.C. 196–187.

(a) { 'Αμμώ—Διο.   Kerchnos[1] or no symbol.
    { 'Αμμώ—Διο.   Cornucopiae.

Period 146–middle of first century B.C.

    { Ξενοκλῆς—'Αρμόξενος   Serpent.
(b) { Ξενοκλῆς—'Αρμόξενος   Trident and dolphin.
    { Ξενοκλῆς—'Αρμόξενος   Metellus(?) seated.

On the whole the evidence of the coins is so inconsistent that it is safest to assume that there was no fixed rule; indeed, the placing of the symbol beside the name was by no means essential, since we find series in which the symbol is either always or sometimes absent[2].

[1] For the significance of this symbol, until lately wrongly called plemochoë, see O. Rubensohn, *Athen. Mitth.*, 1898, pp. 271 ff., especially p. 302.

[2] An arrangement, somewhat similar to the Athenian, is found in a series of coins of Macedonia (regal of Philip V and autonomous of the same time) which have been shown by Gaebler (*Z.f. N.* xx. 1895, pp. 170, 171) to bear three sets of monograms, of which the third is associated with a symbol.

§ 3. *The Office of the Moneyer.*

Who were these magistrates to whom the superintendence of the coinage of Athens was confided? It is impossible with our present information to say [1]. We only know that the first two magistrates were annual, the third (whose signature was by no means essential) enjoyed office during the length of a prytany, and therefore presumably was elected from the prytanizing tribe. The Council being the supreme financial authority at Athens [2], the control of the coinage was naturally in its hands. It seems fair to suppose that the third magistrate is the treasurer (ταμίας) of the prytany [3].

In the case of some federal coinages we are able, thanks to historical records, to recognize the office held by the magistrates who sign the coins. Thus the coins of Phocis in the fourth century bear the names Ὀνυμάρχου and Φαλαίκου, the famous Phocian strategi in the Sacred War (Onymarchus B. C. 354-352, Phalaecus B. C. 351-350). The name Ἐπαμ. or Ἐπαμι. on Theban coins of the period B. C. 379-338 (Pl. IV. 10) almost certainly represents Epaminondas; and it appears that the privilege of coinage belonged to the Boeotarchs who happened to be at the head of affairs [4].

A few cities there are in the pre-Roman period which go so far as to specify on their coins the official title of the magistrate. A unique gold stater of Smyrna, probably of the period when Mithradates the Great controlled the city (B. C. 88-84), bears the inscription ΣΜΥΡΝΑΙΩΝ ΠΡΥΤΑΝΕΙΣ. The earlier coins of the same city (cistophori, tetradrachms, and drachms of the second century B. C.) frequently bear, in addition to a magistrate's name, monograms in which the letters ΠΡΥ or ΠΡΥΤΑ are

---

[1] The various conjectures—they are nothing more—may be found in Lenormant, iii. pp. 41 ff. M. Th. Reinach's tempting theory that the first and second magistrates are the στρατηγὸς ἐπὶ τὰ ὅπλα and the στρ. ἐπὶ τὴν παρασκευήν respectively (*Rev. des Ét. gr.* 1888, pp. 163 ff.) is refuted by Preuner (*Rhein. Mus.* 1894, p. 376 f.).

[2] Gilbert, *Greek Constitutional Antiquities* (Eng. Trans.), p. 341.

[3] Gilbert, op. cit. p. 273.

[4] Lenormant, iii. p. 73, and Head, *Brit. Mus. Catal., Central Greece,* p. xlii. The Euares mentioned in a Delphian decree of proxenia (Perdrizet in *Bull. Corr. Hellén.* 1897, p. 551) is named (EYΓAPA for Εὐfάραο, the Boeotian genitive) on a Theban coin (*Brit. Mus. Catal.* p. 82, no. 140). See *Bull. Corr. Hellén.* xxi. p. 577.

a predominant element. These coins were therefore issued in the former case by the authority of the whole body of the Prytaneis, in the latter by a single Prytanis[1]. It is noteworthy that the officials who sign the coins of the imperial period at Smyrna are not prytaneis but strategi. It follows that, in the matter of titles, we cannot infer from imperial coins to the autonomous period. Such an inference as that drawn by Lenormant from the usage at Rhodes in Imperial times (when coins are signed ἐπὶ τοῦ δεῖνος ταμία) to an earlier period is only justified when we know that the institutions of a city have remained absolutely unchanged.

The same word πρύτ(ανις) occurs in monogrammatic form on the cistophori of Pergamum in the period B. C. 133–67, together with the first two letters of a magistrate's name. It is by no means certain that this magistrate is himself a prytanis. Πρύτ. may simply signify that the prytaneis have authorized the issue of the coin, while the magistrate who signs is the responsible mint master.

The mention of magistrates' names on regal coins is naturally somewhat restricted. The most remarkable instance is perhaps that of Zoilus who signs in full on some tetradrachms of Perseus of Macedon, and in monogram on other coins of Perseus and his father Philip V[2].

An inscription of Sestos[3], recording a decree in honour of one Menas, throws some light on the position of moneyer in this small city of the Thracian Chersonesus. Since the time of Lysimachus, Sestos had depended on foreign currency; now, some time in the latter half of the second century, it decided to issue a bronze coinage of its own (l. 43) : τοῦ τε δήμου προελομένου νομίσματι χαλκίνῳ χρῆσθαι ἰδίωι, χάριν τοῦ νομειτεύεσθαι μὲν τὸν τῆς πόλεως χαρακτῆρα, τὸ δὲ λυσιτελὲς τὸ περιγενόμενον ἐκ τῆς τοιαύτης προσόδου λαμβάνειν τὸν δῆμον, καὶ προχειρισαμένου τοὺς τὴν πίστιν εὐσεβῶς τε καὶ δικαίως τηρήσοντας, Μηνᾶς αἱρεθεὶς μετὰ τοῦ συναποδειχθέντος τὴν καθήκουσαν εἰσηνέγκατο ἐπιμέλειαν, ἐξ ὧν ὁ δῆμος διὰ τὴν τῶν ἀνδρῶν

---

[1] Two of these officials entitle themselves Βαυs, which appears to be an abbreviation for Βα(σιλε)ύs. The head of the prytaneis was therefore the βασιλεύς (see Pauly-Wissowa, Real Enc. iii. p. 71).
[2] Lenormant, iii. 85. Zoilus is unknown to history. In the succeeding pages Lenormant mentions various historical personages whose names are to be recognized, with more or less probability, on regal coins.
[3] Last printed in Ch. Michel, Recueil d'Inscr. gr. no. 327.

δικαιοσύνην τε καὶ φιλοτιμίαν χρῆται τῶι ἰδίωι νομίσματι. The new coinage is that which is classed to the second century B.C.[1]

§ 4. *Magistrates in Imperial Times.*

The mention of magisterial titles is very rare before the time of the Roman domination. The titles which are then given are, however, not merely those of offices actually connected with the issue of money or of eponymous offices. A man may inscribe on coins issued by his authority any titles, however empty, that he may chance to possess, even to the omission of the actual title in virtue of which alone he is enabled to sign his name.

The formulae which occur on coins in connexion with the magistracies are of almost endless variety. In the first place the name of the magistrate may be

1. In the nominative;
2. In the genitive;
    (a) Alone, or with a preposition;
    (b) With a participle or noun in absolute construction, or preceded by a preposition.

(1) στρατηγὸς Κλάρος, Smyrna.
  Ἑκατώνυμος Αἰσχρίωνος, Erythrae.
(2) (a) Αἰγαιανοῦ, Lebedus.
  διὰ Ὀρθρίου Ἱέρωνος, Tabae (Caria).
  (b) ταμία Τειμοστράτου, Rhodes.
  ἐπὶ Τειμοθέου ἄρχοντος, Hyllarima (Caria).
  στρατηγοῦντος Σωστράτου, Dionysopolis (Pl. XIV. 12).

1. The use of the nominative needs little comment. It is very much rarer than the genitive, and would seem, as in pre-Imperial times, to imply some special responsibility or interest on the part of the magistrate. He may, for instance, make the coin a means of paying a compliment to some superior person, or to his city. In this case he uses formulae which may be roughly classified as follows:—

(a) He merely states that he struck the coin. The most curious instances of this class are those rare ones involving the use of the word χαράττειν as Ζώσιμος Φιλόπατρις Ἱεροπολειτῶν ἐχάραξ(εν)

---

[1] Head, *H. N.*, p. 225.

at Hieropolis in Phrygia; with which must be compared the Ephesian legend Ὁ νεω(κόρος) Ἐφε(σίων) δῆ(μος) ἐπεχάρ(αξεν).

(β) He dedicates the coin to a personage or body of persons. Thus Θευδιανὸς στρατη(γῶν) ἀνέθηκε Σμυρναίοις[1]. This 'dedication' probably means that the expense of the issue was borne by Theudianos; it would seem that the issue of coinage was regarded as a leitourgia.

(γ) The name of the person complimented may also be placed in the accusative case, in which circumstances we must understand some such word as ἐτίμησε, e.g. Σεβαστὸν Κεφαλίων γραμματεύων (Pergamum).

2. The use of the genitive is much commoner. The prepositions which are employed are three in number. Ἐπί of course expresses primarily a date, but probably in the case of financial officers also direct responsibility. Other prepositions are restricted to small areas. Διά is confined to part of Caria and south-west Phrygia, occurring at the cities of Laodicea ad Lycum, Attuda, Cidramus, Trapezopolis, Apollonia Salbace and Tabae (at the last two places only exceptionally). Παρά is found once or twice at Apamea in Phrygia (παρὰ Στρατονικιανοῦ). Παρά and διά, like the formulae of dedication, both seem to imply that the person charged himself with the expense of the coinage.

Before passing on to deal with the various magisterial titles that occur, we must consider a few participial constructions which express not an office but a commission or private undertaking which resulted in the issue of coins. The commonest of these is ἐπιμεληθέντος or ἐπιμελήσαντος. This merely implies that the person (whose official title is sometimes mentioned—ἐπιμεληθέντος Φλ. Μύωνος ἄρ(χοντος) at Aphrodisias in Caria) is charged with the issue[2]. The title ἐπιμελητοῦ is probably quite distinct, the ἐπιμελητής being a distinct official[3].

Ψηφισαμένου Φλαυβίου Διομήδους is the inscription on a coin of Stratonicea in Caria of imperial date[4]. The use of the middle

---

[1] Smyrna, *Brit. Mus. Catal., Ionia*, 133. At Temenothyrae in Phrygia nearly all the coins with magistrates' names are inscribed with this formula (omitting ἀνέθηκε).
[2] The phrase is common in inscriptions in connexion with the erection of monuments. Compare also the Sestos inscription (above, p. 125).
[3] He occurs on coins of Mastaura.
[4] *Brit. Mus. Catal., Caria*, p. 153, no. 42.

voice is peculiar, but the analogy of lapidary inscriptions shows the sense to be that the coins were issued in accordance with the terms of a ψήφισμα proposed by Diomedes, or possibly passed under his presidency.

Αἰτησαμένου Φροῦγι occurs on coins of Alia, and similar inscriptions on coins of Ancyra and Eucarpia, all Phrygian towns. The phrase perhaps means that the coins were issued in answer to a request from Frugi for funds to defray certain expenses [1].

Εἰσαγγείλαντος M. Κλ(αυδίου) Οὐαλερινοῦ ἀρχι(ερέως) 'Ασίας is the inscription on a coin of Eumenia. Here of course the participle cannot have the technical sense which it bore in Attic law; most probably the inscription means that the coin was issued 'on the presentation of a report by M. Claudius Valerianus.'

The vaguest in meaning of all the titles is ἄρχων. It may either be, as at Athens, a real title, or, when used in the genitive, may simply mean 'being in office.' Only at those places where no other official title occurs on the coins can we feel sure that the magistrates were called archons, and at any time a magistrate's title may be discovered on a new coin to disprove our theory. Elsewhere, as at Cyzicus, we are able by comparison to arrive at the real title. Thus two coins of Cyzicus (in 'alliance' with Ephesus under Antoninus Pius) read respectively ἐπὶ ἄρχοντος 'Εστιαίου, 'Ομόνοια and 'Ομόνοια, Στρ(ατηγοῦ) 'Εστιαίου [2]. The former inscription, therefore, means 'during the year of office of (the general) Hestiaeus.'

The various titles, and the explanation so far as that is possible, of their meanings, cannot be given in detail here. It is, however, necessary to emphasize the distinction between the various classes of them:—

(1) Regular official titles, of an eponymous character, or giving the bearer right to issue coins.

(2) Regular official titles, but not necessarily implying either of the above rights.

(3) Honorary or fancy titles, or titles expressing social grade.

Of course the same title may at one place belong to class (1),

---

[1] Friedländer (*Hermes*, ix. pp. 492 ff.) refers the words ἐπιμεληθέντος and αἰτησαμένου not to the issue of coins, but to the erection of statues or the like, which are sometimes represented on the coins themselves.

[2] *Brit. Mus. Catal., Mysia*, p. 60.

at another to class (2). The third class, however, stand quite apart.

The regular official titles of the first class may relate to all kinds of offices connected with the administration of the state. The strategos (who of course had no military power), the prytanis or boularchos, and other officials connected with the various municipal assemblies, financial officers like the ταμίας, superintendents of the athletic and musical contests which were celebrated at so many cities under the Empire (panegyriarchs, agonothetae, &c.), and, where sacerdotal and political offices were closely combined, priests and archpriests—all these figure on coins, probably as possessing the right of coinage. But again, it is not in virtue of his office as Asiarch that Τέρτιος Ἀσιάρχης issues coins at Smyrna, but because he holds some other office; Epikrates, son of Xenokrates, calls himself ἱερεὺς δήμου at Plarasa-Aphrodisias, but it is probably as holding some other office that he is entitled to put his name on the coins he issues. Finally, such titles as υἱὸς Ἀφροδισιέων, θυγάτηρ τοῦ δήμου (Smyrna), υἱὸς Ἀσιάρχου, υἱὸς πόλεως are merely honorary titles (sometimes, doubtless, specially conferred by a grateful city); titles like ἱππικός merely betoken a social rank; and Ἄτταλος σοφιστής and Στ. Ἄτταλος ἀρχίατρος indicate professional distinction.

Besides individual magistrates, it would appear that bodies or corporations undertook the issue of coins. Thus we find the Νέοι at Laodicea issuing a coin as a body, while, conversely, the Statilius Attalus already mentioned dedicates a coin Νέοις at Heraclea in Caria. Boards of magistrates are mentioned, though rarely: thus ἐπὶ ἀρχό(ντων) τῶν περὶ Μενεσθέα Ἰσόβουνον at Aphrodisias, or συναρχία at Antiochia in Caria.

§ 5. *The Greek Mint.*

At Athens alone among Greek states do we know anything of the arrangement of the mint. An inscription[1] of Roman but pre-Imperial date speaks of the standards preserved ἐν τῷ ἀργυροκοπείῳ. The same term for the place ὅπου κόπτεται τὸ νόμισμα is quoted from Antiphon, Aeschines Socraticus, and Andocides.

[1] *C. I. A.* ii. 476, § 4 Ἀγέτω δὲ καὶ ἡ μνᾶ ἡ ἐμπορικὴ Στεφανηφόρου δραχμὰς ἑκατὸν τριάκοντα καὶ ὀκτὼ πρὸς τὰ στάθμια τὰ ἐν τῷ ἀργυροκοπείῳ.

A later term was σημαντήριον [1]. The term Στεφανηφόρου δραχμαί in the inscription just mentioned is to be explained by 'drachms fresh from the mint,' which was attached to the shrine of the hero Stephanephoros [2].

Some at least of the workmen in the mint were public slaves. Andocides says of Hyperbolus that 'his father is branded, and is still a public slave in the mint, where, being an alien and a barbarian, he λυχνοποιεῖ [3].' Whatever the last phrase may mean, it certainly denotes some very base office. It does not, however, follow from this passage that the die engravers were slaves, as some would have us suppose.

On the Athenian tetradrachms of the 'new style' we find a number of abbreviations which seem to indicate the various officinae or workshops of the mint. In a time when all the coins were struck by hand there is nothing astonishing in the existence of a great number of workshops in the mint of a city of which the coinage was as extensive as the Athenian. Most of these abbreviations seem to represent names, possibly of gods or heroes after whom the various workshops were named. Five of them occur in all four of the periods into which the coinage of the new style has been divided (namely: AN ; ME or MENE ; ΠΡ ; ΣΦ (Pl. IX. 8), ΣΦΑ or ΣΦΑΙ ; and ΣΩ). A few of the abbreviations can hardly represent names: such are ΦЖ, МФ, MP. In all there are between thirty and forty of these mint marks.

Other cities (with few exceptions) do not seem to have gone so far as Athens in fixing the responsibility of the moneyers. At the same time, the extraordinary differences in the dies which were employed may have acted as a check, if some record was kept of the way in which the dies were used by the various workmen.

In Athens, as we have seen, it is possible, though not proved, that the workmen of the mint were public slaves working in the mint and probably under one roof. It has been suggested (by Lenormant) that elsewhere the moneyers worked in their

---

[1] As Beulé suggests, a more suitable term, when Athens was not allowed to strike in silver.
[2] Who was probably no other than Theseus, one of the mythical inventors of money (Beulé, Les Monn. d'Athènes, p. 349).
[3] Schol. Aristoph. Vesp. 1007.

private workshops, being of course responsible to the state. The difficulty of properly controlling them seems to make this suggestion highly improbable [1]. The mint must always have been strictly under the control of the state, and this would have been thoroughly ineffective if the moneyer were allowed to make coins in his own house.

The artists who engraved the dies of Greek coins are, in a comparatively few cases, known to us by name, owing to their custom of signing their dies. The consideration of this subject belongs more properly to another chapter. Here we may note that, magnificent as some of their productions were, the utter silence of ancient literature in respect to these engravers has suggested to some writers that they were not freemen. Yet, if so, it is hard to see how they can have been permitted to affix their signatures to the state issue. The fact that we find the same artist working for different cities also makes it improbable that he was a slave; the jealousy that always existed between Greek cities, even in times of political alliance, would hardly have permitted an interchange of state servants of this kind.

B. Among the Romans.

§ 6. *Roman Monetary Magistrates.*

The earliest Roman coins bear no mark indicating the moneyer who issued them. As in Greece, so too in Rome, a beginning in the way of indicating the moneyer is made by means of symbols. These are found on some of the old denarii of unreduced weight (therefore before the close of the First Punic war)[2]. Towards the close of the third century B.C. (before 217) appear the names of moneyers, in ligature or otherwise abbreviated. Gradually the name begins to appear at greater length.

---

[1] A passage is quoted by Lenormant (Polyb. ap. *Athen.* v. 193 d) in favour of this arrangement at Antiochia. But the ἀργυροκοπεῖα which Antiochus Epiphanes frequented were merely silversmiths' workshops. This is clear from the context. Ἀργυροκόπος must not *always* be taken in the sense of moneyer. It is parallel in meaning exactly to our word silversmith. There is no reason, for instance, to suppose that Demetrius of Ephesus was a moneyer.

[2] See above, pp. 47, 48.

It is only in the later period that any title is added to the name. This becomes common in the case of extraordinary issues; and sometimes even we find the title (such as IMPER*ator* on a coin of Q. Caecilius Metellus Pius, or Q for Quaestor on a coin struck in 81–80 B.C. under Sulla) without the name. The increasing importance of the moneyers is also shown by the introduction (about 134 B.C.) of types personal to the moneyers (such as the tribune C. Licinius Crassus assembling the people in the *septa*, on a denarius of P. Licinius Nerva, Pl. XII. 1). The authority over the coinage probably belonged in the earliest times to the consuls. About the time of the Second Punic war, when coinage was concentrated within the city, it would seem that a new arrangement was made. The tendency at the time was to restrict the consular power within the limits of the city in various ways. Accordingly the consuls lost the right of coinage within Rome, which was given to a special board of magistrates, *tresviri auro argento aere*[1] (or *aere argento auro*) *flando feriundo* or *tresviri monetales*.

The title of the ordinary monetary magistrate, when expressed, is simply given as IIIVIR (e. g. M. AQVIL*ius* M. F*ilius* M. N*epos* IIIVIR). It is commonest among the moneyers belonging to the exiled Pompeian party, who naturally felt it desirable to call attention to their right to issue coins.

It is probable that when the board of moneyers was first instituted, these officials were appointed not every year, but only when their services were required. The definite establishment of the magistracy is dated by Mommsen between 104 and 89 B.C. As a rule only one magistrate signs a coin. Thus C. Claudius Pulcher, whom we know to have been *IIIvir a. a. a. f. f.*[2] always signs alone: *C. Pulcher*. This practice is fully in accordance with the Roman rule that each official could exercise his power independently, subject to the veto of any one else of equal authority. But there are, nevertheless, coins signed by all three members of the board: thus *M. Calid(ius)*, *Q. Met(ellus)*, *Cn. F(o)l(vius)*. The office of moneyer was one to which, in the ordinary *cursus honorum*, a man might attain at the age of twenty-seven. An appointment does not seem necessarily to have entailed the issue of coins; for we know,

---

[1] The old form of the dative, as in *iure dicundo*.
[2] *C. I. L.* i. p. 279, of 92 B.C.

from the coins dating between the social and civil wars, of some sixty moneyers only[1].

Inscriptions on coins of the Republic bear witness to certain extraordinary issues authorized by the Senate:—

   S(enatus) C(onsulto)
   Ex S(enatus) C(onsulto)
   P(ublice) E(x) S(enatus) C(onsulto)[2]
   D(e) S(enatus) S(ententia)

or by the popular vote:—

   Pu(blice)—M. Lucili(us) Ruf(us) [90 B.C.]
   Rulli—P. Servili M. F(ilii) P(ublice) [89 B.C.]

These issues might be directed by the triumvirs, but most often a special person was commissioned for the purpose. In 82 B.C. an urban praetor was commissioned to melt down all the temple treasures, and struck denarii with the inscription Q. Anto(nius) Balb(us) Pr(aetor) S. C. Other inscriptions of this kind are:—

Fig. 20.—Semuncial bronze *semis.* Obv. Head of Jupiter, S. Rev. L.P.D.A.P. Prow of galley. Weight: 6.11 grammes.

   L. Torqua(tus) Q(uaestor) Ex S. C. [99-94 B.C.]
   A. Plautius Aed(ilis) Cur(ulis) S. C.[3] [54 B.C.]
   M. Fun(nius) L. Crit(onius) P(ublico) A(rgento) Aed(iles) Pl(ebei) [86 B.C.]

The formula Ex A(rgento) P(ublico)—sometimes without the preposition—appears on many denarii issued between 90 and 80 B.C., some of them anonymous. L(ege) P(apiria) D(e) A(ere) P(ublico) is the inscription on the earliest semuncial bronze (Fig. 20).

---

[1] With three moneyers to the year, we should have for this period more than double this number. Possibly, however, the appointment was not annual. Cicero's use of the word *monetalis* in reference to Vectenus (*ad Att.* x. 5 and 11) is a jest, the point of which has escaped Lenormant (iii. pp. 162, 163), who founds on these passages a theory that Vectenus was a triumvir but did not issue coins!

[2] Others write these abbreviations P(ublic)E S(enatus) C(onsulto).

[3] The coins thus signed were probably issued at the expense of the aedile to serve for his games, and naturally he had to obtain permission from the government to issue them.

A set of coins (a special emission for the purposes of the *ludi Apollinares* made by *M. Volteius M. f.* shortly before 74 B.C.) bear the legend S. C. D(e) T(hesauro), and we know that the expenses of these games were defrayed out of a special treasury.

Names of magistrates other than the regular triumvirs do not occur on bronze coins of the city. *Ex S. C.* is found on an anonymous semuncial as, *De S. S.* on an as of *C. Cassius L. Salina(tor)* issued in 85 B.C. Probably all the bronze was issued by ordinary triumvirs.

Julius Caesar increased the number of the moneyers to four (towards the end of 45 B.C.). The first members of this new board were L. Flaminius Chilo, L. Aemilius Buca, M. Mettius, and L. Sepullius Macer, of whom the first seems to have been the head of the board, if we judge by his signature L. FLAMINIVS CHILO IIIIVIR PRI*mus* FLA*vit*.

Hitherto the issuing of gold had not been within the competence of the board of moneyers. When the Senate towards the end of 44 B.C. decreed an issue of this metal, it appointed the praetors C. Norbanus and L. Cestius to superintend it (so that the coins read, for instance, L. CESTIVS C. NORBA*nus* PR*aetores* S*enatus* C*onsulto*). But in the next year the power of striking gold was transferred to the quatuorviri, some of whom added the new distinction to their title (L. REGVLVS IIIIVIR A*uro* P*ublice* F*eriundo*).

The board of quatuorviri as constituted by Caesar had but a short existence. The old triumviral arrangement was restored by Augustus after a brief period (B.C. 41-27) in which no coins signed by regular monetary magistrates were issued. The names of the triumvirs now appeared for a few years until 15 B.C. From this date onward they were discarded on gold and silver, but maintained themselves for about ten years on the bronze coinage, which was instituted in this year. This was the last appearance of a magistrate's name on any Roman coin. Then followed after an interval the change by which the Senate took over the superintendence of all the copper or brass coinage, a fact which is indicated by the letters S C, which henceforward occur on all the small money. The earliest known coin struck under the new conditions belongs to the year A.D. 11. The gold and silver coinages remain in the province of the emperor.

The *vigintivirate*, the magisterial college in which the *tresviri monetales* were included, was established definitively in 11 B.C.

Although the names of the triumvirs vanish from the coins, lapidary inscriptions in plenty attest the existence of the office for at least two and a half centuries[1]. But although they retained the full title of 'triumvirs appointed to cast and strike gold, silver, and bronze,' their competence was restricted to the last metal. The mention of these triumvirs in inscriptions ceases soon after the middle of the third century A.D., and shortly after this time (under Aurelian) the senatorial right of issuing money was suppressed, and presumably at the same time the board of triumvirs ceased to exist. The change is probably connected with the great revolt of the moneyers in 274 A.D.

The coinage of the imperial gold and silver was entrusted to officials of the imperial treasury. We hear of Caesar's having placed private slaves in charge of his coinage; of a *familia monetalis* in the imperial household; of one Julius Thallus, a freedman of Caligula, who was *superpositus auri monetai nummulariorum* under Claudius. In the time of Domitian it was the chief official of the imperial treasury (with the title *a rationibus* or *rationalis*) who superintended the coinage at the mint in Rome, though doubtless not in the various supplementary provincial mints.

Trajan it probably was who centralized the whole system of Roman imperial coinage, both at home and abroad, placing the general management in the hands of a *procurator monetae Augusti*, who had under his orders *dispensatores*, probably all slaves or imperial freedmen. These procurators were men of equestrian rank; and they remained under the control of the *rationalis* (at least it was a *rationalis* Felicissimus who instigated the revolt of the moneyers under Aurelian)[2].

After the suppression of the senatorial coinage, at the close of the third century, we find special procurators appointed under the chief procurator. Such are the *proc. sacrae monetae per Gallias tres et prov. Narbonens.* and *proc. sacrae monetae Trivericae*. This arrangement was finally extended and re-

---

[1] The title is *IIIvir a a. a. f. f*, or *IIIvir monetalis a. a. a. f. f.*, &c. The inscriptions are collected by Lenormant, iii. pp. 185 ff.
[2] Vopisc. *Aurelian*, 38.

gularized by Diocletian. There exist gold bars, of which two are figured here (Figs. 21, 22), bearing stamps which were impressed in the metal before cooling by various officials connected with the mint at Sirmio[1]. The stamps are (1) *Lucianus obr(yzum)*[2] *I sig(navit)*, followed by the Christian monogram; (2) *Fl(avius) Flavianus Pro(curator) sig(navit) ad digma*[3], followed by a palm-branch; (3) *Quirillus et Dionisus* [star] *Sirmi(i) sig(naverunt)* [palm-branch]; (4) DDD NNN (i. e. *Domini nostri*) with three busts; (5) *Sirm(ium)*, with personification of Sirmium seated, holding palm-branch; above star or Christian monogram. The date of these bars can be fixed to some time between 367 and 383 A.D. Flavianus is evidently the *procurator monctae* at Sirmium; Quirillus and Dionisus and Lucianus probably minor officials. The *procurator sacrae monetae Urbis* until Constantine's time was under the *rationalis*; afterwards he was placed under the disposition of the *comes sacrarum largitionum*. We possess the tedious *formula qua moneta committitur*, i.e. the formula of institution of these procurators[4].

§ 7. *Monetary Officials of Roman Colonies.*

In the Roman colonies the formula corresponding to the Roman S. C. is D. D. or EX D. D. (*ex decurionum decreto*)[5]. But, just as at Rome in Republican times it was never considered necessary, save in the case of special issues, to mention the fact that the issue was authorized by a senatus consultum, so in the colonies the letters D. D. or EX D. D. are by no means essential. Much more frequent is the appearance of the titles of the monetary magistrates. The coinage was in the hands of the duumvirs (originally *praetores duumviri*), who are therefore named sometimes singly, sometimes both together[6]. The duumviri

---

[1] See especially *C. I. L.* iii. *Suppl.* 8080; Mommsen, *Z. f. N.* xvi. pp. 351 ff.; *Arch. Ep. Mitth. aus Oest.* vol. xii. The article of H. Willers (*Num. Zt.* xxx. 211), too recently published for consideration here, should be consulted.
[2] Ὄβρυζον, refined gold.   [3] Δεῖγμα, sample or standard.
[4] Cassiodorus, *Var.* vii. 32, quoted by Lenormant, iii. p. 212.
[5] Lenormant, iii. pp. 215 ff.
[6] In the old colony of Carthage (that founded by Julius Caesar) the old title of Suffetes was revived (ARISTO MVTVMBAL RICOCE SVF.) for a time. We also find quatuorviri, as at Parium IIII*viri Iure Dicundo Decurionum Decreto*.

FIG. 21.—Gold Bar from the mint at Sirmio. [Pesth Museum.] Length: 16.5 cm. (6⅜ in.). Weight: 409 grammes.

FIG. 22.—Gold Bar from the mint at Sirmio. [British Museum.] Length: 16.5 cm. (6⅜ in.). Weight: 476 grammes.

were usually elected annually; but in some colonies we meet with duumviri quinquennales who were appointed every fifth year. This quinquennial office was filled as often as three times by the same man (as is shown by the coin of Buthrotum in Epirus reading GRAECINVS QVIN. TERT. BVTHR.[1] The office of quinquennalis was occasionally bestowed in compliment on imperial personages; in which case, like those duumvirs who from some other cause were absentees, they appointed prefects (*praefecti pro duumviris*) to fulfil their duties. Thus at Carthago Nova we have a pair of coins of Augustus and Agrippa respectively reading :—

(1) IMP*erator* CAES*ar* QVIN*quennalis* L. BEN*nio* PRAE*fecto*—HIBERO PRAEF*ecto*.

(2) M. AGRIP*pa* QVIN*quennalis* HIBERO PRAE*fecto*—L. BENNIO PRAEF*ecto*.

From the arrangement of these coins it appears that Bennius was the prefect of Augustus, Hiberus of Agrippa. The prefects are not, however, always named. The honour was also occasionally offered to distinguished strangers outside the imperial circle, as to the two kings of Mauretania, Juba II and Ptolemaeus, who were *duumviri quinquennales* at Carthago Nova.

Occasionally, we find coins signed by aediles or quaestors (as at Carteia). At some towns, as Obulco, the aediles may have been the regular monetary officials; but elsewhere, when we find aediles, we have probably to do with special occasions, such as games.

The magisterial titles are occasionally, though rarely, given alone, without the name of the magistrate: IIIIVIR. D. D., or CE*n*S*or*, or Q*uaestor* at Carteia. The formulae relating to the issue are simple, such as F*aciundum* C*uravit* or other phrases containing the same verb.

§ 8. *Roman Governors.*

The nature of the military coinage of the Romans, in virtue of which the Roman generals or their subordinates placed their signatures on coins, has already been explained (p. 98). These officers hardly enter into the scope of a discussion of

---

[1] Gardner, *Brit. Mus. Catal.*, p. 97, no. 3.

monetary officials. The Roman governors whose names appear on Greek coins of Imperial times are as a rule mentioned merely out of compliment, or for the purpose of a date. Thus we have such formulae as

ἀνθυπάτῳ (=legato proconsule) Φροντείνῳ στρατηγὸς 'Ρηγεῖνος at Smyrna [1], or

ἐπὶ Λ. Ἀντωνίου Νάσωνος ἐπιτρόπου (procuratore) in Bithynia, or

ὑπ(ατεύοντος) Κυντιλιανοῦ in Moesia Inferior.

Occasionally, however, the Roman official signs in the nominatives: thus, at Nicaea Λ. Μίνδιος Βάλβος ἀνθύπατος. It is possible that in such cases the money may have been struck by the orders of the Roman governor for his own purposes, or at any rate that he was directly responsible for the issue.

§ 9. *The Roman Mint.*

Little more is known of the Roman mint than of the Greek. The letters and monograms which occur on the early Republican coins denote extra-Roman mints (KA for Capua and the like). When these mints were closed, letters, monograms, and symbols representing the monetary magistrates were placed on the coins. Finally, when it became the custom for the magistrates to sign at greater length, mint-marks properly so called were introduced. They have been classified by M. Babelon[2] as

(1) Symbols.
(2) Latin letters or syllables.
(3) Greek letters.
(4) Monograms.
(5) Numbers, rising in large issues as high as CC, and on the coins of L. Calpurnius Piso Frugi to CCIƆƆ (10,000).
(6) Dots, generally placed in a certain connexion with letters or symbols.

The object of these various marks was the same as that served at Athens by the letters below the amphora.

Towards the end of the third and beginning of the fourth

---

[1] It has recently been suggested (by Pick, *Journ. Internat.* 1898, p. 461, note 2) that these datives are incorrect representations of the Latin ablative absolute. For this view there is certainly much to be said; but at the same time there is nothing improbable in the theory of a dedication.

[2] *Monn. de la Rép.* I. pp. l, li.

century A.D. we meet on Roman coins with a curious series of mint-marks, which have only revealed their secret after patient collation of various issues [1]. Two examples must suffice. Three coins of Diocletian, of one and the same type, and struck at the same place, bear in their exergues:—

XXI · A · I, XXI · B · O, and XXI · Γ · BI.

Three corresponding coins of Maximian bear in their exergues:—

XXI · A · HP, XXI · B · KOY, and XXI · Γ · ΛI.

The XXI, which is constant, is a mark of value. The A B Γ represent three different workshops. The remaining letters put together read, in the case of Diocletian, IOBI, and in that of Maximian, HPKOYΛI. These words represent the genitives of the Latin titles assumed by the two emperors, *Iovius* and *Herculius*.

A set of coins struck in Rome during the period of the tetrarchy with the legend SAC(ra) MON(eta) VRB(is) AVGG(ustorum) ET CAESS(arum) NN(ostrorum) give us the following exergual letters:—

    Coin of Diocletian (First Augustus)   R P
    ,,   Maximian (Second ,,)   R S
    ,,   Constantius (First Caesar)   R T
    ,,   Galerius (Second ,,)   R Q.

The R of course stands for the city name. The remaining letters are the initials of prima, secunda, &c. (officina). There were thus four workshops in Rome, one devoted to each of the four rulers.

At Alexandria also at this same time there were apparently four workshops, but not devoted each to producing the coins of one of the four rulers. For, taking only the coins in the British Museum collection, we find A and Δ on coins of Diocletian, A, B, and Γ on those of Maximian, A? on a coin of Constantius Caesar, and A or Δ, and Γ on coins of Galerius Maximianus. The use of these mint-marks seems to begin in the eighth year of Diocletian (A.D. 291-2).

Of the workmen in the mint (*familia monetalis*) we have,

---

[1] Mowat, *Combinaisons secrètes*, Rev. Num. 1897, pp 67 f., 127 f.

during Imperial times, many classes mentioned. The significance of their titles is by no means always clear.

Officinatores was the usual word for the officials who supervised the mints. Before the creation by Trajan of the office of *procurator monetae* these, and the officials to be mentioned, were perhaps under the general direction of a *superpositus*[1]. Under Constantine their director was known as *praepositus*.

The *conductores flaturae* directed the *flaturarii* who cast the bars of metal and the blanks for coining. The *signatores* have been explained as officials who attested by their signature the exactness of the weight and quality of the blank. But at the period at which we hear of these functionaries (the second and third centuries A.D.) signatures of any sort are conspicuous by their absence from the coins. Further, as we find *signatores* mentioned together with *suppostores* and *malliatores*[2], it would seem that they were concerned with the actual striking of the coin. It may be suggested that as the *suppostor* was the person who placed the blank between the dies, while the *malliator* brought the hammer down on the upper die, the *signator* was the person who held the upper die in position. *Signum* means device or type, and this person could well be said *signare monetam*[3]. The testing of the accuracy of weight of the blanks was probably the work of the *aequator*. Finally, there were the *scalptores*, who engraved the dies.

All the officials of whom we hear under these names were members of the Imperial household[4]. The titles and organization of the workmen who produced the senatorial coins were doubtless similar. All, in any case, worked together in the mint attached to the temple of Juno Moneta, which occupied on the Capitol the site where once had stood the house of Manlius[5].

The organization of the mint at the beginning of the second century A.D. can best be realized from three inscribed bases

[1] In 115 A.D. we find the whole familia of officinatores under an *optio et exactor auri argenti et aeris* (*C. I. L.* vi (1), nos. 42-44). See below.
[2] See the inscriptions described below.
[3] No inference must be drawn from the connexion between this title *signator* and the verb *sig(navit)* on the gold bars described above; for the subject of the latter is a procurator and a high official.
[4] Julius Caesar *monetae publicisque vectigalibus peculiares servos praeposuit*, and thus began the practice (Suet. *Div. Iul.* 76).
[5] Livy, vi. 20.

found near the site of the ancient mint[1]. The first is a dedication to Apollo by *Felix Aug. lib. Optio et Exactor auri argenti et aeris.* The second, to Fortuna by the *Officinatores monetae aurariae argentariae Caesaris n(ostri)*. The list contains the names of (1) the Felix already mentioned; (2) Albanus lib(ertus) optio; (3) sixteen liberti, who are described as off(icinatores); and (4) nine slaves. The third inscription is a dedication by the same Felix and the *signatores suppostores malliatores monetae Caesaris n(ostri)*. The list of these officials contains thirty liberti and thirty-six slaves. The inscriptions belong to the year 115 A.D.

[1] *C. I. L.* vi (1), nos. 42-44.

BOOK II

CHAPTER VI

FABRIC AND STYLE

§ 1. *Struck Coins.*

The word fabric is loosely employed in numismatics to denote the form given to a coin by the peculiar methods employed to produce it. These methods and their results varied at different times and places, and on a proper acquaintance with them depends to a large extent the power of distinguishing the genuine coin from the forgery, ancient or modern, as well as the possibility, in many cases, of attributing a coin to its true place of origin. The ancient literary authorities on this part of our subject are meagre in the extreme, and our knowledge of it is largely founded on inference.

Metal of the proper quality and homogeneity having been obtained, the first process was to divide it into the requisite quantities. Where the method of coinage employed was that of casting, the process of division coincided with the final stage of giving the coin its proper form and type.

For the purpose of striking[1] coins, the blanks of metal had first to be prepared of the requisite shape and weight. This could most easily be done by casting them; and in all probability this was the process usually adopted[2].

---

[1] Χαράττειν, ἐπιχαράττειν, κόπτειν, *ferire, cudere, percutere, signare* (see Blümner, *Technol.* iv. pp. 258, 259). The type, and apparently even the struck coin, may be called χαρακτήρ or κύμμα (*Neue Jahrb. f. Phil.* 1896, p. 538; *Num. Chr.* 1897, p. 287).

[2] Pieces of gold have been found of the same quality and weight as the Roman *aurei*, with one side more convex than the other, to allow of

In many struck coins the traces of the original casting of the blank are still apparent, as in the projections at the edge marking the channels by which the metal entered the mould (see below, § 4). The traces of casting are present, again, in the sloping edges which are characteristic of the bronze issues of Syria and Egypt (Fig. 23). The moulds were made with the edges slanting slightly outwards, so that the blanks when cool would easily drop out. The edges of the gold bars described above (p. 136) are sloped for a similar cause. Any roughness

FIG. 23—Bronze coin of Antiochus IV of Syria (B.C. 175-164). *Obv.* Head of Zeus-Sarapis. *Rev.* Βασιλέως 'Αντιόχου Θεοῦ ['E]πιφανοῦ[s]. Eagle.

left on the edge of the blank by the casting was trimmed off; hence a secondary chamfer is often apparent.

The Pompeian wall-painting from the Domus Vettiorum, which is reproduced on pp. 146, 147 (Fig. 24 *a, b*) is of the utmost importance as illustrating the methods of coining employed by the ancients[1]. Its date is some time in the first half-century of our era, but the methods it illustrates are probably in all essentials the same as those of an earlier period. The peacocks above the scene are probably purely ornamental, but they may possibly symbolize the presidency of Juno Moneta over the operations of the mint, which are carried on, in the artist's

the high relief in which the head was represented (Mongez, *Mém. de l'Acad. des Inscr.* ix. 1831. p. 207). There exist also several proofs of coins struck in lead (e.g. *Brit. Mus. Catal., Lycia*, p. 283, no. 16 A). It has been suggested (Friedländer, *Ann. d. Inst.* 1859, p. 407) that from these proofs moulds were made in which the blanks were cast.

[1] First published by Mr. T. Ely, *Num. Chr.* 1896, Pl. VI. The view of Mau (*Röm. Mitth.* 1896, p. 78) and others (*Rev. Num.* 1896, p. 360; 1899, pp. xvi ff.) that this painting represents a goldsmith's workshop, is, I venture to think, untenable. Jewels are not made with sledge-hammers.

fancy, by amoretti. Beginning at the right we see a furnace (surmounted by a head of Vulcan). On one side stands a Cupid who examines a ladle full of metal which he withdraws from the furnace [1]. On the other, another *flaturarius* with a pair of tongs holds in the flame a blank of metal which he is heating with the help of a blowpipe. When heated the blanks are passed on to a third Cupid, who reduces them to a proper shape by means of a hammer and anvil. The next object in the picture is a cabinet with shelves containing various coins and pieces of metal and balances. A fourth Cupid holds a pair of scales with which he is testing the weight of a blank before a seated figure who appears to be female. It would, however, in spite of the apparent 'eyes' on her wings, be rash to identify her with the presiding goddess. The final stage is represented on the extreme left, where one Cupid (the *suppostor*) holds with the tongs the die, which another (the *malliator*) strikes with a sledge-hammer on top of the blank which—though not seen in the representation—is lying on the anvil [2]. The coins are throughout represented as of gold.

On the coins (Pl. XII. 6) of T. Carisius (denarii struck about 48 B.C., and 'restored' by Trajan) are represented four objects which are generally supposed to represent the instruments of the moneyer—anvil, hammer, tongs, and a wreathed conical object, generally described as a coin die. Others explain this object as the cap of Vulcan, and the presence of the wreath appears to favour this view. So far as its shape is concerned, either explanation will serve [3]. The hammer is absurdly small for the size of the die, but accuracy in a matter of this sort can hardly be expected.

The only other external evidence of the methods of striking coins is derived from a small bronze coin of Paestum, alluding

---

[1] This, Mr. E. J. Seltmann's explanation (*Num. Chr.* 1898, p. 295), is undoubtedly right. This Cupid was previously explained as stoking the fire.

[2] The depression in the anvil, necessary to prevent the blank slipping aside, accounts for the invisibility of the blank. Or it is possible, as Mr. Seltmann suggests, that the dies are actually fastened into the tongs. See ch. ix. § 3, note.

[3] Cp. the die of a coin of Augustus; Caylus, *Rec. d'Ant.* i. 284, Pl. 105, no. 1. The case against the explanation of the object as a die is given by Friedländer, 'Welche sind die ältesten Medaillen?' p. 26; cf. *Ann. d. Inst.* 1859, pp. 407 f.

apparently to the right of coinage specially accorded to this place by the Romans in 89 B.C. On this piece we have on the obverse a pair of scales, on the reverse a workman (*malliator*)

Fig. 24 a.—Wall-painting in the House of the Vettii, Pompeii. (Right-hand portion.)

striking the die with a hammer as on the painting; in front of him stands another person (the *optio*?) directing his work (Fig. 25)[1]. Other bronze coins of the same place represent what appears to be the mint building.

[1] Garrucci, *Le Monete dell' Italia*, Pl. 123, nos. 5 (the specimen here figured) and 6.

FABRIC AND STYLE

The Pompeian picture somewhat incompletely suggests that casting was the method by which flans were originally prepared.

FIG. 24 b.—Wall-painting in the House of the Vettii, Pompeii. (Left-hand portion.)

If so, the process of re-fusing with the blowpipe and hammering seems somewhat unnecessary unless it be to remove irregularities of the kind already mentioned. If, on the other hand, the blanks were obtained not by casting, but by cutting off equal lengths from a bar of metal of uniform thickness, we can understand that it would be necessary to touch up the blanks before they could be struck [1].

The actual process of striking would be much facilitated by heating the blank, and the reticulated surface which some early Greek coins present is evidence that in at least some cases coins were struck while hot [2].

FIG. 25.—Bronze coin of Paestum. *Obv.* Scales. *Rev.* The striking of money.

But this raises a further difficulty in the interpretation of the picture. If the blanks were heated before being struck, a second furnace episode might be expected; for during the touching-up and the weighing the flans would have become cold. The omission may be due to obvious artistic reasons; or again, the order of the scenes from right to left may not correspond to the actual order in time.

The lower die—that of the obverse of the coin—was let into the anvil [3]; the blank was laid over it; the reverse die—consisting in the earliest times merely of the end of a bar,

---

[1] In mediaeval times the blanks were clipped into shape with shears. This of course was possible only when coins were thin, although Lenormant thinks that the process of punching out the flans was occasionally adopted in ancient times. The blanks of the square Indo-Greek coins were perhaps cut out of sheets of metal.

[2] Mongez (op. cit. pp. 208, 209) states that, until the time when steel dies came in, all blanks were heated before striking. This he holds was necessary so long as the dies were made of so soft a material as bronze (i. e. throughout the good period of ancient coinage). The eccentricity of the impressions was also partly due to the great haste which was necessary, if the blank was to be struck before it became cool. Coins which were left too long after heating usually split under the hammer. Mongez and Lenormant hold that coins were taken away between the blows and reheated, but the evidence for this, never very strong, is still more weakened by the Pompeian wall-painting.

[3] This is the generally accepted view. By some it has been supposed that the incuse square was produced by an elevation on the anvil, and consequently that the obverse die was the upper one (Blümner, *Techn.* iv. p. 261, note 1). The rude, unequal nature of some of the incuses shows that the position of the blank would be somewhat insecure on such an elevation.

roughened so as to grip the blank—was placed over all; and the hammer being brought down caused an impression to be made on both sides. No collar appears to have been used to prevent the metal spreading or slipping. The upper die being driven deeply into the blank by the first blow (thus producing the incuse impression) served fairly well to keep the coin in place, and at each blow the security of the position of the blank was of course increased. But, although kept in place, the metal was able to spread freely; and to this we owe the irregular shapes and split flans which can hardly be said to detract from the charm of Greek coins.

§ 2. *Ancient Dies.*

The way in which dies were prepared in ancient times can only be conjectured from the appearance of the coins struck with them. Mongez[1] maintains that the instrument employed for engraving gems was also employed for coin dies, viz. the wheel[2]. The graving tool was not introduced until late Roman times, in the fourth or fifth century. That the wheel was used for sketching out the main design cannot be doubted[3]; the circular sinkings produced by the instrument were often left, and the bosses resulting from them are obvious, especially in the lettering, on the less carefully finished coins. Very often these bosses are so large as to considerably increase the difficulty of deciphering the letters; and the types of barbarous imitations often reduce themselves to a meaningless conglomeration of bosses or pellets of this kind. The more careful engraver supplemented the wheel with the graving tool, and smoothed away the circular sinkings until the whole intaglio appeared to have been produced by the graving tool alone.

A few ancient dies exist; one used for striking coins of Faustina II, in the Lyon Museum, has been illustrated more than once[4], and is reproduced here (Fig. 26). It is made of

---

[1] Op. cit. p. 204.
[2] i.e. a small metal wheel with a cutting edge, worked by means of a drill. See *Brit. Mus. Catal. of Engraved Gems*, p. 11.
[3] The Italians of the Renaissance, who imitated Roman coins, used the graver wholly (Mongez, op. cit. p. 204).
[4] Friedländer in *Z. f. N.* v. p. 121; Gardner, *Types*, p. 20.

soft iron, except for the part which contains the actual design, which is in steel. Other dies exist of hardened bronze; a few made for striking Gaulish coins are entirely of bronze or soft iron. It is doubtful whether any of the coin dies supposed to be Greek can be regarded as genuine[1].

On the coins of the Seleucidae (Fig. 23 and Pl. X. 4), on some of the contemporary bronze coins of Syrian and Palestinian cities, on the coins of the Lagidae with sloping edges, and on a number of Greek imperial coins, there occur punctures in the very centre of the field. These are generally supposed to have been caused by a pin inserted in the centre of the die, in order to prevent the blank from shifting. It is odd that so simple a thing as a collar should not have occurred to those who are supposed to have adopted this barbarous expedient. The supposition is however without foundation; for in two coins from the same die the hole is in different places, thus showing that the object which produced the hole was not fastened into the die[2].

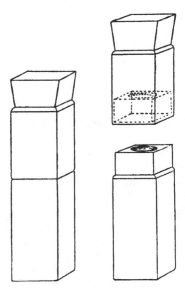

FIG. 25.—Die for striking coins of Faustina II. Lyon Museum. [From the *Zeitschrift für Numismatik*, vol. v. p. 121.]

Instruments made of soft metal naturally wore out very quickly, and it is indeed not common, before imperial times, to find two coins from the same die[3]. To this fact we owe the

---

[1] One with the type of Berenice is published in the *Mon. d. Inst.* v. 51, no. 9; *Annali*, 1853, p. 128.

[2] E. g. Wroth, *Brit. Mus. Catal., Galatia,* &c., pp. 20, 21, nos. 16, 20. I know of no satisfactory explanation of this fact.

[3] Though commoner than at first sight appears. Naturally collectors do not care to have two specimens from the same dies. At the same time, the value of noting the community of dies is considerable. The chronological relation between a number of coins can be partly ascertained

extraordinary variety in design which is characteristic of ancient coins. In imperial times, however, it is not uncommon in any large collection to find two coins sharing one die between them, although it is still rare to find both obverse and reverse of two coins from the same dies.

Traces of the mending of dies sometimes appear on imperial coins, in the shape of circular lines parallel to the edge of the coin. The die has cracked at the edge, and the edge has been replaced by a band of fresh metal, which, not being truly adjusted, leaves traces of the join (Pl. XIII. 7).

But if the soft dies wore out quickly, it was also possible to produce them with great rapidity. This speed of execution accounts for the not infrequent blunders on ancient coins, and for the careless workmanship which is too common even in the period of the finest art. It also explains the fact that emperors whose reigns were short—sometimes limited to a few days—are represented by large and various issues[1].

§ 3. *The Development of Form of Struck Coins.*

The lower die, as we have seen, produced what is known as the obverse of the coin, the upper die the reverse. The reverse continued for some time to receive merely a rude impression from the punch; the idea of ornamenting the latter, however, was not late in arising, and by the middle of the sixth century the practice of having what might properly be called a type for both sides of the coin was fairly well established[2]. Before this

by making such a list of common dies as that drawn up for Elis by Mr. Wroth (*Num. Chr.* 1892, pp. 12, 13). The sharing of common dies by different cities is evidence of a political connexion between them. Thus Mr. Arthur Evans possesses two coins of Croton and Metapontum from the same obverse die. Prymnessus and Synnada in the time of Gallienus used the same obverse die. See Imhoof-Blumer, *Zur Münzkunde Grossgriechenlands &c., mit besonderer Berücksichtigung einiger Münzgruppen mit Stempelgleichheiten, Num. Zeit.* xviii.

[1] Mongez, op. cit. p. 210.
[2] If the accepted attribution of the earliest double-type coins of Athens to Solon is correct—and it has not been disproved—Athens was a generation in advance of other states in this matter. In any case, these earliest double-type coins are not later than the middle of the sixth century (Von Fritze in *Z. f. N.* xx. 1896, pp. 142 ff.). Some of the earliest electrum coins of Asia Minor bear minor types on their reverses (Pl. I. 3, 7; Head, *Coins of the Ancients*, Pl. I. 3, 4).

was the case, various methods of modifying the monotony of the incuse square had been adopted. A combination of two squares of unequal size, or of an oblong with a square, is very characteristic of the earliest pieces of the west coast of Asia Minor (Pl. I). In the south-east corner of the Aegean we find two narrow oblongs side by side. Another method of diversification—not common in these early times in Asia— was to divide up the square into quarters (square or triangular) or eighths. By leaving every other eighth level with the surface, there was produced the pattern known as the mill-sail incuse (Pl. I. 5)[1]. Some of these forms were retained by certain states long after the practice of using two types had become established elsewhere; in other cases a transition was effected by placing small types or letters in the division of the incuse, preparatory to abolishing the divisions and filling the whole space with one type.

One great exception, however, to the use of the incuse square on the reverse must be mentioned. This is met with in Southern Italy[2]. At the time when coinage was introduced into this district the double type had become established; but instead of a new type being placed on the reverse, the type of the obverse was repeated in incuse in a slightly modified form[3]. This was an advance on the practice prevalent in Northern Italy (Etruria) and in other outlying districts, such as some parts of Cyprus, where the reverse was sometimes left perfectly plain. The object of the Italian fabric was to make it possible to pack or pile coins. A number of coins of this peculiar fabric can be piled one on top of the other to some height. With ordinary coins of which both sides are in relief this is impossible. But from an artistic point of view the form was due to a naive attempt to enable one, so to speak, to look through the coin and see the obverse type from behind. Thus on early coins of Poseidonia (Pl. III. 2) the figure of Poseidon on the obverse is seen from the front, advancing to the right; on the reverse the god is seen from

---

[1] Peculiar forms of incuse, Head, *Coins of the Ancients*, Pl. 1. 5; 6. 31; 9. 33 (a variety of the mill-sail); 13. 24.
[2] And at Zancle in Sicily in the earliest times (Evans, *Num. Chr.* 1896, pp. 101 ff.).
[3] The coins have thus the deceptive appearance of being small pieces of repoussé work, and are indeed very thin.

behind (as is clear from the representation of the chlamys) advancing to the left. Small details were usually omitted on the reverse, although the inscription was sometimes, as in the case just mentioned, repeated. Even where the reverse type was a different one, it was usual in this district to represent it in incuse. The use of an incuse design on the reverse is also found in the electrum coinage of Lesbos in the fifth century[1]. But here the designs are always different on obverse and reverse.

The reverse die, in Southern Italy and in Sicily, was as a rule from the first made circular instead of square in form. The result of this was a circular impression on the reverse instead of the incuse rectangle of Hellas proper and the East. As in many other things, the Western colonies were thus considerably in advance of their mother-cities. For in Hellas proper and the East, the incuse square continued to be usual until the end of the fifth century B.C. Before this, however, the experiment had sometimes been made of using the round-headed punch for the reverse. Shortly after 400 B.C. this circular incuse very generally displaced the square, and it was not long before it disappeared in its turn, except so far as the excessive size of the blank caused the edges to swell up under pressure and form a rim round the type. The transition from the incuse square to the flat reverse was often effected without the intermediate stage of the incuse circle.

It was doubtless for commercial reasons that a state such as Cyzicus refused to do away with the incuse square on its reverse, but retained it till late in the fourth century. But the sudden reappearance of a well-defined incuse square in the second century B.C. at Rhodes, and certain places under Rhodian influence (mainly in Caria and Lycia, Pl. IX. 5), was not due to any such reasons, and must be attributed to a tendency to archaize.

So far as fabric is concerned, there are few changes to chronicle in the fourth century. In spite of the disappearance of the incuse, coins continued to be made of a considerable thickness. The earliest coins were almost bean-shaped; but the thick oval dump gradually gave way to the round, flat, but still comparatively thick piece. Towards the end of the fourth

[1] Wroth, *Brit. Mus. Catal., Troas*, &c., Pl. XXXI.

century may be noticed a tendency to spread the flan and make the relief lower. At the same time more care is taken to strike the coin, so far as concerns the placing of the type in the centre of the flan; and the types of the coins of this and the succeeding period show up well in the centre of the flan, surrounded by a comparatively broad field. From the beginning of the second century B.C. dates the introduction of the 'spread tetradrachms' which were struck in such numbers, especially in Asia Minor. This spreading was often carried to excess, as for instance in the coinage of Maronea, Thasos, and Byzantium (Pl. IX. 2).

A few of the varieties of fabric in struck coins which are met with from the fourth century onwards must be mentioned here. Some of these were perhaps due to fancy merely. To this class must probably be assigned the famous Roman *serrati* (Pl. XII. 4), denarii with notched edges which gained a considerable reputation in distant parts of the world [1]. The serrate fabric was employed by the Carthaginians (who perhaps invented it), the Seleucidae (Pl. X. 4), and the Macedonians about 200 B.C.[2]. Since there are bronze coins of this fabric, its object can hardly have been to show that the coins were solid and not plated.

Another class of coins owed their shape to the method by which the blanks were prepared. Such are, for instance, the square Indo-Greek coins (which were cut from a strip or sheet of metal), and the circular coins with sloping edges which have been mentioned above[3]. The varieties so far described are distinguished by the nature of their edges; as regards surface, there were very few departures from the usual form. The earliest coins are lentoid, and highly convex; a very slight convexity is as a rule preserved, even on the reverse, throughout the later periods of Greek and Roman coinage,

---

[1] Tacitus (*Germ.* 5) says of the Germans in his time (long after the *serrati* had ceased to be issued): *pecuniam probant veterem et diu notam, serratos bigatosque*. This statement is confirmed by finds.

[2] Babelon, *Rois de Syrie*, pp. clxxxviii ff.

[3] See p. 144. Lenormant thinks (i. p. 264) that the blanks of the large bronze coins of the Lagidae were not cast but cut out with a punch. But I fail to see in them the regularity of edge on which he bases this theory. In fact, they present every appearance of being cast, and many of them have the characteristic projections at the side.

sufficient to prevent the piece from looking too flat. But there are a few instances of a slight concavity[1] although never attaining to the peculiar *scyphate* fabric of late Byzantine coins.

§ 4. *Cast Coins.*

The process of casting[2] coins was similar to that used for all other metal work which was cast solid. With hollow-casting we are not concerned. The first step was to make a model of the coin—we will suppose in wax or fine clay. On this a mould was made in two parts, which were then joined together. Apertures were left, by one of which the liquid metal could be introduced, while the air escaped by the other. These apertures are represented in the actual coin by projections from the sides, to remove which, in some cases, no trouble seems to have been taken[3]. A number of coins could be cast at the same time by placing the moulds side by side, and allowing the molten metal to run from one into another by means of channels. It is natural to suppose that the moulds were

---

[1] For instance, the bronze coins struck for Cyprus, with the head of Antoninus Pius on the obverse, and that of Marcus Aurelius on the reverse; and a bronze coin of Mytilene (*Brit. Mus. Catal.*, *Troas*, &c., Pl. XLI, no. 3).

[2] Χανεύειν, διαχεῖν, *fundere*, (con)*flare*. The last word is the only one of the four which is actually used of coins: *aes antiquissimum, quod est flatum, pecore est notatum*, Varr. *R. R.* ii. 1. 9; *flata signataque pecunia*, Gell. ii. 10. 3; *IIIviri auro argento aere flando feriundo*, Inscr. (Wilmann's *Exempla*, 611 c, 1189, &c.). Pomponius (Dig. I. 2, 2) speaks of the *triumviri monetales aeris, argenti, auri flatores*; and we have denarii of L. Flaminius Chilo with IIII. VIR PRI(*mus*) FLA(*vit*), and of Cn. Cornelius Lentulus Marcellinus CVR(*ator*) ✱ (*denariis*) FL(*andis*). But the use of the word *flare* refers partly to the casting of bars of metal which were afterwards made into struck coins (some of these bars have been found bearing the names of functionaries of the mint; see above, p. 136, and Blanchet in *Rev. Num.* 1896, p. 17; 1893, p. 285), and partly to the casting of the flans of the coin.

[3] Others have given a different explanation of these projections which, as we have seen, occur frequently in struck coins of which the blanks were cast. It is supposed (Blümner, *Techn.* iv. p. 259) that, the mould being made in two parts, a raised edge was left where these two parts joined. On the face of the coin this disappeared in the process of striking, but at the rim two projections would remain. Now (1) the object of making the mould of a coin which was afterwards to receive a type from the hammer in two parts is not apparent, unless it was made from a proof, which is a matter of conjecture. The mould of the blank was more probably

made in such a way that they could be employed more than once; otherwise the labour and cost of producing a number of coins would have been immense[1]. When, however, the first mould was broken or otherwise spoilt, it was easy to make another from one of the coins already cast. The effect of this on the fabric would be important. For, as metal contracts in cooling, each coin when cool would be slightly smaller than the capacity of its mould. A second mould made from this coin would be of the same size as the coin, and therefore by an equal amount smaller than the original mould. A repetition of the process would produce a still smaller mould and coin, and the effect of these successive reductions would in the course of time become easily appreciable[2]. This is in all probability one cause of the curious degeneration in size and weight, which we meet with in the early Roman coinage—the largest series of cast coins in existence.

The usual shape of cast coins, as of struck ones, is circular. Among the earliest coins of Central Italy, however, are the large quadrilateral bricks known as *aes signatum* (Fig. 10); and even earlier than these are the *aes rude* (Fig. 9), and *massae*, large pieces of metal often presenting the appearance of fragments of cast bronze bars. Another exceptional fabric is found at Olbia in Sarmatia, where pieces were cast in the shape of fish (Fig. 1).

In ancient times the process of casting was almost entirely limited to Italian coins of the early period. Of early Greek coins, only the large bronze pieces of Olbia in Sarmatia were produced by this process; for the *aes grave* of Sicily must be classed with the cast coins of Italy. Among the coins issued by Greek cities in imperial times are a number of pieces

---

a mere sinking, like the holes in a coin-tray. This may be considered as certain in the case of coins with a sloping edge (see above, p. 144). (2) If the mould were made in two parts, the only practical method would be to make one part for one face, the other for the other face, of the coin. This could never leave a raised edge *across the face* of the blank, but only round the rim.

[1] In later times, in the case of medals, it is quite possible that the original moulds were not used more than once. C. F. Keary, *Guide to the Exhib. of Italian Medals in the B. M.* p. xii.

[2] With regard to cast medals, see the calculations by N. Rondot, *Rev. Num.* 1895, pp. 403-416.

which have been cast. Their genuineness has often been doubted. But some light is thrown on this point by two coins of Sillyum in Pamphylia (*obv.* Head of Salonina; *rev.* Tyche seated), one of which is cast from the other, which is struck. It would be fair to suppose that the cast was made in modern times, were it not that the original is in some places more worn than the cast, and must therefore have been in circulation after the cast was made [1]. In addition to evidence such as this, the existence of clay moulds (Fig. 27) proves that many ancient coins were cast. It has been suggested that

FIG. 27.—Clay moulds for casting coins of Maximianus Herculeus and Constantius Chlorus. Found at Duston, Northampton.

the moulds formed part of the plant of false moneyers; but there is reason to suppose that they were used by the authorities [2]. In deciding whether a coin is cast or struck, the presence of air-holes is of course a good test; but it must be remembered that, the blanks having been originally cast before the die was impressed, the second process may sometimes have failed to eliminate all traces of the first.

[1] *Brit. Mus. Catal.*, *Lycia*, &c., p. 169, no. 21, and p. 298, no 21 A.
[2] Mongez (op. cit. p. 207) considers that they are so numerous that they cannot have been used only by the authorities. Large quantities have been found in England, in France, and on the Rhine. See Caylus, *Rec. d'Ant.* i. p. 286, Pl. 105, no. ii; Mommsen, iii. p. 15. The casting process was severely forbidden by various ordinances of the fourth century.

§ 5. *The Composition of the Type.*

Regarded from the point of view of a design, the types of Greek and Roman coins went through a regular development. At first the type was usually impressed on the metal, without any particular regard for its decorative properties. Even in the earliest period, however, we may note cases in which some attempt was made to adapt the type to the field. Such a simple expedient as reverting the head of an animal (Pl. I. 7, 12), in order to make the whole design more suitable to the circular field, is the most obvious instance of this attempt. A similar motive inspires the 'heraldic' arrangement, by which a type is represented doubled, so as to produce a symmetrical arrangement (Pl. I. 6). The so-called kneeling (really running) figures, so common in early Greek art, were for a similar reason also suitable for coin-types (Pl. I. 5). An advance on this stage was made when the figure was represented in its natural attitude, and the circular field filled up by adjuncts, either purely ornamental or taking the shape of legends or symbols expressing the authority under which the coin was issued. The addition of a border enhanced the artistic appearance of the coin. In the case of the reverse, the type was sufficiently enclosed by the incuse square[1], although in some places a border was added on the reverse long before the obverse was thus decorated. In Greek Italy a border was usual from the first on both sides of the coin, although in Sicily it was as a rule dispensed with where the incuse circle was employed. These borders most frequently take the shape of a row of dots; occasionally we find a plain line, a cable pattern (Pl. III. 2), a radiate border, a row of dots between two lines, or two lines with the interval between them filled with parallel cross-strokes. These are the chief forms of the purely decorative border; but there are also instances of the adaptation to the purposes of a border of something organic to the type. The best instance of this is the use of the wreath (Terina, Pl. VI. 8); we also find a conventional wave-pattern enclosing the head

---

[1] The early coins of Calymna (Pl. I. 14) are interesting for the way in which the shape of the incuse is adapted to the shape of the type—a chelys.

of a water-nymph¹; and even the legend is sometimes disposed in a strikingly decorative way. The Greek artist, however, left himself a free hand in these matters, and we have examples in which he allowed some portion of the type to escape from the border; the good effect thus produced is to be remarked on the obverse of the coin of the Sicilian Naxos (Pl. VI. 1), the reverse of which is at the same time a fine example of the adaptation of the type, without distortion, to a circular field.

An instance of the way in which what was once an organic part of the type may come to have merely a decorative importance is seen in the use of the shield. On the early coins with the type of a shield bearing a device² the whole design from the first strikes the eye as representing a shield. On the late coins of Macedon³, however, the shield is so treated that the part of it not covered by the head has the effect of an elaborate border. This is more evident in the coins of Macedon under the Romans (Pl. X. 5) than in the coins of Philip V of the preceding period (Pl. VIII. 7).

Of the adjuncts to the type which occur in the field, those above described as purely ornamental are the exception in Greek coins; and indeed it may sometimes be doubted whether a better knowledge of the meaning of these adjuncts would not reduce still further the number of those which can be called purely ornamental. It is enough to instance as adjuncts of this kind the volute ornaments on Cypriote coins and the floral ornaments in the corners of the square border in coins of Posidium in Carpathus⁴, and Rhaucus in Crete⁵. But by far the greater number of the adjuncts have a distinct meaning. The discussion of this, however, belongs to a different chapter⁶. On the early coins the symbols are often represented with undue prominence; but in the best period they are made smaller and do not interfere with the effect of the type. Compare for instance the dolphins on the Demareteion and its companion tetradrachm of B.C. 480 (Pl. III. 5, 6) with those on the decadrachms of a later date (Pl. VI. 4, 6). Similarly,

[1] Gardner, *Types*, Pl. VI. 13.
[2] E. g. at Elis, Head, *Coins of the Ancients*, Pl. 14, no. 33. In Lycia, *Brit. Mus. Catal., Lycia*, Pl. VII, nos. 7, 10.
[3] Head, *Coins of the Ancients*, Pl. 54, nos. 10, 12.
[4] *Ibid.*, Pl. 3. 32.
[5] Svoronos, *Num. de la Crète anc.* Pl. 29. 9.   [6] Ch. vii. § 10.

an exaggeration of the border is visible on early coins as compared with later[1].

Legends at first appear on Greek coins in a much abbreviated form. The initial letter of the name of the community served to indicate the authority by which the coin was issued, such initials being in fact used as the city arms on other objects besides coins[2]. Not even the earliest inscriptions, however, are limited to the city name; a legend explanatory of the type occurs on the earliest inscribed coin (Pl. I. 4). As with the spread of writing the legends became longer, it became necessary to arrange them decoratively so as to fill the vacant spaces of the field or form a border. The former arrangement is obvious on most coins; the latter is perhaps best illustrated by the coins of the Macedonian and Thracian region, such as Amphipolis (Pl. V. 1). As time went on, a tendency showed itself to overcrowd the field with inscriptions, of which good instances may be found on the Athenian tetradrachms and the regal coins of late times. On the latter the employment of the inscription to enclose the type as a border, whether square (Pl. X. 1) or round[3], was still usual, and on imperial coins the circular arrangement became almost invariable, and has lasted down to modern times. In imperial times the border of dots is almost universal.

§ 6. *Development of Style.*

It is not proposed to deal here in any great detail with the artistic development of Greek and Roman coin-types[4]. The treatment of the relief in coins follows more or less closely the general lines on which Greek sculpture in relief developed[5]. The Greeks soon advanced beyond the stage in which the decoration of their coins consisted of a mere pattern, to that in which they represented some object natural or artificial. As

---

[1] E.g. on coins of Tarentum: Head, *Coins of the Ancients*, Pl. 7, no. 4, &c.
[2] E. Curtius, *Ueber den rel. Char. der gr. Münzen*, Ges. Abh. ii. p. 457, cf. 91; Imhoof-Blumer, *Z. f. N.* i. 130.
[3] Head, *Coins of the Ancients*, Pl. 62, nos. 20, 21.
[4] For Greek coins this has already been done at length in Professor Gardner's *Types of Greek Coins*; for a brief summary of the development of style, see also Head, *Hist. Num.* pp. lx ff.
[5] The development of coins, however, very often, though not always, lags somewhat behind that of sculpture.

the human figure is the last object to the satisfactory treatment of which any art attains, we are prepared to find that the subjects represented on the earlier coins are more frequently of another kind; in fact, animal types are by far the most common. Next to these, perhaps, in frequency come monstrous types (with which may be classed the head of the Gorgon), consisting of fantastic combinations either of two or more animals, such as the chimaera, pegasus, griffin, winged boar, or of animals and human beings, such as the centaurs. The most fertile imagination in regard to these *monstra horrenda* seems to have belonged to the die engravers of Cyzicus. The human head is naturally much less represented in this early period than the human figure as a whole. But from the middle of the sixth century we are able to trace the development of style as shown in the treatment of both head and figure. This treatment, down to the time of the Persian wars, cannot be called anything but primitive. The head, where represented, is extremly rudely made; the eye is an elliptical swelling, plastered, as it were, on to the face, and of an excessive size. The ear is placed rather too high. The swelling of the cheek is exaggerated by the emphasizing of the defining line below it, the transition from cheek to jaw being not gradual, but marked by a depression which lends to the face the 'archaic grin.' The swelling of the nostril, also, is too sharply defined. The hair is frequently represented by rows of dots. The best instances of this style are to be found in the early coins of Athens (Pl. II 2). The treatment of the human figure errs by a similar exaggeration of the various features, and failure to blend them, as is clear from the early coins of Lete in Macedon [1] and Caulonia in Italy (Pl. III. 3). But even before the Persian wars the rudeness of primitive art begins to be refined. There is a considerable advance from the coin of Caulonia just mentioned to that of Poseidonia (Pl. III. 2). The human-headed bull at Gela (Pl. III. 7), or the female head at Syracuse (Pl. III. 5) brings us very near to the most remarkable coin of the 'early transitional' period—the Demareteion of 480 B. C. (Pl. III. 6). In this coin, all the primitive exaggerations are toned down; the eye, though still shown in full, no longer projects from the face; the ear, however, is still set

---

[1] Head, *Coins of the Ancients*, Pl. 4. 5.

too high. The cheek merges naturally into the jaw, and the archaic grin becomes a smile. The hair is still represented with formality, but by means of wavy lines instead of dots. The formality which is characteristic of the period on which we have now entered is not the result of long movement in a groove; it is, on the contrary, instinct with life. Before it could reach its full freedom Greek art had, so to speak, to go through this period of rigid training, in which extraordinary care is devoted to thoroughness of detail, and grace and refinement ($\chi\acute{a}\rho\iota s$) are put before every other aim. Some twenty years later than the Demareteion is the Naxian head of Dionysus (Pl. VI. 1). A curious feature of this head is the contrast between the hair, the treatment of which is not surpassed on any Greek coin, and the formal beard and moustache. The somewhat unpleasant leer, intensified by this treatment, is unusual in Greek representations of the wine-god who, though not always dignified, is almost always humane. A striking contrast to the two pieces of Syracuse and Naxos is furnished by the archaistic coins of Athens (Pl. IV. 3). In these we see the result of a mental conflict in the artist, who is really capable of much better work, but who is bound to produce a piece which shall resemble the genuinely archaic Athenian coins. The result entirely fails to carry conviction; it is neither primitive nor advanced; it is lifeless, and formal for formality's sake.

The change in the treatment of the human figure at this period is sufficiently apparent from a study of such representations as the discobolus on coins of Cos[1], or, again, the remarkable Silenus on the reverse of the coin of Naxos already described. It is difficult to imagine how the pectoral and abdominal muscles (above all in a Silenus!) could in a position of repose take the tense form given them. There is some excuse for the exaggeration of the anatomy in cases of energetic action[2], but the only muscles which should stand taut in this figure are those of the legs. The proper modelling of the muscles in this pose is to be found in the later coin of Naxos with the same type (Pl. VI. 3), where all the dryness of the transitional period is replaced by the supple modelling and

---

[1] Head, *Coins of the Ancients*, Pl. 11. 36.
[2] An obvious instance of such exaggeration is to be found in the Amazon frieze of the Mausoleum.

ῥυθμός of the artist who understands anatomy, and understands it well enough to keep it in its proper place.

By the middle of the fifth century, the eye is shown in profile; the top of the ear is level with the line drawn from corner to corner of the eye. The general characteristic of the style of this period is a severe simplicity. The trammels of archaic refinement— for with increasing power the artist begins to work more boldly—are thrown off, and a larger, freer treatment results. Of the noble, severe style of this period there is perhaps no better instance than one of the earliest coins of Thurium, dating from 443 B.C. or a few years later (Pl. VI. 5). But this style is of comparatively short duration. At the culminating period of the art of Greek coins, which may be placed at the close of the fifth century, the severity of which we have spoken had completely given way before a softer, though still dignified and ideal treatment. The little coin of Terina (Pl. VI. 8), a masterpiece in its chastity of design, serves best to illustrate this stage. The most popular monuments of this time are, however, the Syracusan decadrachms and tetradrachms (Pl. VI. 4, 6, 7). Many of these, however, marvellous as they are, lack the simplicity and reserve of the coin of Terina; some indeed are almost extravagant. Still, of none of the best coins of this period can it be said that they are merely pretty. The facing head of Apollo on the coin of Amphipolis (Pl. V. 1) has a tendency towards effeminacy, but it is still a noble head. At the same time with the loss of severity, the artists have learned to be realistic and picturesque. The young hunter at Segesta with his leash of hounds [1], the Cretan goddess seated in her tree (Pl. IV. 2), the Victory of Elis, seated on a basis, watching the contest (Pl. V. 2), the two eagles at Acragas, βοσκόμενοι λαγίναν ἐρικύμονα φέρματι γένναν, the one tearing his prey, the other with his head raised, shrieking (Pl. III. 9)—all these are instances of the new power of expression belonging to the coin engraver. And the frequent occurrence at this time of the facing head is another proof of power [2].

---

[1] Head, *Coins of the Ancients*, Pl. 17, no. 31.
[2] The wear to which a full-face representation was exposed soon reduced a beautiful relief to a caricature. It was therefore little loss to art when, about the middle of the fourth century, this form of representation

The art of the first half of the fourth century maintains most successfully the level now attained. It is not really until we pass the middle of the century that any serious change is visible. The portrait of a Persian satrap (Pl. V. 9), on a coin struck about 390 B.C., ranks among the finest Greek coins; the same is true of many of the Lampsacene gold staters (Pl. V. 10), and some of the silver staters of Philip II of Macedon (Pl. VII. 2). But the head of Zeus on a silver coin (Pl. VIII. 3) of Alexander of Epirus (B.C. 342-325) illustrates the tendency to weakness which now begins to set in. It would be easy to find other examples from the same period. The tendency, it should be remembered, is naturally first felt in purely ideal heads. In the idealized portraits of the close of the fourth century, it is not apparent; for the very reason that the personality of the original gives force and character to the portrait, idealized though it may be.

In the third century, the work, although often clever, is also often careless. The more careful portraits, as those of Antimachus of Bactria (Pl. VIII. 4), Mithradates II of Pontus (Pl. VIII. 2), or Hiero II of Syracuse (Pl. XI. 6), are equal to anything of the kind produced by Renaissance medallists.

The large flans which became usual, especially in Asia Minor, after the fall of Antiochus in 190 B.C. gave excellent opportunity for showy work. Some of the heads—notably that of the turreted city goddess at Smyrna (Pl. VIII. 10), or that of Artemis at Perga (Pl. VIII. 9), strike the eye at first as fine, but the impression does not last. Nor can such portraits as those of Philip V or Perseus (Pl. X. 3) be rated very highly. The best efforts of the time are devoted to producing pretty, conventional decorative effects. There is little to be said of the art of Greek coins during the last century before Christ. Occasionally a remarkable coin is met with—such as those

became less common. The form was unsuited to coins, and was only adopted by a magnificent blunder. There are some curious instances on early coins of faces represented full or nearly full, notably in Arcadia (*Brit. Mus. Catal., Peloponn.*, Pl. 31, 10; 37, 24. 25). Side by side with these must be put the remarkable representations of riders and chariots seen from the front (*Journ. Hellen. Studies*, 1897, pp. 80 ff., Pl. II, nos. 5, 6). The bold examples of foreshortening from Naxos (Pl. VI. 1, 3) and Gortyna (*Brit. Mus. Catal., Crete*, Pl. 9, no. 6) belong to a later period, and owing to the comparative lowness of their relief are not subject to the criticism just made on the full-face.

with the clever if theatrical portrait of Mithradates the Great (Pl. X. 7), or the striking but hardly pleasing head of Cleopatra at Ascalon (Pl. X. 8)—but the general mass of Greek coins at this time is, from an artistic standpoint, absolutely devoid of interest. The art of portraiture revives slightly towards the time of Augustus. The portrait of Archelaus, king of Cappadocia from B.C. 36 to A.D. 17 (Pl. X. 9), is one of the best works of its time, and deserves to rank with the youthful head on an aureus of Augustus (Pl. XII. 10). The latter was probably, like the former, the work of a Greek artist.

Rome, whose coinage begins in the middle of the fourth century, offers nothing remarkable from an artistic point of view, but falls into line with the artistically poorer districts of the Greek world. The occurrence of portraits is rare until the approach of the Empire. With the concentration of all political power in Rome a distinct improvement, due presumably to Greek influence, is manifest, and the series of portraits on Roman coins, beginning with Augustus, is unrivalled for extent, interest, and skill of execution. The improvement, however, can hardly be said to have extended to the Greek world. The highest point was reached in the time of the Flavian and Antonine emperors (Pl. XV. 1-3, 5); thenceforward there is a gradual decline to the time of Constantine, after which a conventional portrait is all that the die engraver is able to produce. At the beginning of the fifth century A.D, when even the profile portraits had become almost unrecognizable, the full-face representation again begins to prevail (Pl. XV. 11), and in the Byzantine coinage it is the rule (Pl. XV. 12).

CHAPTER VII

THE MEANING AND CLASSIFICATION OF COIN-TYPES

§ 1. *The Religious Theory and the Commercial Theory.*

THE meaning of the great variety of types which appear on Greek and Roman coins has been made the subject, in recent years, of some discussion, arising out of a theory enunciated by Professor Ridgeway in his brilliant work on the *Origin of Metallic Currency*[1]. Mr. Ridgeway believes that modern scholars 'have directed all their efforts to giving a religious signification to everything' that occurs as the type of a coin; whereas a truer view is that stated long ago by Leake, who remarked that the types of Greek coins generally related 'to the local mythology and fortunes of the place, with symbols referring to the principal productions or to the protecting numina.' Mr. Ridgeway himself goes further than Leake. In his general statement of the case [2] there is little with which it is possible to find fault. But several types which he adduces in support of his theory can with equal plausibility be explained from the religious point of view [3].

There can be no doubt that many of the objects which figure as coin-types are articles of commerce or symbols of commercial products. The tunny figures on the coins of Cyzicus (Pl. I. 3),

---

[1] Pp. 313 ff.
[2] 'I do not for a moment mean that mythological and religious subjects do not play their proper part in Greek coin-types. But it is just as wrong to reduce all coin-types to this category as it would be to regard them all as merely symbolic of the natural and manufactured products of the various states.'—p. 314.
[3] See the discussion in the *Classical Review*, 1892, p. 470 f.; 1893, pp. 79 ff.

and there is no doubt that the tunny fishery was the staple industry of that city. The wine-cup figures on the coins of the island of Naxos (Pl. II. 3), and it will not be disputed that wine was a product of the island. Mr. Ridgeway holds that these and similar types appear on coins because, and only because, they relate to commerce, and because exchange by means of a currency has replaced an earlier stage of exchange by barter in the object represented or alluded to. The coin with the wine-cup is the representative of an amount of wine; the coin with the tunny of a certain amount of tunny fish, and so on. The 'orthodox' view is that these types appear because they are connected in some way with the presiding deities of the various states, and the genuineness of the coin is guaranteed by its bearing on it the religious symbol of the state that issues it. The truth, probably, in the greater number of cases, lies between, or rather behind, these two views. The type, whatever its character may be, appears on coins because it is the badge by which the issuing authority is recognized. The religious sense of the Greeks led them, whatever the staple industry of any state might be, to place it under the protection of their chief deity. Obviously, therefore, the object of the industry could be regarded as a symbol of the presiding deity. In early times the difficulty of representing the human form was sufficient reason for placing on a coin not the actual deity, but that object which most readily recalled him or her to the mind of a citizen. This is the primary reason for the appearance of the wine-cup on the coin of Naxos. It is only a happy accident that the type of the coin at the same time suggests the staple industry[1]. The fact that the tunny at Cyzicus is decorated with fillets (Pl. I. 3) proves conclusively that the type is meant to have a religious significance.

In addition to what I have already said as to the commercial allusion of the type not being, as a rule, the primary one, it is necessary to make clear two points which militate against the commercial theory. One coin on which Mr. Ridgeway lays great stress is the well-known electrum stater which, according to a more than doubtful interpretation, bears an inscription stating

[1] It is exceedingly difficult to accept Mr. Ridgeway's ingenious interpretation of the commercial significance of such types as the double axe of Tenedos or the shield of Boeotia.

it to be the *sema* or badge of Phanes (Pl. I. 4)[1]. The type is a stag browsing. 'The stag is nothing more than the particular badge adopted by the potentate Phanes, when and where he may have reigned, as a guarantee of the weight of the coin and perhaps of the purity of the metal[2].' Such is Mr. Ridgeway's own explanation, and it gives away his case. For if his explanation is true, then other types may also be 'particular badges' adopted by states and rulers as guarantees of the weight of the coin and of the purity of the metal. It will not be suggested that Phanes was a dealer in venison. But it would be fair to suppose that Artemis was his tutelary deity, and he adopted her symbol as his badge. And in the same way a city which worshipped Artemis would use the same symbol on its coinage.

Secondly, did the types which Mr. Ridgeway explains as having a commercial significance represent an old barter-unit, that is to say a fixed amount of the commodity in which the issuing city traded, we should expect, at least in some cases, to find in the types one feature which, at any rate in the earliest times, is entirely absent. The smaller denominations would not bear the same type as the larger, but that type halved or divided according to the requisite proportion. If for instance the early Lycian staters, of which the constant type is a boar or the forepart of a boar, represents a certain amount of ham, how is it that the whole boar and its half appear on coins of the same weight? If the earliest silver drachm of Athens 'was equated to the old barter-unit (either of corn or of oil)[3],' why was not the olive-spray varied on the larger and smaller denominations in order to indicate an equation with more or less of the old barter-units? And why, above all, was the olive-oil unit indicated by a mere adjunct in the field, instead of occupying the main position on the coin? The halving of the shield on Boeotian coins does not correspond to the denominations as it should, if the barter-unit theory were correct. Thus, on the earliest coins of Thebes, we have the whole shield on the didrachms, drachms, triobols, obols; the half-shield on hemi-obols; and the whole shield again on the quarter-obol.

---

[1] The genitive has been rightly explained by Sir C. T. Newton and Fränkel as equivalent to 'of the bright one' (meaning probably Artemis; see above, p. 79, note 1).
[2] Ridgeway, p. 320.   [3] Id. p. 324.

CH. VII] MEANING AND CLASSIFICATION OF COIN-TYPES 169

The half-shield is used as the type of the hemi-obol, simply because the name hemiobelion suggests the *halving* of the type, not because the coin represented the worth of half a shield. A well-known statement of Aristotle would seem, at first sight, to favour Mr. Ridgeway's interpretation, but the true translation of the passage is not 'the stamp was put on the coin as an indication of value,' but 'was put on a coin to show that the value was present'; in other words, to guarantee that it was of full weight and true [1], not to state the weight or value of it.

The type then does not indicate that the coin represents an old barter-unit; but it must be admitted that there are many types which cannot be explained as religious symbols, and that some of these have a commercial significance, in that they symbolize an industry. Nevertheless, owing to the extraordinary penetration of religion into all the affairs of life among the Greeks and Romans, it is by no means entirely unscholarly to read a religious sense into what often at first sight appears to be something very different.

With this understanding, an attempt may be made to classify types according to the principles which induced the issuing state or ruler to adopt them as badges.

§ 2. *Religious Types.*

(a) First among those types which can only have a purely religious meaning must be mentioned the deities, represented either directly or by means of symbols. Zeus and Dione in Epirus, Zeus at Elis, Messene, and Mylasa, Poseidon at Poseidonia (Pl. III. 2) and Potidaea, Apollo at Lacedaemon and Delphi (Pl. V. 7) and in Lycia, Hera at Samos (Pl. XIII. 8), the Cyprian Aphrodite at Paphos, Athena at Corinth (Pl. IV. 6) and Athens (Pl. II. 2), Artemis at Ephesus (Pl. XIII. 9) and Perga (Pl. VIII. 9), Hermes at Pheneus (Pl. V. 12) and Aenus, Helios at Rhodes (Pl. V. 5), Baal-Tars at Tarsus (Pl. IV. 12), Cybele at Smyrna (Pl. VIII. 10, identified with the city), are among the more famous instances of the

---

[1] Arist. *Pol.* ii. 1257 a 41 ὁ γὰρ χαρακτὴρ ἐτέθη τοῦ ποσοῦ σημεῖον. See above, p. 67, note 2, and the definition of σημεῖον in *Anal. Pr.* ii. 27. 2 οὗ γὰρ ὄντος ἔστιν ἢ οὗ γενομένου πρότερον ἢ ὕστερον γέγονε τὸ πρᾶγμα, τοῦτο σημεῖόν ἐστι τοῦ γεγονέναι ἢ εἶναι.

great deities employed as types in the most obvious way. Deities and heroes, again, are constantly represented in their mythological connexions. At Pheneus Hermes is shown carrying the infant Arcas (Pl. V. 12); Apollo slays the Python on the coins of Croton; Cydon is suckled by a bitch on the coins of Cydonia; at Phaestus, Heracles attacks the Hydra, which is assisted by a crab, or Talos hurls his stone (Pl. IV. 11). Castor and Pollux are represented on the early Roman silver (Pl. XI. 8, 10, 11) charging on horseback, as they appeared at the battle of lake Regillus. At the Lycian Myra (Pl. XIV. 4) a cultus-statue of the form of Artemis known as Eleuthera is represented in the branches of a tree which is attacked by two men with axes and defended by snakes which dart forth from its roots[1]. At Apamea Κιβωτός ('the ark') in Phrygia (Fig. 28) we find a representation of the deluge, Noah (ΝΩΕ) being represented with his companions in an ark floating on the waters[2]. Occasionally the myth which is represented has no known connexion with the place; thus, at Cyzicus, Gaia rises from the earth and holds up Erichthonius[3]. It would be easy to multiply the instances of obscure and complex myths which figure on coins, especially in the rich series of the cities of the provinces in imperial times. And a complete enumeration of the symbols which represent deities would fill a volume—such symbols as

FIG. 28.—Reverse of bronze coin of Septimius Severus struck at Apamea (Phrygia). Ἐπὶ ἀγωνοθέτου Ἀρτεμαγ. Ἀπαμίων. Νῶε. From a specimen in the Bibliothèque Nationale, Paris.

[1] The type probably has some reference to the story of Myrrha, who was transformed into a tree. Her father split open the trunk with his sword, and Adonis was born. Head, *H. N.* p. 578.
[2] For the tradition of the deluge localized at Apamea, where there was a strong Jewish element in the population, see Babelon, *Mélanges*, i. p. 172; W. M. Ramsay, *Cities and Bishoprics*, pp. 669 ff.
[3] The so-called types of Cyzicus are, however, really moneyer's symbols (see above, pp. 119 f.). In any case, this type is probably copied from a well-known monument; the counterpart to it appears in the figure of Cecrops on another Cyzicene stater, and the two are combined on a terra-cotta relief at Berlin (Baumeister, *Denkmäler*, i. p. 492), where, however, Athena is present.

the thunderbolt or eagle of Zeus, the trident of Poseidon, the owl of Athena, the stag or bee of Artemis, the lyre or the triskeles symbol of Apollo, the ram or the caduceus of Hermes, and, to come down to the end of the period which concerns us, the cross of Christ on late Imperial coins (Pl. XV. 12). That by means of such symbols the coins were marked as the property of the authorities which issued them is proved by parallels outside the sphere of coinage. Marble vessels in the temple of Apollo at Cnidus were marked with a lyre; in the Samian war the Athenians branded their prisoners with an owl, the Samians theirs with the *Samaina* or Samian galley. And just as the various states, so did kings and rulers of all kinds place on their coins their guardian deities and heroes, or their symbols. Zeus, Athena, and Heracles figure on the coins of Philip II (Pl. VII. 1) and Alexander the Great (Pl. VII. 4, 5), Perseus on the coins of Philip V (Pl. VIII. 7)[1], Venus on those of Sulla (Pl. XII. 2). Even the minor details and instruments of cults are used for the purpose of types, such as the fire-altar on the coins of Persis. the great altar at Amasia, the tripod of Apollo at Croton. Local features of various kinds are personified. Thus, at Caulonia, Apollo stands holding on his outstretched arm a little wind-god, personifying probably the wind which blew off the east coast of Bruttium (Pl. III. 3). But the most frequent instance of this kind of personification is the river-god (Pl. III. 7; XIV. 12), who appears in various forms, from the ordinary bull to the reclining male figure, on coins of all periods[2]. On an imperial coin of Laodicea in Phrygia the two rivers Lycos and Capros are represented by a wolf and a boar respectively (Pl. XIV. 6).

§ 3. *Types representing the Issuing Authority.*

(*b*) The above may suffice for an indication of the nature of the coin-types belonging to the more strictly religious class. It was, however, possible for a badge to be used which expressed the identity of the original authority in a way which was less

---

[1] Who actually named one of his sons after his favourite hero. On the coin illustrated in Pl. VIII. 7, this son is represented in the guise of the hero. See *Num. Chr.* 1896, pp. 34 ff., Pl. IV.

[2] P. Gardner, *Greek River-Worship, Proc. of Roy. Soc. of Lit.*, April 19, 1876.

obviously connected with religion. When the authority in question was a king, the type might express his royal power. Thus, on the Persian coins (Pl. I. 10, 11), the Great King is represented in person hastening through his dominions armed with spear and bow. At Sidon the king proceeds in his car. At Tyre his power is symbolized by the owl with crook and flail. Possibly the lion of Sardes is also a symbol of royalty[1]. In the same way various types of Victory were associated with the supreme power, especially in late Roman times, when they almost ousted other types from the field. This kind of type was, however, not possible within Hellas proper until the time when the Greeks also became accustomed to the representation on their coinage of the supreme power of a single ruler. Thus it was that portraits were placed on coins, at first half-disguised under divine attributes—as when Alexander the Great appears in the guise of Heracles (Pl. VII. 4)—afterwards boldly and unconcealed. Personal symbols also, such as the capricorn on the coins of Augustus (who was born under this sign), or the sphinx, which the same ruler used both on his signet-ring and on his coins, come under the present head.

The forms of activity, commercial, political, military, agonistic, and the like, which are expressed by coin-types are of course infinitely various. The cities of Thessaly which were famous for their cavalry forces are represented by appropriate types, such as the bridled horse on the coins of Larissa. The horsemen of Tarentum (Pl. XI. 1) furnished a well-known type for the coins of that city. The warriors of Aspendus were sufficiently famous to figure on the early coinage of their city. Many forms of athletics are represented: the discobolus on the coins of Cos, the wrestlers on those of Aspendus, the athletes casting lots on coins of Ancyra in Galatia and other cities, the race-torch (Pl. V. 1) on the beautiful staters of Amphipolis, are well-known instances of this kind of type. More famous still are the chariot-types at cities such as Syracuse (Pl. III. 5, 6; VI. 6, 7). The naval importance of a city is often represented, notably, for instance, by means of the prow or stem of a galley on the coins of Phaselis, or by a plan of the harbour buildings

---

[1] According to others (Gardner, *Types*, p. 42) it is a symbol of Astart or of the Sun.

as at Zancle or Side. The Roman who filled an important religious office used as his badge the instruments of sacrifice or augury (Pl. XII. 2). The municipal life of the cities of Asia Minor is symbolized by representations of their Council, Senate, or Demos [1].

In this connexion may be mentioned the symbolic representations of various attributes belonging to rulers or states. The idea of Liberty was sometimes expressed by an unbridled horse, as on the coins of Termessus Major in Pisidia, a city to which a kind of freedom was accorded by Rome. To the same category belongs the type of the infant Heracles strangling the serpents (Pl. IV. 13), which symbolized the rise of the power of Thebes against the Spartan supremacy, and was employed by various other states, such as Rhodes and Samos, to express their sympathy with the new power (see above, p. 112).

The Roman coinage is especially rich in this kind of type. The personifications, however, of Abundantia, Felicitas, Concordia, and the like may, perhaps, be better classed with the more strictly religious types.

§ 4. *Types representing Local Features.*

(c) Closely allied with the second class of types is a class many of the varieties of which have been explained as having a purely commercial significance. The prevalence in a certain district of some animal or plant was sufficient to induce its adoption as a badge by the cities of that district. That the object was sometimes of commercial importance was a mere accident, so far as its adoption as type for the coinage was concerned. The mussel of Cumae in Campania, the corn of Metapontum, the wine of Naxos, Mende, Maronea, the wild celery of Selinus (Pl. VI. 2), the cow of Euboea, the sepia of Coresia, the silphium of the Cyrenaica (Pl. V. 3) all belong to the same category; and that some of these types are punning types, while others represent articles of commerce, is not, it must be insisted, the reason for their appearance. To the same class belong types or symbols relating to other local features, such as the warm springs of Himera (represented by

---

[1] See above, p. 91, and below, ch. viii. § 2.

a small satyr bathing in a fountain). The lion tearing a bull at Acanthus[1] is evidently as appropriate where lions were abundant, as is the boar in the mountains of Lycia or at Laodicea in Syria. How rivers were represented has already been stated; neighbouring mountains may also be made to furnish types, as Mt. Argaeus at Caesarea in Cappadocia (Pl. XIV. 2), or Mt. Viaros at Prostanna in Pisidia.

§ 5. *Types representing Monuments.*

(*d*) Types of a class which may be called monumental are naturally not wanting, but are almost confined to imperial times. An anticipation, however, of this class of types is found in early times in the representation of the harbour at Zancle (Pl. III. 4)[2]. A harbour, with porticoes running round it, is represented in much later times at Side. The bridge over the Maeander, with the river-god reclining on the parapet, and a stork perched on the gateway, furnishes one of the most remarkable types at Antiochia in Caria (Fig. 29). The Acropolis at Athens, the Forum of Trajan at Rome (Pl. XV. 2), are other similar types. The commonest type of this class is, however, the temple, such as those which occur at Ephesus (temple of Artemis, Pl. XIII. 9), or at Paphos (temple of Aphrodite). The great altar at Amasia has already been mentioned. Finally, a most important instance of this class of type is the representation of famous statues which decorated the city that issued the coin: statues such as

FIG. 29.—Reverse of a bronze coin of Gallienus struck at Antiochia in Caria.

---

[1] Cf. Herod. vii. 125: in this district lions attack the camels of Xerxes' commissariat. These parts, says the historian, abound in lions and wild bulls.

[2] Usually explained as a sickle, and therefore a canting type; for ζάγκλον was the local name for a sickle, and the place was sickle-shaped (Thucyd. vi. 4). But the object on the coins is either a mere semicircular bar (not with a cutting edge) or a flat object with blocks upon it, which perhaps are meant for buildings on the quay.

the Zeus of Pheidias at Elis (Pl. XIV. 1) or the Aphrodite of Praxiteles (at Cnidus). This class of types is naturally of the utmost importance to archaeologists, and sometimes forms the only basis for the restoration and reconstruction of lost works of sculpture and architecture [1].

§ 6. *Historical Types.*

(*e*) History, legendary or other, also furnished its quota of types. The foundation of Tarentum by Taras, who arrived at the spot on a dolphin sent by his father Poseidon to save him from shipwreck, is alluded to on the coins, where Taras is seen riding on a dolphin (Pl. XI. 1 [2]). The hare on the coins of Rhegium and Messana may possibly be placed there in commemoration of the interest which the tyrant Anaxilas took in this animal [3]. The mule-car on the coins of the same places is certainly commemorative of the success which Anaxilas attained with mules at Olympia. In a similar way the naval victory won in 306 B.C. by Demetrius Poliorcetes over Ptolemy is commemorated by representations of Nike standing on a prow and blowing a trumpet (Pl. VII. 10) [4], and Poseidon wielding his trident. A remarkable type on a late coin of Sagalassus, which was taken by Alexander the Great, probably represents the capture of the city. A statue (of Zeus?) stands in the middle; on the left is Alexander (ΑΛΕΞΑΝΔΡΟC) charging on horseback; on the right is a warrior fleeing from the conqueror and holding up his hand in supplication to the statue of his tutelary deity [5]. To return once more to legendary history, the story of Hero and Leander

---

[1] Their utility may best be realized from the works of Imhoof-Blumer and Gardner, *Numismatic Commentary on Pausanias*, and Donaldson, *Architectura Numismatica*. See also Gardner, *Types of Greek Coins*, Pl. XV.

[2] The beautiful type of Pl. XI. 2 may perhaps have some reference to the appeal of Tarentum to Sparta, which led to the expedition of Archidamos in 338 B.C. See Evans, *Horsemen of Tarentum*, p. 66.

[3] Aristotle (ap. Poll. v. 75) says that he introduced it into Sicily. But the type has, perhaps rightly, been connected with Pan, who on a coin of Messana is seen caressing a hare (see Head, *H. N.* p. 93).

[4] This type happens also to belong to the preceding class, for it represents the well-known 'Nike of Samothrace' in the Louvre.

[5] This type again has the appearance of reproducing a piece of sculpture in relief, or a painting.

is naively told on the Imperial coinage of Abydos (Pl. XIII. 5) and of Sestos, and Aeneas is represented on the coins of New Ilium carrying Anchises from the burning city. Roman denarii are rich in historical types. On the reverse of a denarius struck between 134 and 114 B.C. by M. Caecilius Metellus is a Macedonian shield with an elephant's head in the centre, the whole surrounded by a laurel-wreath: a two-fold allusion, to victories won by L. Caecilius Metellus in 250 B.C. in Sicily, and by another ancestor in Macedonia between 148 and 146 B.C. The surrender of Jugurtha by Bocchus to Sulla, again, is commemorated on a denarius of the dictator's son, Faustus Cornelius Sulla (Pl. XII. 3). Among Imperial Roman types may be mentioned those commemorating the subjection of Judaea (IVDAEA CAPTA, Pl. XV. 1) or the visits of Hadrian to the various provinces of the empire (ACHAIA RESTITVTA and the like).

Of the representation of famous persons connected, either by legend or by history, with the history of the city, the most common is Homer, of whom we have busts or figures at no less than seven cities. The largest series of portraits of this kind is found at Lesbos[1].

§ 7. *Canting Types.*

(*f*) The most obvious of all forms of badge was the *type parlant* or canting or punning type, which represented the issuing authority by means of a pun on his or its name. If we consider the number of possibilities of this kind, the canting type will be found to be comparatively scarce in ancient coinage. Famous instances are the seal (φώκη) at Phocaea (Pl. I. 2), the rose (ῥόδον) at Rhodes (Pl. V. 5) and Rhoda, the lion's head at Leontini, the wild celery (σέλινον) at the Sicilian Selinus[2], the pomegranate (σίδη) at Side, the apple (μῆλον) at Melos, the table (τράπεζα) at Trapezus (Pl. IV. 7)[3]. Possibly the

[1] See below, ch. viii. § 3.
[2] But this, like the head of Athena at Athens, really belongs to another class; see above, p. 173.
[3] The objects piled on the table have usually been called grapes; it is possible, however, that they are meant for coins, and that the table is that of a banker (τραπεζίτης).

race-horse ridden by a jockey on the silver coins of Philip II of Macedon (Pl. VII. 1) embodies a punning allusion to his name.

§ 8. *Ornamental Types.*

(*g*) The types so far classified were adopted for reasons which are or ought to be capable of explanation. But there is another class the adoption of which seems to be purely arbitrary, and that is the ornamental class, which merely consists of a meaningless decorative design. The simplest instance of this is to be found on one of the earliest of all coins (Pl. I. 1). As a matter of fact the instances of this class are comparatively few, and some of them, as the double stellar design on the coins of Corcyra (Pl. II. 7), or the star at Erythrae, may be connected with some religious ideas with which we are not familiar. The arrangement of the reverses of many series of coins—as at Aegina, Cyzicus, and in Lycia in early times—seems, however, to be purely decorative.

§ 9. *Imitative Types.*

(*h*) Finally, it must not be forgotten that a number of types are purely imitative, and were adopted by states in order to obtain currency for their own issues. Striking instances of this practice are to be found in the Asiatic imitations of the coinage of Philip II and Alexander III, or the Gaulish imitations of the gold staters of the former king (Fig. 4, p. 10), or the Himyarite copies of the Athenian coinage. In these, and similar cases, the types have of course no proper relation to the authorities which issued them. Further, among barbarous nations, unintelligent copying led to the production of a meaningless type or pattern, out of which eventually the barbarian engraver evolved some animal or figure. Thus out of the profile head copied by the Anglo-Saxons from Roman coins was developed, through successive degradations, the type of a bird[1]. As a rule, however, the final result is a mere

---

[1] C. F. Keary, *Morphology of Coins*, *Num. Chr.* 1886, Pl. III [Pl. IV. of separate edition], nos. 74-78. In the same way the British Iceni metamorphosed a human head into a boar. Evans, *Ancient British Coins*, Pl. XVI.

pattern, such as that developed by the Gauls out of the rose on the coins of Rhoda in Spain[1].

§ 10. *Classification of Symbols.*

The classification here adopted for types will also serve for what in numismatic language are called symbols. These are, to define them roughly, subsidiary types, and may be broadly divided into two classes, according as they are attributes of the main type, or are disconnected from it, and serve a separate purpose of their own.

The first division needs no discussion. A deity is constantly accompanied by his or her attributes, or attendant objects. These are sometimes brought into direct connexion with the figure, as when Zeus holds a Nike or an eagle on his outstretched hand (Pl. VII. 4)[2]. Or else they are simply placed in the field, as is the sphinx of Artemis on the earliest coins of Perga.

The second division of symbols comprises those which were meant to identify the coin in a further degree than was made possible by the main type alone. In the case of coins issued by a state or ruler through mint officials a symbol was frequently placed on the coin in order to fix the responsibility on the proper person[3].

Another very large division of the second class of symbols comprises those which denote a mint. Such are many of the symbols on the coins struck in imitation of the tetradrachms of Alexander the Great. On these, for example, the rose is the mint-mark of Rhodes, the helmet of Mesembria, the race-torch of Amphipolis, the bee of Ephesus. The imitations of the tetradrachms of Lysimachus are similarly differentiated, those of Byzantium, for instance, bearing a trident (Pl. IX. 2). But the usage of symbols is guided by much less fixed principles than

---

[1] C. F. Keary, *Morphology of Coins*, *Num. Chr.* 1885, Pl. VIII, (I) nos. 20-22.

[2] These types are sometimes described as Zeus Nikephoros and Aëtophoros respectively. But it may be noted that νικηφόρο·, in its concrete sense of 'holding Nike,' has no classical authority; and ἀετοφόρος is only used to signify a standard-bearer.

[3] See above, p. 119.

is the usage of types, and it must be admitted that the great majority of symbols are unexplained.

It has already been noted [1] that in some cases the main type degenerates into a mere mint symbol, while the greater part of the field is occupied with the magistrate's symbol. Occasionally, at least at Cyzicus, the symbol is combined with the main design in a curious way; thus the winged running figure on the stater figured in Pl. I. 5 is represented holding up the tunny by its tail.

[1] Above, pp. 119, 120.

CHAPTER VIII

COIN-INSCRIPTIONS

§ 1. *Inscriptions naming the Issuing Authority.*

THE varied nature of the inscriptions on coins will be better realized from a study of the problems of numismatics in which those inscriptions are adduced as evidence, than from any formal classification. Nevertheless, for the sake of completeness, it is worth while, at the risk of repetition, to distinguish the various motives underlying the inscriptions which were put upon ancient coins.

The first and most obvious object of the inscription was to state the fact that the coin was issued by a certain people or person—to give, in fact, authority to the coin. The ordinary way of doing this was to inscribe the name in the genitive (Ἀκράγαντος, Συρακοσίων [1], *Romano(m)*, Ἀλεξάνδρου). But an adjective would effect the same object. Adjectives constructed from the name of a people or city are not rare (Ἀρκαδικόν from Ἀρκάδες, Σολικόν from Σόλοι, Δερρωνικόν from Δέρρωνες (?), Ῥηγῖνος, Λαρισαία (understanding possibly δραχμή) and the like). Men's names furnish a smaller number. Thus we have Ἀλεξάνδρειος from the name of Alexander tyrant of Pherae in Thessaly (369-357 B.C.). These adjectives, like the genitives, imply a noun, which may either be a general term for 'struck coin' as νόμισμα, παῖμα(?), κόμμα, χαρακτήρ, ἀργύριον [2], or a more special denomination, as στατήρ, δίδραχμον, δραχμή. The staters of Alexander of Pherae accordingly read Ἀλεξάνδρειος, the drachms

---

[1] Before the introduction of ω the genitive plural often has the appearance of a nominative neuter singular.

[2] Φαιστίων τὸ παῖμα (Phaestus Cretae); Σεύθα ἀργύριον (Seuthes of Thrace, end of fifth century), Σεύθα κόμμα, Κότυος χαρακτήρ (Cotys of Thrace, first century B.C.) are instances.

Ἀλεξανδρεία. Certain tetradrachms (τετράδραχμα) of Attic weight struck by Ptolemy I read Ἀλεξάνδρειον Πτολεμαί(ου?), i.e. 'Ptolemy's tetradrachm of Alexander.' The inscription Φαινοῦς or Φαενοῦς εἰμὶ σῆμα (Pl. I. 4) is a modified form belonging rather to the class of descriptive inscriptions to be discussed below, than to the present group. In addition to the use of the genitive and the adjective, there is a rare use of the nominative case. Most of the names in the nominative found on pre-imperial coins seem to be descriptive of types; but such an inscription as ΑΘΕ Ο ΔΕΜΟΣ (Ἀθηναίων ὁ δῆμος) is an undoubted instance of the use of the nominative in place of the ordinary genitive. ᗡΑΝΚᒪᕮ on the early coins of the city afterwards known as Messana (Pl. III. 4) is descriptive, in as much as the type represents the harbour of the city. Τάρας, on Tarentine coins, is usually descriptive, as when it is written beside the figures riding on a dolphin (Pl. XI. 1); but it is also found with types of which it is not a description[1]. Other instances are ΚΥΜΕ (Cumae in Campania), ROMA.

§ 2. *Varieties of Titulature.*

The simple naming of the person or people on their coins is the rule in the pre-Alexandrine period. After Alexander's assumption on his coins of the title king[2], the custom of writing oneself down as king begins to prevail in most of the monarchies. The steps taken by various tyrants to throw off constitutional hindrances are marked in this way. Thus the coinage of Agathocles falls into three periods, marking by their inscriptions the gradual increase of his confidence :—

Period I. B.C. 317–310. Inscription, Συρακοσίων on all metals.

Period II. B.C. 310–307. Inscription, Ἀγαθοκλέος on gold; Συρακοσίων Ἀγαθόκλειος, (Κόρας) Ἀγαθόκλειος or Ἀγαθοκλέος on silver; Συρακοσίων on bronze.

Period III. B.C. 307–289. Ἀγαθοκλέος Βασιλέος on gold and bronze.

---

[1] E.g., Head, *Coins of the Ancients*, Pl. 7, no. 6 rev.
[2] As early as the beginning of the fifth century, however, on the coins of Getas, king of the Edoni (Pl. II. 9), we find the inscriptions: Γέτα Βασιλέως Ἠδωνᾶν, Γέτα Βασιλεύ Ἠδωνίων, and ΓΕΤΑΣ ΗΔΟΝΕΟΝ ΒΑΣΙΛΕΥΣ. See Babelon in *Journ. Internat.* i. p. 7.

Similarly the tyrant Nabis begins with his name alone (Νάβιος), but on the later tetradrachm in the British Museum he uses the style Βαιλέος Νάβιος [1].

The strings of names characteristic of the later period of the Greek regal coinage, and of the third century A.D., are in curious contrast to the good taste of the early inscriptions.

The titles of Roman emperors on Roman and Greek coins present enormous variety of arrangement, almost every permutation of names being employed, especially on the Greek coins of the imperial epoch. Titles such as Augustus, Caesar (Σεβαστός, Καῖσαρ) are sometimes found alone on coins of the early Empire. In time, however, greater particularization became necessary. Then the simplest form comprised merely the name with the title *Caesar* or *Augustus*: thus *Antoninus Augustus, Gallienus Augustus*, Αὐρήλιος Καῖσαρ.

On coins issued after the death of an emperor or empress, the style is DIVVS ANTONINVS, DIVA DOMITILLA AVGVSTA, DIVO TRAIANO &c., and the reigning emperor is frequently described as DIVI F(ilius).

More commonly than the simpler appellations are found the long strings of titles such as *Pontifex Maximus, Tribunicia Potestate, Consul, Imperator, Pater Patriae*, to mention only the more usual; and to these had to be added the complimentary titles such as Britannicus, Germanicus, Parthicus. We thus meet with inscriptions such as:—

Imp(eratori) Caes(ari) Ner(vae) Traian(o) Optim(o) Aug(usto) Ger(manico) Dac(ico) Parthico P(ontifici) M(aximo) Tr(ibunicia) P(otestate) Co(n)s(uli) VI P(atri) P(atriae) S(enatus) P(opulus) Q(ue) R(omanus).

By the time of Vespasian it had become usual to put *Imp(erator)* first in the inscription, followed by *Caes(ar)*, as in the inscription just quoted, then by the other names. The most usual arrangement in the Greek coins was similarly (to take an instance from Antoninus Pius)

Αὐτοκράτωρ Καῖσαρ Τίτος Αἴλιος Ἀδριανὸς Ἀντωνῖνος Εὐσεβὴς Σεβαστός,

variously abbreviated. But on the whole the titles of emperors on Greek coins are more modest than on Roman [2].

---

[1] See above, p. 82, n. 1.
[2] It is rare, except on semi-Roman issues such as those of Antiochia and

Besides the titles already mentioned, there are others which play a considerable part at a later period. *Pius* (Εὐσεβής) is not uncommon after its introduction by Antoninus, and *Felix* (Εὐτυχής) occurs from the time of Commodus. From this time onwards the conjunction of *Pius Felix* slowly becomes more usual, until after the time of Gallienus it is the rule. At the same time it becomes not unusual to drop the *Im-p(erator)*; the Caesar is called *Nob(ilissimus) Caes(ar)*[1]. In the time of Constantine I we find the style *D(ominus) N(oster)*, and the regular formula is now **D. N. CONSTANTINVS P. F. AVG.** In the fifth century the end of the formula is modified to *Perp(etuus) Aug(ustus)*, often abbreviated to **PP. AVG.**

The titles assumed by kings and emperors mostly explain themselves. But among those belonging to cities, especially in Asia Minor, under the Romans and earlier, there are titles of which the meaning is less evident, and which throw some light on Greek life[2]. The title νεωκόρος (or νεοκόρος), often conferred on men, was also granted to cities. It means apparently 'temple-keeper,' and *par excellence* keeper of the temple of the Augustan cult, νεωκόρος τῶν Σεβαστῶν[3]. When the title was confirmed, as in the case of Ephesus, a second, third, or fourth time, this was duly noted; so that we read **B, Γ,** or **Δ ΝΕΩΚΟΡΩΝ**, at various times, on the coins of Ephesus.

The title πρώτη, according to the most probable explanation, refers to the precedence accorded to the city in the great games of the various κοινά. That the same city did not always hold the first place is clear from the fact that, for instance, both Ephesus and Smyrna call themselves 'first in Asia.' Magnesia in Ionia is content with the somewhat paltry title of ἑβδόμη τῆς Ἀσίας.

Μητρόπολις is a title which usually implies little more than our word metropolis — the chief city of a district. It is doubtful

---

Caesarea, to find the consulship, pontificate, &c., mentioned. I give, however, the inscription of a coin of Trajan struck at Antiochia in Syria: Αὐτοκρ(άτωρ) Καῖσ(αρ) Νέρ(βας) Τραϊανὸς Σεβ(αστὸς) Γερμ(ανικὸς) Δημαρχ(ικῆς) Ἐξ(ουσίας) Ὕπατ(ος) β′ (i. e. *Tr. Pot. Cos.* II).

[1] Rarely on Greek coins Ἐπιφ(ανέστατος) Καῖσαρ.
[2] See the list in Head, *H. N.* pp. lxxiv f.
[3] See P. Monceaux, *de Communi Asiae Provinciae*, Paris, 1885.

whether it even always bore this sense; thus, when Anazarbus, in close proximity to Tarsus, the chief city of Cilicia, calls itself *metropolis*, it is possible that the title is nothing more than a boast.

Ἱερά and ἄσυλος are usually combined in such a formula as Ἀντιοχέων Μητροπόλεως τῆς ἱερᾶς καὶ ἀσύλου. The combination is commonest in Syria and Cilicia from late Seleucid times onwards. The number of sanctuaries with the right of asylum was very considerably restricted by Tiberius, in 22 A.D., since the asyla had become harbours for all sorts of criminals.

Αὐτόνομος, in pre-Roman times, implies certain privileges of self-government conferred by kings on cities in their district. It is confined to southern Asia Minor (from Pisidia eastwards) and Syria. The privilege of autonomy conferred by the Romans was of course of a limited kind. It was embodied in a written constitution (*lex*), which preserved as far as possible all the old constitution of the state, and granted independence in jurisdiction and finance, and freedom from Roman garrisons.

Ἐλευθέρα is found as a title on Roman imperial coins of a few cities in Asia Minor[1], many of which (such as Termessus in Pisidia) also call themselves αὐτόνομος. Strictly ἐλευθέρα is the translation of *libera*. The free cities with this title were known as *civitates sine foedere immunes et liberae*, and their position rested on a law or *senatus consultum*[2].

Σύμμαχος (with or without Ῥωμαίων) is a rare title on Greek imperial coins; it is evidently equivalent to the Latin *civitas foederata*.

Among the titles assumed by cities are some expressing their boasted origin, such as Λακεδαιμονίων, which is the standing addition to the ethnic Ἀμβλαδέων at Amblada in Pisidia. Others are adopted as a compliment to Emperors, as Σευηριανὴ Μακρεινιανὴ Μητρόπολις Ταρσός.

The most magniloquent of all inscriptions is probably that found at Pergamum on a coin of Caracalla: Ἡ Πρώτη τῆ[ς

---

[1] Also on coins of Chersonesus Taurica, though possibly the word ἐλευθέρας is there an epithet of Artemis.

[2] See for instance the *SCtum de Aphrodisiensibus* (Bruns-Mommsen, *Fontes*³, p. 167). Termessus Major received its privileges (*leiberi amicei socieique p. R. sunto*) by the *lex Antonia* of 71 B.C. (op. cit. p. 91).

'Α]σίας, καὶ Μ[ητρό]πολις Πρώτη, καὶ τρὶς Νεωκόρος Πρώτη τῶν Σεβαστῶν, Περγαμηνῶν πόλις.

If the inscription of the name of the supreme authority was found necessary as a guarantee, that of the official who was directly or indirectly responsible for the issue was, in many places, found to be desirable as early as the fifth century. The principles which governed these inscriptions have however been described elsewhere[1]. After the beginning of imperial times, they are practically confined to the Province of Asia.

§ 3. *Inscriptions naming the Type.*

The most interesting and, to archaeologists in general, the most important class of coin inscriptions comprises those which name or explain the type. These may be roughly classified as:—

1. Names of persons and personifications;
2. Names of objects.

1. Names of persons and personifications.

(*a*) Real persons. The names of rulers are of course the most common of this class (see above, pp. 181 f.). With them may be classed personages such as Octavia, Antinoüs, and others connected with the rulers. The deification of kings and emperors has already been alluded to. In the case of the kings the most interesting inscriptions of this class are found on the coins of the Seleucidae and Ptolemies. Thus the word Θεῶν accompanies the heads of Ptolemy Soter and Berenice on coins struck by Philadelphus and Arsinoë (Pl. VII. 8). Ptolemy Philometor calls himself Πτολεμαίου Βασιλέως Φιλομήτορος Θεοῦ. Antiochus IV of Syria has the title Βασιλέως 'Αντιόχου Θεοῦ 'Επιφανοῦς Νικηφόρου.

Personages of historic fame, in proportion to the number of coins extant, are not to any extent commonly named on coins unless they happen to be rulers[2]. Homer is, however, named on coins of Amastris, Nicaea, Cyme in Aeolis, Smyrna, Chios,

---

[1] Above, ch. v.
[2] L. Bürchner, 'Griechische Münzen mit Bildnissen hist. Privatpersonen,' *Z. f. N.* ix. pp. 109 ff.

and Ios (at the last island in the genitive, Ὁμήρου). Of famous persons of a less vague antiquity named on coins we may mention Pittacus (Φιττακός), Alcaeus (Ἀλκαῖος), and Sappho (Ψαπφώ) at Mytilene. Mytilene in fact can reckon more portraits of historical persons than all other Greek towns put together [1]. On Roman coins it was a common custom for a moneyer to name any famous ancestor of his. To this we owe, for instance, the fancy portrait of L. Junius Brutus, with the inscription *L. Brutus Prim. Cos.*, on the aureus of his descendant M. Junius Brutus.

(*b*) The names of deities are among the most important inscriptions of this class, as they enable us to identify many types which would otherwise remain, in numismatic phraseology, 'uncertain deities.' The names occur in all four cases, the nominative (Διόνυσος Κτίστης at Tium) having no special significance, the genitive (Διὸς Ἐλευθερίου at Syracuse) implying that the coin, or possibly the object represented on it, is the sacred property of the deity, the dative (*Sanct. Deo Soli Elagabal.* on coins of Elagabalus with the stone of Emisa, Pl. XV. 6) meaning that the coin is dedicated to the deity [2]. The accusative is very rare, in any cases except of divinized human beings; as Ἰου(λίαν) Πρόκλαν ἡρωίδα (at Mytilene), Θεὰν Αἰολὶν Ἀγριππίναν (also at Mytilene), or personifications of Rome, or the Senate (Θεὰν Ῥώμην, Θεὸν Σύνκλητον, common in Asia). The inscription Δία Ἰδαῖον Ἰλιεῖς is, however, found on a coin of New Ilium. This limitation would appear to show that with the accusative is supposed to be understood ἐτίμησαν ἡ βουλὴ καὶ ὁ δῆμος or some other of the similar phrases found in honorary inscriptions, and not a word expressing *worship* [3].

---

[1] See W. Wroth, *Brit. Mus. Catal., Troas*, &c., pp. lxx ff. To his list add Σέξτος νέος Μάρ(κου?) and Ἀνδρομέδα νέα Λεσβώ(νακτος), Imhoof-Blumer, *Z f. N.* xx. p. 286.

[2] Sometimes, however, the deity is not represented, but only an attribute or a temple, in which case the genitive would imply that the thing represented was the deity's property, the dative that the thing was dedicated to the deity.

[3] The phrase Δία Ἰδαῖον Ἰλιεῖς must be explained by the supposition that the type represents a statue set up by the city, so that we may understand some such word as ἀνέστησαν. Kubitschek has shown (*Oesterr. Jahreshefte*, i. pp. 184 ff.) that this and similar types, occurring at Ilium in the time of Commodus and his successors, belong to a series of statues of which the inscribed bases of three are extant.

It is common to find epithets of the gods without their proper names; such as Δερρωναῖος (Apollo) on a coin of the Paeonian king Lycceius; Σώτειρα (Persephone) at Cyzicus; Σωσίπολις (Tyche?) at Gela.

A very large number of the deities named on coins are, as we have already noticed, river-gods. The figure of the god is quite commonly accompanied by his name, as Ἀμενανίς at Catana, Μέανδρος at Dionysopolis (Pl. XIV. 12), and *Anthius* at the Pisidian Antioch. A pretty instance of the personification of rivers is given by the coin of Laodicea in Phrygia, already mentioned, where the two rivers Λύκος and Κάπρος are represented by a wolf and a boar respectively (Pl. XIV. 6).

The names of heroes and heroines like Αἴας the son of Oïleus on the coins of the Opuntian Locrians, or the Sicanian hero Λεύκασπις at Syracuse (Pl. XI. 4), are comparatively uncommon, except perhaps when the hero gave his name to the city. Such was the case with Τάρας at Tarentum (although, as we have already seen, the inscription sometimes refers to the town rather than to the hero). In later times the word Κτίστης is sometimes added (Μενεσθεὺς Κτίστης at Elaea in Aeolis). The founder of course is frequently nothing more than a late invention, and a mere personification of the state, of the same kind as the helmeted goddess who is called ROMA (Pl. XI. 8, 10, 11; XV. 3), or the goddess wearing a turreted crown whose bust is one of the commonest types on Greek imperial coins (Αἰγή or Αἰγᾶς at Aegae in Aeolis, Πόλις at Prostanna in Pisidia). Countries of course may be named as well as cities; thus a coin of Lucius Verus struck at Alexandria, of which the type is a captive seated at the foot of a trophy, reads Ἀρμενία [1].

Elaborate personifications belong chiefly to a late stage of art (though also, to a certain extent, to a very primitive stage). Therefore, although personifications such as Victory (ΑΚΡΜ, i.e. Νίκα, she is named on a coin of Terina struck early in the fifth century) range through the whole period of Greek coinage, except the very earliest, it is from the imperial period and from the coins of the Romans, who were forced by their love of the concrete to personify abstractions to an extreme degree that we must seek examples of names of this class. Of

[1] On this whole subject, see P. Gardner, 'Countries and Cities in Ancient Art,' *Journ. of Hellen. Stud.* ix. (1888) pp. 47 ff.

the personifications of the various elements of the constitution of Greek cities, we find the names—

Βουλή and Ἱερὰ Βουλή (Pl. XIV. 11),
Γερουσία and Ἱερὰ Γερουσία,
Δῆμος (Pl. XIV. 9, 10), Ἱερὸς Δῆμος, Ἐλεύθερος Δῆμος,
Ἐκκλησία [1].

The Roman Senate appears as—

Σύνκλητος,
Ἱερὰ Σύνκλητος,
Θεὸν Σύνκλητον (Pl. XIII. 6),
Θεὰν Σύνκλητον ⎱ rare.
Θεὸς Σύνκλητος ⎰

The solecism *Sacra Senatus* on the coins of the colony of Mallus in Cilicia is evidently due to an attempt to translate the phrase ἱερὰ Σύνκλητος.

Personification is carried to no further degree on Greek coins than on a coin of Pautalia in Thrace, where the river Strymon is represented surrounded by four children named Βότρυς, Στάχυς, Χρυσός, and Ἄργυρος—the chief products of the district.

At Rome conceptions like Liberty were early personified; but not before the Empire do we meet with personifications of the more subtle character of *Abundantia, Laetitia, Aeternitas* (Pl. XV. 5). The desirability of adding the names to these types was less often felt by the Roman die-sinkers than numismatists would wish.

These more elaborate personifications, or at least their artistic forms, were probably due in some part to the influence of Alexandria. On the coins of this city a number of obscure personifications occur and are named (Σημασία, and the like); but quite as remarkable as these are Στόλος at Nicomedia (a nude male figure wearing a rostral crown and holding a rudder) or τὸ Ἀγαθόν at Ephesus (a nude male figure standing with clenched hands).

2. The titles descriptive of things are on the whole less common than the titles we have just classified. The most important are those which name local monuments, such as temples and statues. The form of the monument of Themistocles at

[1] At Aegeae in Cilicia, Imhoof, *J. H. S.* 1898, p. 161.

Magnesia has recently become known to us by the discovery of a bronze coin of Antoninus Pius, on which the hero, who is represented sacrificing, is actually named Θεμιστοκλῆς. Temples not uncommonly are accompanied by an inscription naming the deity to whom they belong, or otherwise identifying them. So the cistophoric 'medallion' struck under Augustus (B.C. 19), for circulation in the province of Asia, bears a representation of the façade of the temple in which the religious union of the Asiatic cities (κοινὸν 'Ασίας) celebrated the cult of Rome and Augustus. In the field stands COM*mune* ASIAE, on the frieze ROM. ET AVGVST. (Pl. XII. 8). More naive is the inscription on a coin of Ephesus struck in the reign of Elagabalus: 'Εφεσίων οὗτοι ναοί. On Roman coins inscriptions such as FORVM TRAIAN*i* (Pl. XV. 2) occasionally describe a type, but they are rare. Of smaller objects it is sufficient to mention the ἱεραπήμη or ἀπήμη ἱερά, the sacred wagon in which the images of Artemis were carried round the city of Ephesus on festal occasions[1]; the τειμαὶ βασιλέως (ivory chair, golden crown, and sceptre, sent to the king by the emperor and senate) on coins of the kings of Bosporus; and the ship 'Αργώ at Magnesia in Ionia.

§ 4. *Inscriptions giving the Reason of Issue.*

Side by side with the legends descriptive of the type must be set the large class of legends explaining the circumstances of the issue. Coins may be issued for a commemorative purpose, much like one class of our modern medals; or the issue may be complimentary, in which case there is again a parallel in the modern personal medal. The public ordinance in virtue of which the coin is issued, or the purpose for which the issue is required, may need commemoration.

Commemorative inscriptions are fairly common, more so, however, on Roman coins than on Greek. 'Ιουδαίας ἑαλωκυίας on the Judaean, and *Iudaea capta* on the Roman coins of Vespasian (Pl. XV. 1) and Titus commemorate the fall of Jerusalem in A.D. 70. 'Ομόνοια is a common inscription on imperial coins, commemorating a more or less complimentary alliance between two or more cities. The first Roman denarius on which a

---

[1] *Journ. He'len. Studies,* 1897, p. 87, Pl. II. 17.

contemporary event is alluded to was struck by the aediles M. Aemilius Scaurus and C. Plautius Hypsaeus in B.C. 58 (Pl. XII. 5). On the obverse is Aretas (*Rex Aretas*) king of the Nabathaeans, who submitted to Scaurus, governor of Syria, in 62 B.C. He kneels beside his camel. The rest of the inscription is *M. Scaur(us) Aed(ilis) Cur(ulis). Ex S(enatus) C(onsulto)*. On the reverse is commemorated the capture of Privernum— *Preiver(num) Captu(m)* — in 341 B.C. by *C. Hypsae(us) Co(n)s(ul)*, ancestor of the moneyer *P. Hypsaeus Aed(ilis) Cur(ulis)*. On an aureus of Augustus, struck in B C. 17, the legend *Quod viae mun(itae) sunt* refers to the restoration of the Via Flaminia. Among the commonest of the inscriptions on Roman imperial coins are some which refer to the decennial and similar sacrifices. Annual festivals were held, at which vows were offered for the safety of the emperors; and at recurring periods of five years special importance was attached to these festivals. Some of the inscriptions simply mention the vows or games—*Quinquennales, Primi decennales, Votis decennalibus, Votis vicennalibus, Votis X et XX, Votis XX sic XXX, Votis V multis X*.

Others commemorate more specifically the offering of the vows—*Vota suscepta decenn. III, Vota suscepta XX*, or their fulfilment—*Vot. solut. dec.*

On the Greek coins struck by the Roman provincial administration at Alexandria, we meet with inscriptions such as περίοδος δεκάτη, περίοδος δεκαετηρίς, or δεκαετηρὶς Κυρίου.

The commencement of a new age (*Saeculum novum*) is recorded on an aureus of the Emperor Philip issued in 248 A.D [1].

The complimentary significance of many of the inscriptions in which magistrates' names occurred has already been pointed out (p. 139). It will suffice here to enumerate some of the complimentary inscriptions addressed to emperors. On Roman coins we have such inscriptions as *Augusto ob c(ives) s(ervatos), equester ordo Principi Iuventutis*. On Greek coins, we may note at Nicopolis in Epirus, Νέρωνι δημοσίῳ πάτρωνι Ἑλλάδος : at Caesarea in Cappadocia and Nicaea, Κομόδου βασιλεύοντος ὁ κόσμος εὐτυχεῖ: at Caesarea and Tarsus, εἰς ἐῶνα (αἰῶνα) τοὺς Κυρίους [2] : at Cius in Bithynia, Σευήρου βασιλεύοντος ὁ κόσμος εὐτυχεῖ, μακάριοι Κιανοί. These

---

[1] The thousandth year of the city began, according to Varro, on the day equivalent to our April 21, 247 A.D.

[2] See B. Pick in *Journ. Internat.* i. p. 459.

'loyal' inscriptions are the nearest approximation furnished by ancient coins to the modern coin-motto[1].

Except at Rome, where the brass and copper coins under the Empire, and a number of other coins under the Republic, were issued by decree of the Senate — usually recorded S(enatus) C(onsulto) — the ordinance commanding the issue is not commonly mentioned. To the Latin phrase corresponds the Greek Δόγματι Συνκλήτου, which is found at Laodicea in Phrygia. Why this particular city should have required the special sanction of the Roman Senate—for Σύνκλητος always means that body—or, if that sanction was necessary for all cities of the Empire, why it should be mentioned here alone, is a mystery[2].

But the actual object for which coins were issued is sometimes mentioned, often indirectly, directly seldom. Coins struck in Sicily about B.C. 340, when Timoleon united the Sicilians, bear the inscription Συμμαχικόν, denoting that the issue was intended to serve the needs of the allies. The inscription Συν on the alliance coins of the early fourth century (above, p. 112) is of the same kind. The little coin issued by Miletus for the purposes of the Didymean sanctuary, and the crowds who doubtless frequented it, is inscribed ἐγ Διδύμων ἱερή[3]. The occasion which prompted the issue of coins is most distinctly stated on the coins struck by the urban quaestors L. Calpurnius Piso Caesoninus and Q. Servilius Caepio in 100 B.C. out of a special grant made by the Senate for the purchase of corn: *Piso Caepio Q(uaestores) ad fru(mentum) cmu(ndum), ex S(enatus) C(onsulto)*.

The most fertile source of coinage in the provinces of the Roman Empire, and a very rich source in Rome itself, was found in festivals. These festivals—and no city of slight importance

---

[1] They are foreign to the pre-Roman period. The reading of a gold stater supposed to bear the inscription Κυραναῖοι Πτολεμαίῳ is very uncertain (*Brit. Mus. Catal., Ptolemies*, p. xx).

[2] Pick (in *Journ. Internat.* i. p. 459, note 1) has pointed out that the abbreviations Γ. B. and Γ. Γ. on coins of Tarsus and Anazarbus cannot mean (as they have hitherto been supposed to mean) γράμματι or γνώμῃ βουλῆς and γερουσίας, but that the first letter must signify some title of honour like νεωκόρος (possibly γυμνασίαρχος), and B and Γ 'for the second' and 'third time' respectively.

[3] The weight is only 1.75 g., i.e. half a Phoenician drachm. The sacred drachm may, it has been suggested (Head, *H.N.* p. 504), have been only half the weight of the trade drachm, so that we may complete the inscription δραχμή.

seems to have been without one, just as fairs were once universal in England—drew together a great concourse of people. Money was therefore needed for their convenience; and as a great number of the athletic and musical contests were for pecuniary rewards, money was also needed for the prizes[1].

The festivals mentioned on Greek coins may be divided into the following classes:—

(i) The four great Hellenic games and festivals named after them: Ὀλύμπια, Πύθια (Fig. 30), Ἴσθμια, Νέμεα.

(ii) Festivals named after divinities: Ἀσκληπιεῖα, Ἥλια, Καβείρια, Καπετώλια—from Jupiter Capitolinus—and the like.

FIG. 30.—Reverse of bronze coin of Delphi (Obv. Bust of Faustina I θεά): ΠΥΘΙΑ Agonistic table, with wreath, vase, five apples, and raven.

(iii) Those named after historical persons, kings, emperors, &c., as: Ἀλεξάνδρεια, Ἀττάληα, Σευήρεια, Γορδιάνηα, Οὐαλεριάνα, Τακίτιος (scil. ἀγών).

(iv) District festivals, as: Κοινὸν Ἀσίας, Κοινὸς τῶν τριῶν Ἐπαρχιῶν, Κοινὸν Μητροπολειτῶν τῶν ἐν Ἰωνίᾳ.

(v) Festivals commemorating a great event, such as Ἄκτια, the battle of Actium, Saeculares Augg(ustorum) the new century (in 1001 A. U. C.).

(vi) General names descriptive of the conditions, nature, or locality of the games. Οἰκουμενικά are games open to all comers; Θεμίδες, games in which a θέμα or money-prize is offered; Εἰσελαστικά, those which involve the triumphal entry (εἰσελαύνειν) of the victor into his native city; Ἰσοπύθια are games in which the conditions and rewards are the same (so far as local importance could make them!) as at the great Pythian games; Periodicum is a game recurring at fixed intervals; ἱεροί are the ἀγῶνες which centred round a sanctuary, or in which the prize consisted of some consecrated thing, such as a wreath pulled in the sacred enclosure, or oil from sacred olive-trees[2]; titles like ἄριστα, μεγάλα merely express importance, πρῶτα that the games were held in the 'first' city of the district.

[1] Still the money-prizes would hardly have been given in anything but gold, so that the local coinage cannot have been issued to this end.

[2] As a matter of fact all these contests are ἱερά (hence the customary neuter termination of their names), so that the expression of the adjective is really unnecessary.

These inscriptions do not occur always singly. In fact we find the various titles combined in such groups as Αὐγούστεια Ἄριστα Ὀλύμπια, Ἱερὸς Ἀτταλέων Ὀλύμπια Οἰκουμενικός, *Certamina Sacra Capitolina Oecumenica Iselastica Heliopolitana*. A combination such as Ὀλύμπια Πύθια may imply that some of the contests were ordered after the Olympian, the rest after the Pythian model; but the piling on of epithets was as a rule a mere advertisement, intended to attract competitors or satisfy local ambitions.

The titles of the games are not infrequently written on the spheroidal vases which were given as prizes, or on the edge of the table on which the prizes were preserved in the temple of the presiding deity until the time came to distribute them.

Besides the titles of the games, a few inscriptions must be mentioned here as having an agonistic significance. Such are ἀγωνοθεσία, γυμνασιαρχία, the offices of agonothetes or president of the games, and gymnasiarch, the director of the gymnasium. The inscription γυμνασιαρχία is usually associated with a large basin, from which the oil was supplied to athletes[1]—an illustration of the fact that the chief duty of the gymnasiarch in imperial times was to supply oil to the people.

The earliest inscription on a Greek coin having direct reference to games is probably the ΑΘΛΑ of the Syracusan decadrachms of Cimon and Evaenetus (Pl. VI. 4, 6). These coins, as recent researches tend to show[2], are to be connected with the victory of the Syracusans over the Athenians at the Assinarus. The word Ἆθλα is written below the panoply (two greaves, helmet, shield, and cuirass) displayed on the basis of the chariot group, which may be taken to represent either victory in general, or the chariot-race which would form the chief event at the games celebrated in commemoration of the victory.

Indirectly connected with games may be a series of names of boats which occur on the bronze coinage of Corcyra in

---

[1] As at Syedra, Anazarbus, and Colybrassus in Cilicia. These are not prize-vases. Pick (*Journ. Intern.* i. 1898, p. 459, note 1) points out that ΓΥΜΝΑϹΙΑΡΧΙΑ cannot be the name of a festival. As regards form, compare ϹΥΝΑΡΧΙΑ at Antiochia in Caria (Head, *Brit. Mus. Catal., Caria*, p. 18, nos. 27, 28) where, apparently, the coins are issued by all, or a number, of the magistrates in combination.

[2] A. J. Evans, *Syracusan Medallions and their Engravers* in *Num. Chr.* 1891, pp. 205 ff.

O

the third century B.C. — names such as Θήρα, Κῶμος, Νεότης, Φωσφόρος. These names are written above the forepart of a galley. The coins, it has been suggested [1], are perhaps connected with races of galleys; the names may, indeed, be those of the galleys victorious in the years in which the coins were struck. At a later period, the word Νίκα is written on the side of the galley—'a still more unmistakable allusion to a victory won in galley-racing.'

§ 5. *Mint-marks and Artists' Signatures.*

Inscriptions relating to the actual production of coins fall into two main divisions; those relating to the engraving of the die (in other words, artists' signatures), and mint-marks. The latter are either the actual names of cities — usually abbreviated, as BY for Byzantium, CON for Constantinople, TR for Trier, SIS for Siscia [2];—or marks indicating the officina which produced the coin (such as the abbreviated names on the Athenian tetradrachms of the 'new style') or the number of the issue [3].

Artists' signatures are confined to a comparatively short period, and that the finest in the history of Greek coins. The list of known names which can be regarded as belonging to engravers is small enough to be reproduced here [4].

```
'Α...           Terina.
*'Αλ.. or Δα..  Elis.
'Αναν...        Messana (Num. Chr. 1896. p. 123).
*'Αρ...         Leontini (Num. Chr. 1894, pp. 207, 214).
'Αριστόξε(νος)  Metapontum.
*Δα... or 'Αλ... Elis.
'Εξακεστίδας (and abbreviations)  Camarina.
Εὐαίνετο (and abbr.)  Camarina, Catana, Syracuse.
Εὐαρχίδας       Syracuse (Evans, Syracusan Medallions, p. 189).
Εὐθ...          Syracuse, *Elis.
Εὐκλείδα (and abbr.)  Syracuse.
Εὐμήνου (and abbr.)  Syracuse (sometimes written with ε for η).
```

[1] P. Gardner, *Brit. Mus Catal*, *Thessa'y to Aetolia*, p. xlix, and *J. H. S.* ii. p. 96.
[2] See Appendix III.
[3] For further details see above, ch. v.
[4] See A. von Sallet, *Die Künstlerinschriften auf griech. Münzen*, 1871; R. Weil, *Die Künstlerinschriften der sicil. Münzen*, 1884. An asterisk is affixed to those names which may possibly belong to magistrates, and not engravers.

Ἥρα...	Velia.
Ἡρακλείδας	Catana.
Θεύδοτος ἐπόει	Clazomenae.
Ἰμ... or Ἰμ...	Syracuse (*Brit. Mus. Catal., Sicily*, p. 181, no. 233).
Ἱπποκράτης	See Κρατησίππο.
*Ἴστορος	Thurium (*Num. Chr.* 1896, p. 138).
Κ... ἐ(πύει?)	Rhegium.
Κίμων the elder	Himera (Evans, op. cit. p. 175).
Κίμων the younger	Messana, Metapontum, Syracuse (Evans, op. cit. pp. 180, 187, &c.).
Κλευδώρου	Velia.
Κρατησίππο or Ἱπποκράτης	Rhegium.
Μαι...	Himera (Evans, op. cit. p. 180, and *Num. Chr.* 1896, p. 138).
*Μολοσσύς	Thurium (*Num. Chr.* 1896, p. 138).
Μυρ...	Agrigentum.
Νεύαντος ἐπύει	Cydonia (*Num. Chr.* 1894, p. 9).
*Νίκανδρο	Thurium (*Num. Chr.* 1896, p. 138).
*Ὀλυμ...	Arcadia.
Π...	Terina.
Παρμε...	Syracuse.
*Πο...	Elis.
Πολυ...	Metapontum.
Προκλῆς	Catana, Naxos (Sicil.).
Πυθόδωρος	Aptera and Polyrhenium (Crete).
Σώσων	Syracuse.
*Τετ...	Olynthus.
Φ...	Thurium, Heraclea Lucan., Neapolis, Velia, Terina, Pandosia (*Num. Chr.* 1896, p. 139).
Φιλισ...	Terina.
Φιλιστίων or Φιλιστίωνος	Velia.
Φρυ...	Thurium (*Num. Chr.* 1896, p. 138).
Φρύγιλλος (and abbr.)	Syracuse.
*Χαρι...	Arcadia.
Χοιρίων	Catana.

It will be noticed that the practice of signing coins is almost confined to Sicily and southern Italy; of names certainly belonging to engravers, there are none from Greece Proper, two from Crete, and only one from Asia Minor.

The difficulty of judging whether the names represent engravers or not is caused by the fact that it is very rare to find the verb ἐπόει, which (or the equivalent of which) is universal in the signature of sculptors. As a general rule the names of engravers are abbreviated and written in smaller characters than those of magistrates, and sometimes in places where the latter would not inscribe their names (as on the ampyx of Cimon's Arethusa, or on a tablet held by the flying Victory, &c. —instances, these, of somewhat doubtful taste on the part of the artist).

§ 6. *Names and Values of Coins.*

Inscriptions are employed, though not very commonly, to give the denominations of coins. The general terms such as κόμμα, ἀργύριον have already been mentioned. More definite denomination is expressed by inscriptions such as ὀβολός, τετράχαλκον, ἀσσάρια τρία, ἀσσάριον ἥμυσυ (= ἥμισυ, 1½ assaria) and the like at Chios, δίδραχμον (Ephesus, Rhodes), ἑξᾶς (HEΞΑΣ, Segesta), ἡμιοβέλιν (= ἡμιοβέλιον, Aegium). The letter T repeated three times represents the value τμιτεταρτημόριον at Pale; in Arcadia, ὐδ is the dialectal form of ὐβ(ελός); at Colophon the letters ημ combined in a monogram represent ἡμιοβώλιον, and τε, similarly combined, τεταρτημόριον. X is χαλκοῦς at Clazomenae[1]. Similarly, in Italy, L is a common abbreviation for *litra* or *libra*, and S for *semis*.

The method of indicating value by means of numerals is twofold; the figures either mean that the coin weighs so many units, or that its weight is an aliquot part of a greater weight. The sign • • • • is equivalent to *four unciae* or a *triens* (⅓ of a libra); the sign ⁚· to five ounces (πεντόγκιον). On the other hand, the Greek numerals OB, on the late Roman coins, indicate that they are struck at seventy-two to the pound[2].

§ 7. *Dates.*

Inscriptions relating to dates, with the exception of those which merely give the date in numerals[3], are rare. Such as are found really refer only to anniversaries, and are therefore to be classed among commemorative inscriptions. Περίοδος δεκάτη, *Saeculum novum*, and others similar have already been mentioned. Ἔτους ἱεροῦ (Caesarea in Cappadocia), ἔτους νέου ἱεροῦ (Antiochia in Syria), ἔτους δεκ. ἱεροῦ all have reference to the decennalia or similar occasions.

---

[1] These abbreviations all occur on specimens published by Imhoof-Blumer, *Num. Chr.* 1895, pp. 269 ff. See also the Indices to his *Monnaies grecques* and *Griechische Münzen*.

[2] Further instances may be found in ch. ii.

[3] See ch. ix. § 2, pp. 201 ff.

§ 8. Graffiti.

Like other antiquities, coins sometimes bear graffiti, or inscriptions more or less rudely incised upon them with a point, and having no relation to the proper use of the coin. The great majority of such graffiti seem to be dedicatory formulae, and are usually limited to the letters ΑΝΑΘ, or a shorter abbreviation of the word ἀνάθεμα or ἀνάθημα. The most remarkable of all such inscriptions occurs on a stater of Sicyon (Fig. 31), on which is punctured (not, as usual, scratched) an inscription showing that the coin is dedicated as an offering to Artemis: τᾶς 'Αρτάμιτος τᾶς ἐλκεδμονι, i.e. apparently, τᾶς 'Αρτάμιτος

FIG. 31.—Silver Stater of Sicyon with punctured inscription.

τᾶς ἐ(ν) Λ(α)κεδ(αί)μονι[1]. Others, such as Πόρτις καλ. (?) and Φιντέρα, recall the love-inscriptions on vases.

§ 9. Abbreviations.

The foregoing classification of coin-inscriptions deals with them only from the point of view of their significance. But they are valuable for another reason, as offering to the student of epigraphy a quantity of evidence which is the more important because it can usually be dated with accuracy. As regards the forms of the letters, the disposition of words, the use of monograms and ligatures, some idea of the usage on coins is given in Chapter IX. Here we may touch on one other small point. This is the method of abbreviation adopted in order to get legends into a confined space. The punctured inscription on the coin of Sicyon already mentioned is an instance of abbreviation of a peculiarly clumsy kind. Syncope of this kind is excessively rare on Greek coins; the form Βα υς for Βασιλεύς at Smyrna being the only certain instance among official coin inscriptions earlier than imperial times. The

---

[1] J. H. S. 1898, p. 302, where references are given to the literature of the subject.

form Αὐτκρα for Αὐτοκράτωρ is so common on Greek imperial coins that it must be no blunder, but a deliberate syncopation. The form CB for Σεβαστός, though easily explicable as a blunder, may perhaps be another instance of this method. The forms IC XC, and the like, of course become common in Byzantine times. A monogrammatic abbreviation of Καῖσαρ, consisting only of the letters KA and P, is found in early imperial times at Chalcedon and Byzantium [1].

The common method of abbreviation is, however, that in which a certain number of letters are dropped from the end of the word. The Latin *cos* for *consul* stands halfway between this and the syncopated form.

In later Roman times, in the third century A.D., a form of abbreviation for the expression of the plural is introduced. This is the familiar doubling of the last consonant in the abbreviation, of which the form AVGG or AVGGG for two or three Augusti is the commonest. From coins struck in the Greek part of the Roman world it is sufficient to quote Γαλλιηνὸς Οὐαλεριανὸς Π. Λικίννιοι Σεββ. from a coin of Adada in Pisidia, and *Victoriae DDD. NNN.* (*i.e. trium dominorum nostrorum*) from a coin of Pisidian Antioch with the portrait of Caracalla [2].

[1] Imhoof-Blumer in *Journ. Intern.* 1898, pp. 15 f.
[2] The three *domini* are presumably Septimus Severus, Caracalla, and Geta.

CHAPTER IX

THE DATING OF COINS

The numismatist is often heard to boast that, of all objects of antiquity, coins can be the most surely dated. At the worst, few experienced numismatists will differ by more than half a century in ordinary cases as to the date of a particular coin. There are of course instances, as in the case of the early electrum coinage, where opinions may diverge more widely. But in the ordinary series of Greek coins it is seldom that such a difficulty can occur.

In view of this fact—for the boast is largely justified—the importance of coins as affording criteria for the dating of other works of art can hardly be over-estimated. It is worth while, therefore, to analyze, so far as is possible in a brief space, the principles according to which the age of a coin is decided. Some of these are sufficiently obvious, others less so. The cataloguer, it must be admitted, does not always state definitely to himself his reasons for placing one coin later than another. His reasons, as a rule, are complex. It is impossible, therefore, in what follows, to give more than a slight indication of the many kinds of evidence which have to be taken into account.

§ 1. *Dating by the Evidence of History.*

The most obvious means of dating a coin is naturally the external evidence of history. The coins of Himera must all be earlier than 408 B.C., since in that year the city was utterly destroyed. The large flat coins of Sybaris for a similar reason belong to a period previous to 510 B.C. The gold coin of Athens bearing the name of King Mithradates and his partisan Aristion (Pl. IX. 7) must belong to the year 87-86 B.C. when the latter was in power. And the large ten-drachm piece of Syracuse, of early style (Pl. III. 6), must be the Demareteion said to have been struck out of the present of money made to Demarete by the grateful Carthaginians for her intercession after the defeat of Himera.

The earliest coins of Alabanda in Caria, as is clear from their style, are not earlier than the beginning of the second century B.C. These coins bear for types a head of Apollo and a Pegasos. with the inscription ΑΛΑΒΑΝΔΕΩΝ and a magistrate's name. Now there exist a number of coins of the same fabric and with the same types, but with the inscription ΑΝΤΙΟΧΕΩΝ. We know that in 197 B.C. 'Antiochus III, after having made himself master of Ephesus, proceeded to plant colonies in various towns of Asia Minor, and in his honour these towns adopted for a time the name of Antioch. Among them was doubtless Alabanda, which bore the name of Antiochia for a short period between B.C. 197 and the defeat of Antiochus at the battle of Magnesia in B.C. 190.... After the defeat of Antiochus... Alabanda resumed its original name[1].' It is to this short period of seven or eight years, therefore, that the group of coins, with the types of Alabanda and the name of Antioch, must be referred.

A second case of a change of name attested by history, and enabling us to date a group of coins, is furnished by Catana in Sicily. In 476 B.C. Hiero expelled the original Naxian inhabitants, and replaced them by Syracusans, changing the name of the city to Aetna. In 461 B.C. the Syracusan colonists were themselves expelled, and the city reverted to its old name. The small group of coins with a head of Silenus and the inscription ΑΙΤΝΑΙΟΝ or (abbreviated) ΑΙΤΝΑΙ must, therefore, be attributed to the period B.C. 476–461, and interpolated in the series with the name of Catana. At the same time they must be distinguished from the coins of Aetna-Inessa, the place to which the Syracusans expelled from Catana retired, and from which coins were not issued until a considerably later period.

The city of Termessus Major, in Pisidia, received certain privileges from the Romans in 71 B.C. In the year 39 B.C.

[1] Head, *Brit. Mus. Catal., Caria*, pp. xxvii, xxviii.

Pisidia was added to the territories of the Galatian king Amyntas. Both events are of a kind likely to cause changes of some sort in the coinage of the place affected. Now a series of coins, which their style alone would enable us to assign to the first century B.C., bear dates ranging from 1 to 32. They therefore exactly fit the interval between 71 and 39 B.C., to which period we are justified in assigning them [1].

It would be easy to multiply instances of this method of dating; but it must be remembered that as a rule it is only possible to date isolated coins or groups of coins in this way. From the *points d'appui* thus obtained, it is possible to work backwards or forwards, with the help of other criteria.

§ 2. *Coins bearing Dates.*

The custom of actually placing a date on coins, now universal, is of sporadic occurrence in ancient times. The dates, when they do occur, are computed according to eras or regnal years. The mention of an eponymous official is of course equivalent to giving a date, and it is only our want of information that prevents this indication being of any value except in rare cases. Some coins are even dated to a month; such are the Athenian tetradrachms of the 'new style' bearing letters indicating the month in which they were issued [2].

Of the eras [3] some were computed from the foundation of a dynasty, others from some event of local or universal importance. For instance, the Seleucid era was calculated from October 1, 312 B.C.—from the victory of Seleucus and Ptolemy over Demetrius at Gaza. The Actian era began with the defeat of M. Antonius at Actium in B.C. 31.

It is often impossible to discover the exact date from which an era is reckoned. But the following will serve as an illustration of the method to be adopted.

We have coins of Macrinus struck at Aegeae in Cilicia, and bearing the dates ΓΞC and ΔΞC. Macrinus was proclaimed emperor on April 11, 217. He died in July, 218. ΓΞC = 263, ΔΞC = 264.

---

[1] *Brit. Mus. Catal., Lycia,* &c., p. lxxxix.   [2] See above, p. 122.
[3] See the list in the Index (pp. 792, 793) of Head's *Historia Numorum.*

July 218 A.D. was in the 264th year of the era.
Therefore   ,,   1 A.D.   ,,   ,,   47th   ,,   ,,
            ,,   1 B.C.   ,,   ,,   46th   ,,   ,,
            ,,   46 B.C. ,,   ,,   1st   ,,   ,,
Again April 11, 217 A.D. ,,   ,,   263rd ,,   ,,
therefore ,, ,, 46 B.C. ,,   ,,   1st   ,,   ,,

Therefore the era was reckoned from some day between July 47 B.C. and April 11, 46 B.C. Now it was in the autumn of 47 B.C. that Caesar settled the affairs of Asia Minor after the battle of Zela. The era of Aegeae, therefore, probably dates from this epoch.

For the purpose of finding a date, given according to a known ancient era, in terms of years B.C. or A.D., it is useful to have a table giving the exact correspondence. Or, from such a table as follows, it is easy to construct formulae for obtaining the exact equivalent.

In this table, we assume two imaginary eras, one beginning July 1, B.C. 6, the other beginning July 1, A.D. 2.

				In terms of era beginning July 1, B.C. 6	In terms of era beginning July 1, A.D. 2
July 1, B.C. 6, to June 30, B.C. 5				= Year 1	
,,	5	,,	,, 4	= ,, 2	
,,	4	,,	,, 3	= ,, 3	
,,	3	,,	,, 2	= ,, 4	
,,	2	,,	,, 1	= ,, 5	
,,	1	,,	A.D. 1	= ,, 6	
July 1, A.D. 1		,,	,, 2	= ,, 7	
,,	2	,,	,, 3	= ,, 8	= Year 1
,,	3	,,	,, 4	= ,, 9	= ,, 2
,,	4	,,	,, 5	= ,, 10	= ,, 3
,,	5	,,	,, 6	= ,, 11	= ,, 4

It is necessary, however, to remember that an era was not always computed from the actual date at which the epoch-making event happened, but the current year in which it happened was often regarded as the first year of the new era. Thus, in that part of the world where the year began in September, if the event happened in June, A.D. 30, the first year of the new era would probably run from September A.D. 29 to September A.D. 30.

Regnal dates are merely eras on a small scale, and have to be calculated with the allowances already mentioned.

Dates may be recognized by the word ΕΤΟΥΣ (often abbreviated to ΕΤ); in Alexandria, and occasionally elsewhere, by the sign L (derived from an Egyptian sign which signifies that the letters following it represent numerals). Numerals are frequently surmounted by a horizontal line.

§ 3. *Dating by Style and Fabric.*

The safest of all internal criteria, within certain limits, is style. Style for purposes of dating must, of course, be used in conjunction with fabric. It is here that the numismatist has an advantage over the student of sculpture or of gems. The raw material of sculpture or gem has been more or less the same at all periods. But when a type of late style is found on a flan of early fabric, the combination must be false; and when a type of early style occurs on a flan of late fabric, the combination is either false or due to archaism. The latter can easily be detected. Fabric and style together, therefore, form a most valuable criterion, because of the counter-checks which they furnish. There are, however, several pitfalls in the path of the unwary. The tendency to archaism in some states—notably Athens—is the most serious. In the case of Athens, the archaic fabric and style continue down to the introduction of the 'new style' about 220 B.C. In other states, such as Cyzicus, the archaism is restricted to fabric, the old-fashioned 'mill-sail' incuse square being preserved on Cyzicene electrum down to the middle of the fourth century. At Rhodes, again, and in the neighbouring ports of Asia Minor, the incuse square reappears in the second century B.C. Conversely an archaic type—usually representing some revered cultus-figure, such as the Artemis of Ephesus—may be represented down to quite a late date in imperial times.

A second danger lies in the fact that the progress of art is not regular. There are times when the general execution becomes slipshod; then there may be a revival for a short period, and then a relapse. Barbarous imitations may not be very far removed from the original in time, although artistically the two are far apart. The most striking instance of this fact may be found in the coinage of Crete, at such a city as Gortyna, where in the course of about a century the type of the goddess seated in a tree is treated in every possible degree between the extremes of fine work and utter barbarism (Pl. IV. 2 and 4).

Of course there are numerous small features in the fabric and style of coins which are helpful to the numismatist in coming to a decision as to date. It is a curious fact, for instance, that for a long period after about 200 B. C. the large silver regal coins are almost invariably so struck that both types are in the same position relatively to the flan, whereas on the silver coins of the previous period this regularity is not observed[1]. There are also various changes in fashions; thus the border of dots is practically an invariable feature of coins of imperial date; the Greek coins from the close of the first century B. C. to the time of Nero are usually small and neat in style; they then begin to increase in size and reach their maximum (more than an inch and a half in not a few places) about and shortly after 200 A. D.

On the whole, the most difficult period in which to date Greek coins is comprised in the last two centuries before our era. As a rule, style neither progressed nor went backward during this period, and we are obliged to resort to other criteria.

§ 4. *Weight and Quality.*

A slight indication of date can be obtained from the weights of coins. Standards (for reasons explained above) have a tendency to fall. Supposing the same standard to be used or intended, a group of coins differing from another group by a reduced average weight will presumably be somewhat later. This is, however, a most uncertain criterion, Greek coin-standards being proverbially treacherous, and the weights of individual coins depending so largely on their condition. An example,

---

[1] The regularity may be due to the hinging together of dies, as Mr. Seltmann has suggested (*Num. Chr.* 1898, p. 300), or simply to the exercise of care on the part of the workmen. A pair of dies of late Roman coins of the mint of Antioch, hinged together, are figured in M. Babelon's *Notice sur la Monnaie* (Grande Encyclopédie), p. 112.

showing how the criterion at once answers and fails to answer, may be taken from the coins of Rhodes [1].

AVERAGE WEIGHTS IN GRAMMES.

	I. B.C. 400-333	II. B.C. 333-304	III. B.C. 304-166	IV. B.C. 166-88
Tetradrachms	15·065 (15 specimens)		13·251 (11 specimens)	
Didrachms	6·687 (13 specimens)	6·512 13 specimens	6·538 (24 specimens)	
Drachms	3·496 (3 specimens)	3·116 (5 specimens)	2·49 (35 specimens)	2·67 (56 specimens)

It appears that the general rule of decline in weight is broken by the slight rise of the didrachms in the third and of the drachms in the fourth period.

A sudden change of standard often has historical significance, and thus helps to furnish a date. The change from the Euboic-Attic standard to the Phoenician in certain cities of the Chalcidian district of Macedon, such as Acanthus and Mende, is probably to be connected with the failure of Athenian influence in that part owing to the expedition of Brasidas in 424 B.C. So too the less violent change, by which at Syracuse the Corinthian silver stater replaced the Euboic-Attic tetradrachm as the chief silver currency, is to be connected with the mission of the Corinthian Timoleon in 345 B.C.

Analogous to the fall in weight is the degradation of the metal in some series. This is particularly noticeable in Roman coins, or in the series of the semi-Roman mints of Caesarea, Alexandria, and Antioch.

§ 5. *Types.*

The character of the subjects used as types, though a very vague criterion, counts for something in the dating of coins. A glance at the early plates in Mr. Head's *Guide to the Coins of the Ancients*, will show the great predominance of animals and monsters on the earliest coins, and the comparative rarity

---

[1] The weights are taken from the coins in the British Museum, which are sufficiently numerous to afford a basis for calculation.

of the human figure. The early types are also, as a rule, simpler than the later[1]. Architecture is rarely represented on coins before imperial times (the walled cities on coins of Tarsus, Pl. IV. 12, and Sidon are among the rare exceptions to this rule). Copies of actual statues may be said to become frequent in the third century B.C., although doubtless they occur earlier. At Aenus, for instance, there appears, in the first half of the fourth century, a representation of a little terminal statue of Hermes set up on the seat of a throne. And such a figure as the seated Athena on the coin of the Lycian dynast Kheriga[2] (about 410 B.C.) has every appearance of being suggested by a relief. It is, however, probable that very few of the copies of statues on coins before the imperial period are faithful copies, except where the originals are archaic cultus-statues. And these do not appear in great numbers on coins of the fine period, for the simple reason that the artist's sense forbade him to reproduce ugly idols. Xoana such as the Apollo of Amyclae on coins of Sparta[3] are therefore uncommon on coins until imperial times. The copies of fine statues, such as the Cnidian Aphrodite, bear little resemblance to the originals. The head of Aphrodite on one of the Cnidian tetradrachms of the fourth century[4] has, however, distinctly Praxitelean qualities, free as the copy is. So long as the die-sinker's art remained creative, it could hardly be expected to content itself with mere copies. But under the Empire the artist's poverty of invention gave him no choice. In the same period the personifications of qualities and states such as Concord, Hope, Peace, also became more frequent. This is partly due to Alexandrian and Roman influence. The artistic skill required for these personifications was small, their identity being established by means of attributes. Hardly greater was the skill required for the complex historical, mythological, and agonistic subjects in which the coinage of the provinces under the Empire abounds.

All these facts, however, are so vague as to be of little value for purposes of dating within close limits. They, and others

[1] Such pictorial types as the 'Satyr and Nymph' or 'Centaur and Nymph' in Macedonia (*Coins of the Ancients*, Pl. 4, 1-5) are exceptional in the early period.
[2] *Brit. Mus. Catal.*, Lycia, Pl. vi. 5.
[3] Head, *Coins of the Ancients*, Pl. 43. 27; Gardner, *Types*, Pl. xv. 28.
[4] *Journal of Hellenic Studies*, xvii. Pl. II. 15.

like them, can only be employed for making the first rough classification of a large series. The case is different when a type alludes to some historical event. We then have a *terminus post quem*; but it must be remembered that historical types may be used to commemorate events which have long since become ancient history. A well-known instance of a fact which enables us to date the end as well as the beginning of an issue is found in the history of Himera. In 482 B.C. the Agrigentine Theron captured Himera, which he ruled until his death in 472 B.C., when his son Thrasydaeus was expelled. It is to this decade that the coins of Himera which combine the Himerean type of the cock with the Agrigentine crab must be assigned.

Datings of this kind, however, properly come under the class already described in § 1.

§ 6. *Epigraphy.*

The epigraphic evidence of the dates of coins is of two kinds. In the first place, the general character of the inscription may be taken into account. Early inscriptions are usually short and simple; monograms, and abbreviations of two or three letters, precede, as a rule, the writing out of words in full. Thus most of the coins of the 'new style' at Athens bearing monograms are earlier than those with the magistrate's names written in full. Similarly, the city name, or even a king's name in early times is abbreviated. As time goes on it becomes customary to write the name at length; and in the imperial age it is most uncommon to find the name abbreviated. The desire to get as much as possible on to the coin (the heaping up of titles is characteristic of the more Oriental monarchies and of such fictitious importance as was enjoyed by the Greek cities under the Empire [1]) made it useful to employ ligatures in the

---

[1] The style of Vologeses III (77-138 A.D.) of Parthia is Βασιλέως Βασιλέων Ἀρσάκου Ὀλαγάσου Δικαίου Ἐπιφανοῦς Φιλέλληνος. That of the city of Sagalassus on a coin of the third century A.D. is Σαγαλασσέων Πρώτης Πισίδων καὶ Φίλης Συμμάχου. The people of Smyrna in Caracalla's reign call themselves Σμυρναίων Πρώτων Ἀσίας γ' Νεωκόρων τῶν Σεβαστῶν κάλλει καὶ μεγέθι (i.e. the foremost in Asia in beauty and greatness, and for the third time temple-keepers of the Augusti). The title on a Pergamene coin has already been quoted (pp. 184, 185).

legends. These are indeed used at all times under the Empire but first become really common in the time of Septimius Severus. Occasionally letters that cannot be conveniently combined in ligature are made into monograms, as ↑ for το, ℙ for γρ, ४ for ου.

Again, on Roman Republican coins, the disposition of the legends [1] is to a certain extent an indication of date. Thus the word **ROMA** on the earliest denarii occurs only on the reverse in a frame of four lines. As these lines disappear, the word occurs indifferently on either side. Again, when the names of moneyers are written at length, it is very rare to find praenomen, gentile name and cognomen on the same side of the coin ; but on the later denarii this is fairly common.

Secondly, the forms of the letters are necessarily valuable evidence for dates. Thus the form of the letter **B** peculiar to Byzantium (Ϡ) does not occur later than the period B.C. 277-270. A detailed list of the forms in use at various times and places in the Greek world, of the kind worked out for Sicily by Prof. Gardner[2], would be welcome. To the following notes, which deal with only a few of the more important forms, there are, needless to say, innumerable exceptions

In the case of the Greek letters, I have divided the forms into two classes, the first dating roughly before, the second after the general adoption of the Ionic alphabet.

Greek.

A.

(1) The form Α (with the variety Λ) disappears as a rule early in the fifth century; but in Athens it was retained, in accordance with the archaizing tendency of the coinage, until about B.C. 430. Ᾱ is an early form found in Euboea, Boeotia, and Phocis, down to the middle of the fifth century. Λ at Agrigentum and Catana about 480-460 B.C.

(2) Α is common from the closing years of the third century[3] till Nero's time ; thenceforward, save on the coins of the kings of Bosporus, it is rare. Λ in the first century A.D.

---

[1] Mommsen, ii. p. 178 f.
[2] 'Sicilian Studies,' *Num. Chr.* 1876, pp. 38 ff.
[3] An anticipation is found at Agyrium (Sicily) in the fourth century.

B.

(1) Ϸ is common until late in the fifth century, but is confined to the Greek mainland. In some Sicilian cities it occurs occasionally at the end of the third century. ⌐ is peculiar to Byzantium, whence it disappears between 277 and 270 B.C. C and ⟨ are found on coins of the Thraco-Macedonian Bisaltae dating about 500-480 B. C. The former at least is probably due to the influence of the Thasian alphabet.

(2) B comes in perhaps as early as 100 B.C., and is common in Asia Minor under the Empire.

Γ.

(1) C is found until about 440 in Sicily, but lasts as late as the fourth century at Aegae in Achaea. Another early form is ⌐ (Segesta). ⟨ is transitional at Gela and Segesta, in the middle of the fifth century. Elsewhere ∧ is usual, lasting sometimes (as at Gomphi in Thessaly and Gortyna in Crete) down to the end of the fourth century. But as a rule Γ had superseded all the older forms by the close of the fifth century.

Δ.

(1) ▷ is found at Zancle down to 490, and later at Selinus. Another early form is D, also found at Zancle (Messana[1]), in Arcadia, and elsewhere.

E.

(1) The forms ⊫ ⋕ ⋈ and the like are of course early, and probably seldom later than about 480 B.C. E can, in early times, represent ε, η and in certain circumstances, rare on coins, ει. At Athens AΘE is retained on the coins long after the Ionic H had been officially adopted, even on coins of the 'new style,' on which the other words are spelt in the ordinary way. Only on the coins of imperial times is the archaism discarded. Elsewhere, the period of transition from E to H, towards the close of the fifth century, is an uneasy one. The same artist at Syracuse signs EYMENOY and EYMHNOY at times not far removed from each other. Mr. Gardner dates the adoption of H in the West about 425.

---

[1] For its late occurrence there see Evans, *Num. Chr.* 1896, p. 116.

(2) Є is found occasionally before the close of the third century in Sicily, and before 100 B.C. at Apollonia and Dyrrhachium in Illyria. Under the Empire, from about the middle of the first century A.D., it becomes the commonest form. A curious development, anticipating our modern cursive e, is the form used on coins of Rhoemetalces king of Bosporus (A.D. 132-154, Pl. XIII. 3). Є in the first century A.D.

Z.

(1) Ɪ is the usual early form, the middle stroke being seldom if ever slanting. Ɪ on the earliest coins of Zacynthus (before 431 B.C.).

(2) Z comes in with the first century B.C.[1], but is not common until Roman times.

H.

(1) The closed form ⊟ is only found in the earliest times (as on the electrum coin, Pl. I. 4). H of course occurs early in the Ionian district (as at Teos, B.C. 544-400), and also elsewhere, as on coins of Getas king of the Edonians (about 500 B.C.). See above under E.

(2) A slightly ornamented form is H, found in the fourth century in the Peloponnese.

Spiritus asper. The most peculiar form is ⌷ on the earliest coins of Haliartus in Boeotia (before 550 B.C.), which is followed by ⌷ ⌷ and ⊟ (550-480 B.C.). The aspirate is then dropped. ⊟ occurs at Himera in the fifth century. The closed form is followed by the open H, which disappears in Southern Italy and Sicily about 400 B.C. or a little earlier, being partly replaced by Ͱ, which is occasionally found even as late as the third century.

Θ.

(1) ⊕ and similar forms may be said to disappear about the middle of the fifth century, with a few possible exceptions (⊗ at Baletium in the fourth century). Curiously enough the earliest coins of Athens, dating from early in the sixth century,

---

[1] Perhaps earlier; see the coins of Zacynthus, *Brit. Mus. Catal. Peloponnesus*, p. 101.

have ⊙, the ⊕ appearing later in the century, only to disappear again very shortly.

(2) A late form is ⊟ (as on a coin of Aegeae in Cilicia of the reign of Severus Alexander).

I.

(1) ϟ is common on the earliest coins of Southern Italy, and elsewhere, as at Gortyna. Its use as late as the middle and end of the fifth century at Pandosia and Poseidonia is probably an archaism. In some places it takes the form S (as at the Cretan cities of Gortyna, Lyttus, and Phaestus, in the fifth century).

Λ.

(1) The forms Γ and L or V are early. Γ occurs on coins of the Bisaltae about 500 B.C., and elsewhere later, as at Phlius and Lyttus down to the middle of the fifth century. L is rarely found after B.C. 420 in places where Greek influence was strong; but in Campania it lasts down to the early fourth century, when it is found beside Λ. A variety is L (as on the Bisaltian coins and occasionally at Leontini). Λ itself is common at all periods, preceding V, for instance, at Leontini.

M.

(1) The splayed form M is common in early times, but is also found down to the latest period of Greek coinage. It is preceded by forms like M, /~, but these are exceptional.

(2) M appears in the course of the third century. In imperial times, after the period of the Antonines, we often find a form approaching the cursive, viz. ᴍ.

N.

(1) The forms N̓ N N̈ N̑ and the like all go out of use soon after 400 B.C. Exceptional forms are ᴒ, which occurs at Agrigentum about 410 B.C., and N, which is found at Naxos (Sicily) before 480 B.C., and occasionally at other Sicilian cities also in the middle of the fifth century.

Ξ.

(1) According to the class of alphabet, this sound was in early times represented in various ways:

(a) by κσ or χσ. Thus, at Axus in Crete, we find KM or KΣ (on the early fourth-century coins formerly attributed to 'Naxos').

(b) by X, as in the Achaean colonies in the West (Pyxus and Naxos). Even at Naxos it disappears before the end of the fifth century.

(c) by Ξ or (rather later) Ξ. A simpler form, found in Italy and Sicily as early as the fifth century, is Ι.

(2) The middle bar of Ξ tends to become shorter, until in the third and second centuries B.C. it is often reduced to a dot. Ι or Ι becomes common under the Empire, when also we find ornamental forms such as Ξ Ξ Ζ.

O.

(1) After the early years of the fifth century O is regularly written somewhat smaller than the other letters of a word, and occupies either the middle or the upper half of the writing-space.

◊ occurs in Southern Italy and in Crete on coins which are probably in no case later than 450 B.C.

The form ⊙, which is not uncommon in early times, is due to the fact that in lapidary inscriptions the letter was made with a pair of compasses.

The use of O for ου and ω is not properly subsequent to the close of the fifth century or the beginning of the fourth. Apparent exceptions are sometimes due to want of space for the final υ in genitives, sometimes to dialectic peculiarities, as in the Doric βασιλέος on coins of Syracuse.

(2) The rule as to the smallness of O, except in very late or careless inscriptions, is fairly well observed. Sometimes indeed it is made so small as to become a dot. An early instance of this peculiarity is afforded by the coins of Audoleon, king of Paeonia (B.C. 315-286).

☐ is a late form (second and third centuries A.D., as on a coin of Seleucia in Syria of A.D. 157 [1]).—Compare the form ⊟ for θ.

The form ◊ is as unusual in imperial times as in the first period, but may be found, e.g., in the somewhat affected lettering of the obverse of a coin of Apamea (Pl. XIV. 10).

---

[1] Wroth, *Brit. Mus. Catal. Galatia*, &c., p. 272 no. 31, Pl. 32, 10.

Π.

(1) Γ is the usual form throughout the early period. C is confined to Crete.

(2) Instances of Π probably do not occur, except accidentally, before about 250 B.C., nor of Γ after about 200 B.C. Π appears occasionally in the second century B.C., and under the Empire becomes almost universal.

P.

(1) The forms R Ʀ D, it may safely be said, do not occur after 400 B.C., but their general disappearance may be put some twenty or thirty years earlier. Mr. Gardner notes P as late as the middle of the third century at Syracuse and Tauromenium.

(2) P is a product of the first century B.C. and of early imperial times.

Σ.

(1) The early standing form ⑀ is usual until soon after the beginning of the fifth century[1]. At Syracuse it had probably disappeared by 500 B.C. The form S is found until about 476 B.C., e.g., at Messana. The recumbent form M or M lingers on in exceptional cases, as at Poseidonia and Gortyna, to the end of the fifth century. All these forms are finally superseded by Σ or ⑀, which is in use down to the first century B.C., and may occur even later owing to careless writing.

(2) But as early as the fourth century the form Σ occurs[2]. It prevails until the early years of the first century A.D. By the end of that century it may be said to be generally displaced by Ⲉ and C, although it still occurs frequently. Of the two forms, Ⲉ is the less common. Early instances of them are rare; but C occurs on a coin of Cos which is probably earlier than 300 B.C.[3], and on others of the same place which are certainly earlier than 190 B.C.; on a coin of the Illyrian king Monunius about 300 B.C.; on one of Seleucus II of Syria (246-226 B.C.)[4]; at

---

[1] The ⑀ in ΓΑΙⵄΤΑΝΟ about 300 B.C. is Italic, not Greek.
[2] For instance, at Sicyon (*Brit. Mus. Catal., Peloponnesus*, Pl. 8. 21).
[3] *Brit. Mus. Catal., Caria*, p. 195, no. 16.
[4] Imhoof-Blumer, *Monn. Gr.* p. 427.

Salapia, at Agrigentum, and other Sicilian towns before the end of the third century. C is later in appearing; it has been noted on a coin of Antiochus IV[1] (175-164 B.C.). It is fairly common during the early Empire, and again from the middle of the third century onwards.

Y.

V and Y appear to go side by side through the whole history of Greek coinage. The former, however, is probably the earlier of the two. The approximation of one to the other in careless writing, especially when the lines are slightly curved (ϒ), is naturally very close.

Φ.

(1) Φ is not uncommon before the middle of the fifth century. A rare form is ☉, which is only known from two coins, one of Phocaea, dating about 600 B.C. (Pl. I. 2), the other of Phaselis, earlier than 466 B.C.

(2) The tendency in later times is to lengthen the *hasta* of the letter, and make the circle small. A late form is ┼, of which an early instance is found at Phoenice in Epirus about 200 B.C.; but it is commoner in imperial times.

X.

(1) Of the unusual forms Ψ and + both give way to X during the fifth century.

Υ.

(1) The form ↓ (for instance, in the name of the river-god Hypsas at Selinus in Sicily) is earlier than Υ, which is used regularly after the fifth century.

Ω.

(1) In alphabets not belonging to the Ionic group, this sound is represented by O. Ω comes in about 410 B.C. in Sicily; in Greece proper a few years later.

(2) About the middle of the third century Ω begins for a time to be written smaller than the other letters, and the horizontal lines are made longer in proportion. The form ω occurs on a coin of Antiochus II (B.C. 261-246), and this is

---

[1] Imhoof-Blumer, *Monn. Gr.* p. 430.

an exceptionally early instance. It is very common in imperial times. The form Ꙩ is never very common, but is found as early as the first century B. C. The horizontal lines of Ω begin to degenerate into mere serifs in early imperial times, although a well-formed Ω is still often found. W is late, hardly occurring before the time of Septimius Severus.

F.

This letter, in the form F, is kept up as an archaism at Elis, and not discarded until imperial times. At Axus in Crete it lasts to the end of the fourth century. The form Ϲ is also found in Crete, as late as the third century B. C. N is another rare form found in the fourth century B. C. at the Cretan Axus; compare the Pamphylian form Ѡ at Perga in the second or first century B. C.

Ϛ.

Ϛ is only used as a numeral (= 6), but as such has a great variety of shapes. In imperial times it is most commonly Ϲ or Ϭ or Ϲ, sometimes Ϝ; an earlier form is ϟ.

Ϙ.

Ϙ as the initial of the name of Corinth is retained even to the days of the Achaean League. On a few staters of the early fifth century it takes the form φ. In some other places (as in Arcadia and at Syracuse) it disappears early in the fifth century; at Croton it lasts till about 420 B. C. As a numeral (= 90) it continues to be used till the latest times.

San.

This letter is represented on Greek coins by the Ψ of Mesembria. An analogous form seems to be the Pamphylian Ψ (= σσ) on coins of Perga.

ROMAN.

There is much less variety in the forms of letters on Roman than on Greek coins. The development of forms is not therefore of much value for purposes of dating. A few details[1]

---

[1] Based on the unpublished classification of the Roman coins in the British Museum by Count de Salis, and therefore differing in many small points from the results given by Mommsen.

relating to the period 269-50 B.C. are however sufficiently interesting to be noted.

Λ or ʌ is the earliest form. In the word *Roma* it begins to be replaced by A in the period 172-151; in other words, A began to come in during the period 196-173[1]. The diphthongs AI and AE are used indifferently, but AI is on the whole later than AE.

C is the regular form; but occasionally, from about 90 B.C. onwards, it is impossible to distinguish between C (c) and G (g).

EI occasionally represents a long I, as also does E.

H is not found before 91 B.C.

K not before 93 B.C. on Roman coins proper. In words it is only found before the letter A.

Ⱡ is the early form, although an occasional L is found as early as 172-151 B.C. About 102, the latter form becomes invariable. There is sometimes a tendency to make the letter lean slightly to the right (∠). ⌊ is confined to imperial times, and even then is not found on coins of Rome itself.

M or ᴀᴧ is practically the only form in use; but the amount of splaying varies, being sometimes, in and after 67 B.C, very slight. ᴀʌ is the abbreviation for Manius.

N is usual from the first appearance of the letter (196-173); but the slanting form Ν is also found, though rarely.

O is almost invariably written smaller than the other letters. The diphthong OE occurs in 61 B.C.

Γ is the true form, but usually the hook is rounded, so that we get Γ. The letter on Republican coins is *never* closed like the modern P, except owing to careless writing[2].

R does not change its form, but it should be noticed that the upper loop is made small in proportion to the whole, and that the leg comes rather far out to the right.

The sound *x* is occasionally, though not in the earliest times, represented by XS (as in 73 and 65 B.C.).

---

[1] Although Λ disappeared from the coins, it continued to be used in lapidary inscriptions, and from these it won its way back on to the coins of at least one Roman colony in the third century A.D. (Olbasa in Pisidia, *Brit. Mus. Catal., Lycia*, &c., pp. 229, 230, Pl. 36, 14, 15).

[2] The closed form occurs distinctly on coins of Tiberius after about A.D. 25. But it does not supplant the open form until the reign of Claudius I; Γ is even found as late as Galba (on an aureus with *Victoria P. R.*).

Of V there is nothing to remark except that it occasionally bears an accent, being then written V́ or V̇ or V̆ [1].

Y first appears in 69 B.C. In 61 and 58 B.C. the sound is represented by V or Y indifferently.

Numerals. A number of digits (I) combined may be connected by a line above them. When they are preceded by higher numerals, this line is as a rule produced to the left only so far as to connect the first digit with the number preceding it; thus IIII, XVI, VIII. On the other hand, exceptions such as LXVII are found.

X is the only form for 10.

For XVI, in the period 124–103 B.C. the form ✶ comes in.

↓ is the early form for 50. ⊥ appears in 85 B.C., and thenceforward prevails, although ↓ reappears beside it in 73 B.C. L does not occur earlier than on a quinarius of M. Antonius struck at Lyon.

Doubling of consonants is foreign to the early period: we find, e.g. PILIPVS. Double vowels (FEELIX, VAALA) are very rare.

§ 7. *Finds.*

'The discovery of hoards is the only evidence bearing directly on the relative dates of Republican coins; by examining them with care and method we shall be able to determine the chronology of the pieces which occur in them, and even of those which are missing. Before all, we have to fix the date of the burial of the hoard, and then try to discover which are the most recent pieces of the known varieties which we meet with, and the oldest of those which do not occur in the find. To attain this result, we must try to discover from local history the circumstances which may have caused the burial of the hoard, as, for example, the date and character of a war in the locality. The larger the hoard, the easier it becomes to fix with probability the date of its burial, for the greater the number of the coins, the more probable it is that a common piece, if it is not found there, was not struck before the laying

---

[1] Note that on coins of Pomponius Musa the *u* of *Musa* is accented, while that of *Musarum*, on the same coin, is not.

down of the hoard. As to rare pieces, it is clear that their presence is conclusive, while their absence proves nothing. For this reason ... we have as far as possible noted the number of coins of each variety met with in various hoards. It must be remembered also that the difference of standards and the period during which such and such a coin has been in circulation exercise a certain influence on the proportion in which each variety occurs in combination with others [1].'

The rule which Mommsen has laid down for the study of finds in Roman Numismatics, holds equally good for the Greek branch of the subject. But Greek coins were not issued in enormous numbers like Roman. As many as 80,000 Roman gold coins, all struck between 46 and 38 B.C., and of only thirty-two varieties, are said to have been found in a single hoard at Brescello [2], and hoards of more than 10,000 coins of the third and fourth centuries after Christ are not rare. Greek hoards, on the other hand, are usually much smaller, and range over much shorter periods. Typical Greek hoards are the 'Silversmith's hoard' from Naucratis [3] of fifteen coins ranging over about one hundred years; and the Messina find [4] of 1895 of about 185 coins, buried about 493 B.C. and containing coins perhaps as early as 550 B.C. Although only sixty-one coins of this last hoard were actually examined by Mr. Evans, the more important facts seem to be ascertained. The coins examined consisted of:—

No. of Specimens.

1. Coins of Zancle.
    (a) *Obv.* Δανκλε (in the local alphabet) under dolphin contained within raised penannular band (the harbour of Zancle).
    Rev. The same dolphin and band incuse 6
    (b) *Obv.* Δανκλε (sometimes abbreviated) under dolphin contained in raised penannular band, sometimes with four rectangular protuberances on it.
    Rev. Incuse key-pattern with scallop-shell in relief in centre 50
2. Coins of Naxos.
    Obv. Bearded head of Dionysos.
    Rev. Ναξιον. Bunch of grapes 8

The coins were all drachms of the Aeginetic standard (or

---

[1] Mommsen, ii. pp. 120, 121. [2] Ibid., iii. p. 26.
[3] Head, *Num. Chr.* 1886, p. 4.
[4] A. J. Evans, *Num. Chr.* 1896, pp. 101 ff.

thirds of the tetradrachm of the Attic standard, see p. 36). The Naxian pieces were more oxydized than the others, having perhaps been more exposed. This would happen if they were put in at the top of the jar. Most of them were not much worn, and must therefore have been comparatively fresh from the mint when withdrawn from circulation. Many of the Zancle coins of class (*b*) were also in fresh condition. Were there no other means of dating the coins we should from these circumstances place the coins of the class I (*a*) earlier than the others which are less worn.

Now we know that in 493 B.C. Anaxilas of Rhegium induced the Samian and Milesian refugees to seize Zancle, when the name of the place was altered to Messene; and just about the same time, perhaps a little earlier, Hippocrates of Gela laid hands on Naxos. As none of the coins with the name of the Messenians occur in this hoard, we may date its deposit about 498 B.C. It is of course clear for other reasons that the Naxian tetradrachms and drachms of the Attic standard, with the fine archaic head of Dionysus and the squatting Silenus (Pl. VI. 1), cannot be as early as 493 B.C.; but did we not know it already this find would go far to prove it.

Another find made in the Lipari islands[1] consisted of the following coins:—

Cales (circa 334–268 B.C.)	1
Neapolis (c. 340–268 B.C.)	17
Tarentum	
c. 281–272 B.C. (Period 'Evans VII')	22
c. 272–235 B.C. (Period 'Evans VIII')	14—36
Campano-Tarentine after 272 B.C. ?	5
Velia before c. 268 B.C.	2
Rhegium	1
Uncertain	1
	63

The dates here given are those otherwise ascertained as the dates of the classes to which the coins belong. As Mr. Macdonald points out, the hoard must have been buried soon after the beginning of Evans' Tarentine Period VIII, i.e. soon after 272 B.C.; for nearly two-thirds of the Tarentine didrachms belong to Period VII, and one of the didrachms of Period VIII

[1] G. Macdonald in *Num. Chr.* 1896, pp. 185 ff.

was fresh from the mint when it was withdrawn from circulation. The suggestion that the coins were hidden about the beginning of the First Punic War (264 B.C.) is extremely probable, since the Lipari islands were in the centre of the scene of operations.

The solitary coin of Rhegium was unpublished and in good condition. The date of the other coins in the hoard, combined with its own obverse type (head of Apollo) and its weight 1·73 g. (= 2 litrae), enables us to place this coin in the period which begins in 270 B.C.

The two hoards just described are taken at random, and are comparatively insignificant; but they serve to show what sort of evidence can be extracted even from small finds. In dealing with this evidence one may seem sometimes to be arguing in a circle. The fact is, that the various pieces of evidence support each other. There is nothing in the Lipari hoard out of keeping with the dates previously assigned to the various classes of coins concerned; assuming, therefore, that these dates are correct, we proceed to deduce from them the probable date of the coin of Rhegium. We find that this date fits in with the date assigned to other Rhegine coins of the same type and standard, and our whole system of dating is thus confirmed.

Of hoards of Roman coins, that of Montecodruzzo, near San Marino in the Romagna, is thoroughly typical[1]. It must have been buried about 81 B.C. 4,734 pieces coming from this hoard were examined. It may be compared with the Fiesole hoard, which was buried between 88 and 84 B.C. The Montecodruzzo hoard contained a few coins struck in Spain in 82 and 81 B.C., so that it must have been buried before these coins had entered Italy in great numbers. Of Sulla's coins, struck in Greece and Asia Minor in 82 at the latest, it contained none. Now in the Montecodruzzo hoard we find coins of the following moneyers who are not represented in the slightly earlier Fiesole hoard :—

1 { L. Censorinus
    P. Crepusius   } striking together.
    C. Limetanus

[1] Mommsen, ii. p. 135.

2. { Q. Ogulnius Gallus
     Ver(gilius ?)
     Gar(vilius ?) or Car(vilius ?) } striking together.
3. Cn. Lentulus
4. C. Marcius Censorinus } otherwise known to have been triumvirs.
5. L. Rubrius Dossenus
6. C. Norbanus
7. C. Licinius Macer } probably also were triumvirs.

This proves (1) that the Montecodruzzo hoard was at least four years later than the Fiesole hoard, and was probably later; (2) that all the pieces found at Montecodruzzo and wanting at Fiesole were struck between the dates of the deposits of the two hoards.

APPENDIX I.

ANCIENT STANDARDS.

(Weights in grammes.)

THE THREE ORIENTAL STANDARDS.

HEAVY SYSTEM.

[A]. WEIGHTS OF GOLD.

	Norm I	Norm II	Norm III	Norm IV
Tetradrachm	32.72 to 32.84	34.08 to 34.20	34.36 to 34.48	33.60 to 33.64
Didrachm .	16.36 to 16.42	17.04 to 17.10	17.18 to 17.24	16.80 to 16.82
Drachm . .	8.18 to 8.21	8.52 to 8.55	8.59 to 8.62	8.40 to 8.41
Obol . . .	1.36 to 1.37	1.42 to 1.43	1.43 to 1.44	1.40

[B]. WEIGHTS OF SILVER (BABYLONIAN).

Tetradrachm	43.64 to 43.80	45.48 to 45.60	45.84 to 46.00	44.80 to 44.88
Didrachm .	21.82 to 21.90	22.74 to 22.80	22.92 to 23.00	22.40 to 22.44
Drachm . .	10.91 to 10.95	11.37 to 11.40	11.46 to 11.50	11.20 to 11.22
Tetrobol . .	7.27 to 7.30	7.58 to 7.60	7.64 to 7.66	7.46 to 7.48

[C]. WEIGHTS OF SILVER (PHOENICIAN).

Tetradrachm	29.08 to 29.20	30.36 to 30.40	30.56 to 30.68	29.84 to 29.92
Didrachm .	14.54 to 14.60	15.16 to 15.20	15.28 to 15.34	14.92 to 14.96
Drachm . .	7.27 to 7.30	7.58 to 7.60	7.64 to 7.67	7.46 to 7.48
Tetrobol . .	4.85 to 4.87	5.05 to 5.07	5.09 to 5.11	4.97 to 4.99

ANCIENT STANDARDS

LIGHT SYSTEM.
[A]. WEIGHTS OF GOLD.

	Norm I	Norm II	Norm III	Norm IV
Tetradrachm	16.36 to 16.42	17.04 to 17.10	17.18 to 17.24	16.80 to 16.82
Didrachm	8.18 to 8.21	8.52 to 8.55	8.59 to 8.62	8.40 to 8.41
Drachm	4.09 to 4.10	4.26 to 4.27	4.29 to 4.31	4.20
Obol	0.68	0.71	0.71 to 0.72	0.70

[B]. WEIGHTS OF SILVER (BABYLONIAN).

Tetradrachm	21.82 to 21.90	22.74 to 22.80	22.92 to 23.00	22.40 to 22.44
Didrachm	10.91 to 10.95	11.37 to 11.40	11.46 to 11.50	11.20 to 11.22
Drachm	5.45 to 5.47	5.68 to 5.70	5.73 to 5.75	5.60 to 5.61
Tetrobol	3.63 to 3.65	3.79 to 3.80	3.82 to 3.83	3.73 to 3.74

[C]. WEIGHTS OF SILVER (PHOENICIAN).

Tetradrachm	14.54 to 14.60	15.16 to 15.20	15.28 to 15.34	14.92 to 14.96
Didrachm	7.27 to 7.30	7.58 to 7.60	7.64 to 7.67	7.46 to 7.48
Drachm	3.63 to 3.65	3.79 to 3.80	3.82 to 3.83	3.73 to 3.74
Tetrobol	2.42 to 2.43	2.53	2.55 to 2.56	2.49

GREEK STANDARDS.

	Aeginetic Heavy Norm IV	Aeginetic Light Norm III	Attic Heavy (Solonian)	Attic Light	Corinthian Full	Corinthian Early	Corinthian Later	Italic
Tetradrachm	26.88	25.20	34.88	17.44				
Tridrachm					8.73	8.40	8.66	8.164
Didrachm	13.44	12.60	17.44	8.72	5.82	5.60	5.76	5.442
Drachm	6.72	6.30	8.72	4.36	2.91	2.80	2.88	2.721
Obol	1.12	1.05	1.45	.73				

	Tarentine Early	Tarentine Later	Velia	Other Campanian Cities	Campanian Later	Chios (silver)	Rhodes (silver)
Tetradrachm						15.94	14.90 to 15.55
Didrachm	8.16 7.77	6.61	7.76	7.41	6.82	7.97 Tetrobol, 2.66	7.45 to 7.77
Drachm	4.08 3.88	3.30	3.88	3.70	3.41		3.72 to 3.88

	Miletus (electrum) Norm I	Samos (silver)	Cistophori
Tetradrachm	[28.36 to 28.48]	13.3	12.73
Didrachm .	14.18 to 14.24	6.6	6.36
Drachm . .	7.09 to 7.12		3.18
Tetrobol . .	4.73 to 4.75	2.2	
Diobol . .	2.37	1.1	

SICILIAN WEIGHTS.

Weight in grammes	Native System	Euboic-Attic System
.072	ὀγκία	
.145	ἑξᾶς	
.217	τριᾶς	
.290	τετρᾶς	
.362	πεντόγκιον	
.364		ἡμιωβόλιον
.435	ἡμίλιτρον	
.73		ὀβολός
.87	λίτρα	
1.09	1¼ λίτραι	τριημιωβόλιον
1.305	1½ ,,	
1.45		διώβολον
1.64	2 ,,	
2.075	2½ ,,	τριώβολον
2.61	3 ,,	
3.48	4 ,,	
4.366	5 ,,	δραχμή
5.22	6 ,,	
5.83		ὀκτώβολον
6.96	8 ,,	
8.7	δεκάλιτρος στατήρ	στατήρ δίδραχμον
13.05	15 λίτραι	
12.18	16 ,,	
15.66	18 ,,	
17.4	20 ,,	τετράδραχμον
20.88	24 ,,	
24.36	32 ,,	
26.10	πεντηκοντά-λιτρον	δεκάδραχμον

ROMAN WEIGHTS.

Weight in grammes	In terms of Roman pound	
327.45	1	libra = 12 unciae
300.16	1$\frac{1}{12}$	deunx = 11 unciae
272.88	1$\frac{1}{6}$	dextans = 10 unciae
245.59	1$\frac{1}{4}$	dodrans = 9 unciae
218.30	1$\frac{8}{12}$	bes = 8 unciae
191.02	1$\frac{7}{12}$	septunx = 7 unciae
163.73	1$\frac{6}{12}$	semis = 6 unciae
136.44	1$\frac{5}{12}$	quincunx = 5 unciae
109.15	1$\frac{4}{12}$	triens = 4 unciae
81.86	1$\frac{3}{12}$	quadrans = 3 unciae
54.58	1$\frac{2}{12}$	sextans = 2 unciae
40.93	$\frac{3}{24}$	sescuncia = 1½ unciae
27.288	1$\frac{1}{12}$	uncia = 4 sicilici
13.644	$\frac{1}{24}$	semuncia = 2 sicilici
6.822	$\frac{1}{48}$	sicilicus = 2 drachmae
4.548	$\frac{1}{72}$	sextula = 4 scripula
3.411	$\frac{1}{96}$	drachma = 3 scripula
2.274	$\frac{1}{144}$	dimidia sextula = 2 scripula
1.137	$\frac{1}{288}$	scripulum = 2 oboli
0.568	$\frac{1}{576}$	obolus = 3 siliquae
0.189	$\frac{1}{1728}$	siliqua

WEIGHTS OF SOME ROMAN GOLD AND SILVER COINS.

Weight in grammes	Proportion of Roman pound	Name, &c.
10·915	1/30	Aureus of Sulla
9·09	1/36	Aurei of Sulla and Pompeius
8·18	1/40	Aureus of Caesar
7·80	1/42	Aureus of Augustus
6·55	1/50	Aurei of Caracalla and Diocletian
5·46	1/60	Aureus of Diocletian
4·68	1/70	Aureus of Diocletian
4·55	1/72	Solidus of Constantine
6·82	1/48	Double Victoriatus
5·12	1/64	Antoninianus
4·55	1/72	{ Denarius (earliest) { Miliarense of Constantine
3·90	1/84	Denarius (first reduction)
3·41	1/96	{ Victoriatus { Denarius (Neronian) { Denarius of Diocletian
2·27	1/144	{ Quinarius (earliest) { Siliqua of Julian II
1·95	1/168	Quinarius (first reduction)
1·70	1/192	{ Half Victoriatus { Quinarius of Diocletian
1·137	1/288	{ Sestertius (earliest) { Half-siliqua of Julian II

APPENDIX II

TABLE OF EQUIVALENTS

IN TROY GRAINS OF THE WEIGHTS MENTIONED IN THE TEXT UP TO 20 GRAMMES.

Grammes.	Grains.	Grammes.	Grains.	Grammes.	Grains.
0.09	1.39	1.65	25.46	3.628	55.99
0.18	2.78	1.75	27.01	3.63	56.02
0.233	3.59	1.85	28.55	3.75	57.87
0.27	4.17	1.90	29.32	3.88	59.88
0.35	5.40	2.00	30.86470	3.90	60.19
0.36	5.55	2.073	31.99	4.00	61.72940
0.427	6.59	2.12	32.72	4.146	63.98
0.433	6.68	2.138	32.99	4.20	64.81
0.437	6.74	2.15	33.18	4.25	65.59
0.45	6.94	2.17	33.49	4.276	65.99
0.537	8.29	2.18	33.64	4.30	66.36
0.54	8.33	2.27	35.03	4.32	66.67
0.582	8.98	2.30	35.49	4.35	67.13
0.583	8.99	2.46	37.96	4.36	67.28
0.72	11.11	2.49	38.43	4.45	68.67
0.84	12.96	2.55	39.35	4.55	70.22
0.85	13.12	2.60	40.12	4.60	70.99
0.87	13.43	2.63	40.59	4.63	71.45
0.907	14.00	2.72	41.97	4.67	72.07
1.00	15.43235	2.73	42.13	4.68	72.22
1.09	16.82	2.77	42.75	5.00	77.16175
1.1	16.97	2.79	43.06	5.12	79.01
1.13	17.44	2.82	43.52	5.18	79.94
1.137	17.55	2.85	43.98	5.378	82.99
1.15	17.75	2.90	44.75	5.442	83.98
1.17	18.05	2.91	44.91	5.45	84.11
1.18	18.21	3.00	46.29705	5.461	84.28
1.231	19.00	3.10	47.84	5.56	85.80
1.33	20.52	3.30	50.93	5.60	86.42
1.40	21.60	3.41	52.62	5.68	87.65
1.42	21.91	3.50	54.01	5.70	87.96
1.45	22.38	3.57	55.09	5.75	88.73
1.48	22.84	3.58	55.25	5.80	89.51
1.50	23.15	3.60	55.56	5.82	89.82

TABLE OF EQUIVALENTS

Grammes.	Grains.	Grammes.	Grains.	Grammes.	Grains.
6.00	92.59	8.70	134.26	14.20	219.14
6.02	92.90	8.72	134.57	14.24	219.75
6.30	97.22	8.73	134.72	14.50	223.77
6.40	98.77	8.74	134.88	14.54	224.386
6.55	101.08	9.00	138.89115	14.55	224.54
6.609	101.99	9.072	140.00	14.60	225.31
6.80	104.94	9.10	140.43	14.90	229.94
6.82	105.25	9.20	141.98	14.92	230.25
6.86	105.86	10.00	154.32349	14.96	230.87
6.90	106.48	10.23	157.87	15.00	231.48524
7.00	108.02625	10.36	159.88	15.16	233.95
7.10	109.57	10.70	165.13	15.20	234.57
7.128	110.00	10.72	165.43	15.28	235.81
7.27	112.19	10.91	168.37	15.29	235.96
7.30	112.65	10.95	168.98	15.34	236.73
7.41	114.35	11.00	169.75684	15.50	239.20
7.44	114.82	11.01	169.91	15.55	239.97
7.46	115.12	11.172	172.41	15.68	241.98
7.48	115.43	11.20	172.84	15.94	245.99
7.50	115.74	11.22	173.15	15.96	246.30
7.58	116.98	11.339	174.99	16.00	246.91759
7.60	117.28	11.37	175.46	16.005	246.99
7.64	117.90	11.40	175.93	16.07	248.00
7.67	118.36	11.46	176.856	16.33	252.01
7.76	119.75	11.50	177.47	16.36	252.47
7.77	119.91	11.534	178.00	16.37	252.63
7.80	120.37	11.60	179.02	16.42	253.40
7.97	123.00	11.70	180.56	16.46	254.01
8.00	123.45880	11.87	183.18	16.52	254.94
8.164	125.99	12.00	185.18819	16.65	256.95
8.18	126.23	12.40	191.36	16.77	258.80
8.21	126.70	12.57	193.98	16.80	259.26
8.25	127.31	12.60	194.45	16.82	259.57
8.40	129.63	12.70	195.99	16.93	261.27
8.41	129.78	12.73	196.45	17.00	262.34974
8.42	129.94	12.96	200.00	17.002	262.38
8.46	130.55	13.00	200.62054	17.04	262.97
8.47	130.71	13.08	201.85	17.10	263.89
8.488	130.99	13.30	205.25	17.18	265.13
8.50	131.17	13.40	206.79	17.24	266.05
8.52	131.48	13.44	207.41	17.40	268.52
8.55	131.95	13.45	207.56	17.42	268.83
8.57	132.25	13.64	210.50	17.44	269.138
8.59	132.56	14.00	216.05289	17.46	269.446
8.618	132.99	14.04	216.67	18.00	277.78229
8.62	133.03	14.06	216.98	19.00	293.21464
8.66	133.64	14.18	218.83	20.00	308.64698

APPENDIX III

MINT-NAMES ON ROMAN COINS

The names of mints are combined on the coins with various letters and signs denoting the officinae of the mint and the different issues. Among these are:

P(rima)
S(ecunda)
T(ertia)
Q(uarta)
} written also in full on coins struck at Rome under Valentinian I, Gratian, and Valens.

A, B, Γ, Δ, Є, &c.
I, II, III, &c.
OF I, OF II, OF III = Officina I, &c. (at Arelatum).

To these must be added marks of value, such as KA, XXI, OB, and such abbreviations as P (= pecunia or percussa?), M (= moneta), SM (= sacra moneta). Thus we have such combinations as:

S M TR = Sacra Moneta Trevirensis.
M OSTB = Moneta Ostiensis, from the second officina.
P TRE = Pecunia Trevirensis.
F PLG = Pecunia Lugdunensis, issue F.
CVZICΓ = Cyzicus, third officina.

Eliminating these accessory marks, we obtain the following list of mint-names:—

A = Antiochia (in Syria), Arelatum (*Arles*).
AL, ALE = Alexandria (in Egypt).
AMB, AMBI = Ambianum (*Amiens*).
AN = Antiochia (in Syria).
ANB = Ambianum (*Amiens*).
ANT = Antiochia (in Syria).
AQ, AQVIL = Aquileia.
AR = Arelatum (*Arles*).
ARL = Arelatum (*Arles*).
AVG = Londinium.
C = Camulodunum (*Colchester*), Constantinopolis, Cyzicus.
CL = Camulodunum (*Colchester*).
CON = Arelatum (*Arles*), Constantinopolis.

MINT-NAMES ON ROMAN COINS

CONS = Constantinopolis.
CONST = Arelatum (*Arles*).
CVZ, CVZIC = Cyzicus.
H, HERAC, HERACL = Heraclea (in Thrace).
HT = Heraclea (in Thrace).
K = Carthago, Cyzicus.
KA = Arelatum.
KART = Carthago.
KONSA/ (Konstan.) = Arelatum (*Arles*).
KONT = Arelatum (*Arles*).
KV = Cyzicus.
L, LL = Londinium, Lugdunum (*Lyon*).
LD, LG = Lugdunum (*Lyon*).
LN, LON = Londinium.
LVG, LVGD = Lugdunum (*Lyon*).
MD, MED = Mediolanum (*Milan*).
N, NIK = Nicomedia (in Bithynia).
OST = Ostia.
R, RM, ROM, ROMA = Roma.
RV = Ravenna.
S = Siscia (in Pannonia).
SD, SER = Serdica (in Dacia).
SIR, SIRM = Sirmium.
SIS, SISC = Siscia (in Pannonia).
SM = Sirmium.
T = Tarraco (*Tarragona*), Thessalonica ?, Augusta **Trevirorum** (*Trier*).
TE, TES, THS, ⊙ES = Thessalonica.
TR = Tarsus, Augusta Treviorum (*Trier*).
TRE = Augusta Trevirorum (*Trier*).
TS = Thessalonica.
VRB. ROM = Roma.

APPENDIX IV

THE IMPERIAL FAMILIES

OF THE WESTERN EMPIRE TO A.D. 476.

[Reference numbers and letters are in *italics*. The names of persons represented or mentioned on coins are in **heavy type**. Ad. = adopted. Assoc. Emp. = associated in the Empire. *Aug.* = *Augustus, Augusta*. Ban. = banished. Caes. = *Caesar*. D. = daughter. Dep. = deposed. Div. = divorced. *Fil. Aug.* = *Filius Augusti*. M. = married. S. = son.]

Date of Death.

1. **C. Octavius**, son of C. Octavius and Atia = C. Iulius Caesar Octavianus. **Augustus** B. C. 27 (16 Jan.). . . . . 19 Aug. A.D. 14
  a *Wife* (B.C. 43): Claudia. Div. B.C. 41 . .
  b — (B.C. 40): Scribonia. Div. B.C. 39 .   After B.C. 2
  c — (B.C. 38): **Livia Drusilla**, d. of M. Livius Drusus Claudianus, div. wife of Tib. Claudius Nero. After death of *1* called Iulia Augusta . . . .   A.D. 29
  d *Sister*: **Octavia**, m. C. Marcellus (before B.C. 54), M. Antonius (B.C. 40) who div. her B.C. 32 . . . .   B.C. 11
  e *Daughter* (*b*): **Iulia**, m. Marcellus (*f*) B.C. 25, Agrippa (*g*) B.C. 21, Tiberius (*2*) B.C. 11, div. and ban. B.C. 2 . . . .   A.D. 14
  f *Son-in-Law*: M. Claudius Marcellus, s. of *d*, m. *e* . . . .   B.C. 23
  g — M. Vipsanius **Agrippa**, m. *e* . .   B.C. 12
  h *Grandson* (*e* and *g*): C. (Iulius) **Caesar**, ad. B.C. 17, m. Livia (*2 k*) . . . .   21 Feb. A.D. 4
  i — L. (Iulius) **Caesar**, ad. B.C. 17 . .   20 Aug. A.D. 2
  j — M. (Vipsanius) **Agrippa** (Postumus), ad. A.D. 4 (thereafter called Agrippa Iulius Caesar), ban. A.D. 7 . . . .   Aug. A.D. 14
  k *Granddaughter* (*e* and *g*): (Vipsania) Iulia, m. L. Aemilius Paulus, ban. A.D. 9 . .   A.D. 28
  l — Vipsania **Agrippina** (sen.) m. Germanicus (*2 c*) A.D. 5 (?), ban. A.D. 29 . .   18 Oct. A.D. 33

THE IMPERIAL FAMILIES 231

Date of Death.

2. Ti. Claudius Nero, son of Ti. Claud. Nero and *1c*
   = **Tiberius** (Iulius) Caesar, ad. by *1* A.D. 4.
   Aug. A. D. 14 (August) . . . . 16 Mar. A.D. 37
   a *Brother*: **Nero** Claudius **Drusus** (sen.) Germanicus, m. *b* about 16 B. C. . . Sep. B. C. 9
   b *Brother's wife*: **Antonia** (Minor) d. of M. Antonius and *1d*, m. *a*. Made Augusta A.D. 37 A. D. 37
   c *Nephew* (*a* and *b*): **Germanicus** Iulius Caesar, ad. A. D. 4, m. *1l* . . . . . A. D. 19
   d — Tiberius Claudius Nero Germanicus = *4*
   e *Grand-nephew* (*c*, *1l*): Caius Caesar = *3*
   f — **Nero** Iulius **Caesar**, m. *q* A. D. 20 . . A. D. 31
   g — **Drusus Iulius Caesar** (Drusus Iulius Germanicus) . . . . . A. D. 33
   h *Grand-niece* (*c*, *1l*): Iulia **Agrippina** = *4d*
   i — Iulia **Drusilla** = *3e* . . . . A. D. 38
   j — Iulia **Livilla** = *3f* . . . . . A. D. 41
   k *Niece* (*a*, *b*): (Claudia) **Livia** (Livilla) m. *1h* and *2n*
   l *Wife*: Vipsania Agrippina, daughter of *1g* by Pomponia, div. B. C. 11; m. Asinius Gallus A. D. 20
   m — (B. C. 11) Iulia = *1e*
   n *Son* (*l*): **Drusus** Iulius Caesar (Jun.), m. *k* . A. D. 23
   o *Grandson* (*n*, *k*): Germanicus (Iulius) Caesar) A. D. 23
   p — **Tiberius** (Iulius) Caesar (Nero ?)[1] . . A. D. 37
   q *Granddaughter* (*n*, *k*): Iulia, m. *f* A. D. 20 . A. D. 43

3. **Caius** (Iulius) **Caesar** [**Caligula**] = *2e*. Aug. 18 Mar. A. D. 37 . . . . . 24 Jan. 41
   a *Wife* (A. D. 33): Iunia Claudilla (Claudia) . bef. 37
   b — (38): Livia (Cornelia) Orestilla. Banished 38
   c — (38): Lollia Paulina. Div. 39 . . 49
   d — (39): Milonia Caesonia
   e *Sister*: Iulia Drusilla = *2i* 38
   f — Iulia **Livilla** = *2j* 41

4. Tiberius **Claudius** Nero Germanicus = *2d*. Aug. 25 Jan. 41 . . . . . . 12/13 Oct. 54
   a *Wife*: Plautia Urgulanilla
   b — Aelia Paetina
   c — Valeria **Messalina** 48
   d — (49): Iulia **Agrippina** (Jun.) = *2h*. Formerly (A. D. 28) m. to Cn. Domitius Ahenobarbus. Aug. 50 . . . . 19/22 Mar. 59
   e *Son* (*a*): (Claudius) Drusus . . . 20
   f — (*c*): Ti. Claudius Caesar Germanicus **Britannicus** . . . . . bef. 13 Feb. 55
   g *Daughter* (*a*): Claudia

---

[1] Imhoof-Blumer, *Lydische Stadtmünzen*, p. 120.

		Date of Death.
h	*daughter (b)*: (Claudia) **Antonia**, m. 41 Cn. Pompeius Magnus and (after 46/47) Faustus Cornelius Sulla Felix	65/68
i	— (*c*): Claudia Octavia = 5 *a*	62

5. **Nero** Claudius Caesar Drusus Germanicus, s. of Cn. Domitius Ahenobarbus and *4 d*. Ad. by *4* in 50. *Aug.* 13 Oct. 54 . . . . . 9 Jun. 68
   a *Wife* (53): Claudia **Octavia** = *4 i*. Div. 62 . . 9 Jun. 62
   b — (62): **Poppaea** Sabina. *Aug.* 64 . end of summer 65
   c — (66): Statilia **Messalina**
   d *Daughter (b)*: Claudia Augusta 63

6. L. Clodius **Macer**. 68. 68

7. Servius Sulpicius **Galba**. Accepts Empire 6 Apr. 68. *Caes.* circa 16 Jun. 68 . . . . . 15 Jan. 69

8. M. Salvius **Otho**. *Aug.* 15 Jan. 69 . . . 17 Apr. 69

9. A. **Vitellius** Germanicus. *Aug.* 2 Jan. 69 . After 18 Dec. 69
   a *Father*: L. **Vitellius**
   b *Brother*: L. Vitellius . . . . . ca. 21 Dec. 69
   c *Wife*: Petronia
   d — Galeria Fundana
   e *Son (c)*: (Vitellius) **Petronianus**
   f — (*d*): (Vitellius) **Germanicus**
   g *Daughter (d)*: Vitellia

10. T. Flavius **Vespasianus**, s. of Flavius Sabinus and Vespasia Polla. Accepts Emp. 1 Jul. 69. *Aug.* 21 Dec. 69 . . . . . . 24 Jun. 79
   a *Wife*: Flavia Domitilla
   b *Son*: T. Flavius Vespasianus = *11*
   c — T. Flavius Domitianus = *12*
   d *Daughter*: Flavia Domitilla, husband unknown
   e *Granddaughter*: Flavia Domitilla, m. Flavius Clemens (both banished 95)
   f *Great-grandson*: Flavius **Vespasianus** (jun.)
   g — (Flavius) Domitianus (jun.)

11. **Titus** Flavius Vespasianus = *10 b*. Assoc. Emp. 70. *Aug.* 24 Jun. 79 . . . . . . 31 Sep. 81
   a *Wife*: Arrecina Tertulla . . . . Under Nero
   b — Marcia Furnilla
   c *Daughter*: (Flavia) Iulia m. T. Flavius Sabinus

12. T. Flavius **Domitianus** = *10 c*. *Aug.* 14 Sep. 81   18 Sep. 96
   a *Wife* (70): Domitia Longina. *Aug.* 82

13. M. Cocceius **Nerva**. *Aug.* 19 Sep. 96 . . . 25 Jan. 98

THE IMPERIAL FAMILIES

Date of Death.

14. M. Ulpius (Nerva) **Traianus**. Assoc. Emp. 27 Oct.
    97. *Aug.* Jan. 98 . . . . . bef. Aug. 11, 117
  a *Father*: M. Ulpius **Traianus** . . . . bef. 100
  b *Sister*: **Marciana** m. C. Salonius Matidius . 114
  c *Niece (b)*: **Matidia** 119
  d *Grand-niece (c)*: (Vibia) Sabina = *15 a*
  e *Wife*: Pompeia **Plotina** 122

15. P. Aelius (Traianus) **Hadrianus**, s. of P. Aelius
    Hadrianus Afer and Domitia Paulina. Ad.
    by *14* in 117. *Aug.* 11 Aug. 117 . . 10 Jul. 138
  a *Wife* (ca. 100) (Vibia) **Sabina** = *14 d*. *Aug.* 128 136
  b *Favourite*: **Antinoüs** . . . . . bef. 30 Oct. 130

16. L. Ceionius Commodus = L. **Aelius** Commodus
    Verus, s. of L. Ceionius Commodus. Ad. by
    15 summer 136 . . . . . 1 Jan. 138
  a *Wife*: Avidia Plautia
  b *Son*: L. Ceionius Commodus = *19*

17. T. Aurelius Fulvus Boionius Arrius Antoninus =
    T. Aelius Hadrianus **Antoninus Pius**, s. of
    Aur. Fulvus and Arria Fadilla. Ad. by *15*
    on 25 Feb. 138. *Aug.* same date . . 7 Mar. 161
  a *Wife* (112): Annia Galeria **Faustina** (sen.), d.
    of M. Annius Verus. *Aug.* 138 . . Dec. 140/Jul. 141
  b *Son*: M. Aurelius Fulvus Antoninus
  c — M. **Galerius** Aurelius **Antoninus**
  d *Daughter*: Aurelia Fadilla
  e — Annia Galeria Faustina (jun.) = *18 a*

18. M. Annius Verus = M. Aelius Aurelius **Verus**
    Caesar = **M**. **Aurelius Antoninus**, s. of
    Annius Verus and Domitia Lucilla. Ad. by
    17 on 25 Feb. 138. *Aug.* 7 Mar. 161 . 17 Mar. 180
  a *Wife* (145): Annia Galeria **Faustina** (Jun.) =
    17 e. *Aug.* 147 176
  b *Son*: M. **Annius Verus**. *Caes.* 12 Oct. 166 . autumn 169
  c — L. Aurelius Commodus = *20*
  d *Daughter*: Annia Galeria Aurelia Faustina
  e — Annia Lucilla m. *19* (164) and Claudius
    Pompeianus Quintianus (169) . . . 183
  f *Mother*: Domitia Lucilla . . . bef. 7 Mar. 161

19. L. Ceionius Commodus = L. Aurelius **Verus** =
    16 b. Ad. by *17* on 25 Feb. 138. *Aug.*
    7 Mar. 161 . . . . . . Jan. 169
  a *Wife* (164): **Annia Lucilla** = *18 e*

20. M. Aurelius = L. Aelius Aurelius = L. Aurelius
    Commodus Antoninus = *18 c*. *Caes.* 12 Oct.
    166. Assoc. Emp. 176. *Aug.* 177 . . 31 Dec. 192
  a *Wife* (178): Bruttia **Crispina**. Ban. 182

Date of Death.

21. P. Helvius **Pertinax.** *Aug.* 1 Jan. 193 . . 28 Mar. 193
   a *Wife*: **Flavia Titiana**
   b *Son*: P. Helvius **Pertinax** . . . . under Caracalla

22. M. **Didius Iulianus.** *Aug.* 28 Mar. 193 . . 1 Jun. 193
   a *Wife*: **Manlia Scantilla**
   b *Daughter*: **Didia Clara**

23. C. **Pescennius Niger.** *Aug.* May 193. . . Nov. 194

24. D. **Clodius** Septimius **Albinus.** *Caes.* Jun. 196.
     Aug. 196 . . . . 19 Feb. 197

25. L. **Septimius Severus** Pertinax. *Aug.* Apr. or
     May 193 . . . . 4 Feb. 211
   a *Wife*: **Iulia Domna** 217
   b *Son*: M. Aurelius Antoninus = 26
   c — P. Septimius Geta = 27

26. M. Aurelius Severus Antoninus [**Caracalla**] =
     25 *b*. *Caes.* aut. 196. *Aug.* bef. 3 May 198 8 Apr. 217
     Wife (202): Fulvia **Plautilla**, d. of Plautianus.
     Ban. 205 212

27. P. (or L.) Septimius **Geta** = 25 *c*. *Caes.* 2 Jun. 198.
     Aug. 211 . . . . 27 Feb. 212

28. M. Opellius Severus **Macrinus.** *Aug.* 11 Apr. 217 Jul. 218
   a *Son*: M. Opellius Antoninus **Diadumenianus.**
     Caes. 11 Apr. 217. *Aug.* Apr. 218 . . Jul. 218

29. Varius Avitus = M. Aurelius Antoninus [**Elaga-
     balus** or **Heliogabalus**]. *Aug.* 16 May 218 11 Mar. 222
   a *Grandmother*: Iulia **Maesa**, sister of 25 *a*, m.
     Iulius Avitus 223
   b *Mother*: Iulia **Soaemias** Bassiana . . . 11 Mar. 222
   c *Wife*: Iulia Cornelia **Paula**
   d — (220/221): Iulia **Aquilia Severa**
   e — (221): **Annia Faustina**, granddaughter of
     18 *d*

30. M. Aurelius **Severus Alexander.** Ad. as *Caes.*
     by 29 on 10 Jul. 221. Assoc. Emp. 222.
     Succeeded 11 Mar. 222 . . . 18/19 Mar. 235
   a *Mother*: Iulia Avita **Mamaea**, m. Gessius
     Marcianus. *Aug.* 222 . . . . 18/19 Mar. 235
   b *Wife*: **Memmia**
   c — Gnaea Seia Herennia Sallustia Barbia
     Orbiana

APP. IV]   THE IMPERIAL FAMILIES   235

Date of Death.

31. C. Iulius Verus **Maximinus**. *Aug.* bef. 25 Mar. 235 . . . .   17 Jun. 238
  a *Wife*: Caecilia **Paulina**
  b *Son*: C. Iulius Verus **Maximus**. *Caes.* 236 .   17 Jun. 238

32. M. Antonius **Gordianus** (I) Sempronius Romanus Africanus. *Aug.* Feb. (?) 238 . . .   Mar. (?) 238
  a *Son*: M. Antonius **Gordianus** (II) Sempronius Romanus Africanus. Assoc. Emp. Feb. (?) 238 . . . .   Mar. (?) 238
  b *Daughter*: Maecia Faustina m. Iunius Balbus

33. D. Caelius Calvinus **Balbinus**. *Aug.* Mar. (?) 238   Jun. (?) 238

34. M. Clodius **Pupienus** Maximus. *Aug.* Mar. (?) 238   Jun. (?) 238

35. M. Antonius **Gordianus** (III) Pius, s. of *32 b*. *Caes.* Mar. 238. *Aug.* Jun. 238 . . .   Feb. 244
  a *Wife* (241): Furia Sabinia **Tranquillina**

36. M. Iulius **Philippus** (sen.). *Aug.* Feb. 244 . . .   249
  a *Wife* (bef. 238): Marcia Otacilia **Severa**
  b *Son*: M. Iulius Severus **Philippus** (jun.). *Caes.* 244. *Aug.* 247   249
  c *Father*?: **Marinus**

37. Marinus in Moesia and Pannonia, 248; prob. = 38 .   249

38. Tiberius Cl(audius) Mar(inus) **Pacatianus** in Moesia or Pannonia; prob. = 37 . . .   249

39. M. F ... Ru ... **Iotapianus** in the East, 248 . .   248

40. C. Messius Quintus **Traianus Decius**. *Aug.* end of 248 . . . .   summ. 251
  a *Wife*: Herennia Cupressenia **Etruscilla**
  b *Son*: Q. Herennius **Etruscus** Messius Traianus Decius. *Caes.* 250. *Aug.* 251 . . .   summ. 251
  c — C. Valens **Hostilianus** Messius Quintus. *Caes.* 250. *Aug.* Nov. 251 . . . .   Dec. 251

41. C. Vibius **Trebonianus Gallus**. *Aug.* summ. 251   253
  a *Wife*: Afinia Gemina Baebiana
  b *Son*: C. Vibius Afinius Gallus Veldumnianus **Volusianus**. *Caes.* Nov. 251. *Aug.* Jul. 252   253

42. L. Iulius Aurelius Sulpicius **Uranius Antoninus** 253/4 in the East   •

43. M. Aemilius **Aemilianus**. *Aug.* May/Jun. 253 .   29 Aug./22 Oct.
  a *Wife*: C. Cornelia Supera   [253

Date of Death.

44. P. Licinius **Valerianus** (sen.). *Aug.* Aug. 253.
   Captured by Persians 261
   a   *Wife* ? : **Mariniana** . . . . bef. 253 ?
   b   *Son* : (Licinius) Valerianus 268
   c   — ? Marinianus
   d   — P. Licinius Egnatius Gallienus = *45*

45. P. Licinius Egnatius **Gallienus** = *44 d*. Aug. 253 ?   4 Mar. 268
   a   *Wife* : Cornelia **Salonina**
   b   *Son* : P. Licinius Cornelius (or Corn. Lic.)
          Valerianus. *Caes.* 255 259
   c   — P. Licinius Cornelius (or Corn. Lic.) **Saloninus** (or Salon. Valerianus) 268
   d   — ? Q. Iulius **Gallienus**
   e   *Cousin* : (Licinia) **Galliena**

46. Cyriades (Mareades) in the East. 258 . . . 258

47. D. Laelius **Ingenuus** in Moesia. 258 . . . 258

48. P. C . . . **Regalianus** in Illyricum. 258
   a   *Wife* : Sulpicia **Dryantilla**

49. M. Fulvius **Macrianus** (sen.). *Aug.* 261 . . bef. Aug. 262
   a   *Son* : T. (or M.) Fulvius Iunius **Macrianus** (jun.). *Aug.* 261 . . . . . bef. Aug. 262
   b   — T. Fulvius Iunius **Quietus**. *Aug.* 261 . . 262

50. Ballista, contemporary with *49*

51. (Calpurnius ?) Piso Frugi in Thessaly. 261 . . 261

52. P. Valerius **Valens** in Macedon. 261 . . . 261

53. Tib. Cestius Alexander Aemilianus in Egypt. 262 . 263

54. Saturninus. 263

55. Celsus in Africa. 264–5

56. C. Annius **Trebellianus** in Isauria. 265

57. M. Cassianius Latinius **Postumus** (sen.) in the West. *Aug.* 259 (?) . . . . . 269 (?)
   a   *Son* : Postumus (jun.)

58. Ulp(ius) Corn(elius) **Laelianus** in Gaul. 268 . . 268

59. Lollianus = *58* ?

60. M. Piavonius **Victorinus** (sen.) in Gaul. ca. 265 . 268
   a   *Wife* : **Victori(n)a** 268
   b   *Son* : (Piavonius) **Victorinus** (jun.)

61. M. Aurelius **Marius** in Gaul. 268 . . . 268

THE IMPERIAL FAMILIES

Date of Death.

62. C. Pius Esuvius **Tetricus** (sen.) in Gaul. 268.
   Dep. 273 275
   a   Son: C. Pius Esuvius **Tetricus** (jun.). *Caes.*
       268

63. M'. Acilius **Aureolus** in Rhaetia. 267 . . . 268

64. M. Aurelius **Claudius** (II) **Gothicus**. *Aug.* 268 . bef. 29 Aug. 270
   a   Brother: M. Aurelius Claudius **Quintillus.**
       Aug. Apr./May 270 . . . . . Apr./May 270

65. L. Domitius **Aurelianus.** *Aug.* Apr./May 270 . 275
   a   Wife: Ulpia **Severina**

66. Septimius **Odenathus** in Palmyra. *Aug.* 265 . Aug. 266/Aug.
   a   Wife: Septimia **Zenobia**: ruled with c. [267
       Aug. 270
   b   Son (mother unknown): Herodes or Herodianus   Aug. 266/Aug.
   c   — (a): I(ulius) A(urelius) Septimius **Vaballa-** [267
       thus Athenodorus, succ. betw. 29 Aug. 266
       and 28 Aug. 267; recogn. by Aurelian 270;
       captured with *b* not later than 29 Aug. 271
   d   — (a): Herennianus (Haeranes)
   e   — Timolaus
   f   Cousin: Maeonius

67. Antiochus in Palmyra. 273

68. **Firmus** in Egypt. 273 273

69. M. Claudius **Tacitus.** *Aug.* 25 Sept. 275 . . spring 276
   a   Brother: M. Annius **Florianus.** *Aug.* spring 276   summ. 276

70. M. Aurelius **Probus.** *Aug.* spring 276 . . aut. 281

71. Iulius **Saturninus** in the East. 280 . . . 280

72. **Proculus** in Gaul. 280 (?) . . . . . 280 ?

73. **Bonosus** in Gaul. 280 (?) . . . . . 280 ?

74. M. Aurelius **Carus.** *Aug.* Oct. 282 . . . summ. 283
   a   Son: M. Aurelius Carinus = 75
   *b   — M. Aurelius Numerius **Numerianus.** *Caes.*
       Oct. 282. *Aug.* summ. 283 284

75. M. Aurelius **Carinus** = 74 *a*. *Caes.* 282. *Aug.*
       summ. 283 . . . . spring 285
   a   Wife: **Magnia Urbica**
   b   Son ?: (M. Aurelius) **Nigrinianus**

76. M. Aurelius **Iulianus** in Transpadana, &c. ca.
   283-285

Date of Death.

77. C. Valerius **Diocletianus.** *Aug.* 284. Abd.
   1 May 305 313
   a *Wife*: Prisca 314
   b *Daughter*: Galeria Valeria = *85 a* 314

78. M. Aurelius Valerius **Maximianus** Herculeus.
   Caes. 285. *Aug.* 286. Abd. 1 May 305.
   Rest. 306. Flies from Rome 307. Rest. 308.
   Dep. 308 310
   a *Wife*: Eutropia
   b *Son*: M. Aurelius Valerius Maxentius = 88
   c *Daughter*: Fausta = *93 b*
   d *Step-daughter*: Theodora = *84 b*

79. Amandus } in Gaul. 284-286
80. Aelianus }

81. M. Aurelius Maus . . . **Carausius** in Britain. 286 . 293

82. **Allectus** in Britain. 293 296

83. Achilleus = L. **Domitius Domitianus** in Egypt.
   296 297

84. Flavius Valerius **Constantius** (I) [Chlorus] ad.
   by 78 in 292. *Aug.* 1 May 305 . . . . 25 Jul. 306
   a *Wife* (274): Flavia Iulia **Helena.** Div. 292.
   Aug. 306 328
   b — (292): Flavia Maximiana Theodora = *78 d*
   c *Son* (*a*): Flavius Valerius Constantinus = 93
   d — (*b*): Iulius Constantius, m. Galla and Basilina
   e — (*b*): Delmatius = 97
   f *Daughter* (*b*): Flavia Constantia = *90 a*
   g — (*b*): Eutropia

85. **Galerius** Valerius **Maximianus** ad. by 77 in 292.
   Aug. 1 May 305 . . . . 5 May 311
   a *Wife* (292): Galeria **Valeria** = *77 b* . . . 314

86. Flavius Valerius **Severus** (II). Caes. 1 May 305.
   Aug. 306 (after 25 Jul.) . . . . . 2 Apr. 307

87. C. Galerius Valerius **Maximinus** (II) **Daza**, neph.
   of 85. Caes. 1 May 305. Fil. *Aug.* 307.
   Aug. 308 313

88. M. Aurelius Valerius **Maxentius** = *78 b.* *Aug.*
   27 Oct. 306 . . . . Oct. 312
   a *Son*: Romulus . . . . bef. 312

89. L. Domitius **Alexander** in Africa. 308 . . 311

90. C. Flavius Valerius Licinianus **Licinius** (sen.).
   Aug. 11 Nov. 307 324
   a *Wife* (313): Flavia **Constantia** = *84 f* . . 330
   b *Son*: Flavius Valerius Constantinus Licinianus
   Licinius (jun.). Caes. 317 326

THE IMPERIAL FAMILIES

Date of Death.

91. Aurelius Valerius **Valens**. *Caes.* 314 314

92. Sex. Marcius (?) **Martinianus**. *Caes.* 323 . . . 323

93. Flavius Valerius **Constantinus Magnus** = *84 c.*
    Caes. 306. *Fil. Aug.* 307. *Aug.* 307 . . . 22 May 337
  a *Wife*: Minervina
  b — (307): Flavia Maxima **Fausta** = *78 c* . . . 326
  c *Son* (*a*): Flavius Iulius **Crispus**. *Caes.* 317 . . 326
  d — (*b*): Flavius Claudius Iulius Constantinus = *94*
  e — (*b*): Flavius Iulius Valerius Constantius = *95*
  f — (*b*): Flavius Iulius Constans = *96*
  g *Daughter*: Constantina m. *97 a* and *101* . . . 354
  h — Flavia Iulia Helena = *103 a*

94. Flavius Claudius Iulius **Constantinus** (II) = *93 d*.
    Caes. 317. *Aug.* 337 340

95. Flavius Iulius Valerius **Constantius** (II) = *93 e*.
    Caes. 323. *Aug.* 337 361
  a *Wife* (361): Faustina
  b *Daughter* (*a*): Constantia = *108 a*

96. Flavius Iulius **Constans** (I) = *93 f*. *Caes.* 333.
    Aug. 337 350

97. Flavius Iulius **Delmatius**, s. of *84 e*. *Caes.* 335 . . 337
  a *Brother*: Flavius **Hanniballianus**, m. *93 g* . . 337

98. Flavius Iulius Popilius **Nepotianus** Constantinus
    s. of *84 g*. *Aug.* 350. Dep. 350

99. **Vetranio** at Sirmium. *Aug.* 1 Mar. 350. Dep. 350

100. Flavius Magnus **Magnentius**. *Aug.* 350 . . . 353
  a *Wife*: Iustina. See *105 b* 383
  b *Brother*: Magnus **Decentius**. *Caes.* 351 . . 353
  c — Desiderius. *Caes.* 351 353

101. Flavius Claudius Iulius **Constantius Gallus**, s.
    of *84 d*. *Caes.* 351. Assoc. Emp. 351 . . 354
  a *Wife* (351): Constantina = *93 g* . . . 354

102. Flavius **Silvanus** in Gaul. 355 355

103. Flavius Claudius **Iulianus** (Philosophus or **Apostata**) son of *84 d* and Basilina. *Caes.* 355.
    Aug. 360 363
  a *Wife* (355): Flavia Iulia **Helena** = *93 h* . . 360

104. Flavius **Iovianus**. *Aug.* 363 364

	Date of Death.
105. Flavius Valentinianus (I) s. of Gratianus. *Aug.* 364	375
a *Wife*: Valeria Severa Marina. Div. 368	
b — (368): Iustina = *100 a*	388
c *Son* (*a*): Flavius Gratianus = *108*	
d — (*b*): Valentinianus = *109*	
e *Daughter* (*b*): Iusta	
f — (*b*): Galla = *110 b*	
g — (*b*): Grata	
106. Flavius Valens, brother of *105*. Assoc. Emp. and *Aug.* 364	378
a *Wife*: Albia Dominica	
b *Son*: Valentinianus Galatus	
c *Daughter*: Carausa	
107. Procopius *Aug.* 365.	366
108. Flavius Gratianus = *105 c*. *Aug.* 367. Succ. 375	383
a *Wife*: Constantia = *95 b*	
109. Valentinianus (II) = *105 d*. *Aug.* 375	392
110. Flavius Theodosius. *Aug.* 379.	395
a *Wife* (376): Aelia **Flaccilla**	385
b — (386): Galla = *105 f*.	394
c *Son* (*a*): Flavius **Arcadius.** *Aug.* 383. [Emperor of the East]	408
d — Honorius = *113*	
e *Daughter* (*a*): Pulcheria	
f — (*b*): Aelia Galla Placidia, m. Ataulph (414) and *114*	
111. Magnus Maximus. *Aug.* 383.	388
a *Son*: **Flavius Victor.** *Aug.* 383.	388
112. Eugenius. *Aug.* 392.	394
113. Flavius Honorius = *110 d*. *Aug.* 393. Succ. 395	423
114. Constantius (III). Assoc. Emp. 421	421
a *Wife* (417): Aelia Galla Placidia = *110 f*	450
b *Son*: Valentinianus = *120*	
c *Daughter*: Iusta Grata Honoria = *120 a*.	after 454
115. Flavius Claudius Constantinus (III). *Aug.* 407. Recogn. by *113* in 409	411
a *Son*: Constans. *Aug.* 408.	411
116. Maximus, in Spain. 409. Dep. 411	
117. Iovinus. *Aug.* 411.	413
a *Brother*: Sebastianus. *Assoc. Emp.* 412.	413

THE IMPERIAL FAMILIES

Date of Death.

118. **Priscus Attalus.** *Aug.* 409-410; again 414. Dep. 415

119. **Iohannes.** *Aug.* 423 425

120. **Placidius Valentinianus** (III) = *114 b.* *Caes.*
424. *Aug.* 425 455
  a Sister: Iusta Grata **Honoria** = *114 c.* *Aug.* 433   after 454
  b Wife (437): Licinia **Eudoxia.** See *121 a*
  c Daughter: Aelia Placidia = *126 a*

121. **Petronius Maximus.** *Aug.* 455 455
  a Wife (455): Licinia Eudoxia = *120 b*

122. **Eparchius Avitus.** *Aug.* 455. *Abd.* 456

123. **Iulius Maiorianus.** *Aug.* 457 461

124. **Libius Severus** (III). *Aug.* 461 . . . 465

125. **Procopius Anthemius.** *Aug.* 467 . . . 472
  a Wife: Aelia Marcia **Eufemia**

126. **Anicius Olybrius.** *Aug.* 472 472
  a Wife: Aelia Placidia = *120 c*

127. **Glycerius.** *Aug.* 473. *Dep.* 474

128. **Iulius Nepos.** *Aug.* 474. *Dep.* 475 . . . 480

129. **Romulus Augustulus.** *Aug.* 475. *Dep.* 476

R

APPENDIX V

SELECT BIBLIOGRAPHY

A. Works of a General Character.

E. BABELON : *Monnaies de la République romaine.* 2 vols. Paris, 1885, 6.
Mélanges numismatiques. 2 vols. Paris, 1892, 3.
Récentes acquisitions du Cabinet des Médailles. Rev. Num. 1893.
Les Origines de la Monnaie. Paris, 1897.
Inventaire de la Collection Waddington. Rev. Num. 1898.

M. BAHRFELDT : *Nachträge und Berichtigungen zur Münzkunde der römischen Republik* (im Anschluss an Babelon's Verzeichniss der Consular-münzen). Vienna, 1897.

BERLIN, *Königliche Museen, Beschreibung der antiken Münzen,* by J. Friedländer, A. von Sallet, H. Dressel. See § B 4, 6, 7.

BIBLIOTHÈQUE NATIONALE, Paris : *Catalogue des Monnaies grecques,* by E. Babelon. See § B 2, 19, 21, 22, 23, 26.

J BRANDIS : *Münz-, Mass- und Gewichtswesen in Vorderasien.* Berlin, 1866.

BRITISH MUSEUM : *Catalogue of Greek Coins.* By R. S. Poole, B. V. Head, P. Gardner, W. W. Wroth, G. F. Hill. See § B *passim*
Guide to the principal Gold and Silver Coins of the Ancients. By B. V. Head. 2nd ed. (with 70 plates). London, 1881. [Also issued with 7 plates only.]
Catalogue of Roman Coins. See § B 30.

H. COHEN : *Monnaies frappées sous l'Empire romain.* 2nd ed. Paris, 1880-1892. 8 vols.

C. COMBE : *Nummorum vet. populorum et urbium qui in Mus. Gul. Hunter asservantur descriptio.* London, 1782.

E. CURTIUS : *Ueber den religiösen Character d. griech Münzen.* (*Gesamm. Abh.* Vol. II.) Translated by B. V. Head. Num. Chr. 1870.

T. L. DONALDSON : *Architectura Numismatica.* London, 1859.

H. DRESSEL : *Erwerbungen des Kön. Münzcabinets.* 1890-1897. Z. f. N. XXI.

SELECT BIBLIOGRAPHY

J Eckhel: *Doctrina Numorum Veterum.* Vienna, 1792 1798. 8 vols.
C. R. Fox: *Engravings of unedited or rare Greek Coins.* London, 1856, 62.
J. Friedländer: *Die Erwerbungen des kön. Münzkabinets.* Z. f. N. I–XII, 1874-1885.
 Repertorium zur antiken Numismatik. Ed R. Weil. Berlin, 1885.
J. Friedländer u. A. von Sallet: *Das kön. Münzkabinet.* 2nd ed. Berlin, 1877.
P. Gardner: *The Types of Greek Coins.* Cambridge, 1882.
 Greek River-worship. Proc. of Roy. Soc. of Lit. 1876.
 Pollux' Account of Ancient Coins. Num. Chr. 1881.
W. Greenwell: *Rare Greek Coins.* Num. Chr. 1880, 85, 90, 93.
 On a Find of Archaic Greek Coins in Egypt. Num. Chr. 1890.
B. V. Head: *Historia Numorum.* Oxford, 1887.
 The same in Modern Greek, by J. N. Svoronos. Vols. 1, II. Athens, 1898. [Supplement in preparation]
 Metrological Notes on ancient Electrum Coins. Num. Chr. 1875.
 Coins discovered on the site of Naucratis. Num. Chr. 1886.
 Electrum Coins and their Specific Gravity. Num. Chr. 1887.
F. Hultsch: *Griechische und Römische Metrologie.* Berlin, 1882.
 Metrologicorum Scriptorum Reliquiae. 2 vols. Lipsiae, 1864, 66.
 Die Gewichte des Alterthums nach ihrem Zusammenhange dargestellt. Abhandl. d. K. Sächsischen Gesellsch. d. Wiss. xviii. ii. Leipzig, 1898.
F. Imhoof-Blumer: *Choix de Monnaies grecques.* [Plates only.] Winterthur, 1871.
 Beiträge zur Münzkunde u. Geographie von Altgriechenland u. Kleinasien. Z. f. N. 1873.
 Griechische Münzen in dem kön. Münzkabinet im Haag. Z. f. N. 1876.
 Griech. Münzen in der Sammlung in Karlsruhe. Z. f N. 1880.
 Monnaies grecques. Paris and Leipzig. 1883.
 Griech. Münzen aus dem Museum in Klagenfurt. N. Z. 1884.
 Beiträge zur griechischen Münzkunde. Z. f. N. 1885.
 Porträtköpfe auf antiken Münzen hellenischer u. hellenisierter Völker, mit Zeittafeln, &c. Leipzig, 1885.
 Griechische Münzen. Abh. d. kön. bayer. Akad. XVIII. München, 1890.
 Porträtköpfe auf römischen Münzen. 2nd ed Leipzig, 1892.
 Griechische Münzen. Num. Chron. 1895.
 Zur griechischen Münzkunde. (Asia Minor and Syria.) Rev. Su. 1898.
F. Imhoof-Blumer and P. Gardner: *Numismatic Commentary on Pausanias.* Journ. Hellen. Stud. 1885, 1886.
F. Imhoof-Blumer u. O. Keller: *Tier- u. Pflanzenbilder auf Münzen und Gemmen des klass. Altertums.* Leipzig, 1889.
W. M. Leake: *Numismata Hellenica.* London, 1854; Suppl. 1859.

C. F. LEHMANN: *Alt-babylon'sches Maas u. Gewicht.* Verhandlungen der Berl. Ges. f. Anthrop. &c., 1889.
   Zur Ἀθηναίων Πολιτεία (Cap. X). Hermes, 1892.
   Das alt-babylonische Maass- und Gewichts-system als Grundlage d. antiken Gewichts-, Münz- u. Maass-systeme. Leyden, 1893.
F. LENORMANT: *La Monnaie dans l'Antiquité.* Paris, 1878, 9. 3 vols.
A. LÖBBECKE: *Griech. Münzen aus meiner Sammlung.* Z. f. N. X-XXI.
H. DE LUYNES: *Choix de Médailles gr.* [Plates only.] Paris, 1840.
G. MACDONALD: *Catalogue of Greek Coins in the Hunterian Collection, University of Glasgow.* Vol. I (Italy, Sicily, Macedon, Thrace, and Thessaly). Glasgow, 1899.
T. E. MIONNET: *Description de Médailles antiques grecques et romaines.* Paris, 1807-1837. 15 vols.
T. MOMMSEN: *Histoire de la Monnaie romaine*, trans. by Blacas and de Witte. Paris, 1865-1875. 4 vols.
H. MONTAGU: *Unpublished and Rare Greek Coins.* Num. Chr. 1892.
A. ORESCHNIKOW: *Description of ancient Greek Coins in the Imperial Museum, Moscow.* [Russian.] Moscow, 1891.
M. PINDER: *Ueber die Cistophoren.* Berlin, 1856.
M. PINDER u. J. FRIEDLÄNDER: *Beiträge zur älteren Münzkunde.* Berlin, 1851.
A. POSTOLAKAS: Κατάλογος τῶν ἀρχαίων νομισμάτων . . . τοῦ ἐθνικοῦ νομισματικοῦ Μουσείου. I. Athens, 1872.
A. VON PROKESCH-OSTEN: *Inedita meiner Sammlung autonom altgriech. Münzen.* [Wien. Kais. Akad. Denkschr. V.] Vienna, 1854.
J. C. RASCHE: *Lexicon universae rei numariae veterum.* 6 vols. (11 parts). Leipzig, 1785-1804; Suppl. 2 vols. 1802-1804.
TH. REINACH: *De la valeur proportionnelle de l'or et de l'argent dans l antiquité grecque.* Rev. Num. 1893.
W. RIDGEWAY: *The Origin of Metallic Currency and Weight Standards.* Cambridge, 1892.
J. SABATIER: *Monnaies byzantines.* Paris, 1862. 2 vols.
A. VON SALLET: *Zu den Künstler-inschriften auf griech. Münzen.* Z. f. N. II (1875).
   Die Erwerbungen des kön. Münzcabinets. Z. f. N. XIII-XVIII (1885-1891).
J. P. SIX: *Monnaies grecques inédites ou rares.* Num. Chr. 1888 ff.
S. W. STEVENSON, C. ROACH SMITH, F. W. MADDEN: *Dictionary of Roman Coins.* London, 1889.
W. H. WADDINGTON: *Voyage en Asie Mineure au point de vue numismatique.* [Rev. Num.] Paris, 1853.
   Mélanges de Numismatique. [Rev. Num.] Paris, 1861-1867.
J. L. WARREN: *Greek Federal Coinage.* London. 1863.
W. W. WROTH: *Greek Coins acquired by the British Museum.* [Annual Articles since 1888 in the Num. Chron.] London, 1888 f.

Periodicals.

Annuaire de la Société française de Numismatique. Paris, 1866-1896.
Berliner Blätter für Münz-, Siegel- u. Wappenkunde. Berlin, 1863-1873.
Journal International d'Archéologie Numismatique. Athens, 1898 ff.
Mélanges de Numismatique. Paris, 1875-1882.
Numismatic Chronicle. London, 1838 ff.
Numismatische Zeitschrift. Vienna, 1870 ff.
Revue belge de Numismatique. Brussels, 1880 ff.
Revue Numismatique française. Paris, 1836 ff.
Revue suisse de Numismatique. Geneva, 1891 ff.
Rivista Italiana di Numismatica. Milan, 1888 ff.
Zeitschrift für Numismatik. Berlin, 1874 ff.

B. BOOKS AND ARTICLES DEALING WITH THE NUMISMATICS OF DISTINCT PARTS OF THE GREEK AND ROMAN WORLD.

1. Spain.

A. HEISS: *Monnaies antiques de l'Espagne.* Paris, 1870.
A. DELGADO: *Medallas autonomas de España.* Seville, 1871-1876.
J. ZOBEL DE ZANGRONIZ: *Estudio historico de la Moneda antigua española.* Madrid, 1878-80.

2. Gaul.

SAUSSAYE: *Numismatique de la Gaule Narbonnaise.* Paris, 1842.
DUCHALAIS: *Description des Médailles gauloises.* Paris, 1846.
HUCHER: *L'Art gaulois.* Paris, 1868.
ROBERT: *Monnaies gauloises.* Paris, 1880.
E. MURET et M. A. CHABOUILLET: *Catalogue des Monnaies gauloises de la Bibliothèque Nationale.* Paris, 1889.
H. DE LA TOUR: *Atlas de Monnaies gauloises.* Paris, 1892.

3. Britain.

J. EVANS: *Ancient British Coins.* London, 1864; Suppl. 1890.

4. Italy.

[In addition to the works on Roman Coins, for which see § A and § B 30.]

F. CARELLI: *Numorum Italiae veteris Tabulae CCII,* ed. Cavedoni. Leipzig, 1850.

J. Friedländer: *Die oskischen Münzen.* Leipzig, 1850.
L. Sambon: *Monnaies de la Presqu'île italique.* Naples, 1870.
R. S. Poole, B. V. Head, P. Gardner: *British Museum Catalogue.* London, 1873.
W. Deecke: *Etruskische Forschungen*, II. Stuttgart, 1876.
W. Corssen: *Die etruskischen Münzaufschriften.* Z. f. N. 1876.
R. Garrucci: *Le Monete dell' Italia antiqua.* Rome, 1885.
A. J. Evans: *The 'Horsemen' of Tarentum.* Num. Chr. 1889.
L. A. Milani: *Aes rude, signatum e grave rinvenuto alla Bruna presso Spoleto.* Riv. Ital. IV. (1891).
H. Dressel: *Berlin Museum Catalogue,* III. part 1. (Aes rude, aes signatum, aes grave; die geprägten Münzen von Etrurien bis Calabrien.) Berlin, 1894.

5. Sicily.

G. L. Castelli: *Siciliae nummi veteres.* Palermo, 1781.
A. Salinas: *Le monete delle antiche città di Sicilia.* Palermo, 1871.
B. V. Head: *Coinage of Syracuse.* Num. Chr. 1874.
R. S. Poole, B. V. Head, P. Gardner: *British Museum Catalogue.* London, 1876.
P. Gardner: *Sicilian Studies.* Num. Chr. 1876.
R. Weil: *Die Künstlerinschriften der sicilischen Münzen.* (Winckelmannsfest-Progr. xliv.) Berlin, 1884.
A. J. Evans: *Syracusan Medallions and their Engravers.* Num. Chr. 1890, 1891.
Some New Artists' Signatures on Sicilian Coins. Num. Chr. 1890.
Contributions to Sicilian Numismatics. Num. Chr. 1894.
E. Gabrici: *Topografia e Numismatica dell' antica Imera.* Riv. Ital. 1894.
Th. Reinach: *Sur la Valeur relative des Métaux monétaires dans la Sicile grecque.* Rev. Num. 1895.
A. Holm: *Geschichte des sicilischen Münzwesens bis zur Zeit des Augustus* [in vol. iii of his *Gesch. Siciliens im Alterthum*]. Leipzig, 1898.
Du Chastel de la Howardries (Comte Albéric): *Syracuse, ses Monnaies d'argent et d'or au point de vue artistique.* London, 1898.

6. Thrace, &c.

[See also under Bosporus, § 15.]

B. Koehne: *Description du Musée Kotschoubey.* 2 vols. St. Petersburg, 1857.
L. Müller: *Die Münzen des thrakischen Königs Lysimachus.* Copenhagen, 1858.

B. V. HEAD, P. GARDNER: *British Museum Catalogue.* London, 1877.

A. M. PODSCHIWALOW: *Beschreibung der unedirten u. wenig bekannten Münzen von Sarmatia Europaea, Chersonesus Taurica, u. Bosporus Cimmerius aus d. Sammlung A. M. P.'s.* Moscow, 1882.
Catalogue of Coins in the Public and Rumjantzov Museum at Moscow. I. (Sarmatia, Chersonesus Taurica, Bosporus Cimmerius, &c.) [Russian.] Moscow, 1884.

P. BURACHKOV: *Catalogue of Coins belonging to the Greek Colonies on the Coast of Southern Russia,* &c. [Russian.] Odessa, 1884.

J. FRIEDLÄNDER, A. VON SALLET: *Berlin Museum Catalogue,* I. (Taurische Chersonesus, Sarmatien, Dacien, Pannonien, Moesien, Thracien, Thracische Könige.) Berlin, 1888.

B. DOBRUSKÝ: *La Numismatique des Rois thraces.* [Bulgarian, with summary in French.] Sofia. 1897.

B. PICK: *Die Personen- u. Götter-Namen auf Kaisermünzen von Byzantion.* Num. Zeit. xxvii (1895).
Thrakische Münzbilder. Jahrb. d. k. deutsch. Arch. Inst. 1898.
Die antiken Münzen Nord-Griechenlands, unter Leitung von F. Imhoof-Blumer, herausg. v. d. kgl. Akad. d. Wiss. Band I. Dacien u. Moesien. 1ter Halbband. Berlin, 1898.

7. Macedon.

L. MÜLLER: *Numismatique d'Alexandre le Grand, suivi d'un App. contenant les Monnaies de Philippe II et III.* 2 vols. Copenhagen, 1855.

E. H. BUNBURY: *Some unpublished Tetradrachms of Alexander.* Num. Chr. 1868.
Additional Tetradrachms of Alexander. Num. Chr. 1883.

VON PROKESCH-OSTEN: *Liste des Alexandres de ma Coll. qui ne se trouvent pas dans le Catal. de M. Müller.* Num. Zeit. I. (1869).
Suite des Monnaies inéd. d'or et d'arg. d'Alexandre le Grand. Num. Zeit. III. (1871).

F. BOMPOIS: *Examen chronologique des Monnaies frappées par la Communauté des Macédoniens.* Paris, 1876.

B. V. HEAD: *British Museum Catalogue*: Macedon (Paeonia, Macedonia, Thraco-Macedonian tribes, Kings of Macedon to Perdiccas III). London, 1879.

J. FRIEDLÄNDER, A. VON SALLET: *Berlin Museum Catalogue,* II. (Paeonien, Macedonien, die macedonischen Könige bis Perdiccas III). Berlin, 1889.

H. GAEBLER: *Zur Münzkunde Makedoniens.* Z. f. N. XX. (1897).

8. Thessaly to Aetolia.

A. POSTOLAKAS: Κατάλογος τῶν ἀρχ. νομισμάτων τῶν νήσων Κερκύρας, Λευκάδος, κ.τ.λ. . . . συλλεχθ. ὑπὸ Π. Λαμπροῦ. Athens, 1868.

F. IMHOOF-BLUMER: *Die Münzen Akarnaniens.* Num. Zeit. X. (1878).

R. WEIL: *Die akarnanischen Bundesmünzen.* Z. f. N. VII. (1880).
A. J. EVANS: *On some recent discoveries of Illyrian Coins.* Num. Chr. 1880.
P. GARDNER: *British Museum Catalogue,* Thessaly to Aetolia. (Thessaly, Illyria, Epirus, Corcyra, Acarnania, Aetolia.) London, 1883.
J. BRUNŠMID: *Die Inschriften u. Münzen d. griechischen Städte Dalmatiens.* (Abhandl. des arch-epigr. Seminares d. Univ. Wien.) Vienna, 1898.

9. Central Greece and Euboea.

E. IMHOOF-BLUMER: *Zur Münzkunde Boeotiens.* Num. Zeit. III. (1871) and IX. (1877).
Die euböische Silberwährung. Monatsber. d. k. Akad. d. Wiss. Berlin, 1881.
B. V. HEAD: *History of the Coinage of Boeotia.* Num. Chr. 1881.
British Museum Catalogue, Central Greece. London, 1884.
J. N. SVORONOS: Νομισματικὴ τῶν Δελφῶν. Bull. Corr. Hellén. 1896.

10. Attica, Megaris, Aegina.

E. BEULÉ: *Monnaies d'Athènes.* Paris, 1858.
G. RATHGEBER: *Silberne Münzen d. Athenaier.* Weissensee, 1858.
C. L. GROTEFEND: *Chronolog. Anordnung d. athen. Silbermünzen.* Hanover, 1872.
J. G. DROYSEN: *Zum Münzwesen Athens* (Sitzungsber. d. k. Akad. d. Wiss.). Berlin, 1882.
B. V. HEAD: *British Museum Catalogue*: Attica, Megaris, Aegina. London, 1888.
E. BABELON: *Les Monnaies d'or d'Athènes.* Rev. des Ét. gr. 1889.
H. VON FRITZE: *Die Münztypen von Athen im 6. Jahrh. v. Chr.* Z. f. N. XX. (1895–7).
G. GILBERT: *Die älteste Münze Athens.* Neue Jahrbücher f. Philologie. 1896.
U. KÖHLER: *Die attische Goldprägung.* Z. f. N. XXI. (1898).
J. E. KIRCHNER: *Zur Datirung d. athen. Silbermünzen d. beiden letzten vorchristl. Jahrh.* Z. f. N. XXI. (1898).

11. Corinth and Colonies.

E. CURTIUS: *Studien zur Gesch. von Corinth.* Hermes X. (1876).
B. V. HEAD: *British Museum Catalogue*: Corinth and Colonies. London, 1889.

12. Peloponnesus.

J. LEICESTER WARREN: *Greek Federal Coinage.* London, 1863.

A. POSTOLAKAS: Κατάλογος τῶν ἀρχ. νομισμάτων τῶν νήσων Κερκύρας, Λευκάδος, Κεφαλληνίας, Ζακύνθου καὶ Κυθήρων συλλεχθ. ὑπὸ Π. Λαμπροῦ. Athens, 1868.

A. VON SALLET: *Arkadische Münzen.* Z. f. N. II. (1875).

J. FRIEDLÄNDER: *Ueber die für arkadisch gehaltene Münze des achaeisch Bundes.* Z. f. N. II. (1875).

P. GARDNER: *The Coins of Elis.* Num. Chr. 1879.
Zacynthus. Num. Chr. 1885.
British Museum Catalogue: Peloponnesus (excluding Corinth). London, 1887.

U. KÖHLER: *Peloponnesisches Eisengeld.* Athen. Mitth. 1882.

R. WEIL: *Das Münzwesen des achaeischen Bundes.* Z. f. N. IX. (1882).
Arkadische Münzen. Z. f. N. IX. (1882).

J. P. LAMBROS: Ἀναγραφὴ τῶν νομισμάτων τῆς κυρίως Ἑλλάδος. Πελοπόννησος. Athens, 1891.

M. G. CLERK: *Catalogue of the Coins of the Achaean League.* London, 1895.

13. Crete.

W. W. WROTH: *Cretan Coins.* Num. Chr. 1884.
British Museum Catalogue: Crete, &c. London, 1886.

J. N. SVORONOS: *Monnaies crétoises inédites.* Rev. Num. 1888.
Études sur la Numismatique crétoise. Rev. Num. 1889.
Προσθῆκαι εἰς τὸ βιβλίον *Numismatique de la Crète ancienne.* Ἐφημ. ἀρχ. 1889.
Numismatique de la Crète ancienne. Macon, 1890.

14. Cyclades and Sporades.

P. LAMBROS: Νομίσματα τῆς νήσου Ἀμόργου. Athens, 1870.

W. W. WROTH: *The Santorin Find of 1821.* Num. Chr. 1884.
British Museum Catalogue: Crete and Aegean Islands. London, 1886.

W. GREENWELL: *On a Find of archaic Greek Coins, principally of the Islands of the Aegean Sea.* Num. Chr. 1890.

J. N. SVORONOS: Νομισματικὴ καὶ ἱστορία τῆς ἀρχαίας Μυκόνου. Bull. Corr. Hellén. 1893.

D. P. PASCHALIS: Νομισματικὴ τῆς ἀρχαίας Ἄνδρου. Journ. Intern. 1898.

15. Bosporus, Pontus, Paphlagonia, Bithynia.

[See also under Thrace, § 6.]

B. KOEHNE: *Description du Musée Kotschoubey.* 2 vols. St. Petersburg, 1857.

A. VON SALLET: *Numismatik der Könige des Bosporus und Pontus.* Berlin, 1866.

A. ORESCHNIKOW : *Zur Münzkunde des cimmerischen Bosporus.* Moscow, 1883.

J. P. SIX : *Sinope.* Num. Chr. 1885.

W. W. WROTH : *British Museum Catalogue*: Pontus, Paphlagonia, Bithynia, and the Kingdom of Bosporus. London, 1889.

TH. REINACH : *Trois Royaumes d'Asie Mineure, Cappadoce, Bithynie, Pont.* Paris, 1888 ; Suppl., Rev. Num 1891.
Un nouveau roi de Paphlagonie. Rev. Num. 1894.
Un nouveau roi de Bithynie. Rev. Num. 1897.

F. IMHOOF-BLUMER : *Zur Münzkunde des Pontos, von Paphlagonien,* &c. Z. f. N. XX. (1897).
Bithynische Münzen. Journ. Intern. 1898.

16. Mysia, Troas, Aeolis, Lesbos.

W. W. WROTH : *Asklepios and the Coins of Pergamon.* Num. Chr. 1882.

F. IMHOOF-BLUMER: *Die Münzen der Dynastie von Pergamon.* Abhandl. d. k. Akad. d. Wiss. Berlin, 1884.
Zur Münzkunde des Pontus, von Paphlagonien, Tenedos, Aiolis, und Lesbos. Z. f. N. XX. (1897).

W. GREENWELL : *The Electrum Coinage of Cyzicus.* Num Chr. 1887.

W. W. WROTH : *British Museum Catalogue* : Mysia. London, 1892.
British Museum Catalogue : Troas, Aeolis, and Lesbos. London, 1894.

17. Ionia, Caria, and Islands.

B. V. HEAD : *History of the Coinage of Ephesus.* Num. Chr. 1880, 1881.
British Museum Catalogue : Ionia, Satrapal Coinage of the West Coast of Asia Minor, Islands of Ionia. London, 1892.
British Museum Catalogue : Caria, Cos, Rhodes, &c London, 1897.

P. GARDNER : *Samos and Samian Coins.* Num. Chr. 1882.

18. Lydia and Phrygia.

F. KENNER : *Phrygische Münzen.* Num. Zeit. IV. (1872).

F. LENORMANT : *Monnaies royales de Lydie.* Ann. de Num. IV. (1873).

B. V. HEAD : *The Coinage of Lydia and Persia.* London, 1877.

F. IMHOOF-BLUMER : *Lydische Stadtmünzen.* Geneva and Leipzig, 1897.

19. Lycia, Pamphylia, Pisidia.

CH. FELLOWS : *Coins of Ancient Lycia.* London, 1855.

J. L. WARREN : *Greek Federal Coinage.* London, 1863.

J. FRIEDLÄNDER : *Die pamphylischen Aufschriften auf Münzen.* Z. f. N. IV. (1877).

J. P. SIX: *Münzkunde Pisidiens u. angrenzender Länder.* Z. f. N. VI. (1878).
Monnaies lyciennes. Rev Num. 1886, 1887.
TH. BERGK: *Zur Geschichte des griechischen Alphabets in Pamphylien.* Z. f. N. XI. (1884).
E. BABELON: *Bibliothèque Nationale, Catalogue*: Les Perses Achéménides, les Satrapes, &c. Paris, 1893.
G. F. HILL: *British Museum Catalogue*: Lycia, Pamphylia, Pisidia. London, 1897.

20. Lycaonia, Isauria, Cilicia.

W. H. WADDINGTON: *Numismatique de l'Isaurie et de la Lycaonie.* Rev. Num. 1883.
W. W. WROTH: *Coins of Isauria and Lycaonia.* Num. Chr. 1883.
F. IMHOOF-BLUMER: *Mallos, Megarsos,* &c. Ann. de Num. 1883.
Zur Münzkunde Kilikiens. Z. f. N. X. (1883).
Coin-types of some Kilikian Cities. Journ. Hellen. Studies, 1898.
[See also § 26.]

21. Galatia, Cappadocia, Armenia.

V. LANGLOIS: *Numismatique de l'Arménie.* Paris, 1859.
E. THOMAS: *Armenian Coins.* Num. Chr. 1867, 1863, 1871.
O. BLAU: *Die Herren von Sophene u. ihre Münzen.* Num. Zeit. IX. (1877).
Zwei Mithradate von Armenien. Z. f. N. VII (1880).
TH. REINACH: *Trois Royaumes d'Asie Mineure.* Paris, 1888; Suppl., Rev. Num. 1891.
E. BABELON: *Bibliothèque Nationale, Catalogue*: Les Rois de Syrie, d'Arménie et de Commagène. Paris, 1890.
F. IMHOOF-BLUMER: *Zur griech. Münzkunde—Eusebeia Kaisareia,* &c. Rev. Su. 1898.
W. W. WROTH: *British Museum Catalogue*: Galatia, Cappadocia, Armenia, and Syria. London, 1899.

22. Syria.

M. DUANE: *Coins of the Seleucidae.* London, 1803.
A. VON SALLET: *Die Fürsten von Palmyra.* Berlin, 1866.
F. DE SAULCY: *Mémoire sur les Monnaies datées des Séleucides.* Paris, 1871.
Numismatique palmyrénienne. Rev. Arch. 1872.
Numismatique de la Terre Sainte. Paris, 1874
P. GARDNER: *British Museum Catalogue*: Seleucid Kings of Syria. London, 1878.

E. H. BUNBURY: *Unpublished Coins of the Kings of Syria.* Num. Chr. 1883.

E. BABELON: *Bibliothèque Nationale, Catalogue*: Les Rois de Syrie, d'Arménie et de Commagène. Paris, 1890.

W. W. WROTH: *British Museum Catalogue*: Galatia, Cappadocia, Armenia, Syria (Koinon, Commagene, Cyrrhestica, Chalcidice, Palmyra, Seleucis and Pieria, Coele-Syria, Trachonitis, Decapolis). London, 1899.

23. Cyprus and Phoenicia.

H. DE LUYNES: *Numismatique et Inscriptions cypriotes.* Paris, 1852.

J. P. SIX: *Observations sur les Monnaies phéniciennes.* Num. Chr. 1877.
Du Classement des Séries cypriotes. Rev. Num. 1883.

E. BABELON: *Marathus.* Rev. Num. 1888.
Aradus. Rev. Num. 1891.
Les Monnaies et la Chronologie des Rois de Sidon. Bull. Corr. Hellén. XV. (1ᶜ91).
Bibliothèque Nationale, Catalogue: Les Perses Achéménides... Cypre et Phénicie. Paris, 1893.

24. Galilea, Samaria, Judaea.

F. DE SAULCY: *Numismatique de la Terre Sainte.* Paris, 1874.

E. MERZBACHER: *Jüdische Aufstandsmünzen.* Z. f. N. 1874.
Untersuchungen über alt-hebräische Münzen. Z. f. N. III-V. (1876-1878).

F. W. MADDEN: *Coins of the Jews.* London, 1881.

TH. REINACH: *Les Monnaies juives.* Paris, 1888.

L. HAMBURGER: *Die Silber-Münzprägungen während des letzten Aufstandes der Israeliten.* Z. f. N. XVIII. (1891).

25. Arabia.

H. DE LUYNES: *Monnaies des Nabatéens.* Rev. Num. 1858.

M. DE VOGÜÉ: *Monnaies des rois de Nabatène.* Rev. Num. 1868.

F. DE SAULCY: *Lettre ... sur la Numismatique des Rois nabathéens de Petra.* Ann. de Num. 1873.
Numismatique de la Terre Sainte. Paris, 1874.

B. V. HEAD: *On Himyarite and other Arabian Imitations of Coins of Athens.* Num. Chr. 1878.
On a Himyaritic tetradrachm and the Trésor de San'â. Num. Chr. 1880.

G. SCHLUMBERGER: *Le Trésor de San'â.* Paris, 1880.

J. H. MORDTMANN: *Neue himjarische Münzen.* Num. Zeit. XII. (1880).

A. ERMAN: *Neue arabische Nachahmungen griechischer Münzen.* Z. f. N. 1882.

A SORLIN-DORLIGNY: *Monnaies nabatéennes inédites.* Rev. Num. 1887.
E. BABELON: *Monnaies nabatéennes inédites.* Rev. Num. 1887.

26. Mesopotamia, Babylonia, Parthia, Persia, and Satraps.

H. DE LUYNES: *Numismatique des Satrapies et de la Phénicie.* Paris, 1846.
A. DE LONGPÉRIER: *Rois Parthes Arsacides.* Paris, 1853-1882.
A. D. MORDTMANN: *Erklärung d. Münzen mit Pehlvi-Legenden.* Abth. I. Sasaniden. Zeit. d. deutsch. morgenländ. Gesellsch. 1854.
W. H. WADDINGTON: *Numismatique et Chronologie des Rois de la Characène.* Rev. Num. 1866.
P. GARDNER: *The Parthian Coinage.* London, 1877.
B. V. HEAD: *The Coinage of Lydia and Persia.* London, 1877.
A. VON SALLET: *Die Münzen d. Könige v. Characene.* Z. f. N. VIII. (1881).
J. P. SIX: *Le Satrape Mazaios.* Num. Chr. 1884.
E. DROUIN: *Monnaies à Légendes araméennes de Characène.* Rev. Num. 1889.
E. BABELON: *Numismatique d'Édesse en Mésopotamie.* Rev. Belge, 1892.
Les Monnaies des Satrapes. Rev. Num. 1892.
Bibliothèque Nationale, Catalogue: Les Perses Achéménides, les Satrapes, &c. Paris, 1893.
La Numismatique et la Chronologie des Dynastes de la Characène. Journ. Intern. 1898.
E. J. RAPSON: *Markoff's unpublished Coins of the Arsacidae.* Num. Chr. 1893.
F. IMHOOF-BLUMER: *Die Münzstätte Babylon.* Num. Zeit. 1896.

27. Bactria and India.

A. CUNNINGHAM: *Coins of Alexander's Successors in the East.* Num. Chr. 1868-70.
A. VON SALLET: *Nachfolger Alexanders d. Gr. in Bactrien u. Indien.* Z. f. N. VI-X. (1879-83).
P. GARDNER: *British Museum Catalogue*: Greek and Scythic Kings of Bactria and India. London, 1886.
E. J. RAPSON: *Indian Coins.* [Bühler's Grundriss d. indo-arischen Philol. u. Altertumskunde.] Strassburg, 1898.

28. Egypt.

A. VON SALLET: *Die Daten d. alexandrinischen Kaisermünzen.* Berlin, 1870.

F. FEUARDENT: *Numismatique.—Égypte ancienne.* Paris, 1870-1873.
J. DE ROUGÉ: *Monnaies des Nomes d'Égypte.* Rev. Num. 1874, and Ann. de Num. VI. (1882).
R. S. POOLE: *British Museum Catalogue*: the Ptolemies, Kings of Egypt. London, 1883.
British Museum Catalogue: Alexandria and the Nomes. London, 1892.
F. LENORMANT: *Lettre ... sur les Monnaies égyptiennes.* Ann. de Num. VIII. (1884).
E. REVILLOUT: *Lettres ... sur les Monnaies égyptiennes.* Ann. de Num. VIII-XIX. (1884-1895).
B. P. GRENFELL: *The Silver and Copper Coinage of the Ptolemies.* [Revenue Laws of Ptolemy Philadelphus, Appendix III.] Oxford, 1896.
L. SCHWABE: *Die kaiserlichen Decennalien u. die alexandrinischen Münzen.* Tübingen, 1896.

29. Africa (excluding Egypt).

L. MÜLLER: *Monnaies de l'ancienne Afrique.* 4 vols. Copenhagen, 1860-1874.
F. BOMPOIS: *Médailles grecques autonomes frappées dans la Cyrénaïque.* Paris, 1869.
ZOBEL DE ZANGRONIZ: *Estudio historico de la Moneda antigua española* (Hispano-Carthaginian coins). Madrid, 1879.
E. DROUIN: *Les Listes royales éthiopiennes et leur Autorité historique.* Rev. Arch. 1882.
R. S. POOLE: *British Museum Catalogue*: the Ptolemies (Cyrenaica under the Ptolemies). London, 1883.
W. F. PRIDEAUX: *Coins of the Axumite Dynasty.* Num. Chr. 1884.
E. BABELON: *Monnaies de la Cyrénaïque.* Rev. Num. 1885.
A. MAYR: *Die antiken Münzen der Inseln Malta, Gozo, u. Pantelleria.* Munich, 1894.

30. Roman and Byzantine.
[See also § A.]

BARON D'AILLY: *Recherches sur la Monnaie romaine depuis son Origine jusqu'à la Mort d'Auguste.* Lyon, 1863.
A. MISSONG: *Zur Münzreform unter d. röm. Kaisern Aurelian u. Diocletian.* Num. Zeit. I. (1869).
H. A. GRUEBER: *British Museum Catalogue of Roman Coins*: Roman Medallions. London, 1874.
TH. MOMMSEN: *Römische Denarschätze.* Z. f. N. II. (1875).
P. BROCK: *Numismatische Untersuchungen über die spätere röm. Kaiserzeit mit besonderer Beziehung auf die Münzmarken.* Z. f. N. II, III. (1875, 76).

F. LENORMANT : *Études sur les Ateliers monétaires et leurs Marques dans la Num. romaine.* Ann. de Num. V. (1877).

W. FROEHNER : *Les Médaillons de l'Empire romain.* Paris, 1878.

M. BAHRFELDT : *Ueber die ältesten Denare Roms.* Z. f. N. V. (1878).

A. MISSONG : *Die Vorläufer der Werthzahl* OB *auf röm. Goldmünzen.* Z. f. N. VII. (1880).

A. DE BELFORT : *Recherche des Monnaies impériales romaines non décrites dans l'Ouvrage de H. Cohen.* Ann. de Num. VI. (1882)—XIV. (1890).

M. BAHRFELDT u. K. SAMWER : *Geschichte des älteren römischen Münzwesens.* Vienna, 1883.

M. BAHRFELDT : *Die gefutterten Münzen aus d. Zeit der römischen Republik.* Num. Zeit. XVI. (1884).

A. MARKL : *Die Reichs-Münzstätten unter der Regierung Claudius II. Gothicus u. ihre Emissionen.* Num. Zeit. XVI. (1884).

B. PICK : *Zur Titulatur der Flavier.* Z. f. N. XIII. (1885); XIV. (1887).

F. KENNER : *Moneta Augusti.* Num. Zeit. XVIII. (1886).

F. KENNER : *Der römische Medaillon.* Num. Zeit. XIX. (1887).

TH. MOMMSEN : *Die fünfzehn Münzstätten der fünfzehn diocletianischen Diöcesen.* Z. f. N. XV. (1887).

F. GNECCHI : *Appunti di Numismatica romana.* Rivista Italiana di Numismatica, I ff. (1888 ff.).

F. KENNER : *Römische Goldbarren mit Stempeln.* Arch.-epigr. Mitt. aus Oest., XII. = Num. Zeit. XX. (1888).

A. MARKL : *Die Reichsmünzstätten under der Regierung des Quintillus u. ihre Emissionen.* Num. Zeit. XXII. (1890).

O. SEECK : *Die Münzpolitik Diocletians u. seiner Nachfclger.* Z. f. N. XVII. (1890).

O. VOETTER : *Erste christliche Zeichen auf römischen Mün en.* Num. Zeit. XXIV. (1892).

M. BAHRFELDT : *Ueberprägte Münzen aus d. Zeit d. röm. Republik.* Z. f. N. XIX. (1895).

R. MOWAT : *Les Ateliers monétaires impériaux en Gaule.* Rev. Num. 1895.

R. MOWAT : *Combinaisons secrètes de Lettres dans les Marques monétaires de l'Empire romain.* Rev. Num. 1897.

J. W. KUBITSCHEK : *Beiträge zur frühbyzantinischen Numismatik.* Num. Zeit. XXIX. (1897).

O. SEECK : *Sesterz und Follis.* N. Z. XXVIII. (1897).

H. WILLERS : *Römische Silberbarren mit Stempeln.* Num. Zeit. xxx. 1898.

KEY TO THE PLATES

PLATE I

No.	Metal	Weight in Grammes		Page
1	EL	10.81	**Lydia?** Striations. *Rev.* Oblong incuse between two squares. *Babylonic Stater.* Early VII c. B.C.	177
2	N	16.516	**Phocaea.** Seal r. Below, ☉. *Rev.* Two incuse squares of unequal sizes. *Phocaic Stater.* Early VI c. B.C. . . 8, 33, 176,	214
3	EL	16.33	**Cyzicus.** Tunny-fish bound with fillets. *Rev.* Two incuse squares; in smaller, scorpion. *Cyzicene Stater.* Early VI c. B.C.	167
4	EL	14.01	**Ephesus?** AMΉϟIMΉϟOWϡAΦ. Stag grazing r. [*Rev.* Oblong incuse between two squares.] *Phoenician Stater.* Early VI c. B.C. . . 79, 160, 168, 181,	210
5	EL	16.04	**Cyzicus.** Winged female figure running l., raising hem of chiton with l.; in extended r. tunny. *Rev.* Incuse square of mill-sail pattern. *Cyzicene Stater.* B.C. 500–450. . . . 119, 152, 158,	179
6	EL	14.22	**Uncertain of Ionia.** Two lions' scalps combined inversely. [*Rev.* Oblong incuse between two squares.] *Phoenician Stater.* VII c. B.C.	158
7	EL	13.92	**Miletus.** Lion with head reverted, couchant r., within frame. *Rev.* Three incuses; in first, square, stag's head r.; in second, oblong, fox running l. and three pellets; in third, quatrefoil, five pellets arranged on two lines in saltire. *Milesian(?) Stater.* VII c. B.C.	7
8	N	8.03	**Sardes (Croesus?).** Foreparts of lion and bull confronted. *Rev.* Two incuse squares. *Croesean Gold Stater.* B.C. 568–554	7
9	R	10.30	**Sardes (Croesus?).** Similar to preceding. *Babylonic Stater.* B C. 568–554	7
10	R	5.44	**Persia.** The Great King running r. with bow and spear. [*Rev.* Incuse square.] *Siglos.* V c. B.C. 30,	172
11	N	8.36	**Persia (Darius I).** Similar to preceding. *Daric.* B.C. 521–486 . . . 30,	172

KEY TO THE PLATES 257

PLATE I (*continued*).

No.	Metal	Weight in Grammes		Page
12	EL	14.06	**Samos?** Forepart of bull r., head reverted. [*Rev.* Quadripartite incuse square.] *Milesian* (?) *Stater.* Late VI c. B.C. . . 39,	158
13	Billon	14.37	**Lesbos.** Gorgoneion. *Rev.* Incuse square. *Phoenician Stater.* ca. B.C. 500 . .	70
14	AR	10.11 (pierced)	**Calymna.** [Rudely represented archaic bearded head l., in crested helmet.] *Rev.* Chelys, in incuse impression adapted to its shape. *Babylonic Stater.* Early VI c. B.C. .	158n
15	AR	17.22	**Cyrene.** Silphium, silphium-seed, and lion's head l. *Rev.* Eagle's head r. with serpent in beak; in field, floral ornament; the whole in dotted incuse square. *Euboic Tetradrachm.* Late VI c. B.C.	114
16	AR	7.94	**Chios.** Sphinx seated l.; in front, amphora. *Rev.* Quadripartite incuse square. *Chian didrachm.* Early V c. B.C.	39

PLATE II.

No.	Metal	Weight in Grammes		Page
1	AR	12.44	**Aegina.** Sea-tortoise. *Rev.* Incuse square, divided into eight triangles. *Aeginetic Stater.* Early VII c. B.C.	8
2	AR	17.16	**Athens.** Head of Athena r. *Rev.* [A]ΘE. Owl and olive-spray in incuse square. *Attic Stater.* ca. 560 B.C. . . 8, 161,	169
3	AR	12.12	**Naxos.** Cantharus decorated with ivy and grapes. *Rev.* Quadripartite incuse square. *Aeginetic Stater.* VI c. B.C. . . . 8,	167
4	AR	16.48	**Euboea.** Gorgoneion. *Rev.* Bull's head facing, in incuse square. *Euboic Tetradrachm.* Late VI c. B.C.	8
5	AR	8.51	**Corinth.** Pegasus bridled, wing curved, walking l.; below Ϙ. *Rev.* Incuse of swastika form. *Corinthian Stater.* B.C. 625–585	41
6	AR	2.75	**Corinth.** Similar to preceding, but Pegasus flies. *Corinthian Drachm.* B.C. 625–585 .	41
7	AR	11.32	**Corcyra.** Cow l. suckling calf. *Rev.* Two oblong incuses, each containing floral device. *Corcyraean Stater.* B.C. 585–500. 9, 40, 117,	177
8	AR	2.93	**Arcadia.** Zeus Aphesius seated l. with sceptre and eagle. *Rev.* ΝΟϞ[Ι]ΔΑϞ[ЯΑ]. Head of Artemis r. in incuse square. *Aeginetic Triobol.* 480–417 B.C. . . 81,	107
9	AR	27.70	**Edoni** (Getas). Man r., wearing causia, between two oxen. *Rev.* ΓΕΤΑΒΑΣΙΛΕΩ-ΣΗΔΩΝΑΝ within an incuse square and enclosing raised quadripartite square. *Phoenician Octadrachm.* ca. B.C. 500 . 24, 65,	181n

s

PLATE III.

No.	Metal	Weight in Grammes		Page
1	R	8.39	Populonia (Etruria). Gorgoneion; beneath, X. *Rev.* plain. *Euboic-Syracusan piece of 10 units.* ca. 480 B.C.	56 n
2	R	7.48	Poseidonia. MOΠ (=Ποσ) Poseidon r. wielding trident. *Rev.* MOΠ (in raised letters). Similar type l., incuse, and seen from behind. *Campanian Stater.* 550–480 B.C.	104, 152, 158, 161, 169
3	R	8.29	Caulonia. KAVI⸗ Apollo r. with branch in raised r., on extended l. winged figure running r.; in field r. stag. [*Rev.* Similar type l. incuse, but winged figure absent, no inscr.] *Italic Stater.* 550–480 B.C.	103, 161, 171
4	R	5.55	Zancle. ᗞANKVE Dolphin l. within harbour of Zancle. *Rev.* Incuse square divided into many compartments; in central square, shell. *Aeginetic (?) Drachm.* Before B.C. 493.	174, 181
5	R	17.08	Syracuse. Quadriga r., above which Nike laying hand on head of one of the horses. *Rev.* ΣYRAϘOΣION Female head r. (Arethusa ?) surrounded by four dolphins. Incuse circle. *Attic Tetradrachm.* B.C. 485–478	159, 161, 172
6	R	44.43	Syracuse. Quadriga r., horses crowned by flying Nike. In exergue, lion r. *Rev.* ΣYRAKOΣION Laureate head r. (Nike) surrounded by dolphins. Incuse circle. *Demareteion (Attic Decadrachm).* B.C. 480	65, 159, 161, 172, 200
7	R	17.17	Gela. [Quadriga r., horses crowned by flying Nike.] *Rev.* ⟨EΛAΣ Forepart of human-headed bull r. Incuse circle. *Attic Tetradrachm.* ca. B.C. 485.	161, 171
8	R	0.85	Sybaris and Poseidonia. VM (=Συ) Poseidon r. wielding trident. *Rev.* MOΠ Bull standing r. Concave field. *Italic Litra.* ca. B.C. 453–448.	115
9	R	17.37	Agrigentum. AKPAΓ Two eagles r. on hare. *Rev.* AKPAΓAN[TI]NON Crab; below, Scylla l. [Formerly in Ashburnham Collection.] *Attic Tetradrachm.* Late V c. B.C.	163
10	R	3.95	Velia. Female head r *Rev.* VEΛH Owl on olive-branch; in field r., Δ. *Campanian Drachm.* 500–450 B.C.	61

No.	Metal	Weight in Grammes		Page

PLATE IV.

1. ᴀʀ — 8.56 — **Magnesia ad Maeandrum.** ΘΕΜΙΣ-ΤΟΚΛΕΟΣ Apollo standing r., holding long laurel-branch. *Rev.* ΜΑ Eagle flying, in dotted incuse square. [Bibliothèque Nationale, Paris.] *Attic Didrachm.* ca. 460 B.C. — 71 n

2. ᴀʀ — 11.88 — **Gortyna.** Goddess seated in tree. *Rev.* Traces of inscription ΜΟΙΜVΤϞΟΛ. Bull l. Incuse circle. *Aeginetic Stater.* ca. 431-400 — 163, 204

3. ᴀʀ — 17.18 — **Athens.** Head of Athena r. *Rev.* ΑΘΕ Owl and olive-branch, in incuse square. *Attic Tetradrachm.* Mid. V c. B.C. — 162

4. ᴀʀ — 11.67 — **Gortyna.** Goddess seated in tree. *Rev.* Bull r., licking r. hind-leg. Concave field. *Aeginetic Stater.* Early IV c. B C. — 204

5. Æ — — **Eleusis.** Triptolemos l. in winged car drawn by serpents. *Rev.* [Ε]ΛΕΥΣ[Ι] Pig r. standing on 'bacchos.' In exergue, pig's head r. and ivy-leaf. Mid. IV c. B.C. — 81

6. ᴀʀ — 8.55 — **Corinth.** Pegasus l. Below, Ϙ. *Rev.* Helmeted head of Athena l.; behind, palmette. Concave field. *Corinthian Stater.* ca. 400-338 B.C. — 169

7. ᴀʀ — 5.70 — **Trapezus.** [Male head l., wearing wreath.] *Rev.* ΤΡΑ Table, on which bunch of grapes (?). *Babylonic Drachm.* IV c. B.C. — 176

8. EL — 2.55 — **Phocaea.** Female head l., hair in kerchief; beneath, seal. [*Rev.* Mill-sail incuse square.] *Phocaean Sixth.* ca. 400 B.C. — 15, 65, 119

9. EL — 2.52 — **Lesbos.** Female head three-quarters r. [*Rev.* Bull's head l, in incuse square.] *Lesbian Sixth.* Early IV c. B.C. — 15, 105, 120

10. ᴀʀ — 12.21 — **Thebes.** Boeotian shield. *Rev.* ΕΠΑΜΙ (altered in the die from ΕΓΓΑ) above, rose. *Aeginetic Stater.* ca. 378-362 B.C. — 108, 124

11. ᴀʀ — 11.54 — **Phaestus.** ΤΑΛΩ[Ν] Talos hurling stones. [*Rev.* ΦΑΙΣΤΙΩΝ Bull butting r.] *Aeginetic Stater.* IV c. B.C. — 170

12. ᴀʀ — 11.08 — **Tarsus, Satrap Mazaeus.** Baaltars seated l.; his name in Aramaic (בעלתרז). *Rev.* Lion devouring bull; beneath, walls of Tarsus. In Aramaic, מזדי זי על עברנהרא וחלך, Mazaeus, who is over Eber-nahara and Cilicia. *Babylonic Stater.* ca. 362-328 B.C. — 97, 169, 206

13. ᴀʀ — 11.55 — **Samos.** ΣΥΝ Infant Heracles strangling serpents. [*Rev.* ΣΑ Lion's scalp, in incuse circle.] *Rhodian Tridrachm.* ca. 394-365 B.C. — 112, 173

s 2

PLATE V.

No.	Metal	Weight in Grammes		Page
1	AR	14.29	**Amphipolis.** Head of Apollo, three-quarters r. *Rev.* ΑΜΦΙΠΟΛΙΤΕΩΝ in square frame, within which are a racetorch and A. Incuse square. *Phoenician Stater.* ca. 400 B.C.	160, 163, 172
2	AR	11.87	**Elis.** [Eagle to r., tearing a hare. (Countermark, double-axe.)] *Rev.* F A Nike seated l. on basis, holding palm-branch; in exergue, olive-spray. Incuse circle. *Aeginetic Stater.* ca. 400 B.C.	163
3	AR	13.21	**Cyrene.** Head of Zeus Ammon, three-quarters l., in wreath. *Rev.* V⊃ Silphium plant. P A A N *Phoenician Stater.* ca. 400 B.C.	173
4	AV	9.10	**Panticapaeum.** Head of Satyr, three-quarters l. *Rev.* ΠΑΝ Griffin holding spear in mouth; he stands l. on an ear of corn. *Crimean Gold Stater.* ca. 350 B.C.	18, 33, 40
5	AR	15.18	**Rhodes.** Head of Helios, three-quarters r. *Rev.* [P]OΔIO[N] Rose with bud. In field, sphinx l. The whole in incuse square. *Rhodian Tetradrachm.* Early IV c. B.C.	10, 39, 169, 176
6	AR	14.68	**Cyzicus, Satrap Pharnabazus.** ΦΑΡ-[N]ΑΒΑ Head of Pharnabazus r. in Persian head-dress. [*Rev.* Prow l.; below, tunny. Incuse circle.] *Phoenician Stater.* ca. 410 B.C.	96
7	AR	12.14	**Delphi.** Head of Demeter l., veiled and wreathed with corn. *Rev.* ΑΜΦΙΚΤΙΟ-ΝΩΝ Apollo with lyre and laurel-branch seated l. on omphalos; in front, tripod. Concave field. *Aeginetic Stater.* ca. 346 B.C.	118, 169
8	EL	15.95	**Cyzicus.** Bearded head l. in laureate pileus (Cabeiros?); below, tunny. [*Rev.* Mill-sail incuse square.] *Cyzicene Stater*	14, 119
9	AR	15.31	**Iasus? Satrap Tissaphernes?** Head of Satrap r. in Persian head-dress. [*Rev.* ΒΑΣΙΛ Lyre.] *Phoenician Stater.* ca. 412-408 B.C.	164
10	AV	8.37	**Lampsacus.** Bearded head l. as on no. 8. [*Rev.* Forepart of winged horse r. in incuse square.] *Lampsacene Gold Stater.* ca. 394-350 B.C.	120, 164
11	AR	14.44	**Chalcidice.** Head of Apollo l. *Rev.* Χ[Α]Λ-ΚΙΔΕΩΝ Lyre; above, tripod. *Phoenician Stater.* Early IV c. B.C.	108
12	AR	12.03	**Pheneus.** [Head of Demeter l.; behind, ΠΟ.] *Rev.* ΦΕΝΕΩΝ Hermes, caduceus in r., carrying infant Arcas; between legs of Hermes, ʘ. *Aeginetic Stater.* ca. 350 B.C.	169, 170

No.	Metal	Weight in Grammes	PLATE VI.	Page
1	AR	17.44	**Naxos** (Sicily). Head of Dionysus r. wearing ivy-wreath. *Rev.* ΝΑΧΙΟΝ Silenus seated on ground, raising cantharos to his lips. Incuse circle. *Attic Tetradrachm.* ca. 460 B.C. 159, 162, 219	
2	AR	17.43	**Selinus** (Sicily). River-god ΣΕΛΙΝΟΣ l. sacrificing with patera at altar, before which a cock; in his l. a laurel-branch; behind him, selinon-leaf and bull on basis. [*Rev.* ΞΑΙΝΟΜΝΤΙΟΝ Apollo and Artemis in quadriga l., Apollo shooting with his bow.] *Attic Tetradrachm.* ca. 460 B.C. . . 173	
3	AR	17.15	**Naxos** (Sicily). Types similar to no. 1, but on rev. ivy grows beside Silenus, who holds thyrsus. *Attic Tetradrachm.* ca. 415 B.C. . 162	
4	AR	42.83	**Syracuse.** ΣΥΡΑΚΟΣΙΩΝ Head of Persephone l., wearing wreath of corn; around, four dolphins; in field Δ; below, traces of signature ΕΥΑΙΝΕ. [*Rev.* Quadriga l.; above, Nike crowning charioteer; below, on steps, shield, greaves, cuirass and helmet; below which ΑΘ[Λ]Α.] *Attic Decadrachm.* ca. 400 B.C. 65, 159, 163, 193	
5	AR	15.00	**Thurium.** Head of Athena r. *Rev.* ΘΟΥΡΙΩΝ Η Bull butting r. Incuse square. *Italic Distater.* ca. 440 B.C. . . . 117, 163	
6	AR	43.36	**Syracuse.** ΣΥΡΑΚΟΣΙΩΝ Head of Arethusa l.; around, four dolphins, on lowest of which ΚΙΜΩΝ. *Rev.* Similar to no. 4. *Attic Decadrachm.* ca. 400 B.C. 65, 159, 163, 172, 193	
7	AR	17.26	**Syracuse.** ΑΡΕΘΟΣΑ Head of Arethusa facing, dolphins amid her hair. On diadem, ΚΙΜΩΝ. *Rev.* ΣΥΡΑΚΟΣΙΩΝ Quadriga l., Nike above advancing towards charioteer; meta overturned beneath horses' feet; in exergue, ear of corn. *Attic Tetradrachm.* 163, 172	
8	AR	7.74	**Terina.** Head of Nike r. in laurel-wreath; behind head, Φ. *Rev.* ΤΕΡΙΝΑΙΟΝ Nike, holding caduceus and bird, seated r. on hydria. *Italic Stater.* ca. 420 B.C. . 158, 163	

PLATE VII.

| 1 | AR | 14.39 | **Philip II of Macedon.** Head of Zeus l. *Rev.* ΦΙΛΙΠΠΟΥ Youth on horseback to r. carrying palm-branch; in field, bee. *Phoenician Stater.* 359–336 B.C. . . 9, 171 | |

No.	Metal	Weight in Grammes	Plate VII (continued).	Page
2	N	8.62	**Philip II of Macedon.** Youthful male head r. *Rev.* ΦΙΛΙΠΠΟΥ Biga to r. In field, thunderbolt. *Philippeus.* 358–336 B.C.	9, 164, 177
3	N	8.62	**Philippi.** Head of Heracles r. in lion's skin. *Rev.* ΦΙΛΙΠΠΩΝ Tripod; above, palm-branch; to r., Phrygian cap. *Gold Stater.* 358–336 B.C.	20, 83
4	R	17.26	**Alexander III of Macedon.** Head of Heracles r. in lion's skin. *Rev.* ΑΛΕΞ-ΑΝΔΡΟΥ Zeus seated l., with eagle and sceptre. In field l., prow. *Attic Tetradrachm.* 336–323 B.C.	10, 171, 172, 178
5	N	8.62	**Aradus,** imitation of **Alexander III.** Head of Athena r.; on helmet, coiled serpent. *Rev.* ΑΛΕΞΑΝΔΡΟΥ Nike l. with wreath and trophy-stand. In field l. Phoenician inscription א (of A[radus]), r. AP in monogram. *Gold Stater.* ca. 310 B.C.	9, 171
6	R	17.21	**Lysimachus of Thrace.** Head of Alexander the Great r., with ram's horn. *Rev.* ΒΑΣΙ-ΛΕ⌒[Σ] ΛΥΣΙΜΑΧΟ[Υ] Athena seated l. holding Nike. In field, cornucopiae and lyre. *Attic Tetradrachm.* 306–281 B.C.	10
7	R	17.11	**Demetrius Poliorcetes.** Head of Demetrius r., diademed, with bull's horn (as Bacchus). [*Rev.* ΒΑΣΙΛΕ⌒Σ ΔΗΜΗ-ΤΡΙΟΥ Poseidon l. leaning on trident. Two monograms.] *Attic Tetradrachm.* 306–286 B.C.	10
8	N	27.77	**Ptolemy II of Egypt,** and family. ΘΕΩΝ Busts jugate r. of Ptolemy I and Berenice I, diademed. *Rev.* ΑΔΕΛΦΩΝ Busts jugate r. of Ptolemy II and Arsinoë II, diademed. Behind, shield. *Phoenician Octadrachm.* 277 B.C. or later	65, 185
9	R	14.79	**Ptolemy I of Egypt.** Head of Ptolemy I r., diademed. [*Rev.* ΠΤΟΛΕΜΑΙΟΥ ΒΑΣΙΛΕΩΣ Eagle l. on thunderbolt. In field l. ΣΑ in monogram (Sa[lamis] in Cyprus).] *Phoenician Stater.* 305–284 B.C.	10
10	R	17.24	**Demetrius Poliorcetes.** Nike blowing trumpet on prow l. *Rev.* ΔΗΜΗΤΡΙΟΥ ΒΑΣΙΛΕ⌒Σ Poseidon l. wielding trident. Two monograms. *Attic Tetradrachm.* 306–286 B.C.	10, 175
11	R	16.85	**Seleucus I of Syria.** Head of Seleucus r., wearing helmet made of skin of bull's head, and lion's skin round neck. [*Rev.* ΒΑΣΙ-ΛΕ⌒Σ ΣΕΛΕΥΚΟΥ Nike r. placing wreath on trophy.] *Attic Tetradrachm.* 306–280 B.C.	10

PLATE VIII.

No.	Metal	Weight in Grammes		Page
1	N	8.31	**Diodotus of Bactria.** Head of Diodotus r., diademed. *Rev.* ΒΑΣΙΛΕΩΣ ΔΙΟΔΟ-ΤΟΥ Zeus l. hurling thunderbolt, aegis on his arm; in field l., wreath and eagle. *Gold Stater.* ca. 250 B.C.	10
2	R	17.16	**Mithradates II of Pontus.** Head of Mithradates II r., diademed. [*Rev.* ΒΑΣΙΛΕΩΣ ΜΙΘΡΑΔΑΤΟΥ Zeus seated l. with eagle and sceptre; in field l., star and crescent; three monograms.] *Attic Tetradrachm.* 240-190? B.C.	164
3	R	10.71	**Alexander of Epirus.** Head of Zeus r., wreathed with oak. *Rev.* ΑΛΕΞΑΝΔΡΟΥ [ΤΟ]Υ ΝΕΟΠΤΟΛΕΜΟΥ Thunderbolt. In field, eagle r. *Corcyrean Stater.* 342-326 B.C.	164
4	R	17.00	**Antimachus of Bactria.** Head of Antimachus r., wearing diadem and causia. [*Rev.* ΒΑΣΙΛΕΩΣ ΘΕΟΥ ΑΝΤΙΜΑ-ΧΟΥ Poseidon standing to front, with trident and palm-branch. Monogram in field.] *Attic Tetradrachm.* ca. 200 B.C.	164
5	R	16.64	**Side.** Head of Athena r. (Countermark, ΕΦΕ and bow in bow-case). [*Rev.* Nike l. carrying wreath; in field l. pomegranate and ΔΗ.] *Attic Tetradrachm.* ca. 100 B.C.	39
6	R	16.82	**Aetolia.** [Head of Heracles r. in lion's skin.] *Rev.* [Α]ΙΤΩΛΩ[Ν] Aetolia seated r. on pile of shields, r. resting on spear; in field, letters and monogram. *Attic Tetradrachm.* 279-168 B.C.	108
7	R	16.87	**Philip V of Macedon.** On a Macedonian shield, head of the hero Perseus l. in winged bonnet, harpa over shoulder, with features of Prince Perseus. [*Rev.* ΒΑΣΙΛΕΩΣ ΦΙΛΙΠΠΟΥ Club, three monograms. The whole in oak-wreath, outside which, sword.] *Attic Tetradrachm.* 220-178 B.C.	159, 171
8	N	8.63	**Alexander II of Syria.** Head of Alexander r., diademed. *Rev.* [Β]ΑΣΙΛΕΩΣ ΑΛΕΞ-ΑΝΔΡΟΥ ΘΕΟΥ ΕΠΙΦΑΝΟΥΣ ΝΙΚΗΦΟΡΟΥ Zeus seated l. with Nike and sceptre. *Gold Stater.* 128-123 B.C.	12
9	R	16.69	**Perga.** Head of Artemis r., laureate, quiver at shoulder. [*Rev.* ΑΡΤΕΜΙΔΟΣ ΠΕΡ-ΓΑΙΑΣ Artemis l. with wreath and sceptre, accompanied by hind; in field, sphinx r.] *Attic Tetradrachm.* II c. B.C.	164, 169
10	R	16.45	**Smyrna.** Head of Cybele r., turreted. *Rev.* ΣΜΥΡΝΑΙΩΝ and monogram in oak-wreath. *Attic Tetradrachm.* II c. B.C.	11, 164, 169

No.	Metal	Weight in Grammes		Page
			PLATE IX.	
1	ᴀ̄	2.11	**Epidaurus** (Achaean League). Head of Zeus r., laureate. *Rev.* In laurel-wreath AX in monogram. Above monogram, serpent; in field ΣΩ. *Aeginetic Triobol.* III c. B.C. ΣΙ	10, 112
2	ᴀ̄	16.82	**Byzantium** (imitation of Lysimachus). Head of Alexander the Great r. with ram's horn and diadem. *Rev.* ΒΑΣΙΛΕΩΣ ΛΥΣΙ-ΜΑΧΟΥ Athena seated l. holding Nike. In field, monogram; on seat ΒΥ; in exergue, trident. *Attic Tetradrachm.* II c. B.C.	11, 154, 178
3	ᴀ̄	13.41	**Byzantium.** Head of Demeter r. veiled and wreathed with corn. *Rev.* [Ε]ΠΙ ΟΛΥΜ-ΠΙΟΔΩΡ[ΟΥ][1] Poseidon seated r. In field l. ΓΥ, r. monogram. *Phoenician Stater.* ca. 280–270 B.C.	106
4	ᴀ̄	13.97	**Chalcedon.** Head of Demeter r. veiled and wreathed with corn. *Rev.* ΚΑΛΧ Apollo, with bow and arrow, seated r. on omphalos. In field, monogram and ΔΙ. *Phoenician Stater.* ca. 280–270 B.C.	106
5	ᴀ̄	1.81	**Masicytes** (Lycian League). Head of Apollo r. laureate, bow at shoulder. *Rev.* ΛΥΚΙΩΝ ΜΑΣ Lyre in incuse square. *Rhodian* (?) *Drachm.* 168–ca. 81 B.C.	88, 111, 153
6	ᴀ̄	3.4	**Dyrrhachium.** ΜΟΝΟΥΝΙΟΣ Cow r. suckling calf; to r., ear of corn; in exergue, grapes *Rev.* ΔΥΡ ΔΑΜΗΝΟΣ Double floral pattern within square. 229–100 B.C.	121
7	ᴀᴠ	8.23	**Athens.** Head of Athena Parthenos r. *Rev.* ΑΘΕ. ΒΑΣΙΛΕ. ΜΙΘΡΑΔΑΤΗΣ ΑΡΙΣΤΙΩΝ Owl on amphora; in field, star between two crescents. The whole in olive-wreath. 87–6 B.C.	87, 200
8	ᴀ̄	16 65	**Athens.** Head of Athena r. *Rev.* ΑΘΕ. ΑΝΤΙΟΧΟΣ ΚΑΡΑΙΧΟΣ ΜΕΝΑΝ. Owl on amphora; in field, elephant; on amphora Ι; below ΣΦ. The whole in olive-wreath. Shortly before 175 B.C.	11, 130

PLATE X.

| 1 | ᴀ̄ | 14.97 | **Tiridates II of Parthia.** Head of king l., diademed. *Rev.* ΒΑϹΙΛΕΩϹ ΒΑϹΙ-ΛΕΩΝ ΑΡϹΑΚΟϹ ΕΥΕΡΓΕΤ·Υ ΔΙΚΑΙΟΥ ΕΠΙϮΑΝΟΥϹ [Ϯ]ΙΛΕΛ-ΛΗΝΟϹ King seated l., holding Nike. *Debased Attic Tetradrachm.* 33–32 B.C. | 160 |

[1] An Olympiodorus was prostates of Byzantium in 221 B.C., but this coin is probably to be connected with another person of that name.

Plate X (continued).

No.	Metal	Weight in Grammes		Page
2	℞	12.47	**Pergamum.** Cista mystica with serpent issuing from it; the whole in ivy-wreath. *Rev.* ΠΕΡ in monogram. Bow in bow-case between two serpents. In field r., race-torch. *Cistophorus.* ca. 200–133 B.C.	39
3	℞	16.93	**Perseus of Macedon.** Head of Perseus r., diademed. [*Rev.* ΒΑΣΙΛΕΩΣ ΠΕΡ-ΣΕΩΣ Eagle on thunderbolt; in field, three monograms, one of Ι Ωιλος; the whole in oak-wreath, below which, plough.] *Attic Tetradrachm.* 178–168 B.C.	164
4	Æ	—	**Antiochus VI of Syria.** Head of Antiochus r. radiate. [*Rev.* ΒΑΣΙΛ[ΕΩΣ] ΑΝΤΙ-ΟΧΟ[Υ] ΕΠΙΦΑΝΟΥ[Σ] ΔΙΟΝΥ-Σ[ΟΥ] Panther l. holding palm-branch. In field ΣΤΑ.] Serrated edge. 145–142 B.C.	150, 154
5	℞	16.76	**Macedon.** Head of Artemis r. on Macedonian shield. *Rev.* ΜΑΚΕΔΟΝΩΝ Club; above LEG and hand holding olive-branch. The whole in oak-wreath. *Attic Tetradrachm.* After 146 B.C.	11, 88, 159
6	℞	11.51	**Apamea** (Phrygia). [In ivy-wreath, cista mystica, from which issues serpent.] *Rev.* LENTVLVS IMPERATOR ΚΑΣ-ΤΟΡΟ[Σ - - -] Bow-case between two serpents. In field l. bow and [Α]ΠΑ, r. double flute. *Cistophorus.* 56–53 B.C.	88
7	℞	16.8	**Mithradates VI the Great of Pontus.** Head of Mithradates r., diademed. *Rev.* ΒΑΣΙΛΕΩΣ ΜΙΘΡΑΔΑΤΟΥ ΕΥ-ΠΑΤΟΡΟΣ Stag l. browsing. In field, star and crescent, two monograms, and ΒΚΣ (222); below Θ. The whole in ivy-wreath. *Attic Tetradrachm.* 76–75 B.C.	165
8	℞	13.04	**Ascalon.** Head of Cleopatra r., diademed. [*Rev.* ΑΣΚΑΛΩΝΙΤΩΝ ΙΕΡΑΣ ΑΣΥ-ΛΟΥ Eagle l. with palm-branch on thunder-bolt; in field, monogram and LNE (year 55).] 50–49 B.C.	165
9	℞	8.76	**Archelaus of Cappadocia.** Head of Archelaus r., diademed. *Rev.* ΒΑΣΙΛΕΩΣ ΑΡΧΕΛΑΟΥ ΦΙΛΟΠΑΤΡΙΔΟΣ ΤΟΥ ΚΤΙΣΤΟΥ Club. Date ΚΒ. 15–14 B.C.	165

PLATE XI.

No.	Metal	Weight in Grammes		Page
1	AR	7.82	**Tarentum.** Boy on horseback r. placing wreath on head of horse; another boy examining horse's hoof. In field Φ. *Rev.* TAPAΣ, with shield and trident to l. on dolphin; below, E and waves. Concave field. 344–334 B.C.	62, 172, 175, 181
2	AV	8.59	**Tarentum.** Veiled head of Demeter r. In front TAPA and dolphin, behind E. *Rev.* TAPANTINΩN Taras supplicating Poseidon. In field r. T and star; below seat, K; on an incision, I. Concave field. 344–334 B.C.	60, 175 n
3	AV	4.67	**Etruria.** XX Young male head l., wreathed. *Rev.* Bull l., above which, bird flying with wreath in beak; in field l., star; in exergue in Etruscan characters FELZPAPI (retrograde). Concave field. Mid. IV c. B.C.	55
4	AR	4.11	**Syracuse.** ΣYPAKOΣIΩN Head of Athena three-quarter face l.; around, four dolphins. *Rev.* ΣYPAKOΣIΩN ΛEYKAΣ[ΓIΣ] Leukaspis, with shield, helmet, and sword, fighting to r. with spear; behind him, altar; in front, ram lying on its back. *Attic Drachm.* Early IV c. B.C.	187
5	AR	17.11	**Carthage.** Head of Persephone l. wreathed with corn; around, dolphins. *Rev.* Horse's head l.; behind, palm-tree; below, Phoenician letter ([מחנת] = the camp). Concave field. *Attic Tetradrachm.* Mid. IV c. B.C.	9, 97
6	AR	27.77	**Hiero II of Syracuse.** Head of Hiero l., diademed. [*Rev.* BAΣIΛEOΣ IEPΩNOΣ Nike driving quadriga r.; above, star; in field r. K.] *Piece of 32 Litrae.* 270–216 B.C.	10, 164
7	AV	3.41	**Capua.** Janiform head. *Rev.* ROMA Two soldiers taking oath over a slain pig held by a third kneeling between them. *Campanian drachm.* End of IV c. B.C.	60
8	AR	4.32	**Rome.** Head of Roma r.; behind, X. *Rev.* ROMA. The Dioscuri on horseback charging to r. *Denarius.* Shortly after 268 B.C.	47, 53, 170, 187
9	AV	3.37	**Rome.** Head of Mars r.; behind, ↓X. *Rev.* ROMA Eagle r. on thunderbolt. 60 *Sesterces.* ca. 217 B.C.	54, 99
10	AR	1.07	**Rome.** Types as on no. 8; behind head, IIS *Sestertius.* Shortly after 268 B.C.	47, 170, 187
11	AR	2.24	**Rome.** Types as on no. 8; behind head, V. *Quinarius.* Shortly after 268 B.C.	47, 170, 187

KEY TO THE PLATES 267

No.	Metal	Weight in Grammes	Plate XI (continued).	Page
12	R	2·88	**Rome.** Head of Jupiter r. laureate. *Rev.* ROMA Victory r. crowning trophy; at her feet, a sow (moneyer's symbol). *Victoriatus*	47
13	R	3·95	**Italian Allies.** ITALIA Head of Italia r. *Rev.* The Dioscuri riding r. and l. In exergue, in Oscan characters, C. PAPI(us) C. (*filius*). *Denarius.* 90–89 B.C. . 99,	113
14	R	4·05	**Italian Allies.** Head of Italia l.; inscription in Oscan, MVTIL(us) EMBRATVR *Rev.* Two soldiers taking oath over a pig held by a kneeling man. In exergue, inscription as on no. 13. *Denarius.* 90–89 B.C. 99,	113

PLATE XII.

1	R	3·95	**Rome.** ROMA Bust of Roma l. In field l. ✳. *Rev.* Γ. NERVA Three citizens engaged in voting; on a tablet in the background, Γ. *Denarius.* 99–94 B.C. .	132
2	N	10·72	**Rome.** L·SVLLA Head of Venus r. and Cupid l. with palm. *Rev.* IMPER ITE-RVM Two trophies, lituus and ewer. *Aureus.* 87 B.C. . . . 54, 100, 171 *n*,	173
3	R	3·87	**Rome.** FAVSTVS Head of Diana r.; behind, lituus. *Rev.* FELIX Sulla seated l.; before him, Bocchus kneeling, holding up olive-branch; behind him, Jugurtha, hands bound, kneeling. *Denarius.* 62 B.C.	176
4	R	3·92	**Rome.** L. ROSC Head of Juno Lanuvina r. in goat-skin head-dress. Behind, helmet. *Rev.* FABAT Girl bringing food to the dragon of Lanuvium. Behind, club. Serrated edge. *Denarius.* 70 B C. .	154
5	R	4·08	**Rome.** [M S]CAVR AED CVR [E]X S C REX ARETAS Aretas, king of Nabathaeans, kneeling r. beside camel. *Rev.* [P] HVP(S)AEVS AED CVR C HVPSAE COS PREIVER [CA]PTV Jupiter in Quadriga l. *Denarius.* 58 B.C. .	190
6	R	4·02	**Rome.** MONETA Head of Moneta r. *Rev.* T. CARISIVS Moneyer's instruments and cap of Vulcan. The whole in wreath. *Denarius.* 45 B.C. . .	145
7	R	3·64	**Rome.** CAESAR· DICT PERPETVO Head of Julius Caesar r. wreathed. *Rev.* L. BVCA Caduceus, fasces, axe, globe, and clasped hands. *Denarius.* 44 B.C. . .	100

GREEK AND ROMAN COINS

PLATE XII (continued).

No.	Metal	Weight in Grammes		Page
8	AR	11·92	Asia Provincia. [IMP·IX·TR·PO·V Head of Augustus r.] *Rev.* COM ASIAE Hexastyle temple of ROM· ET AVGVST· at Pergamum. '*Cistophoric Medallion.*' 19 B.C.	40, 89, 189
9	Æ	—	Rome. [NERO CLAVD. CAESAR AVG. GER. P.M. TR. P. IMP. II. Head of Nero r.] *Rev.* SECVRITAS AVGVSTI. S. C. Securitas seated r. before an altar, beside which is a torch. In exergue II. *Dupondius.* 54-68 A.D.	15
10	N	7·97	Rome. CAESAR Head of Augustus r. *Rev.* AVGVSTVS Bull l. *Aureus.* 27 B.C.	54, 165
11	Æ	—	Rome. NERO CLAVD. CAESAR AVG. GER. P.M. TR. P. P. P. Head of Nero l. laureate. *Rev.* DECVRSIO. S. C. The Emperor armed with a spear on horseback to r., accompanied by a mounted soldier carrying a vexillum. *Sestertius.* 54-68 A.D.	15

PLATE XIII.

No.	Metal	Weight in Grammes		Page
1	Æ	—	Sardes. MHTPOΠOΛIC · CAPΔIC · ACIAC · ΛVΔIAC · EΛΛAΔOC · A Veiled and turreted bust of the city r. [*Rev.* EΠI COVΛ. EPMOΦIΛOV · A · APX · CAPΔIANΩN · B · NEΩKOPΩN Hades in quadriga r. carrying off Persephone; above horses, Eros.] 238-244 A.D.	91
2	Æ	—	Cyzicus. AVτοκράτωρ KAIσαρ Λούκιος Aίλιος AVρήλιος KOMMOΔOC AVΓουστος CEBαστὸς EVCεβὴς EVTυχὴς PΩM-AIOC HPAKΛHC Bust of Commodus l. laureate, wearing lion's skin. [*Rev.* KVZI-KHNΩN NEΩKOPΩN Cyzicus standing, placing hand on head of horse.] 191-193 A.D.	91
3	N	7·84	Rhoemetalces of Bosporus. Head of Hadrian r. Below, ΘKY (429). *Rev.* BACIΛEωC POIMHTAΛKOY Bust of Rhoemetalces r., diademed; in front, club. 132-133 A.D.	18, 86, 210
4	Æ	—	Bithynia. AVTοκράτωρ KAICαρ TPAIανὸs AΔPIANOC CEBαστός Head of Hadrian r. *Rev.* KOINON BEIΘYNIAC Octastyle temple of the Bithynian Κοινόν; in exergue, prow. 117-138 A.D.	118

KEY TO THE PLATES

No.	Metal	Weight in Grammes	Plate XIII (*continued*).	Page
5	Æ	—	**Abydus.** [ΑΥτοκράτωρ ΚΑΙσαρ Λούκιος CΕΠΤΙΜΙΟC CΕΟΥΗΡΟC ΠΕΡΤΙ-Ναξ Bust of Sept. Severus r.] *Rev.* ΕΠΙ ΑΡΧοντος ΦΑΒΑ. ΠΡΟΚΛΟΥ ΑΒΥΔΗνῶν Leander swimming towards lighthouse of Sestus, in which stands Hero with lighted lamp. 193-211 A.D.	176
6	Æ	—	**Pergamum.** ΘΕΑΝ ΡΩΜΗΝ Bust of Roma r., wearing turreted crown. *Rev.* ΘΕΟΝ CΥΝΚΛΗΤΟΝ Bust of the Roman Senate r. I c. A.D.	91, 188
7	Æ	—	**Conana** (Pisidia). [ΑΥΤοκράτωρ Καῖσαρ ΠΟπλιος ΛΙΚίννιος ΓΑΛΛΙΗΝΟC CΕΒαστός Head of Gallienus r.] *Rev.* ΚΟΝΑΝΕΩΝ Zeus with sceptre; in field, Θ. 253-268 A.D.	151
8	Æ	—	**Samos.** [Μάρκος ΑΥΡήλιος ΚΟΜμοδος ΑΝΤΩνεῖνος Bust of Commodus r.] *Rev.* CΑΜΙΩΝ Cultus statue of Samian Hera, wearing polos, round which serpent twines, and holding patera with pendent fillet in each hand; beside her, Nemesis, with r. hand on her breast. 180-192 A.D.	169
9	Æ	—	**Ephesus.** [ΑΔΡΙΑΝΟC ΚΑΙCΑΡ ΟΛΥΜΠΙΟC Bust of Hadrian r.] *Rev.* ΕΦΕCΙΩΝ Temple of Artemis, containing statue of the goddess, and showing reliefs in the pediment and on the lower drums of the columns. [Bibl. Nat., Paris.] 129-138 A.D.	169, 174

PLATE XIV.

1	Æ	—	**Elis.** [ΑΥΤΟΚΡΑΤΩΡ ΑΔΡΙΑΝΟC Bare head of Hadrian r.] *Rev.* ΗΛΕΙ[ΩΝ] Head of Zeus Olympius of Pheidias r. laureate. [Bibliothèque Nationale, Paris.] 117-138 A.D.	175
2	R	6.73	**Caesarea** (Cappadocia). [ΑΔΡΙΑΝΟC CΕΒΑCΤΟC Head of Hadrian r.] *Rev.* ΥΠΑΤΟC Γ. ΠΑΤΗΡ ΠΑΤρίδος. Figure of the Emperor on Mt. Argaeus; in field, sun and crescent. 119-138 A.D.	12, 89, 174

No.	Metal	Weight in Grammes	Plate XIV (continued).	Page
3	Æ	—	**Antiochia** (Pisidia). [IMPerator CAESar Lucius SEPtimius SEVERVS PERtinax AVGustus. Head of S. Severus r. laureate.] *Rev.* COLonia CAESarea ANTIOCHia. Senatus Romanus (?). Mên, wearing Phrygian cap, crescent at shoulders, stands to front; in l. Nike carrying trophy; r. rests on sceptre; l. foot on bull's head; beside him, cock. 193-211 A.D.	95
4	Æ	—	**Myra** (Lycia). [ΑΥΤοκράτωρ ΚΑΙσαρ Μάρκος ΑΝΤώνιος ΓΟΡΔΙΑΝΟϹ ϹΕΒαστός Bust of Gordian III r. laureate.] *Rev.* ΜΥΡΕΩΝ Simulacrum of Artemis Eleuthera in a tree which is attacked by two men with axes and defended by two snakes. 238-244 A.D.	170
5	Billon	—	**Alexandria** (Egypt). [Αὐτοκράτωρ Καῖσαρ Πόπλιος Λικίννιος ΟΥαλεριανὸς ΓΑΛΛΙΗΝΟϹ ΕΥσεβὴς ΕΥτυχὴς ϹΕβαστός Bust of Gallienus r. laureate.] *Rev.* L Δ (year 4). Bust of Sarapis l., wearing modius; behind, sceptre. 256-257 A.D.	12, 90
6	Æ	—	**Laodicea** (Phrygia). [ΙΟΥΛΙΑ ΔΟΜΝΑ ϹΕβαστή Bust of Domna r. In a countermark, head of an Emperor.] *Rev.* ΛΑΟΔΙΚΕΩΝ ΝΕΩΚΟΡΩΝ Tyche holding patera and statue of Zeus stands between wolf and boar; in field, ΤΠΗ (= 88). 211 A.D.	171, 187
7	Æ	14.87	**Antiochia** (Syria). [ΚΑΙΣΑΡΟΣ ΣΕΒΑΣΤΟΥ Head of Augustus r.] *Rev.* ΕΤΟΥΣ Λ ΝΙΚΗΣ Tyche of Antioch seated r. on rock, holding palm-branch; at her feet, river-god swimming r. In field, ΥΠΑ (in monogram) ΙΓ and another monogram (ΑΝΤΙΟΧ?). 2-1 B.C.	12, 89
8	Billon	—	**Alexandria** (Egypt). [ΝΕΡΩν ΚΛΑΥδιος ΚΑΙΣαρ ΣΕΒαστὸς ΓΕΡμανικὸς ΑΥΤΟκράτωρ Head of Nero r. laureate.] *Rev.* ΝΕΟ. ΑΓΑΘ. ΔΑΙΜ. Serpent Agathodaemon r., wearing skhent, enfolding ears of corn and poppy-heads. In front, LΓ (year 3). 56-57 A.D.	12, 90
9	Æ	—	**Cotiaeum** (Phrygia). ΔΗΜΟϹ ΚΟΤΙΑΕΠΝ Beardless head of Demos r. [*Rev.* ΕΠΙ Π. ΑΙΛίου ΔΗΜΗΤΡΙΑΝΟΥ ΙΠΠΙΚοῦ ΑΡΧοντος ΚΟΤΙΑΕΠΝ (ημη and ων in ligature). Helios in quadriga to front.] 253-260 A.D.	91, 188

KEY TO THE PLATES

No.	Metal	Weight in Grammes	Plate XIV (*continued*).	Page
10	Æ	—	**Apamea** (Phrygia). ΔΗΜΟΣ Bearded bust of Demos r. *Rev.* Π. ΠΕΛΑΓΟΝ-ΤΟC ΠΑΝΗΓΥΡΙΑρχου ΑΠΑΜΕΩΝ Tyche standing to l., in r. rudder, in l. cornucopiae. 244-249 A.D.	91, 188, 212
11	Æ	—	**Docimeum** (Phrygia). ΙΕΡΑ · ΒοΥΛΗ Bust of the Boulé r. [*Rev.* ΜΑΚΕΔΟΝΩΝ [Δ]ΟΚΙΜΕ[ΩΝ] Façade of hexastyle temple.] II c. A.D.	188
12	Æ	—	**Dionysopolis** (Phrygia). ΣΕΥC ΠΟ-ΘΟC ΔΙΟΝΥCΟΠΟΛΕΙΤΩΝ. Head of Zeus Poteos r., wearing taenia. *Rev.* CΤΡΑΤΗΓΟΥΝΤΟC [C]Ω[C]ΤΡΑ-ΤΟΥ Β. ΜΕΑΝΔΡΟC Personification of R. Maeander reclining l., in r. reed, l. rests on overturned urn from which water flows. II c. A.D.	91, 126, 171, 187

PLATE XV.

No.	Metal	Weight in Grammes		Page
1	Æ	25.83	**Rome.** IMP. CAES. VESPASIAN. AVG. P. M. TR. P. P. P. COS. III Head of Vespasian r. laureate. *Rev.* IVDAEA CAPTA. S. C. Judaea seated at foot of palm-tree, guarded by soldier. *Sestertius.* 71 A.D.	165, 176, 189
2	N	7.33	**Rome.** IMP. TRAIANVS AVG. GER. DAC. P. M. TR. P. COS. VI. P. P. Bust of Trajan r. laureate. *Rev.* FORVM TRAIAN Arch of the forum of Trajan. *Aureus.* 117 A.D.	165, 174, 189
3	Æ	24.07	**Rome.** ANTONINVS AVG. PIVS P. P. TR. P. COS. III Head of Antoninus Pius r. laureate. *Rev.* ROMA AETERNA S. C. Roma seated l., holding Palladium. *Sestertius.* 140-144 A.D.	165, 187
4	R	6.54	**Rome.** ANTONINVS PIVS AVG. GERM. Bust of Caracalla r. radiate. [*Rev.* P.M. TR. P. XVIII. COS. IIII. P. P. Jupiter standing r. with sceptre and thunderbolt.] *Argenteus Antoninianus.* 217 A.D.	51
5	N	7.23	**Rome.** DIVA FAVSTINA Bust of Faustina Senior r. *Rev.* AETERNITAS Aeternitas standing l. holding globe and rudder. *Aureus.* In or after 141 A.D.	165, 188

No.	Metal	Weight in Grammes	Plate XV (continued).	Page
6	R	3·15	Roman. [ANTONINVS PIVS FELIX AVG. Head of Elagabalus r. laureate.] Rev. SANCT. DEO SOLI ELAGABAL. Car drawn by four horses, containing stone of Elagabalus shaded by four parasols. [Struck at Antioch.] Denarius. 218-222 A.D.	186
7	N	5·11	Roman. [DIOCLETIANVS AVGVSTVS Bust of Diocletian r., laureate.] Rev. IOVI CONSERVATORI Jupiter with sceptre and thunderbolt standing to l., eagle at his feet; in field Ξ (60), in exergue SMA. [Struck at Antioch.] Aureus. 303-305 A.D.	55
8	R	3·09	Roman. DIOCLETIANVS AVG. Head of Diocletian r., laureate. Rev. VICTORIA SARMAT. Four soldiers sacrificing before the gate of a camp. [Struck at Trier.] Miliarense. 286-305 A.D.	53
9	Æ	—	Roman. [IMP. C. DIOCLETIANVS P. F. AVG. Head of Diocletian r. laureate.] Rev. GENIO POPVLI ROMANI Genius standing to l. with cornucopiae and patera; in field, XX I B; in exergue, ALE. [Struck at Alexandria.] Follis. 296-305 A.D.	51
10	N	4·22	Roman. CONSTANTINVS P. F. AVG. Head of Constantine I r. laureate. Rev. VOTIS · V · MVLTIS · X · Victory writing on shield, supported on column, VICTORIA AVG. In exergue, P TR. [Struck at Trier.] Solidus. 306-337 A.D.	55
11	N	4·45	Roman. Dominus Noster HONORIVS P. F. AVG. Bust of Honorius facing, wearing diadem, and holding in r. mappa, in l. sceptre surmounted by eagle. Rev. VOT. XXX. MVLT. XXXX. Seated figure of the Emperor, holding mappa and sceptre with eagle; in field, R V; in exergue, COMOB. [Struck at Ravenna.] Solidus. 395-423 A.D.	165
12	N	4·39	Constantinople. dominus Noster hERACLIYS PerPetuus AVI (Augustus). Bust of Heraclius I facing, wearing helmet, and holding cross in r. Rev. VICTORIA AVϚysta Є and in exergue CONOB Cross potent on three steps. Solidus. 610-641 A.D.	165, 171
13	R	2·09	Roman. D.N. FL. CL. IVLIANVS P. F. AV. Bust of Julian II r., diademed. Rev. VOT. X. MVLT. XX. in wreath; below which, CONS. [Struck at Constantinople.] Siliqua. 361-363 A.D.	54

INDEX OF SUBJECTS.

ABBREVIATIONS in inscriptions, 197.
Abdera, standard, 34; in alliance with Amphipolis, 116; type of griffin, 117; punning types, 120.
Abydos, Hero and Leander, 176. Pl. XIII. 5.
Acanthus (Macedon), change in standard, 205; lion and bull, 174.
Acarnania, federal coinage, 108.
Accent in Roman inscriptions, 217.
Accusative, names of deities in, 186.
Achaean league, coinage of, 10, 112. Pl. IX. 1.
Acragas : *see* Agrigentum.
Acropolis of Athens as type, 174.
Actian era, 201.
Adada (Pisidia), 198.
Adjectives naming issuing authority, 180.
Adranum (Sicily), 43.
Adulteration of coinage, 31, 68, 71; penalty for, 105.
Aediles, coins signed by, 138.
Aegae (Achaea), form of γ, 209.
Aegeae (Cilicia), era, 201; form of θ, 211.
Aegean Islands, standard, 36.
Aegina, early coinage, 6, 8; quality, 13; electrum of (?), 14; Aeginetic standard, 34 f., 223. Pl. II. 1.
Aegium (Achaea), ἡμιοβέλιν, 196.
Aemilius Scaurus, 190. Pl. XII. 5.
Aeneas at New Ilium, 176.
Aenus (Thrace), standard, 38; type of Hermes, 169, 206.
Aetna, coins of, 200; Aetna-Inessa, *ib.*

Aetolia, federal coinage, 108; personified, *ib.* Pl. VIII. 6.
Africa, alliances in, 118.
Agathocles of Syracuse, 10; titulature, 181.
Agonistic inscriptions, 192 f.; table, 193.
Agrigentum (Acragas), gold coinage, 42; decadrachms, 65; eagles and hare, 163; artists' signatures, 195; forms of α, 208; ν, 211; σ, 214. Pl. III. 9.
Agyrium (Sicily), 43.
Ajax, son of Oïleus, 187.
Alabanda (Caria), 200.
Alaesa (Sicily), 113.
Alba Fucentis, 59.
Alcaeus at Mytilene, 186.
Alexander of Epirus, style of coins, 164. Pl. VIII. 3.
Alexander of Pherae, 81, 180.
Alexander III of Macedon, the Great, coinage, 81, 82; standard, 38; decadrachms, 65; quality, 13; types, 171 : represented as Heracles, 172 ; at Sagalassus, 175 ; imitations of his coins, 10, 11, 38, 177. Pl. VII. 4, 5.
Alexander II of Syria, Zebina, gold coin, 11. Pl. VIII. 8.
Alexandria (Egypt), 12, 14, 89; cessation of Greek coinage, 92; inscriptions, 190; personifications, 188; Roman mint-marks, 140. Pl. XIV. 5, 8; XV. 9.
Alexandria Troas, gold, 87 n.
Alliances, 102 f.; within the union of S. Italy, 104.

INDEX OF SUBJECTS

Alloys, 13, 16; testing of, 24. See also Adulteration.
Altar as type, 171.
Amasia (Pontus), altar of, 171.
Ambianum (Gaul), mint-marks, 228.
Amblada (Pisidia), title, 184.
Amenanus, river, 187.
Amphaxitis, 109.
Amphictiones of Delphi, 81, 117. Pl. V. 7.
Amphipolis (Macedon), standard, 34; a Macedonian mint, 109; mint-mark, 178; facing head, 163; race-torch, 172. Pl. V. 1.
Amyntas of Galatia, gold pieces, 87 n.
Anastasius I, bronze coinage, 53.
Anaxilas of Rhegium, types connected with, 175.
Anazarbus (Cilicia), Γ.Β., Γ.Γ., 191 n.; γυμνασιαρχία, 193 n.
Ancyra (Galatia), 172.
Animal types, 161, 173.
Anthius, river, 187.
Antimachus of Bactria, portrait, 164. Pl. VIII. 4.
Antiochia—Alabanda, 200.
Antiochia (Caria), bridge over Maeander, 174; συναρχία, 193 n.
Antiochia (Pisidia), type of Mên, 95; *Victoriae DDD. NNN.*, 198. Pl. XIV. 3.
Antiochia (Syria), ἀργυροκοπεῖα at, 131 n.; coinage ἀδελφῶν δήμων, 113; silver under the Empire, 12, 14, 89; standard, 34; tetradrachms = 3 denarii, 74; coins with S.C., 94; titles of Trajan at, 182 n.; ἔτους νέου ἱεροῦ, 196; Roman mint-marks, 228. Pl. XIV. 7; XV. 6, 7.
Antiochus II of Syria, form of ω, 214.
Antiochus III of Syria, defeat at Magnesia, 11.
Antiochus IV of Syria, Epiphanes, and the ἀργυροκοπεῖα, 131 n.; titles, 185; Athenian coin, 122; form of σ, 214. Pl. IX. 8.
Antiochus VI of Syria. Pl. X. 4.
Antiochus VII of Syria and Simon Maccabaeus, 85.
Antoninianus, 51, 53.
Antoninus Pius, titles, 182. Pl. XV. 3.

Antonius (M.), quality of coins, 14.
Apamea (Phrygia), Noah's Ark, 170; form of o, 212. Pl. X. 6; XIV. 10.
Apamea (Syria), 113.
Aphrodite as type, 169; temple at Paphos, 174.
Apollo as type of Lacedaemon, 169, 206; Ἀρχαγέτας, 113; at Amphipolis, 163; slaying Python at Croton, 170; with wind-god, at Caulonia, 171.
Apollonia (Illyria), standard, 40; magistrates' names, 121; form of ε, 210.
Aptera (Crete), artist's signature, 195.
Apulia, Tarentine standard in, 63.
Aquileia, mint-marks, 228.
Arabia, standard, 33.
Aradus (Phoenicia), standard, 33, Pl. VII. 5.
Arcadia, federal coinage, 81, 107; full-face coins, 164 n.; artists' signatures (?), 195; δδ(ελός), 196; form of δ, 209; use of *koppa*, 215. Pl. II. 8.
Arcas and Hermes at Pheneus, 170.
Archaisms on coins, 153, 162, 203.
Archelaus I of Cappadocia, 165. Pl. X. 9.
Architectural types, 206.
Archons in Asia Minor, 128.
Arelatum (Gaul), mint-marks, 228.
Aretas of Nabathaea, 190.
Areus of Sparta, 82.
Argaeus, Mount, at Caesarea, 89, 174.
Argo, representation of, 189.
Argos, iron coin, 17, 18.
Ariminum, standard of, 49 n.
Aristotle's conception of money, 67.
Armenia, representation of, 187.
Arsaces I of Parthia, 10.
Artemis as type, 169; coin of Sicyon dedicated to, 197; temple at Ephesus, 174; ἐλευθέρα, 170, 184 n.; the stag her symbol, 79 n., 168. Pl. I. 4.
Artists: see Coin-engravers.
Aryandes, 84 n.
As of Central and Northern Italy, 59; of Luceria and Venusia, 63; of Rome, 45; fall in weight, 46 f.; Roman imperial, 50; of pure copper, 16.

INDEX OF SUBJECTS 275

Ascalon (Judaea), portrait of Cleopatra, 165. Pl. X. 8.
Asia Minor, local standards, 38; restrictions of coinage under Rome, 12, 87. Asia Provincia, Pl. XII. 8.
Asiarch, office of, 129.
Aspendus (Pamphylia), types, 172; convention with Selge, 106.
Asylum, right of, 184.
Athena as type, 169, 171.
Athens, earliest coinage, 8, 151 n.; its quality, 13, 68; gold, 9; weight of gold drachm, 31; electrum (?), 14; denominations of silver, 64; archaism, 162, 203, 209; type of Athena, 169; treatment of head, 161; olive-spray, 168; coinage of 'new style,' 11; mint-marks, 130; monetary officials, 121 f.; 'Αθε. ὁ δεμος, 181; gold of Mithradates, 87, 200; forms of a, 208; θ, 210; type of Acropolis, 174; relation of Athens to subject-allies, 83; Attic standard, 38, 223. *See also* Euboic-Attic. Attic tetradrachms tariffed disadvantageously, 73. Pl. II. 2; IV. 3; IX. 7, 8.
Athletic types, 172.
Attributes of deities as symbols, 178.
Audoleon of Paeonia, form of o, 212.
Augusta Trevirorum, mint-marks, 229.
Augusti, cult of, 183.
Augustus, restores *tresviri monetales*, 134; coin with his portrait, 165; with *quod viae mun. sunt*, 190. Pl. XII. 8, 10; XIV. 7.
Aurei, Roman, 54.
Authority indicated by types, 171; by inscriptions, 180.

Baal-Tars as type, 169.
Babylonian weight-system, 27; standard, 32, 222, 223; distribution, 33.
Bactria, coinage of, 10. *See also* Antimachus, Diodotus, Eucratides. Nickel coins, 16.
Baletium (Calabria), form of θ, 210.
Bankers, supposed private issues, 79.
Barbarous imitations of Greek coins, 9, 203, 204.

Bars of metal as currency, 5; of gold from mint at Sirmio, 136, 137.
Barter, 1.
Basin for oil, 193.
Berenice and Ptolemy I, 185.
Billon, 16.
Bisaltae, standard of, 34; form of β, 209; of λ, 211.
Bithynia, κοινόν of, 118. Pl. XIII 4.
Blanks, preparation of, 143 f., 148.
Boards of magistrates, 129.
Boats, names of, 193. *See also* Galley.
Boeotia, shield of, 168; federal coinage, 107; form of a, 208.
Borders, 158; of dots in imperial times, 204.
Bosporus Cimmerius (Crimean district), gold coinage, 13. 33. 86; τειμαὶ βασιλέως, 189; form of a, 208.
Bottiaea (Macedon), 109.
Boulé personified, 91, 188.
Brasidas in Thrace, 205.
Brass, Roman, 15, 50.
Brescello, hoard of, 218.
Britain, restriction of coinage, 87.
Bronze, as a medium of exchange, 41; first used for coinage, 9; its unpopularity in Crete, 69; quality of, 15; use in Sicily, 43; Italy and Rome, 41, 44 f.; South Italy, 63; Etruria, 57; cessation in Roman Republic, 49; coinage of Roman colonies, 93; of provinces under Empire, 91. *See also* Copper.
Brundisium, standard, 49 n.
Bruttians, coinage of, 61, 109.
Brutus, coins with ΚΟΣΩΝ, 86; with portrait of L. Junius Brutus, 186.
Bull, human-headed, 161. Sardes, Pl. I. 8, 9; Samos (?), Pl. I. 12.
Buthrotum, 138.
Byzantium, iron coinage, 9, 17; standard of silver, 34; convention with Chalcedon, 106; mint-marks, 178, 194; form of β, 208, 209; abbreviation for Καῖσαρ, 198; imperial silver, 90. Pl. IX. 2, 3.

Caecilius Metellus (M.), type, 176.
Caepio: *see* Servilius.
'Caeretan right,' colonies with, 92.

T 2

Caesar, coinage, 100; increases moneyers to four, 134. Pl. XII. 7.
Caesarea (Cappadocia), coinage under the Empire, 12, 14. 89; inscriptions on, 190, 196; Mount Argaeus, 174. Pl. XIV. 2.
Calpurnius Piso Caesoninus, 191.
Calymna, form of incuse, 158 n. Pl. I. 14.
Camarina (Sicily) gold, 42; artists' signatures, 194.
Camirus (Rhodes), electrum, 14.
Camp coinage of Carthage, 98.
Campania, Roman electrum in, 70; Campanian standard, 34, 60, 61, 223. See also Capua.
Camulodunum, mint-marks, 228.
Canting or punning types and symbols, 120, 176.
Capricorn of Augustus, 172.
Capros, river, 171.
Capua, gold, 60; electrum, 15, 61. Pl. XI. 7.
Caracalla, gold, 87; antoninianus, 51, 53. Pl. XV. 4.
Caria, silver in imperial times, 90.
Carisius (P.), 100.
Carisius (T.), 145. Pl. XII. 6.
Carteia (Spain), 138.
Carthage, begins to coin, 9; military coinage, 97; electrum, 15, 71; standard, 34; heavy denominations, 65; Roman colony, 136 n.; Roman mint-marks, 229. Pl. XI. 5.
Carthago Nova, 138.
Cast coins, 73, 155; casting of blanks, 143.
Castor and Pollux on Roman silver, 170.
Catana (Sicily) gold, 42; artists' signatures, 194, 195; form of α, 208; in alliance with Leontini, 115; coins with name of Aetna, 200.
Caulonia (Bruttium), a member of South Italian union, 103; type of Apollo with wind-god, 171; treatment of human figure, 161, Pl. III. 3.
Celenderis (Cilicia), standard, 36.
Centenionalis, 52.
Chalcedon, convention with Byzantium, 106; abbreviation for Καῖσαρ, 198. Pl. IX. 4.

Chalcidice, standard, 34, 38; federal coinage, 108. Pl. V. 11.
Chalcis and the Euboic standard, 37; standard of Chalcidian colonies, 36.
Chalcus. 37, 64.
Chariot-types at Syracuse, 172, 193; to front, 164 n.
Chersonesus Taurica, ἐλευθέρας, 184.
Chios, standard, 39, 223; names of denominations, 196. Pl. I. 16.
Chrysopolis, the plant, 24.
Cilicia, spread of coinage to, 9; under Persia, 84; under Seleucidae, 85.
Cimon, coin-engravers of this name, 193, 195.
Circular incuse, 153.
Cistophori, 12, 39, 87, 88, 224.
Cities personified, 187; titles of, 183.
Cius (Bithynia), 190.
Clay moulds for casting coins, 157.
Clazomenae (Ionia), iron coins, 72 n.; artist's signature, 195; χ(αλκοῦς), 196.
Cleopatra, portrait at Ascalon, 165; at Patrae, 85. Pl. X. 8.
Clodius Macer, 101 n.
Cnidus, coinage of 394 B.C., 112; head of Aphrodite, 206.
Coin, definition of, 2.
Coin-engravers, status of, 131; signatures, 194.
Coining, processes of, 143 f.
Cologne, 94.
Colonies, Greek, 116; Roman, 92; monetary officials, 136.
Colophon (Ionia), ἡμιοβύλιον and τεταρτημόριον, 196.
Colybrassus (Cilicia), γυμνασιαρχία, 193 n.
Commemorative inscriptions, 189.
Commercial alliances, 102 f.; theory of coin-types, 166.
Commodus as Roman Hercules, 91, Pl. XIII. 2. 8.
Common manah, 29; norm, 30, 32.
Complimentary issues, 189; inscriptions, 190; alliances, 102.
Conana (Pisidia), Pl. XIII. 7.
Concave fabric, 154, 155.
Constantine the Great, coinage, 52, 55. Pl. XV. 10.

INDEX OF SUBJECTS

Constantinopolis, mint-marks, 194, 228, 229. Pl. XV. 12, 13.
Consul, authority over coinage, 132; title, 182; abbreviated cos, 198.
Copia = Lugdunum, 93.
Coponius (C.), praetor, 100.
Copper, 15, 16; sources, 22; importance in Italy and Egypt, 22 n.; relation to silver, 37. *See also* Bronze.
Cora (Latium), 59.
Coresia (Ceos), sepia-type, 173.
Corcyra, begins to coin, 8, 9; types, 117, 177; magistrates' names, 121 n.; names of boats, 193, 194; Corcyraean standard, 40, 56, 117. Pl. II. 7.
Corfinium, 113.
Corinth, early coinage, 8; quality, 13; type of Athena, 169; use of *koppa*, 215; a Roman colony, 93, 94 n. Corinthian standard, 41, 223; origin of South Italian standards, 61. Pl. II. 5, 6; IV. 6.
Cornelius Sulla: *see* Sulla.
Corporations, coins issued by, 129.
Cos, discobolus of, 162, 172; form of σ, 213.
Cotiaeum (Phrygia), Pl. XIV. 9.
Cotys of Thrace, Κότυος χαρακτήρ, 180 n.
Countries personified, 187.
Cragus (Lycia), 111.
Crenides (Macedon), gold of, 9, 20.
Crete, standard, 36; cistophori, 39; silver in imperial times, 90.
Crimea: *see* Bosporus Cimmerius.
Croesus, coins ascribed to, 7. Pl. I. 8, 9.
Cross as type, 171.
Croton (Bruttium), a member of South Italian union, 103; in alliance with other towns, 104, 115; shares die with Metapontum, 151; tripod-type, 171; Apollo and Python, 170; use of *koppa*, 215.
Cumae (Campania), gold, 60; type of mussel, 173; form of inscription, 181.
Cybele as type, 169.
Cydon at Cydonia, 170.
Cydonia (Crete), Cydon as type, 170; artist's signature, 195.
Cyprus, spread of coinage to, 9; standard, 33, 36; gold, 84.

Cyrenaica, adopts coinage, 8; electrum, 14; standard, 34; Cyrenians in alliance with Samians and Ialysians, 114; coinage under the Ptolemies, 85; federal coins, 113; silphium type, 173. Pl. I. 15; V. 3.
Cyzicus, electrum coinage, 14; standard, 33; divisional system, 65; discount on electrum, 70: tunny-type, 166 f.; monstrous types, 161; birth of Erichthonius, 170; Heracles and serpents, 112; coin of Pharnabazus, 96; relation of symbol to type, 119 f.. 179; archaistic retention of incuse square, 153, 203; Roman mint-marks, 228, 229. Pl. I, 3, 5; V. 6, 8; XIII. 1.

Damastium (Epirus), mining implements on coins, 21 n.
Daric, 13; weight of, 30.
Datames, satrap, 96.
Dates, how indicated, 201; inscriptions relating to, 196.
Dating of coins, 199 f.
Dative, names of deities in, 186; Greek dative = Latin ablative (?), 139 n.
Debasement of coinage under the Empire, 13, 14. *See also* Adulteration, Degradation.
Decadrachms, 64 f.
Decargyrus, 54.
Decennalia, 190.
Decorative types, 177.
Decussis, Roman, 49.
Dedicatory formulae, 127; graffiti, 197.
Deduction from weights by mint, 30, 31.
Degradation of standards, 26, 31, 156; in size, 156; in quality, 205; a sign of date, 205.
Deification of rulers, 185.
Deities as types, 169; named on coins, 186.
Delphi, coinage of Amphictiones, 81, 117, 169; in alliance with Side, 102. Pl. V. 7.
Demareteion, style of, 159, 161; date of, 200.
Demetrias (Thessaly), 109.

INDEX OF SUBJECTS

Demetrius Poliorcetes, 10, 175. Pl. VII. 7, 10.
Demetrius I, of Syria, Soter, 11.
Demos personified, 91, 188.
Denarius, history of, 47, 48, 53; basis of Western coinage, 86; made universal money of account, 73, 89; double denarius of Diocletian, 51.
Denominations, 64; how far indicated by types, 168; named on coins, 196.
Dextans of Teate and Venusia, 62.
Didrachm, 64, 69.
Didyma, 80, 191.
Dies, 145, 149 f.; hinged together, 204 n.; differences in, 130; community of, 150.
Diobol, 64.
Diocletian, monetary reforms, 51, 53, 54; mint-marks on coins, 140. Pl. XV. 7-9.
Diodotus of Bactria, 10. Pl. VIII. 1.
Dione as type, 169.
Dionysius of Syracuse, debased coinage, 17, 70.
Dionysopolis (Phrygia), 91. Pl. XIV. 12.
Dionysus, head of, type of Naxos, 162; Κτίστης, 186.
Discobolus of Cos, 162, 172.
Discount on silver of Asia Minor, 87; on electrum, 70.
Divisional system of Asiatic standards, 64; of Corinthian, 51. See also Denominations.
Docimeum (Phrygia), Pl. XIV. 11.
Domna, Julia, Pl. XIV. 6.
Drachm, origin of name, 5 n.; of Athens, 64; Didyma, 191 n.
Dupondius, 15, 49, 50.
Duumviri in Roman colonies, 136, 138.
Dyrrhachium (Illyria), standard, 40; magistrates' names, 121; form of ϵ, 210. Pl. IX. 6.

Eagles and hare, type of Agrigentum, 163. Pl. I. 15.
Ecclesia personified, 188.
Edessa (Mesopotamia), imperial silver, 90.
Edoni, Getas king of, 81, 181 n.; use of η, 210. Pl. II. 9.
Egypt, system of weights, 27; standard of coinage, 34. See also Ptolemies, Alexandria.
Elagabalus. Pl. XV. 6.
Electrum, composition of, 14; distribution, 14, 15; early coinage, 8; supposed private issues, 79; divisional system of Asiatic electrum, 65; debased character, 70; at Syracuse, 43; in Campania, 61, 70; at Carthage, 71; at Cimmerian Bosporus, 86.
Eleusis, sanctuary coinage, 81. Pl. IV. 5.
Elis, type of Victory on basis, 163; of Zeus, 169; archaistic use of Ϝ, 125; artists' signatures (?), 194, 195. Pl. V. 2; XIV. 1.
Emesa, silver under Rome, 89.
Emperors, cultus of, 118; titulature of, 182; identified with deities, 91; their families, 230 f.
Epaminondas, coin of, 124.
Ephesus, electrum, 79 n.; gold of 87-84 B.C., 39, 87; cistophori, 39; coinage with Heracles and serpents, 112; imperial silver, 90; τὸ ἀγαθόν personified, 188; type of Artemis, 169; temples, 189; temple of Artemis, 174; ἱεραπήμη, 189; neocorates, 183; ὁ νεω. Ἐφε. δῆ. ἐπεχάρ., 127; δίδραχμον, 196; mint-mark, 178. Pl. I. 4; VIII. 5; XIII. 9.
Epidaurus, Pl. IX. 1.
Epimeletes, 127.
Epirus, type of Zeus and Dione, 169; federal coinage, 108. See also Alexander of Epirus.
Eras, 201 f.
Eretria, 107.
Erichthonius, birth of, 170.
Eryx (Sicily), in alliance with Segesta, 115.
Etruria, spread of coinage to, 9; standards, 38, 55. Pl. III. 1; XI. 3.
Euboea, electrum, 14; early silver, 8; standard, 38; cow-type, 173; types indicating denominations, 66; federal coinage, 107; form of α, 208. Pl. II. 4.
Euboic-Attic standard, 38, 223; discarded in Chalcidice, 205; combined with Sicel system, 42; in Etruria, 56.

INDEX OF SUBJECTS 279

Eucratides of Bactria, 'medallion,' 65.
Evaenetus, coin-engraver, 193, 194.
Exchange, stages in development of, 1.

Fabric, 143; an indication of date, 203.
Facing head on coins, 163; quadriga and riders, 66.
False moneying, 72, 73; moulds used by false moneyers (?), 157.
Familia monetalis, 135.
Faustina I, Pl. XV. 5.
Faustina II, die of, 149, 150.
Federal coinages, 10, 103; under Rome, 88.
Festival coinages, 91, 118, 191 f.; inscriptions, 192.
Fiesole hoard, 220.
Finds as evidence for dating coins, 217.
Fish-shaped coins, 3, 156.
Flaminian Way restored, 190.
Flamininus, T. Quinctius, gold coin, 99.
Flan: see Blank.
Follis, 51 f.
Forgery: see False moneying.
Forum of Trajan, 189.
Founders named on coins, 187.

Gades (Spain), 93, 95.
Galley, as type, 173; racing-galleys, 193.
Gallienus, Pl. XIII. 7; XIV. 5.
Games: see Festival.
Gaulish coinage, origin, 9, 10; imitations of coins of Philip II, 177; of Rhoda, 178; leaden and tin coins, 16; coinage restricted by Rome, 87.
Gela (Sicily), gold coinage, 42; human-headed bull, 161; form of γ, 209. Pl. III. 7.
Genitive, magistrates' names in, 121, 127; deities' names in, 186.
Gerousia, personified, 91, 188.
Getas, king of Edoni, 81, 181 n.; use of η, 210. Pl. II. 9.
Glass coin-weights, 18.
Gold, sources of, 19; quality in coinage, 13; gold-unit equated to ox, 27; gold-standard, 33, 222, 223; relation of gold to silver, 42, 75; becomes important in coinage, 9; in Etruria, 55; at Rome, 54; in South Italy, 60; in Sicily, 42; issued by subjects of Macedon and Persia, 84; disappearance from Greek coinage, 11; regulation of, under Rome, 86.
Gomphi (Thessaly), form of γ, 209.
Gordian III, Pl. XIV. 4.
Gortyna (Crete), goddess in tree, 163; foreshortening of figures, 164 n.; barbarous imitations, 204; introduction of bronze, 69; form of γ, 209; of ι, 211; of σ, 213. Pl. IV. 2, 4.
Graffiti, 197.
Grains of corn used to determine weight-unit, 27.
Grants of right of coinage, 85, 88.
Graeco-Asiatic standard, 32.
Graving-tool used for coin-dies, 149.
Gyges of Lydia, coins ascribed to, 7.
Gymnasiarch, 193.

Hadrian, travels of, 176. Pl. XIII. 3, 4, 9; XIV. 1, 2.
Haliartus (Boeotia), form of *spiritus asper*, 210.
Halicarnassus, Phanes of, 79 n.
Harbours of Zancle and Side, 173, 174.
Hare at Rhegium and Messana, 175; torn by eagles at Agrigentum, 163.
Hatria, standard, 59.
Head, human, treatment on coins, 161 f.
Heliopolis (Syria), silver coinage under Rome, 89.
Helios as type, 169.
Hemiobol, 64.
Hemitetartemorion, 64.
Hera as type, 169.
Heraclea (Lucania), gold, 60; standard of silver, 63; artist's signature, 195.
Heraclea (Thrace), Roman mint-marks, 229.
Heracles, type of Alexander the Great, 171, 172; fighting hydra, 170; strangling serpents, 112, 173; Commodus as Ἡρακλῆς Ῥωμαῖος, 91.
Heraclius I, Pl. XV. 12.

INDEX OF SUBJECTS

Heraea (Arcadia), iron coin, 18; mint of federal coinage, 107.
Heraldic schemes, 158.
Herbessus (Sicily), 43.
Hermes as type, 169, 170.
Hero and Leander, 175.
Hicetas of Syracuse, 10.
Hiero I of Syracuse, founds Aetna, 200.
Hiero II of Syracuse, 10; Σικελιωτᾶν coins, 113; portrait, 164. Pl. XI. 6.
Hieronymus of Syracuse, 10.
Hieropolis (Phrygia), 127.
Himera (Sicily), warm springs at, 173; destruction of the city, 199; coins with Agrigentine type, 115, 207; standard, 36 n.; artists' signatures, 195; form of *spiritus asper*, 210.
Hippias and the Athenian coinage, 41, 69.
Historical allusions in types, 175, 207; dating by historical evidence, 199.
Hoards, as evidence for dating coins, 217.
Holmi (Cilicia), union with Side, 105.
Homer represented on coins, 176, 185.
Homonoia, 115.
Honorius, Pl. XV. 11.
Horse, Thessalian type, 172; symbol of Liberty, 173.
Horseman, type of Tarentum, 172; seen to front, 164 n.
Hot-striking, 148.
Household of Emperor in charge of coinage, 135.
Hyporon (Bruttium) and Mystia, 115.
Hypsaeus : *see* Plautius.
Hyrgalean κοινόν, 107.

Ialysus (Rhodes), allies of Cyrenians from, 114.
Iasus (Caria), coinage of 394 B.C., 112. Pl. V. 9.
Iceni, type of, 177 n.
Ilium, New, type of Aeneas, 176; types and inscriptions, 186.
Imitative types, 177.
Imperator, right of coinage, 98.
Incuse impression, origin of, 148, 149; varieties of, 152, 153; 'mill-sail' square, 203; revival of incuse square, 153, 203; incuse types of South Italy, 152; of Lesbos, 153.
Inscriptions, artistic treatment of, 160; classification of, 180 f.; indications of date drawn from, 207, 208.
Ionian theory of origin of coinage, 7; early coins, Pl. I. 6, &c.
Iron, sources of, 23; coins, 5 n., 6 n., 9 n., 17; at Clazomenae, 72 n.; core of plated coins, 72.
Island-coins, 8.
Isthmian games, 192.
Italia, name of Corfinium, 113.
Italian Allies, federal issues, 86; 113. Pl. XI, 13, 14.
Italic standard, 61, 223.
Italy, bronze in, 44 f.; Northern and Central, standards, 59; Southern, begins to coin, 9; standards, 60; quality of coins, 13; incuse types, 152; monetary union, 103; alliance coins, 114.

Judaea, coinage of procurators, 91; of First Revolt, 34, 85 n.; coins referring to its subjection, 176, 189.
Jugurtha, surrender of, 176.
Julia Procla, 186.
Julian II, Pl. XV. 13.
Junius Brutus (L.), portrait of, 186.
Juno Moneta, temple of, 141.

Kheriga of Lycia, type of Athena seated, 206.
Kikkar, 28.
Kings, coinage of, 10; representation of, 172, Pl. I. 10, 11; titulature, 181.
'Kneeling' figures on coins, 158.
Koina, issues of, 113, 118, 189, 192.
Kupfernickel, 16.

L, numeral sign, 90, 203.
Lacedaemon, iron coinage, 9, 17; type of Apollo, 169, 206.
Lampsacus, electrum coinage, 14, 70; style of staters, 164; types and symbols, 120; Heracles and serpents, 112. Pl. V. 10.

INDEX OF SUBJECTS

Laodicea (Phrygia), rivers of, 171, 187; coins with Δόγματι Συνκλήτου, 91 n., 191. Pl. XIV. 6.
Laodicea (Syria), coinage ἀδελφῶν δήμων, 113; boars at, 174.
Larissa (Thessaly), Thessalian mint, 109; horse type, 172.
Latin language in Roman colonies, 94; colonies with 'Latin right,' 92.
Laurium, mines of, 21.
Laüs (Lucania), 103.
Lead, in bronze coins, 15; coins of, 16.
Leather money, 18.
Legend : see Inscriptions.
Legionary coins, 101.
Leontini (Sicily), canting type, 176; in alliance with Catana, 115; artist's signature (?), 194; form of λ, 211.
Lesbos, standard, 33; debased gold, 70; billon, 70; divisional system of electrum, 65; symbol displaces type, 120 : see also Mytilene. Pl. I. 13; IV. 9.
Lete (Macedon), treatment of human figure, 161.
Letters, forms of, 208 f.; A—N on Athenian coins, 122.
Leucas (Acarnania), 108.
Leucaspis, 187.
Lex Cornelia, 73 n.
Lex Flaminia, 48.
Lex Iulia peculatus, 73.
Lex Papiria, 49.
Libral coinage, 41 f.
Ligatures, 207, 208.
Lindus (Rhodes), Cyrenian allies from (?), 114.
Lion, type of Sardes, 172; head of lion at Leontini, 176; tearing bull, Acanthus, 174.
Lipari islands, find from, 219.
Litra, coinage based on, 41 f., 56, 57, 62.
Local features as types, 173.
Locri (Bruttium) in alliance with Messana, 115.
Locri (Opuntii), type of Ajax, 187.
Londinium, mint-marks, 228, 229.
Luceria (Apulia), standard, 47.
'Lucullan' coins, 100.
Lugdunum = Copia, 93; mint-marks, 229.

Lycia begins to coin, 9; federal coinage, 88, 110; silver under the Empire, 90; type of Apollo, 169; of boar, 168, 174. Pl. IX. 5.
Lycos, river, 171.
Lydia and the invention of coinage, 6, 7; electrum, 14; standard, 32. Pl. I. 1.
Lydian stone, 24.
Lyre, Pl. I. 14.
Lysimachus of Thrace, 10; imitations of his coins, 11, 38. Pl. VII. 6; IX. 2.
Lyttus, form of ι and λ, 211.

Macedon begins to coin, 8; standard, 34; regal coinage, 81 (see also Alexander III, Philip II, Philip V, Perseus); under Philip V, 109, 123 n.; under Perseus, 109; coins of Zoïlus, 125; coinage of the Regions, 12, 88; under Rome, 88, 109. Pl. X. 5.
Maeander, river, 187.
Magistrates, monetary, 119 f.
Magna Graecia, see Italy, Southern.
Magnesia ad Maeandrum (Ionia), coinage of Themistocles, 71 n., 85; monument of Themistocles, 189; representation of the Argo, 189; title ἑβδόμη τῆς 'Ασίας, 183. Pl. IV. 1.
Magnetes (Thessaly), 108.
Mallus (Cilicia), standard, 36; Sacra (l) Senatus, 188.
Manah, 28.
Marks of value in Sicily, 43; Rome, 46 f.; Etruria, 55 f.; Northern and Central Italy, 60; South Italy, 60 n., 62, 63.
Maroneia (Thrace), Dionysiac types, 173.
Marsyas of Roman Forum, 95.
Masicytes, (Lycia), 111. Pl. IX. 5.
Massae, 156.
Massalia, bronze coins, 15; standard, 34.
Maximian, mint-marks of, 140.
Mazaeus, satrap, 97. Pl. IV. 12.
Measures, Pheidonian, 6.
Medal, distinction from coin, 2 n.
'Medallions' of Asia Minor, 40, 89.
Mediolanum, mint-marks, 229.
Medium of exchange, 1, 26.
Melos, canting type, 176.

Memphis, leaden coins, 16.
Mên, the God, 95.
Mende (Thrace), Dionysiac types, 173; change in standard, 205.
Mesembria (Thrace), use of *san*, 215; mint-mark, 178.
Messana (Sicily), type of hare, 175; in alliance with Locri, 115; artists' signatures, 194, 195; form of σ, 213; *see also* Messina, Zancle.
Messene (Peloponnesus), type of Zeus, 169.
Messina, find of 1895, 218. *See* Messana.
Metals, sources of, 18; quality of, 13; testing, 23.
Metapontum (Lucania), a member of South Italian union, 103; gold, 60; type of corn-ear, 173; shares die with Croton, 151; artists' signatures, 194, 195.
Metellus, M. Caecilius, 176.
Miletus, standard, 38, 224; temple-coinage, 81, 191. Pl. I. 7.
Miliarense, 52, 53.
Military issues, 96; in the West, 97; of Rome, 98 f.
'Mill-sail' incuse, 152, 203. Pl. I. 5.
Mina, 28; weight-mina and money-mina, 31.
Mines in antiquity, 19 f.
Mints. Organization, at Athens, 129; at Rome, 139. Building seen on coins of Paestum, 146. Mints closed in Italy, 12; established in provinces, 12; issuing silver under the Empire, 88 f.
Mint-marks, 178, 194; on Athenian coins, 130; on Roman, 139, 228.
Mithradates II of Pontus, portrait, 164. Pl. VIII. 2.
Mithradates of Pontus, the Great, portrait, 165; gold coin struck at Athens, 87, 122, 200. Pl. IX. 7; X. 7.
Monarchs, coinage of, 81.
Money, ancient theory of, 67.
Moneyer, office of, 124 ff.
Monograms, 207, 208.
Monsters as types, 161.
Montecodruzzo hoard, 220.
Monuments as types, 174; named, 188.

Monunius of Illyria, form of σ, 213.
Moulds for casting coins, 156, 157.
Mountain-types, 174.
Mule-car at Rhegium and Messana, 175.
Municipia, coinage of, 93.
Mylasa (Caria), type of Zeus, 169.
Myra (Lycia), type of Artemis, 170.
Mystia (Bruttium), in alliance with Hyporon, 115.
Mytilene (Lesbos), electrum, 15; union with Phocaea, 103 f.; portraits, 186; alliance with Pergamum, &c., 102. *See also* Lesbos.

Nabis of Lacedaemon, 82 n., 182.
Names of coins, 196.
Naucratis, 'Silversmith's Hoard,' 218.
Naxos (Cyclades), wine-cup, 167. Pl. II. 3.
Naxos (Sicily), standard, 36 n.; retains cult of its mother-city, 117; types connected with wine, 173; style of head of Dionysus, 159, 162; of Silenus, 159, 162, 164 n.; artist's signature, 195; coins in Messina find, 218; form of ν, 211; of ξ, 212. Pl. VI. 1, 3.
Neapolis (Campania), artist's signature, 195.
Neapolis (Macedon), standard, 34.
Nemausus (Gaul), ham-shaped coins, 3, 4.
Nemean games, 192.
Neocorates, 183, 185.
Neoi, coins issued by, 129.
Nero, reduces denarius, 53. Pl. XII. 9, 11; XIV. 7.
Nicaea (Bithynia), 190.
Nickel, 16.
Nicomedia (Bithynia), coin with Στόλος, 188; Roman mint-mark, 229.
Nicopolis (Epirus), silver, 90; inscription to Nero, 190.
Nike, personified at Terina, 187; seated on basis, Elis, 163; standing on prow, Demetrius Poliorcetes, 175; type of sovereignty, 172; name of boat (?), 194.
Noah's Ark at Apamea, 170.
Nominative, names of cities in, 181;

INDEX OF SUBJECTS 283

of deities, 186; of magistrates, 121, 126.
Numerals on Roman coins, 217; as indication of value, 196.
Numidia, leaden coins, 16.
Nummus, 42; of Central Italy, 59; of Tarentum, 62.

Obol, 64. *See also* Greek Index, ὀβολός.
Obverse and reverse, 151.
Oecumenical games, 192, 193.
Officinae of Roman and Alexandrian mints, 140.
Officinatores, 141, 142.
Olbasa (Pisidia), form of A, 216 n.
Olbia (Sarmatia), fish-shaped pieces, 3, 156; cast coins, 156.
Oloösson (Thessaly), 109.
Olympian games, 192, 193.
Olynthus, head of league of Chalcidice, 108; artist's signature (?), 195.
Optio, 141 n., 142, 146.
Ornamental types, 177.
Ostia, mint-mark, 229.
Owl with crook and flail, 172. Pl. II. 2.
Oxide, 25.
Ox-unit and gold-unit, 27.

Paestum, mint of, 93; coin representing striking of money, 145-148. *See also* Poseidonia.
Pale (Cephallenia, tritetartemorion of, 196.
Pamphylia, spread of coinage to, 9.
Pandosia (Bruttium), in alliance with Croton, 115; artist's signature, 195; form of ι, 211.
Pannonia, ball-shaped coins, 3.
Panticapaeum (Chersonesus Taurica), gold, 18, 40. Pl. V. 4.
Paphos (Cyprus), Aphrodite of, 169; temple of, 174.
Papius (C.) Mutilus, coinage, 100, 113.
Parlais (Lycaonia), 95 n.
Parthia, beginning of coinage, 10. *See also* Vologeses III, Phraates II, Tiridates II.
Patina, 25.
Pautalia (Thrace), personifications at, 188.

'Pegasi' in Corinthian colonies, 117.
Pentobol, 64.
Perdiccas, base coinage of, 16 n.
Perga (Pamphylia), type of Artemis, 169; style of head, 164; sphinx, 178; form of Ϝ, 215; of san, 215. Pl. VIII. 9.
Pergamum (Mysia), coins struck by prytaneis, 125; gold, 87; cistophori, 39; titles of city, 184; coin with Σεβαστὸν Κεφαλίων γραμματεύων, 127. Pl. X. 2; XIII. 6.
Perrhaebi (Thessaly), 108.
Perseus as type, 171.
Perseus of Macedon, portrait. 164; Macedon under, 109. Pl. VIII. 7; X. 3.
Persia, introduction of coinage, 8; representation of the Great King, 172; coinage of subject dynasts, 84; of satraps, 95 f.; quality of darics, 13. Pl. I. 10, 11.
Persic standard; *see* Babylonian.
Persis, fire-altar, 171.
Personifications as types, 173, 187, 206.
Persons, historical, named on coins, 185.
Phaestus (Crete), types, 170; Φαιστίων τὸ παῖμα, 180 n.; form of ι, 211. Pl. IV. 11.
Phaino-Artemis, 79 n.
'Phanes,' supposed coin of, 79, 168. Pl. I. 4.
Pharnabazus, satrap, 96. Pl. V. 6.
Phaselis (Lycia), galley-type, 172; form of φ, 214.
Pheidon of Argos, 5 n., 6; Pheidonian standard, 40.
Pheneus (Arcadia), type of Hermes, 169, 170. Pl. V. 12.
Pherae (Thessaly), Alexander and Teisiphonus, 81, 82, 180.
Philip II of Macedon, gold, 9; quality of, 13; style of silver staters, 164; types, 171, 177; imitations of, 177; grant of coinage to Philippi, 83. Pl. VII. 1, 2.
Philip V of Macedon, portrait, 164; type of Perseus, 171; Macedon under, 109, 123 n. Pl. VIII. 7.
Philippi (Macedon), 83. Pl. VII. 3.
Phlius (Phliasia), form of λ, 211.

Phocaea (Ionia), standard, 33; gold, 8; debased gold, 70; electrum, 15; divisional system, 65; union with Mytilene, 103 f.; canting type, 176; relation of symbol and type, 119; form of φ, 214. Pl. I. 2; IV. 8.
Phocis, names of strategi on coins, 124; form of α, 208.
Phoenice (Epirus), form of φ, 214.
Phoenician standard, 32, 33, 222, 223; origin of Campanian, 61.
Phraates II of Parthia, 97.
Pietas, Livia as, 91.
Piso, see Calpurnius.
Pittacus at Mytilene, 186.
Plated coins, 71.
Plautius Hypsaeus (C.), 190. Pl. XII. 5.
Political alliances, 102, 106.
Polycrates of Samos, 16 n.
Polyrhenium (Crete), artist's signature, 195.
Pompeius Magnus, 100.
Pontus, see Mithradates II, Mithradates the Great.
Populonia (Etruria), Pl. III. 1.
Portraiture, 10, 164 f.; disguised, 172; idealized, 164; on Roman coins, 100.
Poseidon as type, 169, 175.
Poseidonia (Lucania), fabric, 104, 152; type of Poseidon, 169; treatment of human figure, 161; in alliance with Sybaris, 115; a member of the South Italian union, 104; form of ι, 211; of σ, 213. See also Paestum. Pl. III. 2, 8.
Potidaea (Macedon), 169.
Potin, 16.
Prepositions in magistrates' signatures, 127.
Prerogative of coinage, 78.
Priest ploughing, 95.
Private coinage, 78.
Privernum, capture of, 190.
Provinces under Rome, 88 f.
Proconsuls, names on cistophori, 88.
Procurators, monetary, 135, 136.
Prostanna (Pisidia), Mount Viaros, 174.
Prymnessus (Phrygia) and Synnada share one die, 151.
Prytaneis of Smyrna, 124; of Pergamum, 125.

Ptolemaic drachm, weight of, 30, 31.
Ptolemy I, Soter, 10, 85; called θεός, 185; coin with Ἀλεξάνδρειον, 181. Pl. VII. 9.
Ptolemy II, Philadelphus, gold octadrachms, 65. Pl. VII. 8.
Ptolemy V, Epiphanes, gold, 11.
Ptolemy VI, Philometor, θεός, 185.
Ptolemy XIII, Auletes, 14.
Punning, see Canting types.
Pythian games, 192, 193.
Pyxus (Lucania) in the South Italian union, 103, 104; form of ξ, 212.

Quadrans, Roman imperial, 50.
Quaestors, coins signed by, 138.
Quality of ancient money, 68.
Quatuorvirs, 134.
Quinarius, history of, 47, 48.

Race-horse, type of Philip II, 177.
Race-torch, type of Amphipolis, 172.
Rates of exchange, 74.
Rationalis, 135.
Ravenna, mint-mark, 229. Pl. XV. 11.
Reduction of Roman coinage, 47 f.; of Etruscan bronze, 57.
Regions of Macedon, 88, 109.
Regnal dates, 203.
Relief, treatment of, 160.
Religious alliances, 117; theory of coin-types, 166; types of religious import, 169.
Reverse-types, introduction of, 151.
Rhegium (Bruttium), standard, 36 n.; lion's scalp, 117; hare, 175; coin from Lipari find, 220; artists' signatures, 195.
Rhoda (Spain), canting type, 176; Gaulish imitations, 178.
Rhodes, importance of coinage, 10; standard, 39, 223; weights as a test of date, 205; gold coinage, 9; drachms current under the Empire, 74, 89 n.; canting type, 176; Helios, 169; Heracles and serpents, 112, 173; revival of incuse square, 153, 203; δίδραχμον, 196; mint-mark, rose, 178. Pl. V. 5.
Rhoemetalces of Bosporus, form of ε, 210. Pl. XIII. 3.

INDEX OF SUBJECTS

Rings as currency, 3, 5.
River-gods, 171, 187.
Rome, interference with Greece, 11; regulation of coinage of subjects, 85; military coinage, 98 f.; made a colony, 94; Roman provincial governors, 139; monetary magistrates, 131; colonies, 92; earliest coinage, 9; Roman pound, 41; standards of bronze, 44 f.; of silver, 47, 53; of gold, 54; weight-systems, 224, 225; reduction in size of bronze, 156; quality of bronze, 15, 16; electrum, 15; plated coins, 71; adulteration of imperial coinage, 71; mint-marks, 229; art of coins, 165; personifications, 187; Roma personified, 91, 187; forms of letters, 215 f. Pl. XI. 8-12; XII. 1-7, 9-11; XV. 1-5.
Royal manah, 29, and norm, 30, 32; types, 172.

Sacrificial instruments, 173.
Sagalassus (Pisidia), Alexander at, 175; titles of, 207 n.
Salamis (Cyprus), Pl. VII. 9.
Salapia (Apulia), form of σ, 214.
Samos, standard, 33, 39, 224; early electrum, 38; Samians at Cyrene, 114; coinage with Heracles and serpents, 112, 173; type of Hera, 169. Pl. I. 12; IV. 13; XIII. 8.
San, forms of, 215.
Sappho at Mytilene, 186.
Sardes, personified, 91; lion-type, 172. Pl. I. 8, 9; XIII. 1.
Satraps, coinage of, 84, 95; portrait of satrap, 164.
Scalptores, 141.
Scaurus: see Aemilius.
Scripulum, scruple, 42.
Scyphate fabric, 155.
Secret mint-marks, 140.
Segesta (Sicily), hunter-god, 163; in alliance with Eryx, 115; ἐξᾶς, 196; form of γ, 209.
Seleucia (Cilicia), silver coins, 89.
Seleucia (Syria), coins ἀδελφῶν δήμων, 113; form of o, 212.
Seleucid coinage, 10. See also Antiochus, Seleucus, Syria. Seleucid era, 201.

Seleucus I, Nicator, of Syria, 10. Pl. VII. 11.
Seleucus II of Syria, form of σ, 213.
Selge (Pisidia), convention with Aspendus, 106.
Selinus (Sicily), wild celery of, 173; a canting type, 176; form of δ, 209; of ψ, 214. Pl. VI. 2.
Semis, Roman imperial, 50.
Semuncial standard, 49.
Senate, Roman, bronze coinage, 50, 134, 135; personified, 91, 188.
Serdica, mint-mark, 229.
Serrate fabric, 154.
Servilius Caepio (Q.), 191.
Sesterce, silver, introduction, 47; cessation, 48; bronze and brass, 15, 50; as money of account, 48.
Sestos (Thrace), Hero and Leander, 176; inscription relating to coinage, 125.
Seuthes of Thrace, inscriptions on coins, 180 n.
Severus, Septimius, Pl. XIII. 5; XIV. 3.
Sextantal system, 47 n.
Shekel, 28.
Shield on Boeotian coins, 168; shield-types, 159.
Shrinkage in casting coins, 156.
Sicily, spread of coinage to, 9; weight-system, 224; standards, 36, 38; federal coinage of Timoleon, 113, 191; alliance-coins, 114; Carthaginian coinage, 97; Sicily personified, 113.
Sicinius IIIvir, 100.
Sicyon, form of σ, 213; punctured inscription on stater, 197.
Side (Pamphylia), union with Holmi, 105; 'alliance' with Delphi, 102; canting-type, 176; tariffing and countermarking of tetradrachms, 39, 87; harbour, 173, 174. Pl. VIII. 5.
Sidon, earliest coinage, 9; king in car, 172; walled city, 206.
Siglos, 31.
Signatores, 141, 142.
Signatures of magistrates, 119, 132 f.
Signia, 59.
Silenus, type of Naxos, 162.
Siliqua, 54.

INDEX OF SUBJECTS

Sillyum (Pamphylia), cast coin, 157.
Silphium, 173. Pl. I. 15.
Silver, sources, 20; quality, 13; relation to other metals, 75-77; at Rome, 71, 73; in Etruria, 55; in South Italy, 61; of Roman colonies, 93; restrictions under Rome, 88 f.
Simon Maccabaeus, right of coinage, 85.
Sinope (Paphlagonia), satrapal coins, 95.
Siris (Lucania), 103, 104.
Sirmium, gold bars from, 136; mint-marks, 229.
Siscia, mint-marks, 194. 229.
Sixths of staters, 65.
Slaves in Greek mints, 130.
Sloping edges, cause of, 144.
Smyrna, head of Cybele (city-goddess), 164, 169; coins struck by prytaneis, 124; Ba vs, 197; titles of city, 207 n.; dedication formula, 127. Pl. VIII. 10.
Social War, coinage of, 86, 99, 113.
Soldiers' pay, 48 n.
Solidus of Constantine, 55.
Solon reforms the standard, 40; Solonian weights, 223.
Sovereignty, coinage an attribute of, 82.
Sparta: see Lacedaemon.
Sphinx of Artemis, 178; of Augustus, 172. Pl. I. 16.
Spiritus asper, representation of, 210.
'Spread' tetradrachms, 154.
Square coins, 154.
Stag on electrum stater, 79 n., 168. Pl. I. 4.
Standards, military, as type, 95.
Standards of weight, 26 f.; at Didyma, 191 n.; changes in, 205; tables of, 222.
Statues represented on coins, 174, 206.
Stellar types, 177.
Stephanephoros, 130.
Stratus (Acarnania), 108.
Striking of coins, 143.
Strymon, river, 188.
Style, development of, 160; an indication of date, 203.

Sulla, Faustus Cornelius, 176. Pl. XII. 3.
Sulla, L. Cornelius, military coinage, 100; type of Venus, 171. Pl. XII. 2.
Suppostores, 141, 142.
Sybaris (Lucania), a member of South Italian union, 103; in alliance with Poseidonia, 115; fall of, 199. Pl. III. 8.
Syedra (Cilicia), γυμνασιαρχία, 193 n.
Symbols, classification of, 178; of magistrates, 119; of deities, 170 f.; on Roman coins, 131; artistic treatment of, 159.
Synnada (Phrygia) and Prymnessus share one die, 151.
Syracuse, gold and silver, 42; bronze, 43; electrum, 15; decadrachms, 65; denominations indicated by types, 66; coinage of the tyrants, 10; the Demareteion, 200; chariot-types, 172; ἆθλα, 193; style of head, 161, 163; Corinthian stater, 205; artists' signatures, 194, 195; form βασιλέος, 212; forms of ρ and σ, 213; E and H, 209; use of koppa, 215. See also under the various tyrants. Pl. III. 5, 6; VI. 4, 6, 7; XI. 4, 6.
Syria, Attic standard in, 38; heavy denominations, 65; under Seleucid kings, 85. See also Seleucid coinage.

Table, agonistic, 193; of Trapezus, 176.
Talent, 28.
Talos at Phaestus, 170.
Taras, hero of Tarentum, 175, 181; name of the city, 181.
Tarentum (Calabria), standards, 61, 62, 223; in the South Italian union, 104; gold, 60; Taras, 175, 181; horsemen, 172. Pl. XI. 1, 2.
Tariffing of coins, 73.
Tarraco (Spain), mint-mark, 229.
Tarsus (Cilicia), Baal-Tars, 169; walled city, 206; loyal inscription, 190; titles, 184; Γ. B. and Γ. Γ., 191 n. Pl. IV. 12.
Tauromenium (Sicily), form of ρ, 213.
Taxation, raising of weights for, 30.
Tegea (Arcadia), iron coin of, 18.

INDEX OF SUBJECTS

Teisiphonus of Pherae, 81.
Temenothyrae (Phrygia), 127.
Temesa (Bruttium) in alliance with Croton, 104, 115.
Temple coinages, 80, 191; types, 174, 180.
Teos (Ionia), form of η, 210.
Terina (Bruttium), type of Nike, 187; style of coins, 163; artists' signatures, 194, 195. Pl. VI. 8.
Termera (Caria), 81.
Termessus Major (Pisidia), type of free horse, 173; dating of coins, 200.
Terracotta money, 18.
Tetartemorion, 64.
Tetradrachm and didrachm at Athens, 64, 69.
Tetrobol, 64.
Thasos, standard, 34.
Thebes (Boeotia), coinage of, 315 to 288 B.C., 108; Heracles and serpents, 112, 173; shield and half-shield, 168; names of Boeotarchs on coins, 124. Pl. IV. 10.
Themistocles, satrapal coin, 71, 85; plated, 71 n.; monument at Magnesia, 188, 189. Pl. IV. 1.
Thessaly, horse-types, 172; federal coinage, 108.
Thessalonica (Macedon), Roman mint-marks, 229.
Thibronian money, 97.
Thrace, early coinage, 8; coins of Lysimachus, 10; imitations, 11; standard of south coast, 33; heavy denominations, 65.
Thurium, head of Athena, 117, 163; artists' signatures (?), 195. Pl. VI. 5.
Thyrrheum (Acarnania), 108.
Timarchus of Babylon, gold, 11.
Timoleon in Sicily, 113, 191, 205.
Tin, sources, 23; coins, 16, 17; proportion of, in bronze, 15, 16.
Tiridates II of Parthia, Pl. X. 1.
Tissaphernes (?), Pl. V. 9.
Titles of magistrates, 128; on Roman coins, 132; of rulers, 181; of cities, 183.
Tmolus, electrum of, 7.
Token, nature of, 1, 2.
Torch, type of Amphipolis, 172.
Touch-stone, use of, 24.

Trade, various stages of, 1; colonies and, 116.
Trajan, organizes system of coinage, 135; his Forum, 174; titles, 182. Pl. XV. 2.
Trapezus (Pontus), canting type, 176. Pl. IV. 7.
Tremissis, 55.
Tressis, 49.
Tresviri, monetary, 132.
Trevirorum, Augusta, mint-marks, 194, 229.
Tribal unions, 106.
Triens, 55; triental standard, 49 n.
Trier, mint-marks, 194, 229. Pl. XV. 8, 10.
Trihemiobol, 64.
Trihemitetartemorion, 64.
Triobol, 64.
Tripod, type of Croton, 171.
Triskeles symbol, 110.
Triumvirs, monetary, 132.
Tunny at Cyzicus, 166 f.
Tymnes of Termera, 81.
Types, reason for use of, 67; relative positions on flan, 204; type and symbol, 119 f.; composition of, 158; meaning and classification, 166; inscriptions naming types, 185; character of, as a sign of date, 205 f.; distinguishing denominations, 65 f.; personal, at Rome, 132; of Roman colonies, 95; of Greek colonies, 117.
Tyrants, debased coinage, 70.
Tyre, earliest coinage, 9; type of owl, 172; gold decadrachm, 87; silver under Rome, 89, 90.

Uncial standard, 48.

Values of the metals, relative, 74; of coins, how indicated, 65 f., 67, 196.
Vases given as prizes, 193.
Vassal rulers, treatment by Rome, 92.
Velia (Lucania), standard, 34, 61, 63, 223; artists' signatures, 195. Pl. III. 10.
Venus, type of Sulla, 171.
Vespasian, Pl. XV. 1.
Vettii, wall-painting in house of, 144 f.
Viaros, Mount, 174.

Victoriatus, standard of, 40 ; introduction of, 47 ; cessation, 48.
Victory ; *see* Nike.
Vigintivirate established, 135.
Vologeses III of Parthia, 207 n.

Wave-pattern, 158.
Weighing of precious metal, 5.
Weights and weight-standards, 26 f., 222 f.; weights as a sign of date, 204.
Wheel, engraving, 149.
Wind-god at Caulonia, 171.
Wine-cup at Naxos (Cyclades), 167.
Winged running figure, Pl. I. 5.
Wolf and Twins, 95.

Wooden money, 18.
Wreath, use of, 158.

Zacynthus, form of ζ, 210.
Zancle (Sicily), belongs to South Italian union, 103, 104 ; standard, 36 n.; harbour, 173, 174; in alliance with Croton, 115 ; coins in Messina find. 218 ; form of δ, 209. *See also* Messana. Pl. III. 4.
Zeus as type, 169, 171; attributes of, 178; Eleutherios, 113; Poteos, 91.
Zinc, proportion of, in bronze, 15, 16.
Zoïlus, coins of, 125.

II. GREEK

Ἀγαθόν, τό, 188.
Ἀγωνοθεσία, 193.
Ἀδελφῶν δήμων, 114.
Ἀετοφόρος, 178 n.
Ἀθε. ὁ δεμος, 181.
Ἆθλα, 193.
Αἴας, 187.
Αἰγή, 187.
Αἰτησαμένου, 128.
Ἀκόνη, 24 n.
Ἀκράγαντος, 180.
Ἄκτια, 192.
Ἀλεξάνδρεια, 192.
Ἀλεξανδρεία, Ἀλεξάνδρειος, 180.
Ἀλέξανδρος, 175.
Ἀλεξάνδρου, 180.
Ἀλκαῖος, 186.
Ἀμενανός, 187.
Ἀναθ..., 197.
Ἀνέθηκε, 127.
Ἀνθυπάτῳ, 139.
Ἀπήμη ἱερά, 189.
Ἀργύριον, 180.
Ἀργυροκοπεῖον, 129 f.
Ἄργυρος, 188.
Ἀργώ, 189.
Ἄριστα, 192, 193.
Ἀριστόξε(νος), 194.
Ἀρκαδικόν, 81, 180.
Ἀρμενία, 187.
Ἀρτάμιτος τᾶς ἐλκεδμονι, 197.
Ἀρχίατρος, 129.
Ἄρχων, 128.
Ἀσκληπιεῖα, 192.
Ἀσσάρια τρία, 196.
Ἀσσάριον ἥμυσυ, 196.
Ἄσυλος, 184.
Ἀττάληα, 192.
Αὐγούστεια Ἄριστα Ὀλύμπια, 193.

Αὔτκρα., 198.
Αὐτοκράτωρ Καῖσαρ κ.τ.λ., 182.
Αὐτόνομος, 184.

Βα'ιλέος Νάβιος, 82 n.
Βασανίτης λίθος, 24.
Βασιλεύς, 181; Β. βασιλέων κ.τ.λ., 207 n.; βασιλέος, 212.
Βα υς, 197.
Β. Νεωκόρων, 183.
Βότρυς, 188.
Βουλή, 188.

Γ. Β., 191 n.
Γ. Γ. 191 n.
Γερουσία, 188.
Γέτας Ἠδωνέων Βασιλεύς, 181 n.
Γ. Νεωκόρων, 183.
Γορδιάνηα, 192.
Γυμνασιαρχία, 193; γυμνασίαρχος ?, 191 n.

Δανκλε, 181.
Δάτον ἀγαθῶν, 20.
Δεκαετηρὶς Κυρίου, 190.
Δελφίς, 3.
Δερρωναῖος, 187.
Δερρωνικόν, 180.
Δῆμος, 188.
Διά, 127.
Δία Ἰδαῖον, 186.
Διαχεῖν, 155 n.
Δίδραχμον, 90 n., 196.
Διδύμων (ἐγ) ἱερή, 80.
Διὸς Ἐλευθερίου, 186.
Δίχαλκον, 64.
Δ. Νεωκόρων, 183.
Δόγματι Συνκλήτου, 91 n., 191.
Δραχμή, 5 n., 90 n.

INDEX

Ἑβδόμη τῆς Ἀσίας, 183.
Ἐγ Διδύμων ἱερή, 191.
Εἰς αἰῶνα τοὺς Κυρίους, 190.
Εἰσαγγείλαντος, 128.
Εἰσελαστικά, 192.
Εἰς ἐῶνα τοὺς Κυρίους, 190.
Ἐκκλησία, 188.
Ἐλευθέρα, 184.
Ἐλείθερος δῆμος, 188
Ἐμπορικὴ μνᾶ, 129 n.
Ἐξακεστίδας, 194.
Ἐξᾶς, 196.
Ἐπί, 127.
Ἐπιμεληθέντος, ἐπιμελήσαντος, ἐπιμελητῆς, 127.
Ἐπιτρόπου, 139.
Ἐπιφ. Καῖσαρ, 183 n.
Ἐπιχαράττειν, 127, 143 n.
Ἐπόει, 195.
Ἔτους, 90, 203 ; ἔτους δεκ. ἱεροῦ, ἔτους ἱεροῦ, ἔτους νέου ἱεροῦ, 196.
Εὐαινέτο(υ), 194.
Εὐαρχίδας, 194.
Εὐκλείδα, 194.
Εὐμήνου, 194.
Εὐσεβής, 183.
Εὐτυχής, 183.
Ἐφεσίων οὗτοι ναοί, 189.

Ζάγκλον, 174 n.
Ζεὺς Ἐλευθέριος, 113.

Ἤλεκτρον, ἤλεκτρος, 14.
Ἤλια, 192.
Ἡμιοβέλιν, ἡμιοβόλιον, 196.
Ἡρακλείδας, 195.
Ἡρακλῆς Ῥωμαῖος, 91.
Ἡρκούλι, 140.

Θεὰν Αἰολὶν Ἀγριππίναν, 186.
Θεὰν Ῥώμην, 186.
Θεὰν Σύνκλητον, 188.
Θεὰ Ῥώμη, 91.
Θεὰ Φαυστεῖνα, 90.
Θεμίδες, 192.
Θεμιστοκλῆς, 189.
Θεόδοτος ἐπύει, 195.
Θεὸν Σύνκλητον, 186, 188.
Θεὸς Σύνκλητος, 188.
Θεῶν, 185.
Θήρα, 194.
Θιβρώνειον νόμισμα, 97 n.
Θυ., 3.
Θυγάτηρ τοῦ δήμου, 129.

Ἱερά (city), 184 ; (contest), 192.
Ἱερὰ βουλή, γερουσία, σύνκλητος, 188.
Ἱεραπήμη, 189.
Ἱερεὺς δήμου, 129.
Ἱεροὶ ἀγῶνες, 192.
Ἱερὸς Ἀτταλέων Ὀλύμπια Οἰκουμενικός, 193.
Ἱερὸς δῆμος, 188.
Ἰόβι, 140.
Ἰουδαίας ἑαλωκυίας, 189.
Ἰου(λίαν) Πρόκλαν ἡρωίδα, 186.
Ἱπποκράτης, 195.
Ἴσθμια, 192.
Ἰσοπύθια, 192.
Is. Xs., 198.

Καβείρια, 192.
Καινόν, 113.
Καῖσαρ, 182.
Καπετώλια, 192.
Κα ... ρ = Καῖσαρ, 198.
Καταστρατεῖο, 97.
Κεράτιον, 54.
Κιλίκιον, 84, 96.
Κλευδώρου, 195.
Κοινόν, 113, 118.
Κοινὸν Ἀσίας, 189, 192.
Κοινὸν Μητροπολειτῶν τῶν ἐν Ἰωνίᾳ, 192.
Κοινὸς τῶν τριῶν Ἐπαρχιῶν, 192.
Κόλλυβος, 64.
Κόμμα, 143 n., 180.
Κομόδου βασιλεύοντος ὁ κόσμος εὐτυχεῖ, 190.
Κόπτειν, 143 n.
Κόσων, 86.
Κρατησίππο(υ), 195.
Κτίστης, 187.
Κυμε, 181.
Κυραναῖοι Πτολεμαίῳ?, 191 n.
Κῶμος, 194.

Λ = λίτρα, 196.
Λακεδαιμονίων, Ἀμβλαδέων, 184.
Λαρισαία, 180.
Λεύκασπις, 187.
Λευκὸς χρυσός, 14.
Λίτρα, 41 f.

Μακάριοι Κιανοί, 190.
Μέανδρος, 187.
Μεγάλο, 192.
Μενεσθεὺς κτίστης, 187.
Μῆλον, 176.

II. GREEK

Μητρο. Κολωνία, 94.
Μητρόπολις, 91, 183, 185.
Μνᾶ, 28, 129 n.

Νέα θεὰ Ἥρα, 91.
Νέμεα, 192.
Νέοι, 129.
Νεοκόρος, 183.
Νεότης, 194.
Νέρωνι δημοσίῳ πάτρωνι Ἑλλάδος, 19c.
Νεύαντος ἐπόει, 195.
Νεωκόρος, 183, 185.
Νίκα, 187, 194.
Νικηφόρος, 178 n.
Νόμισμα, 2 n., 180.
Νόμος, 2 n., 62.
Νοῦμμος, 62.

ΟΒ, 55, 196.
Ὀβελίσκοι, 5 n., 6 n., 17.
Ὀβελοί, 17.
Ὀβολός, 5 n., 63 n., 196.
Ὀδ(ελός), 196.
Οἰκουμενικά, -κύς, 192, 193.
Ὁ κόσμος εὐτυχεῖ, 190.
Ὀλύμπια, 192, 193.
Ὀλυμπικόν, 81.
Ὁμήρου, 186.
Ὁμόνοια, 102, 189.
Ὁ νεω. Ἐφε. δῆ. ἐπεχάρ., 127.
Ὀρείχαλκος, 15.
Οὐαλεριάνα, 192.

Παῖμα (?), 180.
Παρά, 127.
Παρμε . . ., 195.
Πεντέχαλκον, 64.
Πεντόγκιον, 196.
Περίοδος δεκάτη κ.τ.λ., 190.
Πόλις, 91, 187.
Πόρτις καλ., 197.
Πρόκλα: see Ἰουλία.
Προκλῆς, 195.
Πρυτάνεις Ζμυρναίων, 124.
Πρῶτα, 192.
Πρώτη, 183; π. τῆς Ἀσίας, 183, 184.
Πρώτης Πισίδων κ.τ.λ., 207 n.
Πρώτων Ἀσίας κ.τ.λ., 207 n.
Πύθια, 192, 193.
Πυθόδωρος, 195.

Ῥηγῖνος, 180.
Ῥόδον, 176.

Ῥώμη, 91 n.: see also Θεὰ Ῥώμην, Θεὰ Ῥώμη.

Σβ = Σεβαστύς, 198.
Σεβαστός, 182.
Σεβαστῶν, νεωκόρος τῶν, 185.
Σεββ = Σεβαστοί, 198.
Σέλινον, 176.
Σευήρεια, 192.
Σευηριανὴ Μακρεινιανὴ Μητρόπολις Ταρσός, 184.
Σευήρου βασιλεύοντος ὁ κόσμος εὐτυχεῖ, 190.
Σημαντήριον, 130.
Σημασία, 188.
Σίγλος, 28.
Σίδη, 176.
Σιδητῶν Δελφῶν ὁμόνοια, 102.
Σικελία, 113.
Σίκλος, 28.
Σολικόν, 180.
Σοφιστής, 129.
Στάχυς, 188.
Στεφανηφόρου δραχμαί, 129 n.
Στόλος, 188.
Συμμαχικόν, 113, 191.
Σύμμαχος (Ῥωμαίων), 184.
Συν = Συνμαχικόν, 112, 191.
Συναρχία, 129, 193 n.
Σύνκλητος, 91, 188.
Συρακοσίων, 180.
Σωσίπολις, 187.
Σώσων, 195.
Σώτειρα, 187.

Τακίτιος, 192.
Τάλαντον, 28.
Τάρας, 181, 187.
Τᾶς Ἀρτάμιτος τᾶς ἐλκεδμονι, 197.
Τειμαὶ βασιλέως, 180.
Τερμερικόν, 81.
Τερσικόν, 84.
Τεσσαρακοστὴ Χία, 39 n.
Τεταρτημόριον, 196.
Τετρασσάριον, 50.
Τετράχαλκον, 196.
Τράπεζα, 176.
Τριτεταρτημόριον, 196.
Τύμνο(υ), 81.

Ὑδαρέστερον, 105.
Ὑιὸς Ἀσιάρχου, Ἀφροδεισιέων, πόλεως, 129.
Ὑπατεύοντος, 139.
Ὑπὲρ νίκης Ῥωμαίων κ.τ.λ., 90.

Φ..., 195.
Φαινοῦς εἰμὶ σῆμα, 79 n., 181.
Φιλιστίων, 195.
Φιντέρα, 197.
Φιττακός, 186.
Φρύγιλλος, 195.
Φωκαΐδες, 70 n.
Φώκη, 176.
Φωσφόρος, 194.

Χ = χαλκοῦς, 196.

Χαλκόκρατον κασσίτερον, 17 n.
Χαλκοῦς, 37.
Χαρακτήρ, 143 n., 180.
Χαράττειν, 126, 143 n.
Χοιρίων, 195.
Χρυσός, 188.
Χωνεύειν, 155 n.

Ψαπφώ, 186.
Ψηφισαμένου, 127.

III. LATIN

A. A. A. F. F.: *see* Tresviri.
Achaia restituta, 176.
Ad fru. emu. ex S. C., 191.
Aequatores, 141.
Aes argento miscere, 72 n.
Aes grave, 45; rude, 44, 156; signatum, 45, 156.
Anthius, 187.
Antoninianus, 51.
A. Plautius, Aed. Cur. S. C., 133.
Argentum Oscense, 21.
As, 41 f, 57 f.
Auggg., 198.
Augusto ob c. s., 190.
Augustus, 182.
Aureus, 54.
Aurichalcum, 16.

Caesar, 182.
Capitolina, 193.
C. Cassius L. Salina., 134.
C. Coponius Pr., 100.
Centenionalis, 52.
Certamina Sacra Capitolina Oecumenica Iselastica Heliopolitana, 193.
Ces = Censor, 138.
C. Hypsae. Cos., 190.
Civitas foederata. 184; sine foedere immunis et libera, *ib.*
Cn. Corn. M. Tuc. Patr., 95.
Col. C. A. A., 94.
Col. Cl. Agrip., 94.
Col. L. Ant. Com., 94.
Col. Nem., 4.
Com. Asiae, 189.
Concordia Militum, 101.
Conductores flaturae, 141.
Conflare, 155 n.

Copia, 93.
Coticula, 24 n.
C. Pulcher, 132.
Cudere, 143 n.
Cuneus, 2 n.
Cur. ✳ Fl., 155 n.

D. D., 136, 138.
DDD. NNN., 136, 198.
Decargyrus, 54.
Decennalia, 190.
Decussis, 49.
Denarius, 47.
Dextans, 62.
Digma, 136.
Dispensatores, 135.
Divi F., 182.
Divus, Diva, 182.
D. N., 183.
D. S. S., 133, 131.
Dupondius, 49, 50, 58, 60.
Duumviri quinquennales, 138.

Empor. Munic., 93 n.
Equester Ordo Principi Iuventutis, 190.
Ex A. P., 133.
Ex D. D., 136.
Ex S. C., 133. 134.

Familia monetalis, 135.
F. C., 138.
Feelix, 217.
Felix, 183.
Felix Aug. lib. Optio et Exactor auri argenti et aeris, 142.
Ferire, 143 n.
Ferrum argento miscere, 72 n.
Fides Militum, 101.

INDEX

Flare, 155 n.
Flaturarius, 141, 145.
Fl. Flavianus Pro sig. ad digma, 136.
Follis, 51 f.
Forum Traian., 189.

Graecinus Quin. Tert. Buthr., 138.

Heliopolitana, 193.
Hibero Praef., 138.

Imp. Caes. Quin. L. Ben. Prae., 138
Imperator, 132, 182.
Imper. iterum, 100.
Indulgentiae Aug. moneta impetrata, 93.
Inficere, 72 n.
Iselastica, 193.
Italia, 113.
Iudaea Capta, 176, 189.

L Bennio Praef., 138.
L. Cestius C. Norba. Pr. S. C., 134.
Leg., 88.
Leg. XIII. Gem. M. V., 101.
L. Flaminius Chilo IIIIvir pri. fla., 134, 155 n.
Libra, 41, 45 f.
Libralis, as, 41.
L. P. D. A. P., 133.
L. Regulus IIIIvir A. P. F., 134.
L. Sulla, 100.
L. Torqua. Q. Ex S. C., 133.
Lucianus obr. I sig., 136.

M. Agrip. Quin. Hibero Praef., 138.
Malliator, 141, 142, 145, 146.
M. Aquil. M. F. M. N. IIIvir, 132.
Massae, 156.
M. Calid. Q. Met. Cn. Fl., 132.
M. Fan. L. Crit. P. A. Aed. Pl., 133.
Miliarense, 52, 53.
Miscere monetam, 72 n.
M. Lucili. Ruf., 133.
M. Scaur. Aed. Cur. Ex S. C., 190.
Municipi Patronus et Parens, 95.
M. Volteius. M. F., 134.

Nob. Caes., 183.
Numisma, 2 n.
Nummus, 42, 59.

Obryzum, 136.
Oecumenica, 193.
Officinatores, 141, 142.

Orichalcum, 16.
Oscense argentum, 21.

Pater Patriae, 182.
Patronus et Parens, Municipi, 95.
Pecunia maiorina, 52.
Percutere, 143 n.
Periodicum, 192.
Permissu Augusti, Caesaris, 93; proconsulis, 94.
P. E. S. C., 133.
P. F., 183.
P. Hypsaeus Aed. Cur., 190.
Pietas, 91.
Pilipus, 217.
Piso Caepio Q. ad fru. emu. ex S. C., 191.
Pius, 183.
Pontifex Maximus, 182.
PP. Aug., 183.
P.P.D.D., 94.
Praefecti pro duumviris, 138.
Preiver. Captu., 190.
Procurator monetae, 135, 136.
P. Servili M. F. P., 133.
Pu(blice), 133.

Q = Quaestor, 132, 138.
Q. Anto. Balb. Pr. S. C., 133.
Quadrans, 46, 50, 57 f., 63.
Quatuorviri monetales, 134.
Quinarius, 47, 48.
Quincunx, 60, 63.
Quincussis, 58.
Quirillus et Dionisus Sirm. sig., 136.
Quod viae mun. sunt, 190.

Rationalis, 135.
Rex Aretas, 190.
Roma, 99, 181, 187, 208.
Romano(m), 180.
Rom. et August., 189.
Rulli, 133.

S = semis, 64, 196.
Sac. Mon. Urb. Augg. et Caess. NN., 140.
Sacra (certamina), 193.
Sacra (!) Senatus, 188.
Saeculares Augg., 192.
Saeculum novum, 190.
Sanct. Deo Soli Elagabal., 186.
S. C., 50, 94, 95 n., 100, 133, 134, 191.
Scalptores, 141.
S. C. D. T., 134.

INDEX. III. LATIN

Scripulum, 42.
Semis, 46, 50, 57 f., 64, 196.
Semuncia, 49, 60.
Senatus sacra (!), 188.
Serrati, 154.
Sescuncia, 60, 63.
Sestertius, 15, 47, 48.
Sextans, 46, 57 f.
Sicinius IIIvir, 100.
Signare, 143 n.
Signatores, 141, 142.
Siliqua, 54.
Sirm., 136.
Solidus, 55.
S. R., 95.
Superpositus, 141; auri monetai nummulariorum, 135.
Suppostores, 141, 142, 145.

Tingere, 72 n.
T. Quincti, 99.

Tremissis, 55.
Tressis, 49, 60.
Tresviri auro argento aere flando feriundo (monetales), 132.
Tribunicia potestate, 182.
Triens, 46, 55, 57 f.

Vaala, 217.
Victoriatus, 47. 48.
Uncia, 46, 48, 57 f., 63 f.
Vota suscepta, votis decennalibus, &c., 190.

IIIvir, 132, 133.
IIII. I. D. D. D., 136 n.
IIIIvir D. D., 138.
IIIIvir pri. fla., 134, 155 n.

THE END

OXFORD: HORACE HART
PRINTER TO THE UNIVERSITY

PLATE I

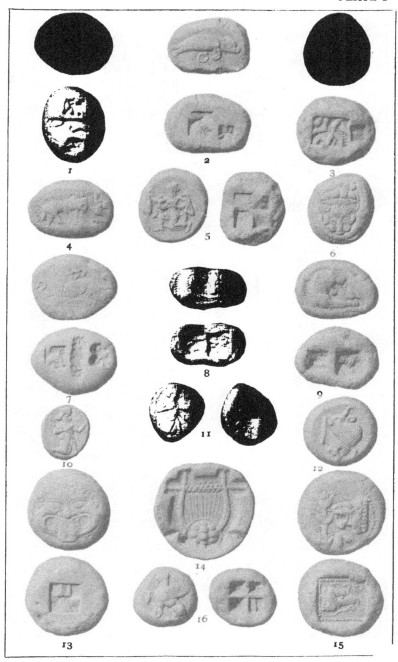

PLATE II

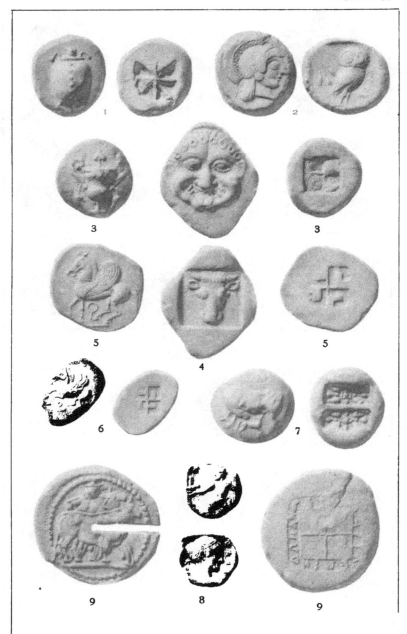

PLATE III

PLATE IV

PLATE V

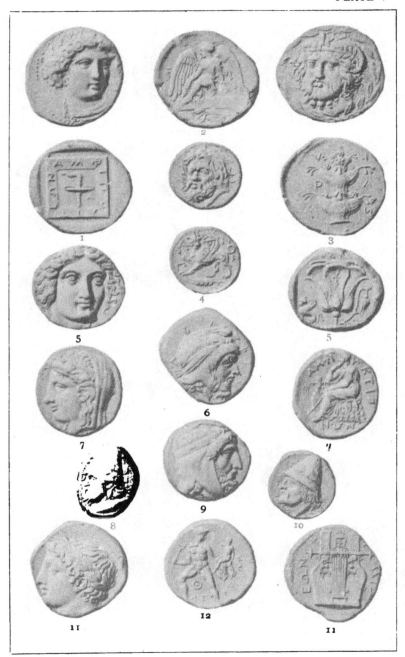

PLATE VI

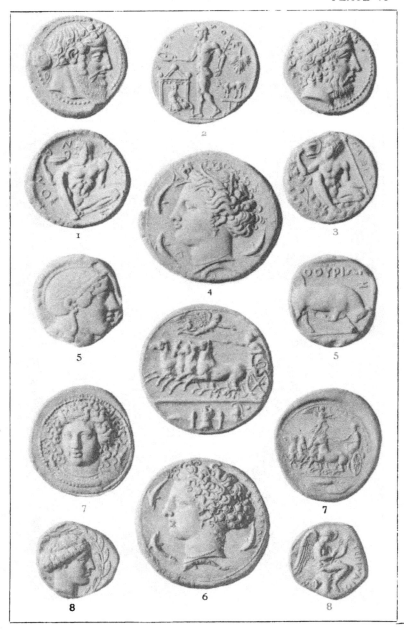

PLATE VII

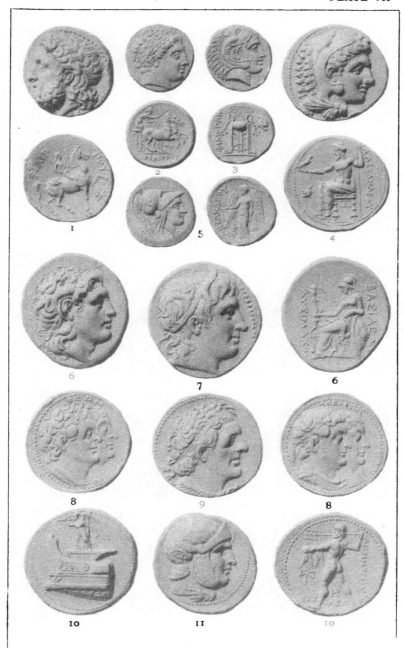

PLATE VIII

PLATE IX

PLATE X

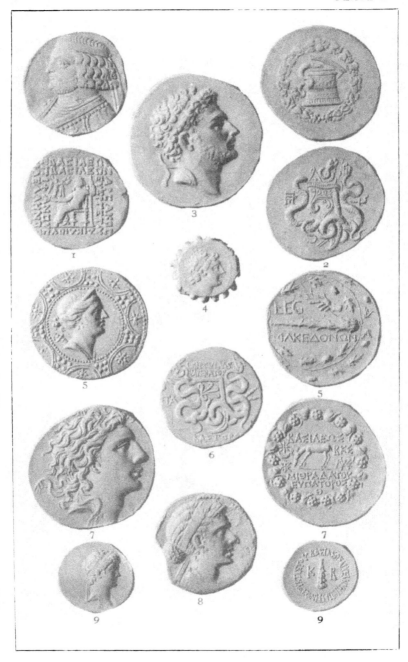

PLATE X

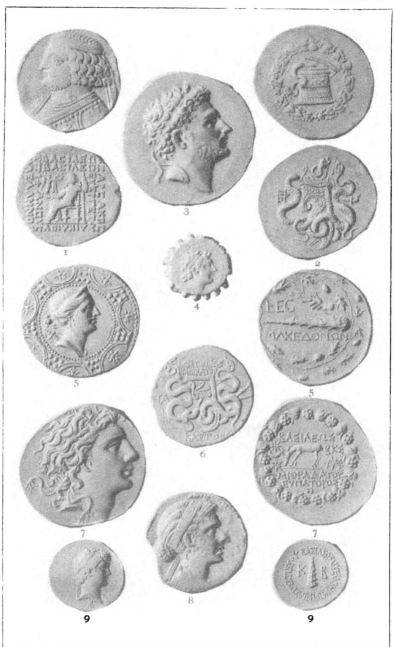

PLATE XI

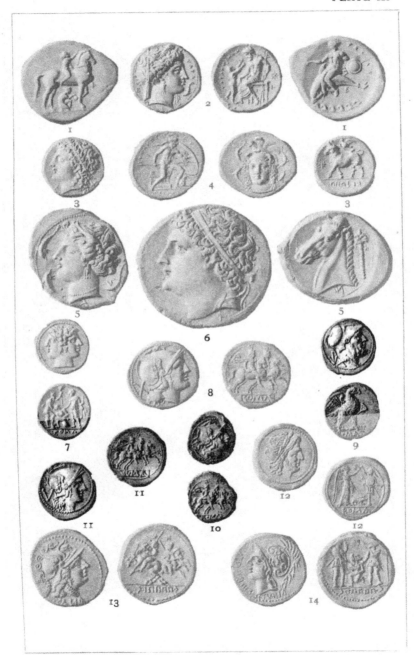

PLATE XII

PLATE XIII

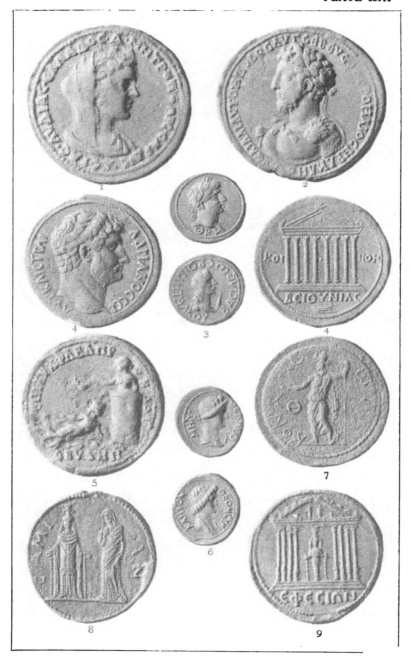

PLATE XIV

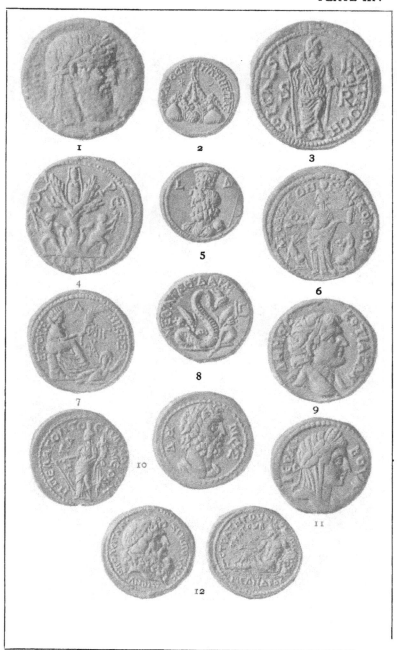

PLATE XV

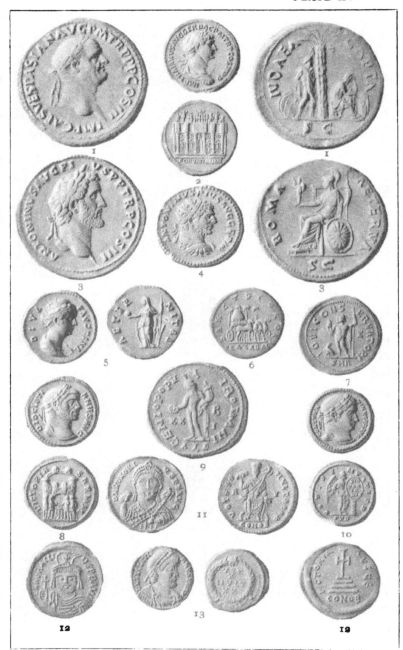

CPSIA information can be obtained
at www.ICGtesting.com
Printed in the USA
LVHW112312070620
657616LV00008B/151